Professional Communication:

Deliver effective written, spoken and visual messages

Fourth Edition

Jane English
Sally Burt
Gabrielle Nudelman

JUTA

Professional Communication
Deliver effective written, spoken and visual messages

First published 2002
Second edition 2006
Reprinted 2010
Reprinted 2011
Third edition 2012
Reprinted 2015
Fourth Edition 2017

Juta and Company (Pty) Ltd
PO Box 14373, Lansdowne 7779, Cape Town, South Africa

ISBN 978-1-48511-712-4

Project manager: Carlyn Bartlett-Cronje
Copy editor: Simone van der Merwe
Proofreader: Niki Sampson
Indexer: Language Mechanics
Typesetter: LT Design Worx
Cover designer: Eugene Badenhorst
Cover photograph: Nina de Jager

Typeset in Rotis Serif Std 10.5pt

TABLE OF CONTENTS

Introduction

This textbook is a long-established aide to anyone needing to hone their communication skills – those skills which are the cornerstone to personal and professional success. This edition has been re-devised in the context of digital communication but keeps the timeless, core elements required in fluent delivery in speech or writing. It has the benefit of long use and feedback from tertiary and commercial users (see the Preface) but also the contributions from two new authors, Sally Burt and Gabrielle Nudelman, both highly qualified and known in their areas of expertise.

The content remains sound in its theoretical base whilst having a strong practical focus: every chapter offers tips and skills – particularly those for using digital tools to your advantage whether in writing, managing, researching, presenting or creating graphics. We as the author team are confident that this edition will be an essential reference to take you to the next stage of your professional journey.

Jane English
Cape Town, 2017

Contributing author

SALLY BURT (chapters 2, 6, 9 and 11) runs a communication consultancy focusing on professional communication including business writing and presentation skills, plain language and document design, reporting strategies and improving digital workplace skills, as well as offering editing services, and materials and template development. She has also written a range of English textbooks and study guides for the South African and various international curricula. She has worked in both the public and private sectors as well as in higher education. Sally obtained her honours and masters in Modern History at Magdalen College, Oxford in England and a postgraduate certificate of education from Roehampton Institute in London.

www.footprintcommunications.co.za

Editor and principal author

DR JANE ENGLISH (chapters 1, 3, 4, 5, 7, 8, 9, 10 and 14) is an Associate Professor at the University of Cape Town (UCT) where she heads up Professional Communication Studies and is responsible for lecturing, administration and curriculum design. Jane lectures on aspects of communication to the UCT Research Office and to master's students across UCT. She obtained her PhD from Glasgow Caledonian University, Scotland. Her research interests are in communication in business and industry and also women working in industry. She is established in her field: publishes in accredited journals and presents regularly at international conferences and for the International Labour Office (ILO).

Jane consults on written, spoken and interpersonal communication to numerous organisations and corporations, such as Anglo American, Aurecon, Botswana National Productivity Centre, Cape Town City Council, Coega, GIBB, Investec, Old Mutual, Parliament, Transnet and Woolworths.

She has been an author on this textbook since its first edition and the editor for the last two editions.

www.janeenglish.co.za

Contributing author

GABRIELLE NUDELMAN (chapters 12 &13) holds a Masters from UCT and is currently undertaking her PhD in Higher Education Studies through Rhodes University. She has taught in a variety of higher education institutions in Cape Town, including Stellenbosch University, CPUT and UCT's Graduate School of Business. She currently teaches in Professional Communications Studies, located in UCT's Faculty of Engineering and the Built Environment. She has, in addition, run team-building and training workshops with various individuals and groups. Gabrielle has worked as a moderator and editor, has presented at conferences and published in academic journals. Her research interests include employability skills development and student learning in higher education.

Preface

Communication may not be the first thing that springs to mind when thinking about entrepreneurship, yet it is certainly one of the handful of factors that separate great entrepreneurs from mediocre ones.

The effective communication of thoughts and ideas lies at the core of entrepreneurial success. Without this, entrepreneurs cannot sell their ideas to early-stage partners and investors, convince clients to use their products or services, or find and retain great team members. Like many engineers, I underestimated this subject while doing it, only realising the importance of the lessons and principles in this book when I needed to raise venture capital.

I have carried four key learnings from university through my career as an entrepreneur: how to look for opportunity, how to solve a wide variety of problems, how to work with others and, lastly, how to communicate professionally. The greater portion of this final lesson was facilitated by reading this book and practising its principles. Effective communication is like any other skill: aptitude helps to get you started, but then it needs a solid foundation of theory, and plenty of practice.

Those who hone this skill inevitably succeed.

JP Kloppers
CEO, BrandsEye

Preface

I am fortunate to have a unique perspective on the textbook, *Professional Communication – Delivering effective written, spoken and visual messages*, having encountered it at both undergraduate level and professional stages in my career. My first contact with the textbook was as a student studying civil engineering at the University of Cape Town. I found it a practical and useful guide to polishing my writing and presenting skills – areas of expertise essential in all professions. My second contact came about as CEO of a company that realises the importance of equipping employees with business communication skills. This proved particularly important as we became a leading African firm competing with the best in the world, where excellence is the norm.

This book is a first-class, comprehensive tool with quality content that reflects the knowledge and experience of the authors. It is a reference work for good management practice in writing reports, managing meetings, writing agendas and minutes, and creating and delivering persuasive presentations. It is, in addition, useful for those who are continuing with studies or who publish as industry specialists, as it incorporates research methods, referencing and writing up papers and theses. The authors have ensured the content of this edition remains relevant, especially in our new world order of digital communication, office and social media. It will add value to your working life.

Richard de Vries
CEO, GIBB

Acknowledgements

The content in the book, the examples and explanations that relate to computer software, refer mainly to the Microsoft Office package. However, the authors acknowledge that a variety of similar packages is available.

We are indebted for the advice and content that has enriched this book. Our thanks go to past and present staff of Professional Communication Studies, UCT, in particular: Vivienne Basckin, Dr Mignonne Breier, Alison Gwynne-Evans, Evelyn Howard, Dr Lara Raffaeli and Nan van der Merwe.

We also thank the students and personal acquaintances who have given us permission to include samples of their work.

Writing effectively

The requirements for effective writing remain the same regardless of the medium used – paper, a computer, a tablet or a mobile phone. Writing emails, reports, minutes and business plans are part of virtually every workday, and, for academics, there are papers and theses to write. We all need to access information quickly and we therefore require clearly organised and well-written messages. Your writing must attract the reader's attention through an appealing layout, hold it through logical content and persuade the reader by using a convincing style. **It is important to remember that the reader has an active role in making meaning out of your message. You therefore need to write as clearly as possible to avoid misinterpretation.**

Good writing at work is not only about correct grammar and spelling, but also about selecting and managing information and using clear reasoning for ease of understanding on the part of the reader. We often write and read in digital spaces and we often write collaboratively (as described in Chapter 2). It therefore becomes increasingly important to write appropriately, as the reader may well have English as a second language. In addition, few readers make contact with the writer for further explanation if something is unclear — they simply lose interest.

Many documents are written but never read. The reason is that they are unreadable; that is, they display some or all of the common errors in the areas of planning and purpose, style and grammar, and presentation and layout. This chapter addresses these areas and is divided into four main sections, namely:

1. Purpose and planning
2. How to produce the document
3. How to write in Plain English
4. How to edit the final draft for visual readability and impact.

Once you have worked through this chapter, you will:
- know the characteristics of effective writing
- have practised selecting relevant information
- have practised writing in clear, simple English
- know how to organise information so that your message is unified, logical and has the right emphasis.

1.1 Purpose and planning

Select information and use visual note-taking tools

In most instances, the first stage of the planning process consists of reading a message that you are responding to, and reading other texts for background and/ or content to use in your document.

Understand the brief

If you are required to write a document in response to a set question, you need to understand the brief, task or question:

1. Read the brief or assignment very carefully.
2. Write a purpose statement; that is, write out the topic in your own words to clarify for yourself what is required.
3. Before you start, choose a format appropriate for the finished product.

Find and record information

Sources of information might include discussions (such as recordings or transcripts of meetings), interviews and other texts, which can be found on the Internet or in printed form. In business writing the referencing of sources has not been done regularly, but today awareness of copyright issues is increasing. Writers should always track and record their sources and, in some cases, reference them in the document. See chapters 12 and 13 for approaches to gathering information, data collection tools and appropriate referencing styles.

Mind mapping is a useful technique for taking notes in lectures and for writing review notes. Essentially, you create a visual diagram that represents all the ideas from a meeting, reading or lecture. Mind maps show how ideas are inter-related and make for accessible, interesting notes. The creation of visual diagrams allows you to avoid rereading notes (left-brain activity), as it provides an instant summary (right-brain activity). There are programs you can use to create mind maps (eg Visio and Freeplane), but hand-drawn mind maps are still considered valuable.

Order your notes in suitably titled folders (electronic or physical) and in a logical sequence so that you can easily access them.

Pitch appropriately to your reader

A message that is appropriate for one receiver (readership or audience) may need to be written in a different style for another receiver, even though it contains the same content. Before you write, ask yourself the following questions:

• Will your reader(s) expect to read about this subject?
• Will your reader(s) be interested in this subject?
• What will your reader(s) know about this subject?

- Will this document be read immediately and only once, thus having a finite period of use, or will it be read over time and referred to years after it was written?
- Will your reader(s) be able to contact you and will you always be available for reference?
- Under what circumstances will your reader(s) read your writing: in what place, at what time and in what psychological state?

Decide on a purpose

Before you begin writing, you have to know **why** you are writing.

Each written message must open with a statement of the purpose of the topic covered. Having a clear purpose or topic statement helps you to select information that will serve this purpose. A clear purpose helps you to decide how to arrange and express information that is most suited to the purpose. For example, if your purpose is to inform and educate your readers, you should keep your information factual and precise. On the other hand, there is no reason to load the reader with heavy technical information if your purpose is to entertain. For a text you are required to write in the course of your studies, the purpose may be to:

- show that you understand the topic
- show that you have read the prescribed references
- score high marks.

In addition to your main purpose, it is common to have a number of secondary purposes. These can overlap at times. For example, if you write a regular blog, your purpose may be to:

- convince your readers to change their points of view
- promote yourself as a forward thinker
- contribute to the professional reputation of the company that employs you.

Other purposes for writing include to describe, explain, inform, instruct, specify, record, evaluate and/or recommend.

Plan the message: mind maps and topic outlines

Now that you have completed your preparation, you should be ready for the planning stage, in which you will:

- organise and create a mind map of your ideas
- arrange your material to suit your purpose and readership
- devise a topic outline.

It is tempting just to start writing with one thought flowing into the next and without organising these thoughts beforehand. The reader then has the task of not only reading, but also trying to find the logic pattern used by the writer, which may not be logical at all. If the writer cannot organise his or her own thoughts and content, it is an indication of how difficult it will be for the reader to fathom the meaning. Most readers will not take on this task and will stop reading.

Organise and create a mind map of your ideas

With mind mapping, messages can be planned in two forms: linear diagrams, in the form of 'trees' with main and sub-branches, or spray-type diagrams. The map can be a hand-drawn sketch which grows organically, as shown in Figure 1.1. From this sketch, the author developed a linear, logical sequence of content. This initial ordering can also be translated into a visual plan by using drawing software such as Visio or Freeplane.

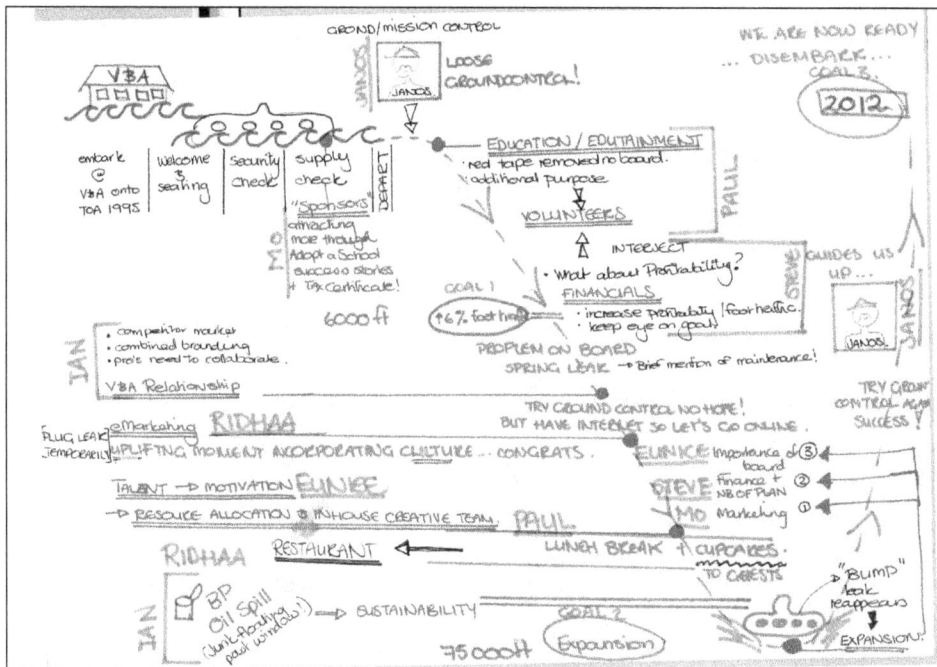

Figure 1.1 An example of a mind map

Arrange your material to suit your purpose and readership

You can arrange your content by using a diagram (eg a mind map), as described above, and then in a list as illustrated in the example that follows.

℮9

Question/task:	Describe the factors that influence empathetic listening and recommend ways to improve this.
Readership:	Non-specialists, teachers, lecturers
Purpose:	To inform, stimulate thinking, persuade

The following is an example of information that a writer may collect on the subject described in the brief above:

- Listening: a definition
- Concentration: techniques
- Barrier: daydreaming
- Mentally summarise as you listen
- Listen for key words
- Barrier: no clear purpose
- Be self-aware
- Bias or prejudice
- Environmental noise
- Non-verbal cues to assist listening
- Speech delivery too fast
- Responsibility of listener and speaker
- Credibility of speaker
- Negative attitude to content
- How to overcome barriers
- Eye contact
- Take notes
- Evaluate the message
- Build empathy
- Tell someone about the message

This information could be arranged as follows:

Listening
Definition

Barriers
- Daydreaming
- Bias
- No clear purpose
- Speech too fast
- Adverse environment
- Poorly organised message
- Negative attitude

How to overcome barriers
- Mentally summarise
- Self-awareness
- Listen for key words
- Tell someone
- Use non-verbal cues
- Positive attitude
- Eye contact
- Take notes
- Concentrate
- Build empathy

Devise a topic outline

A topic outline is a tool that enables you to select and organise your material to develop a logical argument. It serves various functions, namely:

- giving an overview of complex material
- helping you to determine the completeness of your thinking
- allowing you to check your chosen order and make changes
- indicating if any one section is too detailed
- subdividing the material into sections and subsections
- saving you time and effort in the later editing stages.

A topic outline of a piece of writing consists of numbered headings and subheadings. The headings and subheadings give your reader an overview. Good headings tell your reader about the subject in each section. A good structure and appropriate headings will make it easier for your readers to refer back to specific sections of your report.

The headings and subheadings are numbered using a decimal numbering system, showing the hierarchy and the relationship of the topics to each other and to the subject of the document as a whole. However, you should limit the decimal numbering system to three places. Some documents however may have numbering systems of up to four levels, but then only three levels are reflected in the table of contents.

Using a word processor such as Microsoft® Word™, you can create your own template for headings and subheadings, as in the example below. You can also use one of the many variants offered online. A good template uses a variety of fonts (see the section *Use variations between and within typeface families,* on page 25) and usually uses a decimal numbering hierarchy as described. It ensures consistency throughout your document. See Chapter 2 for extensive information on using and creating templates. The following example shows a possible topic outline for the task discussed earlier.

2.	BARRIERS TO EFFECTIVE LISTENING
2.1	Barriers within the Listener
2.1.1	*Physical barriers*
2.1.2	*Psychological barriers*
2.2	Barriers within the Speaker
2.2.1	*Physical barriers*
2.2.2	*Psychological barriers*
2.3	Barriers within the Message
2.4	Environmental Barriers
3.	STRATEGIES FOR OVERCOMING BARRIERS TO EFFECTIVE LISTENING
3.1	Mental Processes and Attitudes
3.2	Note-taking
3.2.1	*Manual notes*
3.2.2	*Electronic notes*

Having a plan such as this will enable you to keep the full document or report in place while you concentrate on parts of it. You will also be able to write up sections in any part of the document.

This type of structure is essential for collaborative work where different people are contributing to the same document, as they will be able to identify the sections that they need to cover. Here it is crucial to use a template which can be uploaded to Google Docs or shared across a cloud system such as Dropbox. General good practice needs to be adhered to by all writers in a collaborative project, such as using the Track Changes feature properly to make changes to the text and using the comments feature to ensure that a record of the dialogue is kept within the document itself rather than in stray conversations or emails. Chapter 2 covers the use of Microsoft® Word™ and templates for collaborative writing.

1.2 How to produce the document

This section deals with the practical steps for effective writing. If you apply these steps carefully, your readers will have material evidence of your ability to write well. This is crucial for establishing your credibility.

Write the draft(s)

No matter how brilliant or unusual your ideas are, if they are poorly expressed in your writing, your readers are unlikely to pay them attention. Write out drafts of sections – according to your topic outline – as quickly as possible in order to create a flow of information. Write those sections that you are most comfortable with first, as this will give you confidence and help you avoid developing writer's block. You do not have to write all the sections of a well-planned document sequentially. However, do use your created or chosen template (topic outline) from the start. You will then avoid later problems with formatting.

Set your draft aside for a while so that you can be more objective when you look at it again. It is more than likely that you will be forced to write within very tight time constraints, but if you plan for this step, it will serve you well in the end.

You need to write well to establish your credibility. You can do so by following these steps (discussed in the rest of this chapter):

- Check the logic of your argument and the structure of the discourse.
- Write in an appropriate style and adhere to the principles of Plain English.

Avoid common abuses of logic

At this point, it is worth stopping to consider one of the most powerful influences on a writer's credibility; that is, the way in which logic is used when arguing a point of view.

In the process of arguing a point, look out for the following flaws:

- The argument must not avoid the issue by:
  - introducing emotive expression instead of concentrating on the facts:

e9

Instead of writing:
Everyone knows that none of the relief aid reached the starving people in the district.

→

Rather write:
It is difficult to know exactly how much of the relief aid has reached the starving people in the district. In an interview last week with the London Times, Red Cross Relief Director Herr Schmidt estimated that not more than 30 of the donated 1 000 tonnes had been distributed.

> ▶ attacking the person rather than the principle:

Instead of writing:
Ms Stone's leadership is distinguished by decisions that, when they are made, are too little and too late.

Rather write:
Decisions by the leadership in the company are often too little and too late.

- The argument must not manipulate the evidence by:
  - ▶ introducing irrelevant data that detracts from the essence of the matter
  - ▶ distorting data, eg when statistics are used out of context
  - ▶ suppressing information that would weaken the argument.

Fear-inducing headlines may attract attention, but Mark Twain was right – we should be wary of meaningless or manipulative statistics, as illustrated in the following example.

Lies, damn lies and statistics
Bread Kills!
...
3. In the 18th century, when virtually all bread was baked in the home, the average life expectancy was less than 50 years; infant mortality rates were unacceptably high; many women died in childbirth; and diseases such as typhoid, yellow fever, and influenza ravaged whole nations.
4. Every piece of bread you eat brings you nearer to death.
5. Bread is associated with all the major diseases of the body.
....
6. Evidence points to the long-term effects of bread eating: Of all the people born since 1839 who later dined on bread, there has been a 100% mortality rate.

Source: Virtual Dr 2016

When you reason from facts rather than from what you suppose, you arrive at stronger conclusions. It is critical that you understand the difference between:

- deductions
- inferences
- assumptions.

Deduction

Deduction is reasoning from facts, from the general to the particular.

℘

Cape Town is in South Africa.
Claremont is in Cape Town.
Therefore, Claremont is in South Africa.

In deduction, you have to be sure that your first premise is true and that the relationship between the premises is valid. The inaccuracy of the following deduction speaks for itself:

℘

Students live in communes.
Nudists live in communes.
Therefore, all students are nudists.

Inference

Inference is based on fact, but is not fact. Look at the example provided and the comparison between inference and deduction outlined in Table 1.1.

℘

Two brands of milk product	A	B
Cost	R5.00	R5.50
Annual sales	3 million	R1.5 million

Inference: A outsells B because it is cheaper.

You ask 500 people if the lower cost of A motivates them to prefer it to B.

Results: 300 say they buy A because it is cheaper; 200 say they buy B because they have not noticed A.

→

This adds strength to your conclusion, but it is still inference, because those interviewed reacted only to the cost feature of the products. There could be many other reasons for buying A rather than B; for example packaging and ingredients.

Table 1.1 Inferences versus facts in argumentation

Inferences	Deductions
are made anytime: before, during or after an observation	follow from observation
go beyond what one observes	are confined to what one observes
represent only some degree of probability	represent a situation as close to certainty as possible
usually generate disagreement	tend to generate agreement
are unlimited in number	are limited in number

Assumption

Assumption is based on common sense or intuition (gut feel). Let us use the previous example again to illustrate this:

eg

Inference: A outsells B because it is cheaper.

Assumption: Consumers prefer lower prices.

When data is unavailable to us, we have to make assumptions. However, we must always ask ourselves whether our assumptions:
- are consistent with available data
- have a reasonable chance of being accurate.

eg

You cannot assume categorically that no one will buy product B if you know that people are buying it. The most you can venture is that it is unlikely that many people will buy B, because it is more expensive.

There are instances in which a writer needs to work from inferences or assumptions. There may be no facts available, and the material may be extrapolated from another area; thus, inferences are drawn or assumptions made for this area. There is nothing wrong with this, as long as the reader is told that these are inferences or assumptions and is not left to assume that they are facts.

Check the discourse structure

Every successful piece of writing has an overall internal shape. This is called the discourse structure. This is achieved by making sure that your message has certain elements, namely:

- unity
- coherence
- emphasis.

Unity

Unity is achieved when the ideas in a piece of writing all relate to the dominant topic, which is stated in the opening topic sentence of the introduction. The conclusion must relate to the objectives set out in the introduction. Each paragraph must also have unity; it must deal with one idea.

Coherence

Coherence is achieved when the ideas in a piece of writing flow logically. This means that the thought or idea contained in one sentence must be clearly linked to that of the preceding sentence.

There are many ways of arranging information according to a sequence that is coherent, namely:

- definition
- order of importance
- question and answer
- problem and solution
- cause and effect
- reasons
- contrast or comparison
- order of familiarity
- order of support
- analysis
- a conclusion followed by supporting data
- presentation of data, followed by a conclusion
- chronological order (ie time)
- order of space
- particular to general
- general to particular.

Coherence is also achieved by links that take the reader from one sentence and idea to the next. Connectors, or transition words and phrases, provide continuity in the content. Transitional words and phrases have different functions, as shown in Table 1.2.

Table 1.2 Some examples of linking words and transitions

Linking words	Function
this, that, it, those	reference
further, another, moreover, and	adding
some, a few, seldom, occasionally	limiting
as a result, consequently, thus	consequence
but, however, whereas, yet	contrast
so that, in order	purpose
still, nevertheless	continuation
because, since, so	reason
finally, thus, therefore	conclusion

Emphasis

When a message has the correct emphasis, the intended scale of importance of the items of information is clear to the reader. This means that minor topics are less important than major topics and are not given prominence or much space.

You can achieve emphasis in your writing by:
- starting and ending with the content you wish to emphasise
- allocating more space to main points and repealing important facts
- supporting an idea with a statistic, quotation or sample
- including an illustration or graphic to support the verbal information.

Include the basic elements of written documents

In general, written documents include the following elements:
1. The **cover page** should provide full information regarding the:
   - title. For example, *The development of a training plan for the project management team*
   - author's name and position
   - author's place of work
   - date of the document.
2. The **introduction** should immediately orientate the reader to the topic. You may do this by restating the topic and your approach to it. For example: 'This document outlines the company procedure for project management training according to the specifications laid out by the Sector Education Training Authority (SETA).' In this example, you may begin by quoting the relevant section from the SETA manual and then linking this content directly to the way in which the company plans to train its project managers.

3. The **body** should clearly reflect the requirements for good readability and style (described later in this chapter).
4. The **conclusion** draws the discussion together and should end on a note of finality.

The following example of an article clearly illustrates the elements of a well-constructed and well-written piece of continuous writing:

℮9

The need for communication courses for engineering students

Introduction

The teaching of communication skills is low in the priorities of most engineering faculties and departments. This phenomenon applies equally in developing and first world countries.

The topic is expressed in the first one or two sentences of the introduction.

It is therefore important to examine why there is a need for communication courses for engineers.

This article will focus on the:

- level of communication required by practising engineers
- communicative ability of engineering students
- feasibility of acquiring competence without a formal course
- need for courses in communication.

The writer now gives the scope of the article and also states the limitations or the areas that the article does not cover.

The design of an appropriate course and the teaching methodology are not considered.

1. The level of communication required by practising engineers

The first point listed in the description of the scope of the article appears as the first item in the body.

The view is sometimes expressed that the writing of engineers and scientists is merely part of the conventional wisdom, a view which is based on the assumption that engineers and scientists are expected to be numerate rather than literate. Supporters of this view contend that technical writing is not particularly difficult or demanding. They argue that experience on the job is sufficient to produce adequate writing ability, that anything beyond this is merely embellishment and that time spent on technical writing is not worth the effort. Such views are frequently expressed by students and recently graduated engineers. Curley [1] discusses these arguments and concludes that they are not valid.

In this paragraph, the word 'view' is repeated to develop a logical connection between sentences.

Three points in support of Curley will be discussed in detail. These are the level of difficulty in technical writing, the need for communication skills and the need for specialised teaching.

1.1 The level of difficulty of technical writing as a subject

1.2 The communication needs of the engineering profession

1.3 The need for specialised teaching

Note how this paragraph forms a clear link between the previous one and the sections that follow, each of which are indicated clearly by a numbered subheading.

→

2. The communicative abilities of engineering students

3. The feasibility of acquiring competence without formal courses

4. The need for courses in communication

In assessing the need for communication courses at university, various aspects need to be considered, namely:

- whether school has prepared the students adequately for university and professional life
- whether the students will acquire the necessary skills at university without formal instruction
- whether communication skills can be more effectively taught during postgraduate training.

4.1 The abilities of students entering university

4.2 The possibility of acquiring communication skills without formal training

4.3 The possibility of teaching communication skills at postgraduate level

Conclusion

If engineers aim to be considered as a professional group, they should ensure that their communicative abilities are on the same level as their technical abilities. *To ensure this*, it is necessary for functional language to be taught at schools. *This teaching* should be followed by formal instruction at university level and further guidance at postgraduate level. *Thus*, while the university is not solely responsible for communicative competence, it should not abdicate its responsibility for teaching some of the communication skills and insights necessary for producing professionally competent engineers.

The connecting words and phrases are italicised. These words show continuity and help the reader follow the argument.

1.3 How to write in Plain English

Plain English is an approach to writing that espouses formal and consultative writing styles that are neither too formal and pompous (also known as 'frozen' as they do not come across as consultative or friendly) nor too casual and intimate to be regarded as professional. Plain English may be described in terms of five different levels, as illustrated in Table 1.3:

Table 1.3 Levels of formality in writing style

Style	Example sentence
Frozen:	It would be appreciated if you would convey the book to the writer.
Formal:	Please give (send) the book to me.
Consultative:	Have you got the book, please?
Casual:	Got the book?
Intimate:	Book?

A formal style is appropriate for essays, articles and case studies, because they are intended to give factual information. A formal style enhances the readability of the message and your credibility as a professional.

The characteristics of effective Plain English are:
- short, crisp sentences
- simple, clear words and the absence of jargon
- the absence of ambiguity
- effective paragraphing and the use of topic sentences
- clear links between and within paragraphs
- good grammar
- the use of direct rather than indirect expression where possible (the active rather than the passive voice).

Each of these will be dealt with in more detail in the sections that follow. Note that Microsoft® Word™ incorporates some style and grammar checks which can aid you. For example, prompts (wavy underlining) appear to indicate style suggestions such as changing passive to active voice and to highlight spelling errors. You need to set the proofing language in Microsoft® Word™ to the version of English you want to use (USA, UK or SA). As these aids differ between versions of Microsoft® Word™, familiarise yourself with what your word processor checks for and follow the prompts. In certain versions of Microsoft® Word™, once the document has been closed, the prompts will not appear again. Thus, it is advisable to respond to the prompts on first appearance. And on top of this, run a full spellcheck when you have finished writing.

Use short, crisp sentences without nominalisation

Effective sentences

If you are writing on a simple topic, you may write a long sentence with various clauses and your readers would have no problem understanding it, provided that they have good language skills. As a rough guide, such a sentence can run to over 25 words. If you are writing on a technical or some other intellectually demanding topic, the reader needs the material to be broken up into one idea per sentence in order to understand it easily. Such sentences need to be 15 to 25 words. Use conjunctions, such as 'since', 'because' and 'when' – they help the reader predict the kind of information that is to follow and also show which ideas are less important than others. Read the following two examples:

The Development Department is interested in the possibility of using resin cloth for electrical insulation, and because overheating of electrical equipment could cause heating of the resin cloth, which could lead to the evolution of flammable gases from the resin, an investigation into the pyrolysis products of the resin was requested.

The following version is much easier to read:

> The Development Department is interested in the possibility of using resin cloth for electrical insulation. However, the overheating of electrical equipment could cause heating of the resin cloth. This could lead to the evolution of flammable gases from the resin. For this reason, an investigation into the pyrolysis products was requested.

Did you notice the way transitional words were used in the second example in order to increase the flow?

In the following sentence of 71 words, there are four different ideas:

> The adoption of an information technology (IT) programme in an organisation can cause work performance to decrease in the short term because staff need to become familiar with it and comfortable in its application, but over time there will be a meaningful improvement in productivity: not productivity aligned to the programme introduced, but rather from the adjustments made to the business systems which evolved from the adoption of the IT programme.

Separate but linked sentences convey the ideas more clearly:

> The adoption of an information technology (IT) programme in an organisation can cause work performance to decrease in the short term. This negative outcome is because staff need to become familiar with the programme and comfortable in its application. Over time, however, there will be a meaningful improvement in productivity. This will not be productivity aligned to the programme introduced, but rather a result of the adjustments made to the business systems which evolved from the adoption of the IT programme.

Nominalisation

You can see how important it is to write sentences containing only one main idea. However, clarity and Plain English are not achieved if the sentences are reduced by simply using a stack of nouns without prepositions. This practice of stacking nouns is called nominalisation. Phrases with prepositions are preferable to nominalisation. Look at the following example:

e9

Early childhood thought patterns misdiagnosis was the cause of problems.

Here, the meaning is unclear, as it is not clear what the adjective 'early' refers to. Was the misdiagnosis made early? Or was the research conducted on very young children, thus in early childhood? Using prepositions to rewrite the phrase would clarify the meaning:

e9

The problems were caused by the thought patterns in very young children being misdiagnosed.
OR
Problems occurred because the misdiagnosis of thought patterns in children was made too early in the study.

Use simple, clear words and avoid jargon

Keep the number of syllables per word as low as possible. It is not clever or professional to deliberately use language that your readers will find hard to understand. This often causes confusion and irritation and can lead to costly delays. The following are a few guidelines you can follow:

- Avoid using unnecessary words. Sometimes writers pad their writing with redundant words and indirect expressions.
- Use concrete, specific terms (eg 'Spaniel') where required rather than vague, emotive or generic terms (eg 'canine breed').
- Use familiar terms (eg 'suitcase') where possible instead of long, foreign or abstract words (eg 'portmanteau').

Clear vocabulary

Use a single adjective or adverb instead of using an adverbial phrase or clause:

e9

A delay which is to be regretted = A regrettable delay
A point which is in doubt = A doubtful point
He spoke in a manner that was courteous = He spoke courteously
The committee which was established to study housing problems = The housing committee

Use the original verb form rather than a phrasal verb or a noun. Original words are more accessible to the reader than derivative words.

> The environmental laws place an emphasis on the need to train farmers in the conservation of water.

This is more direct and easier to understand:

> The environmental laws emphasise the need to train farmers in conserving water.

Use a direct style and avoid double negatives. Double negatives do not exist in many languages, and are therefore particularly difficult for second-language users of English to understand.

> Instead of writing:
>   The institution is not unknown
>   That is not a bad dress on you.
>
> Rather write:
>   The institution is well known.
>   That is a good dress on you.

Avoid unnecessary jargon

Avoid jargon and gobbledygook wherever possible. Gobbledygook – a word coined from the noise a turkey makes – means language that uses, to an unnecessary degree, vocabulary drawn from business, science and technology and that ends up lacking meaning (Wordhippo.com, 2016).

> Instead of writing:
>   The optimum operational capabilities of the computer are contiguous on the parameters of its support systems.
>
> Rather write:
>   The quality of the support systems installed on the computer will affect its performance.

Avoiding jargon does not mean getting rid of necessary technical terms. The correct defining terms need to be used rather than general terms.

e9

Instead of writing:
   The engine is running very fast.
   The additional amount of memory made the computer run faster.

Rather write:
   The engine is running at 30 rpm.
   The additional 20 RAM of memory increased the computer's speed by 20%.

If you are writing for non-specialist readers, one way of accommodating a less technically knowledgeable readership is to include definitions of essential terms within the text or to include a glossary at the start or end of your text.

Measure readability

Chapter 2 deals with the tools offered by Microsoft® Word™ for checking your writing, but the measurement tool for readability is pertinent here. Readability scoring exercises read the weighting of terms used – more sophisticated words have a higher number of syllables – with the length of sentences. High scores indicate dense language, which can be difficult to read. The readability statistics feature in Microsoft® Word™ produces a summary (see Figure 1.2) with statistics, including the Flesch Reading Ease score and the Flesch-Kincaid Grade Level score. See Chapter 2 for a full explanation of how to score the readability of your writing.

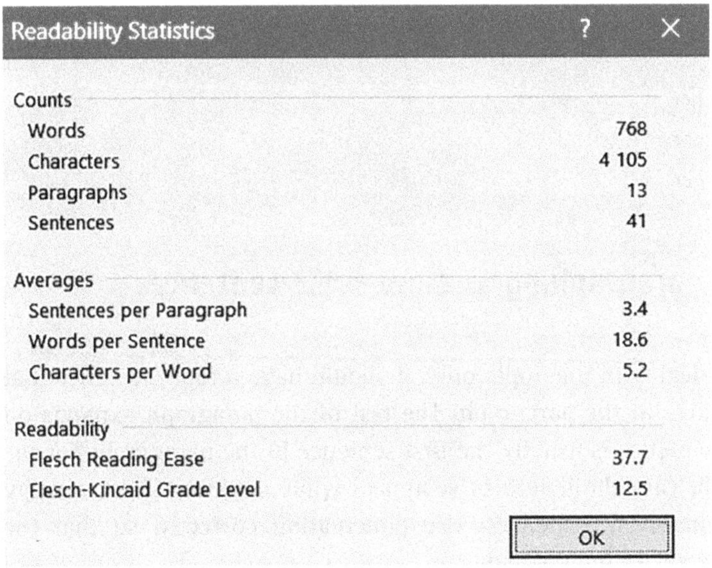

Readability Statistics	? ✕
Counts	
Words	768
Characters	4 105
Paragraphs	13
Sentences	41
Averages	
Sentences per Paragraph	3.4
Words per Sentence	18.6
Characters per Word	5.2
Readability	
Flesch Reading Ease	37.7
Flesch-Kincaid Grade Level	12.5
	OK

Figure 1.2 Readability statistics in Microsoft® Word™

Avoid ambiguity and apply the rule of proximity

Ambiguity

Ambiguity is where there is more than one meaning that can be read into a phrase, sentence or passage. It can occur because a word has more than one meaning.

Find the causes of ambiguity in the following passage:

I must write to tell you how sorry I am that my golf ball narrowly missed you yesterday. I certainly thought for a moment I had hit you behind the bunker. When I got there you had already passed on, so I decided to waste no time in writing. What happened was that as I was about to strike the ball, my eye was caught by a passing squirrel which deflected the ball to the right where you were standing. I have said for years that somebody would get hit there and something needed doing badly about it, so I am particularly distressed at coming so near to offending myself.

The rule of proximity

An important thing to remember is the rule of proximity, of which the passage above also gives examples. A phrase will take its meaning from the phrase closest to it before it takes meaning from the phrase which is separated from it by a comma or colon.

The following three sentences each have a different meaning:

Only I told her I loved her.
I told *only her* I loved her.
I told her I loved *only her.*

Apply effective paragraphing and use topic sentences

The topic sentence

A paragraph should deal with one topic only. It should have a topic sentence that expresses the main idea in the paragraph. The rest of the paragraph expands on this idea. The topic sentence is usually the first sentence in the paragraph. For the rest of the paragraph, vary the length of sentences while avoiding short, choppy sentences or long, involved sentences. Use punctuation correctly, so that the message can be more easily understood.

In the following example the topic sentence is in italics at the start of the paragraph:

Technology has revolutionised activities in the digital business office. For example, messages written on computers or other devices are transmitted instantly. In addition, computer software manages many other kinds of writing, recording, designing, etc.

Clear links between paragraphs

Look at the list of linking words or conjunctions that was given in Table 1.2 on page 12.

Use good grammar

Finite verbs

A complete sentence must contain a finite verb; otherwise it is called a fragment.

The following are incorrect, as some of these are fragments:
In order to succeed in professional sport. Players must train regularly.
Since joining the company and gaining promotion.
Running fast. He planned to win.
The following are all correct, full sentences:
Players must train regularly in order to succeed in professional sport.
Since joining the company, she has gained promotion.
He planned to win by running fast.

Concord between nouns, pronouns and verbs

A singular subject (the noun preceding the verb) takes a singular verb and a plural subject takes a plural verb.

A member of staff is on the Committee of Health and Safety.

If the subject consists of a singular and a plural noun connected by 'or' or 'nor', the rule of proximity applies. This means the noun nearest the verb dictates whether the verb will be singular or plural.

e9

Neither the students nor the lecturer expects a positive set of results. (The singular antecedent is closest to the verb.)

Neither the lecturer nor the students expect a positive set of results. (The plural antecedent is closest to the verb.)

The use of direct versus indirect expression

The English language has two voices: active and passive.

e9

Active voice:
   Janet filed the letter.
   The R&M Group recommends the following steps.

Passive voice:
   The letter was filed by Janet.
   The following steps are recommended by the R&M Group.

A direct, active style is more effective, because it is emphatic and vigorous. The passive voice makes writing indirect, which often makes it long-winded and boring to read.

However, there are sometimes legitimate reasons for using the passive voice, such as:

* when you need to **emphasise the object** of the action, for example: *The lathe has been broken again* is more emphatic than *Someone has broken the lathe again.*
* when you **do not wish to assign blame** to anyone specific, for example: *The required documents were not included* is more neutral than *You failed to include the required documents.*
* in report writing, when you want to convey an **objective point of view**, for example: *It was found that ...* is more objective than *I found that ...*

Check your references and/or bibliography

The reasons for including a list of references and/or bibliography and how to compile it are explained in Chapter 12.

1.4 How to edit the final draft for visual readability and impact

Readability requires that the message be visually pleasing. The physical layout of the text plays a role in attracting and holding a reader's attention. Readability in layout can be created by using:

- readable typefaces
- headings and subheadings that are informative phrases
- bold or italics to emphasise certain words, phrases and sentences
- numbering, spacing and indentation
- white space and wide margins to rest the eye of the reader, help organise the message in the text, create an elegant layout and reduce the eye span required to read the text
- lists and bullets where appropriate:
  - Remember that bulleted lists must be parallel; that is, each bulleted item must begin with the same type of word, such as a verb, noun or gerund.
  - Each of the items in the list must run on from the introductory sentence, or each item must form a full sentence on its own.

Breaks in text are important for readability. Be extravagant with white space; it rests the eye of the reader, helps organise the message in the text and results in a more elegant page.

Include illustrations

Illustrations include photographs, diagrams, pictures, tables and all types of graphs. See Chapter 10 for details on these aspects.

Always remember the following points when including graphics in your message:

- Do not place the illustration before it has been mentioned or introduced in the text. Always prepare the reader, however briefly, for the illustration and its content.
- Once you have placed the illustration, you are in a position to direct your reader's attention to specific aspects contained within the illustration.
- Position illustrations as close as possible to the point in the text at which the readers will need the information provided by the illustration.
- Always acknowledge the source if the illustration is not your own.

An illustration can be judged according to the criteria given in Table 1.4.

Table 1.4 Criteria for readability of illustrations in text

Criterion	Description
Accuracy	If it is not both numerically and visually accurate, the design is at best useless, at worst dishonest.

→

Criterion	Description
Brevity	The message conveyed should be as immediate as possible. Avoid trying to make too many points through one illustration.
Clarity	Make every effort to reduce clutter – numeric or verbal – by carefully selecting information and positioning labels.
Emphasis	Guide the reader to the focus of the illustration by using colour, arrows or symbols.

Choose typefaces for readability

When you choose or create a template for your document, be aware of the factors that will either improve the presentation of your writing or hinder it. This particularly applies to your choice of typefaces.

When choosing a font size, you need to ask yourself if it is easy to read. Printing a well-written email or letter in unreadably small text is self-defeating. Most readers are comfortable reading type in 12 point rather than in 10 point. Fonts have different X sizes – the measure of the body of the letter. Times New Roman (TNR) 12 and Calibri 12 are equivalent to Arial 11 and to Verdana 10, which have a large X size and short ascenders (upward extensions on the h, t, k, etc) and descenders (downward extensions on the y, g, q, etc). Thus, for the smaller fonts, such as TNR and Calibri, anything smaller than 11 point is too small to be read with ease.

Times New Roman

This is 14-point type.

This is 12-point type.

This is 11-point type.

This is 10-point type.

This is 9-point type.

Point size in Calibri

This is 14-point type.

This is 12-point type.

This is 11-point type.

This is 10-point type.

This is 9-point type.

Point size in Arial

This is 14-point type.

This is 12-point type.

Point size in Verdana

This is 14-point type.

This is 12-point type.

→

This is 11-point type.   This is 11-point type.

This is 10-point type.   This is 10-point type.

This is 9-point type.   This is 9-point type.

Serif and sans serif fonts

A typeface that has a serif (a little line or stroke that finishes off a letter) is a traditional typeface. The serif originated from the days of hard copy printing when a letter created out of a small piece of lead imprinted ink onto the page. Times New Roman is an example of a serif font. Arial is an example of a sans serif font. A serif font has more shape.

For older readers, who were educated with textbooks printed in a serif font and who have read serif text most of their lives, a sans serif text is tiring to read. However, for younger readers who have a lot of experience of reading text in sans serif text on screens and in textbooks, it presents no problem. Sans serif is preferred for business documents, such as reports, as it has a more contemporary look. Such documents do not consist of pages filled to the maximum with text; they contain headings and white space, which rests the eye.

For the same reason, always put extensive blocks of text into lower case. Upper case has less variety in shape (BECAUSE IT IS SQUARED OFF) and is harder to read. The ascenders and descenders of lower case text give the line of type shape and this is what catches the reader's eye.

Use variations between and within typeface families

Consider using a second style of typeface to make certain items stand out. For example, for the text of a report you may use a serif typeface, such as:

℮9

Georgia, Times New Roman or Courier New(serif)

However, for headings and captions, you may use a sans serif typeface, such as:

℮9

Arial or **Verdana**

Note from these examples how the typefaces come across as having different point sizes, even though all the examples are in 10.5 point. The typefaces that appear larger have a bigger X height and shorter descenders and ascenders than do the other typefaces. The smaller-looking typefaces have the opposite; that is, a smaller X height with longer descenders and ascenders.

Headings and subheadings

Use headings and subheadings to aid readability – even in a one-page document – to ensure that the overall order of the message is clear to the reader. Headings will also make the inter-relationship of ideas come across; that is, what is more important or less important.

It is also effective to use variations within a font for headings to emphasise the relationship between headings:

- To emphasise headings, for example the subject line and subheadings, you can present them in a larger font size, such as 14 point, in bold, in italics or even in bold and italics.
- Preferably do not use underlining, as it is considered to make the page appear heavy. It is also considered out of date: other forms of emphasising type have taken over.
- In choosing the font for an effective and striking subject line, you may also consider the UPPER CASE of the typeface. However, if the heading or subject line runs over more than one line, it can be too heavy. You may also consider SMALL CAPS.

For example, in designing your overall combination of typefaces, you may choose to use Garamond (a serif font) for the text of the report and Arial (a sans serif font) for headings, which are then also printed in bold and small caps. The variety in size, colour and weight of your typeface will add interest to the page.

Columns

In a document or an attachment that carries extensive text – that is, full paragraphs and pages of text – your column of text can be justified or can run ragged right. When text is set to run ragged right (as this paragraph does), it means that the right side of the column is not justified.

Justification on the right as well as the left of the page (as in this paragraph) gives a more orderly look. The disadvantage, however, is that where there is little text on a page – and thus few words per line – or where text is placed in narrow columns (as in a journal or for captions to illustrations) it can cause ugly spaces to appear in certain lines, as the characters are spaced out to reach to the end of each line. A line printed in 12 point that spans the width of the page will be unlikely to create any gaps (called 'rivers and lakes'). However, if you create your document in two columns, gaps will occur in the spacing across these narrow lines.

The alternative to justifying text on the right as well as the left of the page is to allow words at the end of lines to be split (as shown in the example in this paragraph). This outcome also makes for poor readability.

e9

If you choose narrow columns and a large font size, it is preferable to leave the right side of your page unjustified.	The computer is then able to space the letters naturally without any unnecessary kerning (spacing) or gaps occurring.

✓

Checklist for a well-organised and coherent message

Writing is a skill that can be learnt. The more you practise it, the better you will become as a writer. Bear in mind that your degree or diploma may secure you your first job, but what will determine your promotion and continuing success will be your ability to express yourself well, particularly in your writing.

In order for your message to lead to the outcome you desire, it must be readable. Use the following checklist when you prepare a message:

- Select content according to the purpose of the message and the designated readership.
- Use brainstorming and mind mapping techniques in the initial planning.
- Create a topic outline out of the mind map.
- Make sure the formatting and template are appropriate to the document.
- Use informative headings, subheadings and a numbering system.
- Use logical argumentation with a sound discourse structure (unity, coherence and emphasis).
- Make sure your style is appropriate.
- Use correct grammar.
- Incorporate illustrative matter and give the sources.
- List your references (if required).
- Use a readable layout.

2

The digital footprint: social media, templates, Microsoft® Word™

Living in a digital world gives you access to a wealth of information and knowledge. It also allows you to remain in easy contact with friends, relatives and other followers as well as colleagues. It enables you to create a digital presence. The ease of using social media and other digital platforms can, however, lead to a blurring of the interface between your personal and professional profiles. While some sites are overtly aimed at allowing professionals and businesspeople to network and create public profiles, other more socially oriented sites may still have an impact on your professional reputation, as they also form part of your digital footprint.

This chapter will enable you to become more aware of and learn how to manage your online presence. It also covers tools and techniques for being more professional and efficient when dealing with electronic documentation, both to enhance your personal brand and to support your organisation's brand and reputation. For example, Microsoft® Word™ is an extremely powerful program and we can work faster and more effectively by using it more fully.

By the end of this chapter, you will know how to:
- research and understand social media spaces, separating your personal and professional accounts
- promote your professional profile online
- develop smart digital work skills
- develop smarter documentation skills
- use the tools, features and commands in Microsoft® Word™ to improve your output.

2.1 Research and understand social media spaces

A myriad of platforms already exists through which you are able to communicate with others and develop your online presence. New platforms are created all the time, each of which has a different purpose and audience, with a different combination of content, whether text-based or visual. The spaces in which you choose to operate and how you do so can make an enormous difference to your online reputation. As with any other reputation, once you have damaged your professional reputation it can take a long time to rebuild. Take time to understand the purpose and value of a presence on any platform or online activity and how it really works. Do this to assess whether it is worth your professional time to maintain a presence, and, on a personal level, how much control you will have over what is done with your posts, what happens to information after you post it and what others say and post about you.

Personal versus professional social media accounts

While many of us use social media primarily for social purposes, regularly updating our status, uploading new content and sharing posts, tweets or images, many employers also review the social media accounts of applicants or of employees as part of their policies to maintain their own reputation and integrity. Employers require more from a potential employee than a clean record and good initial references. Many companies and organisations have a code of conduct that seeks to guide employees to behave in a way that is congruent with the organisation's values and image.

Inappropriate content or images, even if they appear in your social space, would negatively affect your image and may even contravene the organisation's code of conduct and so make you a greater risk as an employee. It is not just your own accounts that can create risk: friends and even colleagues can post photographs or share content in which you may be tagged or tracked without your being aware of it.

Even the most cursory online search by a potential or current employer could throw up content that would not necessarily accord with how you wish to present yourself in your workplace. Furthermore, if you are starting out in your working career, you will not have an employment track record to bolster your CV and covering letter, and many recruitment organisations and potential employers will search for your profile on social media to assess you.

Personal versus professional email accounts

If you are in employment or work for yourself, you should avoid using work email for any personal correspondence or transactions. Maintain a personal email account for all personal emails and use your work email account only for work-related issues. While your personal email is your own affair, you still need to maintain a level of awareness; while you can control what you send and to whom, you cannot control how your messages will be forwarded or shared.

Treat an employer's reputation with as much respect as you would wish for your own reputation:
- Always ensure your work-related correspondence, whether internal or external, is courteous and appropriate, even in potentially difficult circumstances. (Also see Chapter 3.)

- Always include a signature at the bottom of your emails, containing your full name, your title or position, the company name, the company logo (if applicable) and the relevant contact details. Electronic signatures may also be specified for staff within an organisation and may include a similar logo and typeface to the company letterhead to confirm the brand. You may also choose to give additional information, such as your qualifications (see Chapter 3). If your organisation has no requirements in this regard, set up your own electronic signature containing the relevant information and use it for all your work correspondence. These pre-set electronic signatures can be dropped in manually or automatically.
- Never add anything personal to the end of an email, such as a quotation or saying. It is inappropriate, as it has not been approved by the company or organisation you work for, and it may not send the message that the company wishes to convey.

See yourself as an employer or client might see you

Without running your own checks, it is impossible to know what is out there online attached to your name or your profile. At any rate, it is a worthwhile exercise to regularly run a search using your name and review what each search turns up, particularly if you are active online. If you have had various social media accounts for some time and you regularly post comments, content, links or images, it is likely that some of this may have been shared and re-shared and thus reached an audience that you are unaware of. In an extreme case, you might have the same name as someone whose online profile portrays an undesirable image, and so it may become necessary to actively differentiate your profile from that of your namesake.

Regardless of the outcome, awareness and a strategy are important: once you are aware of any potential problems, you are better placed to mitigate or manage damaging content. On the flip side, if nothing much turns up, it may indicate to a potential employer or client that you are not active in the social media space. Depending on the industry you are in and the people whom you hope to impress, a lack of presence may not be a good thing. This may indicate that you need to promote your profile and online activity more successfully.

Check your privacy settings

Check, and if necessary customise, the privacy settings on all your social media accounts to ensure you are aware of who is able to see your content and that you are able to review content you are tagged in. Before posting any content on any site where you have an account, click on the privacy button or option, and read the options carefully before selecting how you want to proceed. It is important to know not only who will be able to view your profile but also what the organisation will do with your details and content.

Even on personal accounts, you should be prudent about whom you allow to see your content. Avoid adding people to your network that you do not personally know – quality trumps quantity in most cases.

Promote your professional profile online

In addition to creating a presence on professional networks such as LinkedIn, consider setting up a separate public or professional profile on various social media platforms, such as Facebook and Twitter, and use those accounts to manage your professional online presence. Before you set up your accounts, research various platforms to find out what you like and to locate professional networks or groups that would be useful given your interests and skills. Do not try to be active across too many platforms, however, as managing your profile across all of them becomes extremely time-consuming and it is likely that some will end up becoming inactive or forgotten.

Many working or aspiring professionals set up or maintain a blog, as this allows them to post commentary on industry-related matters or to follow and post links to relevant sites. Sharing links to relevant articles, blogging and commenting on others' posts – courteously and thoughtfully – can be a useful way to boost your profile. For certain industries, a personal blog or personal/individual professional webpage – if carefully managed and compiled – can act as an online portfolio (e-portfolio) of your work and creative talents as well as showcase any relevant or meaningful projects you are or have been engaged in, whether as paid work or voluntarily. It can also act as an extended CV. (See Chapter 4 for more on CVs and Chapter 13 for more on academic blogs and e-portfolios.)

Various easy-to-use, free online platforms are available for creating personal or professional blogs or individual webpages or websites, including WordPress, Wix.com and Blogger. Some are tools for creating simple blog sites or landing pages for dropping images, video, text and links that reflect your profile quickly and efficiently. Others enable you to create full websites allowing more depth of content, which may be more suitable for displaying a portfolio of your working career. Most offer extensive online tutorials via the platforms themselves (or YouTube), as well as a variety of examples you can research to get ideas.

While many platforms already exist and many more are being created all the time, you need to exercise judgement and caution about which platforms you choose to be active on – less is sometimes more. All social media platforms require maintenance and regular updating if they are not to appear irrelevant or out of date. As mentioned, if you have a presence on too many platforms, it is likely to become time-consuming and difficult to maintain this dynamically. It is better to close an account than to have it reappear at an inopportune moment. Finally, it is important to maintain a strict division between social sites and those you set up to promote your online presence for professional or academic purposes.

2.2 Develop smart digital work skills

The concept of the workplace has changed enormously and is likely to continue to do so as new possibilities for communication and collaboration develop and become widespread. Workplace flexibility has increased as people work from home, work flexi-hours or work remotely (such as when on-site or travelling) to suit their personal circumstances. Different businesses obviously require diverse interaction modes, but widespread interconnectivity has expanded collaboration potential and permitted real-time collaboration even across multiple sites.

Online collaboration tools

There are numerous methods of collaborating online, whether in real time or just to collate opinions and expertise on documentation. Facilities such as Dropbox or Google Docs create a shared storage space that is accessible wherever you can access the Internet. These types of collaboration tools allow you to share folders and documents for small projects, or transient and one-off collaborations. While many organisations have shared network drives, it can be cumbersome or even impossible to use remote servers, in which case free tools such as Dropbox, Google Docs and other cloud solutions can provide alternative collaboration options.

Many commercial collaboration tools, such as Microsoft® SharePoint™, allow organisations and project managers to control access and editing rights to documentation and resources through role-based access. These tools also help to manage version control, as a document is effectively 'checked out' and so cannot be worked on by anyone else until it is 'checked in' again. Other tools are more dynamic and allow people in different locations to interact, edit and add commentary while online at the same time. As a professional, it is important for you to get to know and understand how such tools work and how to make the most of them in your career.

In addition to collaboration tools that allow people to share documentation, video- and audioconferencing facilities are common, as well as tools such as Skype and other messaging services that allow multiple participants. These tools allow people to take part in meetings in a meaningful way while in different locations and across time zones.

Other, more informal group options, such as WhatsApp, iMessage or similar, may be very useful for small groups and teams, but their informal nature can lead to inappropriate or overly abbreviated communication, which in turn may lead to misunderstandings. In addition, this informality can allow work communication and requests to spill over too easily into personal time. Groups making use of such communication tools should ensure clear protocols around when people can be contacted or requested to take action, especially if the person making the request is in a senior position.

Note that work decisions need to be recorded so that, if necessary, a clear audit trail can be traced relating to decisions and the responsibility for actions.

Even informal messaging systems can be used as evidence and so it is important to maintain courteous and professional standards at all times.

Online training

Online training is a growing form of professional development. Information is available on almost every subject; and this can assist you to do research, find out about work-related issues and develop your workplace communication skills. It is worth signing up to or following relevant and reputable industry or development sites to increase your knowledge and skills. More and more webinar-based training is being offered on the Internet – and much of it is free. Webinars are an extremely useful way to take part in continuing professional development, as they often allow real-time interactions, unlike straightforward online courses that consist of non-dynamic training videos.

2.3   Develop smarter documentation skills

The increasingly digital nature of the workplace shifts the burden of developing personal skills onto the individual more than ever before. While workplaces will always provide training, particularly for proprietary software or in specific environments, personal knowledge, skills and flexibility are essential due to the rapidly changing environment. While keeping abreast of changing technology is important, it is equally important to ensure that your everyday skills match your communication ability. A well-worded and informative report, proposal or even letter can lose its effectiveness if there are flaws in the document's visual impact or if it is riddled with grammar, spelling and punctuation errors.

Your documents are ambassadors for you and your organisation. Consistency is extremely important and forms a big part of branding. Documents need to look correct and appealing, and must conform to an organisation's style guide. If no style guide is provided, you should, as a professional individual, develop a personal set of templates to guide both your thinking and your presentation. Good templates allow you to concentrate fully on the document's content.

The importance of using templates

Most organisations regularly use a range of documents, for example for minutes, reports, proposals, letters and so on. Rather than set each one up from scratch every time, it is common to find a document similar to the one required, save the file under a new name and then delete whatever content is not required. The difficulty with this is that documents end up being used over and over, each time with slight changes to formatting and layout as well as content. This can often prevent a document from working as you would expect, with numbering and formatting going awry and sometimes being very difficult to fix, especially with multilevel numbering. This problem can be avoided by putting in a little work upfront and setting up templates.

The term 'template' carries a range of meanings, depending on context. Most people think of templates as documents with pre-set layout, formatting and required content. In Microsoft® Word™, however, a template differs from a document. When you open Microsoft® Word™, the blank document is based on the default template 'Normal.dotx'. Effectively, a document (with the file extension .docx) is launched based on the default template. Templates operate exactly like documents in that they can include a defined set of styles, formatting, layout and fixed text or headings. The important difference is that when you double-click on the template icon (see Figure 2.1), a document is launched rather than the template being opened (the function of the .dotx extension). This means that regardless of the changes that are made to that document, the original template remains exactly as it should be, ready to be used again, with all the required text, formatting and layout.

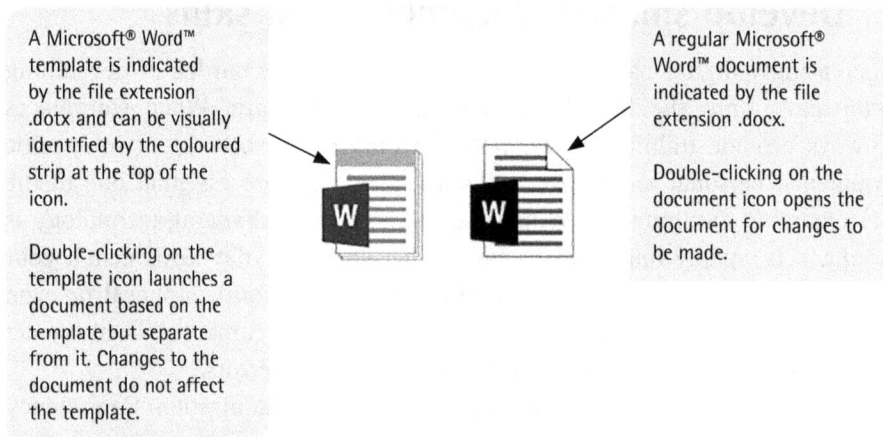

A Microsoft® Word™ template is indicated by the file extension .dotx and can be visually identified by the coloured strip at the top of the icon.

Double-clicking on the template icon launches a document based on the template but separate from it. Changes to the document do not affect the template.

A regular Microsoft® Word™ document is indicated by the file extension .docx.

Double-clicking on the document icon opens the document for changes to be made.

Figure 2.1 Template and document icons in Microsoft® Word™

Using a Microsoft® Word™ template as a base for a new document rather than re-using an old document is the best way to ensure that a document does not degrade from being used repeatedly. Documents carry with them all the formatting changes made in each subsequent version, thereby storing up potential frustration for the user when the old formatting conflicts with the new. Using a template ensures consistency; no one is impressed by poorly or inconsistently laid-out documents.

Furthermore, using templates speeds up the process of creating documents that have to be laid out in a particular way. You can also transform lengthy documents with incorrect or inconsistent formatting in a matter of minutes by dropping them into a template with all the fixed, pre-set styles and applying the correct styles as appropriate. Microsoft® Word™ has a number of built-in styles for text, headings, bullets, numbering and so on. For example, the default style is called 'Normal': it is left-aligned, uses Calibri in 11 point and applies automatic line and paragraph spacing. (Later in this chapter you will learn how to create and modify styles in Microsoft® Word™.)

Each style acts as a base onto which additional formatting may be added. However, each additional formatting change effectively creates a new style, for example 'Normal + bold', 'Normal + bold + italic + 10 pt' and so on. These new styles become associated with the document, together with the original styles, but are not necessarily deleted when the underlying text is deleted in a revised version of the document or when the file is saved using the *Save As* command. This means that if the document has been repeatedly resaved and/or renamed, the formatting changes and resulting styles continue to be part of the document, potentially causing it to become unstable, corrupt or difficult to work with, especially regarding numbering and bullet styles. Furthermore, if text with different formatting is copied and pasted from another document, the styles and formatting from the source document can become associated with the destination document as well as the content – even if the content is reformatted to appear in line with the new document.

Microsoft® Word™ templates

As the discussion above shows, the ideal approach is to create your own Microsoft® Word™ templates that contain only the styles you need for your documents or the documents linked to them. Once this has been done, you can restrict yourself or other users to the specially created styles (accessed via the *Styles* gallery or the *Styles* task pane, as explained later in this chapter) with no muddle, confusion or inconsistency. A template can even appear as a blank document, with no inserted content but all the customised styles ready for use.

Template trees

The best way to create a series of templates is to create a master template with all the styles that may be required in your documents (or your organisation's documents), for example the styles for bullets, numbering and headings, to name a few. Once this has been done, the master template can be used to create a range of documents with additional layout, content or branding built in, and these in turn can be saved as templates. This means the same styles can flow through an organisation's entire range of documents. Figure 2.2 gives an idea of the beginnings of a template tree descending from a single master template.

```
                    ┌─────────────────┐
                    │  Blank master   │
                    │ with all styles │
                    └─────────────────┘
```

Main letterhead	Reports & proposals	Summaries	Policies & procedures
Formal letters for ABC	Short reports	Executive summaries	Policy on XYZ
Regular letters for XYZ	Research reports	Research summaries	Procedure for XYZ
High-level letters	Regular reports	etc...	
etc...	Proposal for XYZ		

Ideally, each template would be either dated or numbered to ensure version control when amendments are made. This also implies the need for a custodian of the templates in any organisation/department.

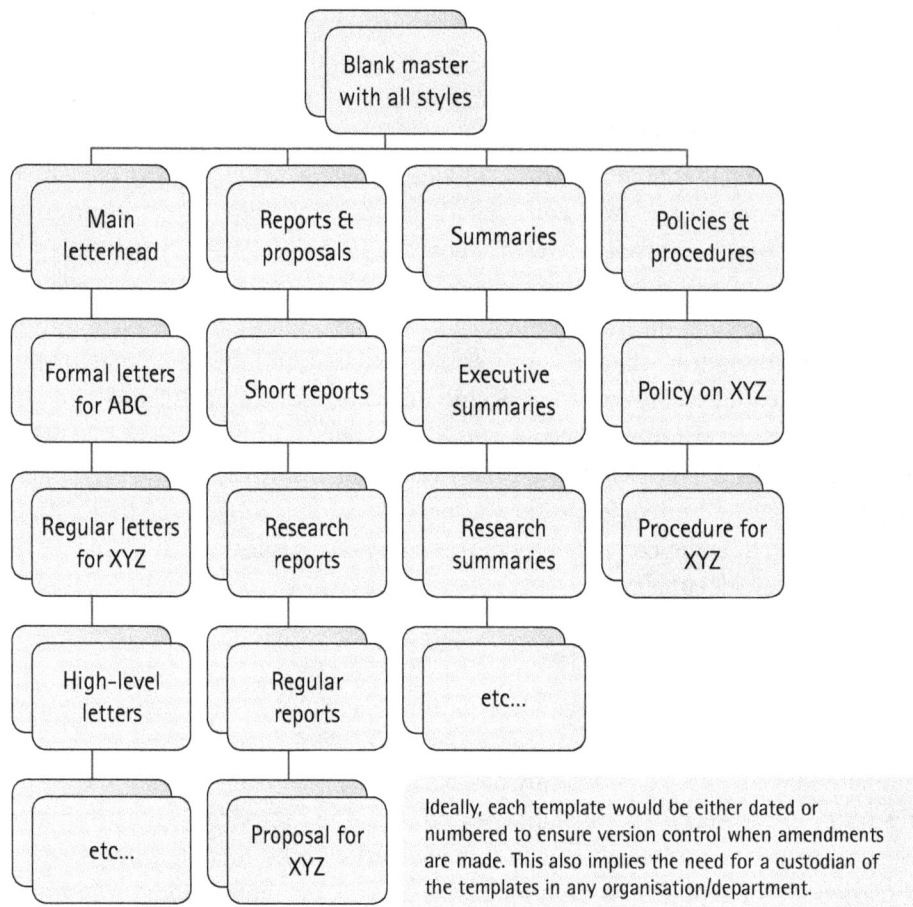

Figure 2.2 A template tree

How to save a document as a template

To save a document as a template rather than as an ordinary document, use the *Save As* command. In the *File* tab, click on *Save As* to bring up the *Save As* dialog box. Give the document an appropriate name and select 'Word Template' from the *Save as type* dropdown box (at the bottom of the dialog box). Before clicking *OK*, select or check the location you want to save the template in, as it usually defaults to a hidden template folder and can be difficult to locate.

This approach to using templates to create consistency and branding across documentation is also useful in Microsoft® Excel™ and PowerPoint™. In the *Save As* dialog box in Microsoft® Excel™, select 'Excel Template' (*.xltx, not *.xlsx) and in PowerPoint™, select 'PowerPoint Template' (*.potx, not *.pptx).

Check the page setup

When you set up a template, you need to confirm the sizes of the page margins and the paper, as well as whether the document or any sections are to be landscape rather than portrait. It is worth setting this up in the template itself rather than document by document, so that you need not worry about it later. One of the most common errors made in this regard is due to people not being aware that in the USA, the default paper size is not A4 but 'Letter' size, which is broader and shorter than A4. While everything will look fine on the screen, when the document is printed it can be problematic, as the margins of the 'Letter' size do not suit A4 and the pages will look truncated. A second issue you have to be aware of is that page margins are often set at peculiar measurements in centimetres; this is because the USA uses imperial measurements and not metric ones.

The first step therefore is to check that your measurements are in centimetres. If they are not, change them in the *Word Options* dialog box (accessed from the *File* tab). In the dialog box, click on *Advanced* and scroll down to the *Display* segment and select centimetres from the list of options in the dropdown menu.

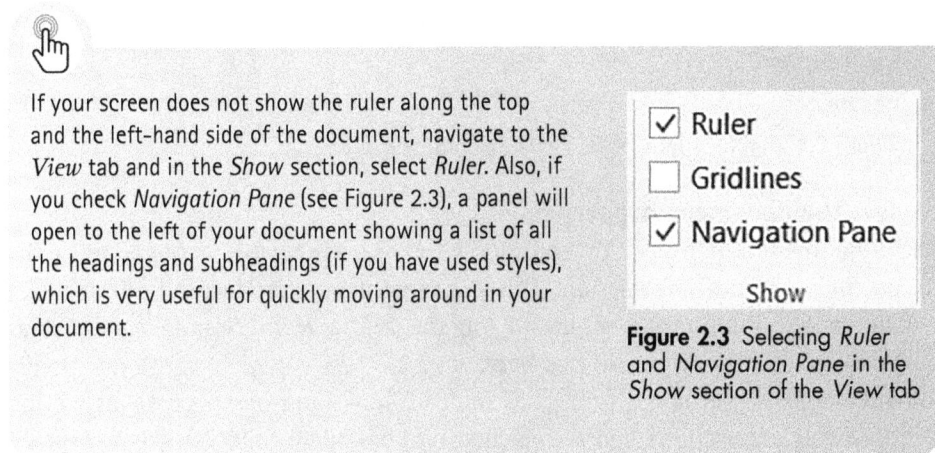

If your screen does not show the ruler along the top and the left-hand side of the document, navigate to the *View* tab and in the *Show* section, select *Ruler*. Also, if you check *Navigation Pane* (see Figure 2.3), a panel will open to the left of your document showing a list of all the headings and subheadings (if you have used styles), which is very useful for quickly moving around in your document.

☑ Ruler

☐ Gridlines

☑ Navigation Pane

Show

Figure 2.3 Selecting *Ruler* and *Navigation Pane* in the *Show* section of the *View* tab

The second step is to open the *Page Setup* dialog box by selecting the mini-arrow at the bottom right-hand corner of the *Page Setup* section of the *Layout* tab. The dialog box has three tabs: *Margins*, *Paper* and *Layout*. Each tab has settings worth checking:

- *Margins:* Check that the page margins are sensible numbers in centimetres. The default page margins are 2.54 cm, which is a direct conversion of one inch. However, 2 cm or 2.5 cm would be more sensible in a metric environment. This tab also allows you to add a gutter if your document will be printed and mirror margins if it will be printed back to back.
- *Paper:* This tab allows you to select the paper size and set it to A4 if it is still in the default 'Letter' size.

- *Layout:* This tab allows you to change the settings for headers and footers, which by default are set 1.27 cm (0.5 inches) from the edge. It also has an option to set a different header and footer for the first page, which is important for letter templates with a logo, address and so on that need to appear on the first page only.

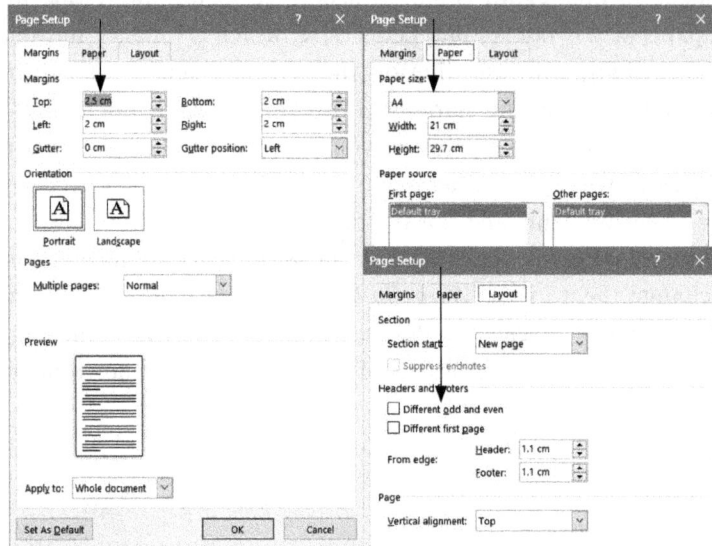

Figure 2.4 The three tabs of the *Page Setup* dialog box

Review the document properties

The final important aspect to consider when working with a template is the document properties information. This is accessed by selecting the *File* tab and looking at the information displayed (on the *Info* screen). Standard as well as advanced properties can be viewed here.

The standard document properties indicate how long has been spent editing the file (which is useful if you are calculating how much time you have spent on a document), who the author is, when it was last modified and by whom it was modified. Here you can also set document protection to restrict who can look at or edit the file, which is useful for confidential documents or ones where certain parts may not be changed.

The advanced document properties can be accessed by clicking on the dropdown arrow next to the *Properties* heading in the top right-hand section of the *Info* page and selecting *Advanced Properties*. All five tabs in the resultant dialog box can be useful to look at or complete, depending on company requirements. Figure 2.5 shows the following three of those tabs:

1. The *General* tab provides information on where the file is stored, what type of file it is, when it was created and when it was last modified. If the *Save As* command has been used a number of times, it can be quite revealing to see when the document was first created.

2. The *Summary* tab should be completed, indicating in particular the author of the document and the company, if relevant. If you are unsure where a document first came from, it is important to check here, because it will retain the name of the original author and company. Ethical problems can arise if documents are used that are effectively the intellectual property of another company or person.

3. The *Statistics* tab provides more detailed information on how much time has been spent on the document and when it was printed and accessed, together with a summary of the content statistics. This tab is often used in forensic investigations when it needs to be established when the document was created, accessed or printed.

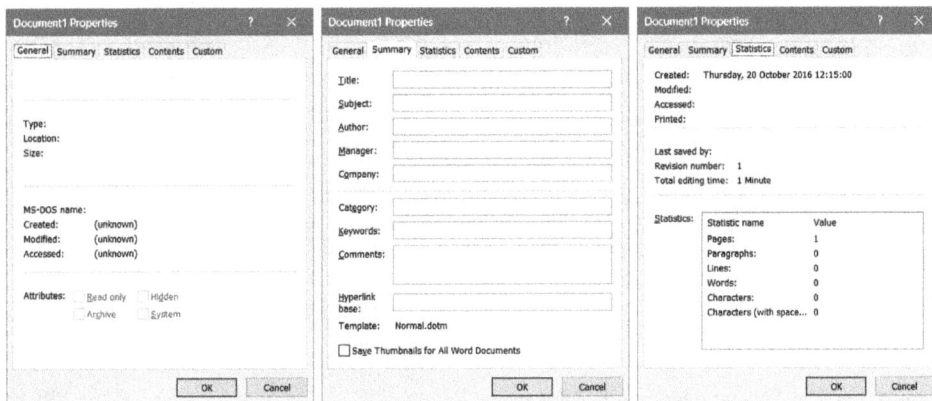

Figure 2.5 Three of the tabs in the *Document Properties* dialog box

Use styles rather than formatting

A style in Microsoft® Word™ is a set of formatting instructions attached to a character or a paragraph so that the text always presents in a particular way. As a style carries all the formatting, spacing and other features you require, you can concentrate on content rather than formatting. The advantage of using styles rather than formatting content manually is that you get exactly the same result every time because you (or your organisation) created the styles, thereby saving time and effort that can always be better spent than on formatting or layout. Microsoft® Word™ has numerous built-in styles, the default being the 'Normal' style.

How to access styles

Built-in or pre-set styles can be accessed either from the *Styles* gallery or from the *Styles* task pane (see Figure 2.6). The advantage of the *Styles* pane is that it remains fully open and therefore visible while working on a document for easy access to the styles. It is easy to forget to use the styles and revert to manual formatting when they are not so obviously available. The *Styles* pane can be opened via the arrow in the bottom right-hand corner of the *Styles* section on the *Home* tab, or by adding a shortcut to the Quick Access Toolbar (see Figure 2.6). When opened for the first time, the *Styles* pane floats over your document. Double-click on the title bar to lock it at the right-hand side, and then tick *Show Preview* to see what the styles look like as well as their names. Next time the pane is opened, it will be locked and showing the preview.

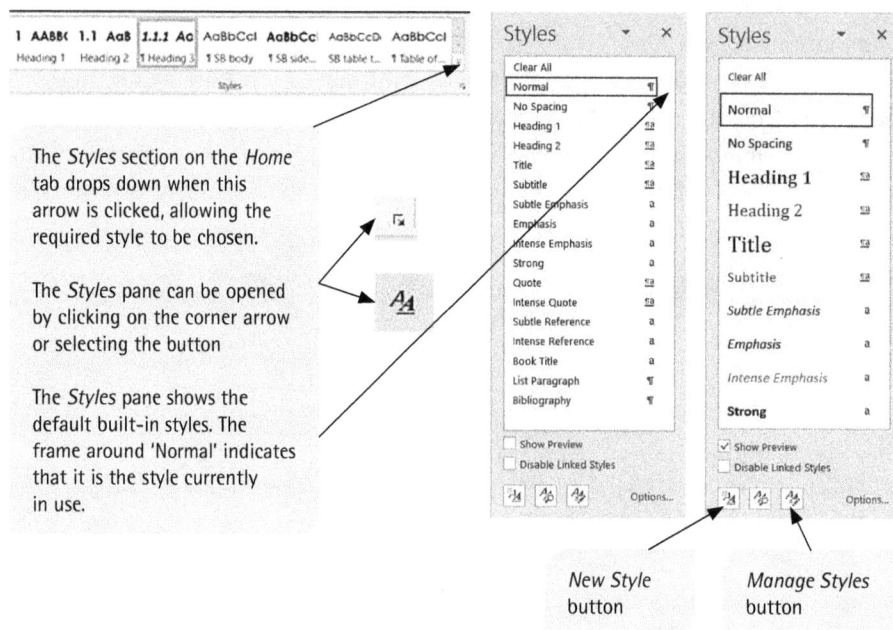

Figure 2.6 The *Styles* gallery and *Styles* pane

To use the *Styles* pane, you can work in either of the following ways:
* Click on the required style in the pane (eg 'Heading 1') and start typing.
* Type the required text, highlight it and then click on the required style.

How to create and modify styles

You can create a new style rather than modify an existing one by selecting the appropriate button at the bottom of the *Styles* pane (see Figure 2.6). This brings up the *Create New Style from Formatting* dialog box.

You can also use the *Modify Style* dialog box (see Figure 2.8) to create or modify a style. This dialog box is identical to the *Create New Style from Formatting Style* dialog box – only the title bar is different. To bring up the *Modify Style* dialog box, open the *Styles* task pane and move the mouse cursor across to the style you want to modify; a dropdown arrow will appear (see Figure 2.7). Click on the arrow and select the *Modify* option to bring up the *Modify Style* dialog box.

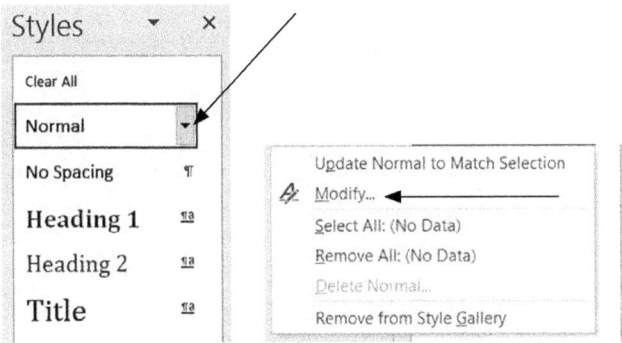

Figure 2.7 The *Modify* option in the *Styles* pane

If you modify a style, leave the name the same.

If you create a style, give it a name. You can use the company name or your personal initials in front of each of the styles you create so you can differentiate styles across different documents.

If you create a new style, ensure the *Style based on* dropdown box is set to 'Normal'.

Here you can select a style for the next new paragraph. For example, after a heading you are likely to want 'Normal' or a body text you have created, not the heading style again.

Now, via the *Format* button, work through the options one by one, only clicking *OK* once all the changes are done. The changes will be reflected in the *Styles* pane. If you created a new style, it will now appear in your *Styles* pane.

Figure 2.8 Modifying a style by using the *Modify Style* dialog box

If you find you have to format text in a particular way more than once, it indicates you should create a new style or modify an existing one. Once you have created a style, if you need to modify it (for example by changing the colour of a heading) all the text in that style will be updated throughout the document, ensuring consistency. The easiest way to work with styles is to take the time to decide what styles you use regularly and then create those styles in a blank document, or as you work in the document. After you have created all your most regularly used styles, save the document as a template. This will make those same styles available every time you create a document based on that template.

The *Format* options in the *Modify Style* dialog box allow you to set the font option and line spacing as well as build in automatic paragraph spacing. Borders can be selected to be part of the style, and the *Numbering* option is where you select bullets or numbering formats to accompany your style.

Remember to select your required language, such as English (South Africa, UK or US). This must be built into the style to ensure the spellcheck runs using the correct language.

If you set up a template with your own styles, start by modifying the style called 'Normal'. Having done this, you can base all the other styles you create on 'Normal', to ensure consistency. It also means that if you need to change the font of the template, all you need to do is modify the 'Normal' style and everything else will be changed automatically.

How to copy and paste from documents with different styles and formatting

The Clipboard

Microsoft® Word™ allows text to be copied or cut and pasted elsewhere, either in the same document or into another document or program. When the selected text is cut or copied, it sits in an area called the Office Clipboard until it is pasted into its destination. Normally, if you copy or cut information, it needs to be pasted into its destination before you can copy or cut another item, or you will lose the previously copied item. This can be annoying when you need to copy several items from a source, as it obliges you to go backwards and forwards between the source and the destination.

However, if you open the Clipboard (see Figure 2.9), a task pane appears to the left of your screen which allows you to copy up to 24 items, which then remain available for pasting once or more whenever you are ready. This allows you to copy several items from a single source without having to paste after each copy. The Clipboard can be very useful when you have to repeatedly use names or terms that are long or difficult to spell – they can be kept on the Clipboard to be used as and when you need them.

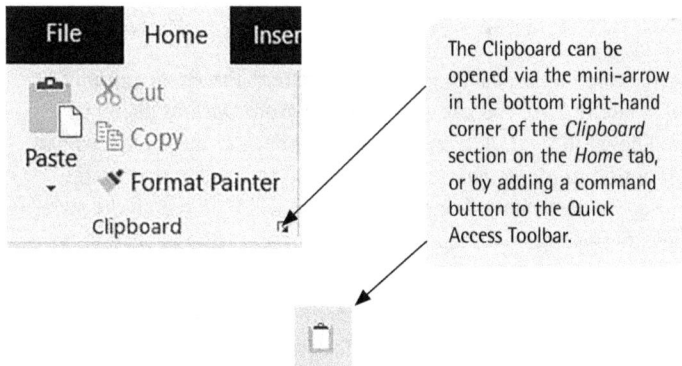

Figure 2.9 Opening the Clipboard

To paste an item from the Clipboard, place the cursor in the correct place in the document and then click on the desired item on the Clipboard. You can paste Clipboard items repeatedly, even into another Microsoft® Office™ program.

The *Paste Options* button

Copying and pasting content from other documents can cause problems when styles or formatting clash. The *Paste Options* button (see Figure 2.10) appears each time something is pasted. By clicking on the dropdown arrow on this button, you can select options such as *Keep Source Formatting, Merge Formatting* or *Keep Text Only*. The options can differ; for example, when pasting numbered or bulleted items, you will be asked whether the list should be continued or not. The options are always quite logical; the important thing is to know that you have to guide Microsoft® Word™ as to what formatting and styles you require.

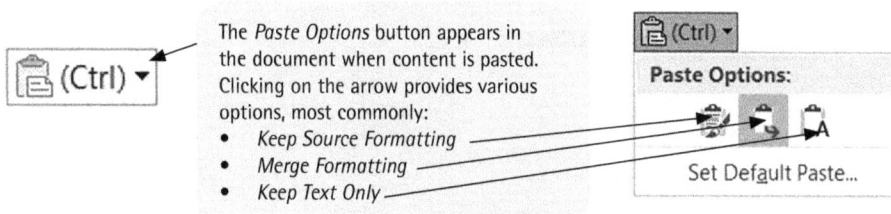

Figure 2.10 The *Paste Options* button and its dropdown menu

If you do not pay attention to the paste options, styles from other documents can be brought in, as well as page setup parameters and different languages (English US, for example), which will affect the spellcheck feature.

You can set the default paste option by choosing *Set Default Paste* in the *Paste Options* dropdown menu, as shown in Figure 2.10. You can also open the *Word Options* dialog box (from the *File* tab) and scroll down to the *Cut, copy, and paste* options in the *Advanced* section. Setting the default option to *Merge Formatting* helps you to avoid importing the styles and formatting from source documents. The pasted content will then match the style that you are in when you paste. This does not stop the *Paste Options* button appearing, so you can still select any of the options.

If a foreign or unwanted style does appear in the *Styles* pane, you can delete it using the dropdown menu that appears beside the style. This helps keep the document clean and consistent.

Paste Special

If pictures or diagrams are copied from elsewhere, they are by default pasted as 'objects', and often cannot be edited. However, if you use the *Paste Special* dialog box (opened by clicking on the dropdown arrow beneath the *Paste* button on the *Clipboard* section of the *Home* tab), you can select options which allow you to paste differently (see figures 2.11 and 2.12). The same applies in all Microsoft® Office™ programs, although the options will vary. For example, you could use this method to prevent a Microsoft® Excel™ table, a bitmap or a picture from being altered when you paste it.

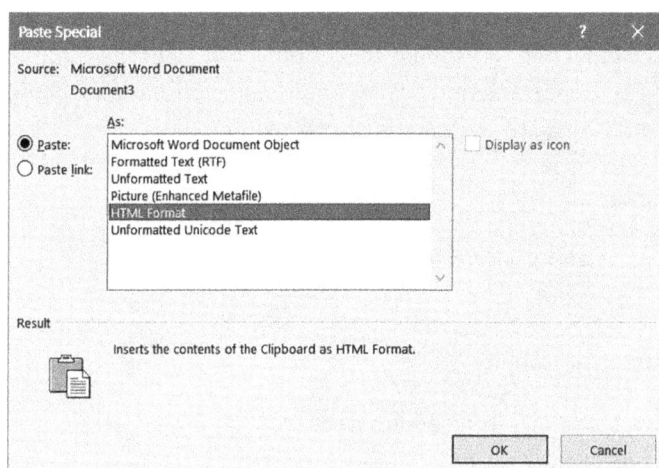

Figure 2.11 The *Paste Special* dialog box when pasting from a Microsoft® Word™ document

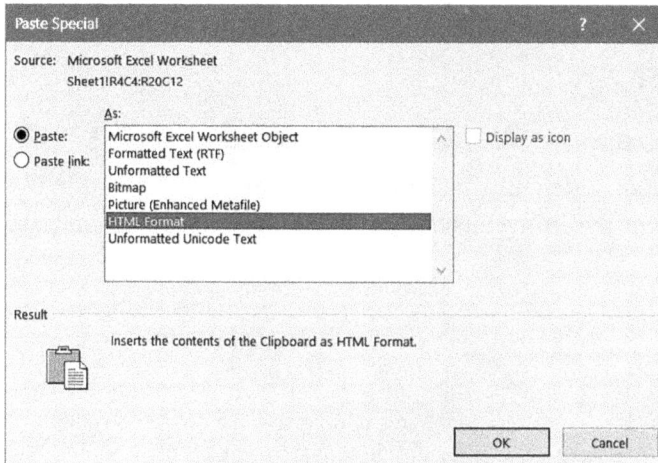

Figure 2.12 The *Paste Special* dialog box when pasting from a Microsoft® Excel™ document

If you select *Microsoft Excel Worksheet Object* (see Figure 2.12) when pasting a table, for example, and then double-click on the pasted table, Microsoft® Excel™ will open inside Word™, allowing you to access the spreadsheet functions. Once you click away, the table appears again as a normal table in Word™.

Ensure the spellings in the source document are correct **before** you copy and paste, especially if you are pasting a Microsoft® Word™ or Excel™ object.

Paste Link

The *Paste Link* option in the *Paste Special* dialog box (see figures 2.11 and 2.12) allows an image or mirror to be copied, rather than embedding the external content into the document. This is particularly advantageous if you present regular reports or presentations containing tables or charts prepared in Microsoft® Excel™. You can set up a template containing a table or chart with a link to the relevant spreadsheet. Each time the document or presentation opens, a message appears asking if you would like the links updated. This will locate the source document, open it and automatically update the linked table or chart to the latest version. For this to work, however, you need to keep the files in the same places; otherwise the link to the source document will be lost and the table or chart will become static.

2.4 How to use Microsoft® Word™ to improve your output

Customise your Microsoft® Word™ environment

We all use a word processor differently, using different options, tools and styles. It is therefore time-efficient and convenient to modify how the program appears, to suit your needs.

> Microsoft® Word™ has been through many versions and doubtless will continue to change, but the essential features of the program have remained the same. Some of these features include styles; automated features such as tables of contents, cross-referencing, bookmarks, captions and hyperlinks; different viewing modes; headers and footers and page numbering. The more familiar you are with how Microsoft® Word™ is laid out and how it operates, the easier it will be to identify where the feature you want has moved to (if it has moved) or how it is accessed in a new version of the program.

The layout of Microsoft® Word™

As with all Microsoft® Office™ programs, everything you need to do can be accessed via the *File* tab and the ribbon (the successor to the toolbars). Rather than toolbars, command buttons are now grouped according to function and organised into tabs (the successors to the menu bar), as shown in Figure 2.13.

Figure 2.13 The tab menus on the ribbon

Other tabs appear automatically when you select a particular item or option. For example:

- If you select a picture, a coloured tab appears called *Picture Tools*, with a *Format* section to allow picture-related actions.
- If you insert or work in a table, two additional *Table Tools* tabs appear: the *Design* and the *Layout* tabs.

In addition, the context-sensitive right-click menus in Microsoft® Word™ automatically offer a selection of options on a small floating toolbar that appears as soon as text is highlighted.

Customise the Quick Access Toolbar

The Quick Access Toolbar, which appears by default above the *File* tab in the title bar, is designed to be customised to contain command buttons for repeatedly used actions. This is where you can gather all the commands that you regularly use to avoid having to move between different tabs to find the commands you need. Ideally, the Quick Access Toolbar should be repositioned below the ribbon (see Figure 2.14) to make it more accessible, to give more space for buttons and to prevent the buttons being blocked by the document name.

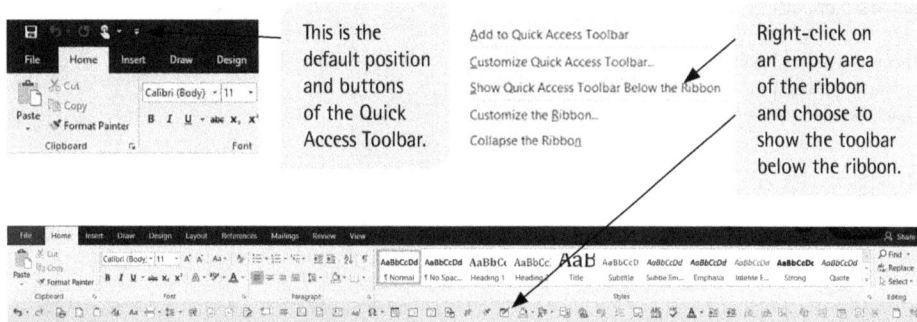

This is the default position and buttons of the Quick Access Toolbar.

Add to Quick Access Toolbar
Customize Quick Access Toolbar...
Show Quick Access Toolbar Below the Ribbon
Customize the Ribbon...
Collapse the Ribbon

Right-click on an empty area of the ribbon and choose to show the toolbar below the ribbon.

Figure 2.14 The Quick Access Toolbar

To customise the Quick Access Toolbar with your personal selection of frequently used commands, do one of the following:

- Right-click on a button on the ribbon that you want to add to the Quick Access Toolbar and select *Add to Quick Access Toolbar.* To remove a button from the Quick Access Toolbar, right-click on it and select *Remove from Quick Access Toolbar.*
- Click on *Options* on the *File* tab menu to bring up the *Word Options* dialog box. From here you select the *Customize Ribbon* section. You can also bring up this dialog box by right-clicking on the ribbon and selecting *Customize Quick Access Toolbar.*

If the option you want
is not in the *Popular
Commands* dropdown list,
use the dropdown arrow
to select *All Commands*
and then scroll through
the alphabetically
organised options.

This is the list of possible
commands to add to the
Quick Access Toolbar.

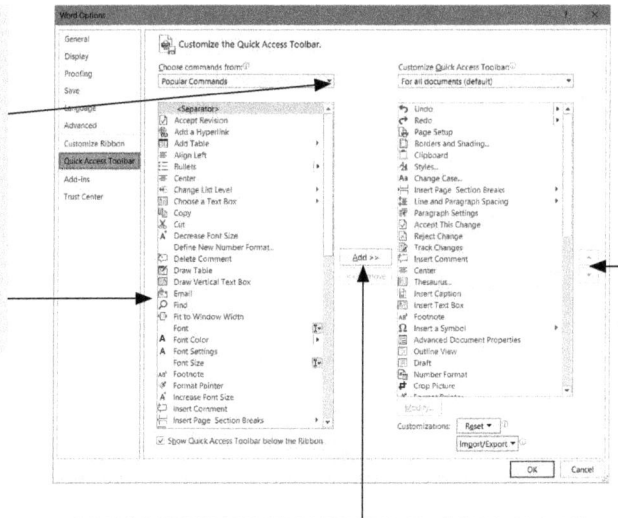

Use the *Add* button to add to the list of commands on
your Quick Access Toolbar, and use *Remove* if you want to
take a command off.

Use the up and down arrows to the right of the column to
re-arrange the buttons displayed on the toolbar.

Figure 2.15 Customising the Quick Access Toolbar via the *Word Options* dialog box

Figure 2.16 shows some suggestions for useful everyday commands for the Quick
Access Toolbar.

Styles		Thesaurus	
Clipboard		Track Changes	
Change Case	Aa	Insert a Comment	
Paragraph Settings		Insert Hyperlink	
Line and Paragraph Spacing		Insert Footnote	AB^i
Page Setup		Insert Caption	
Borders and Shading		Insert Cross-reference	

Insert Picture From File		Restart at 1 (or a)	
Insert a Symbol	Ω ▾	Outline view	
Insert Page and Section Breaks		Draft view	
Draw Table		Repeat Header Rows	

Figure 2.16 Useful options for the Quick Access Toolbar

After customising the Quick Access Toolbar, you can right-click on the ribbon and choose *Collapse the Ribbon* to free up more space for content on the screen. This is especially useful if you are working on a small laptop, notebook or some other device with a small screen.

The *Word Options* dialog box

Microsoft® Word™ is an extremely powerful program. Most of us, however, use very little of what it can do, as our work context tends to dictate the types of documents produced. However, Microsoft® Word™ contains extremely useful features to help you produce professional documents more quickly and so it is worth getting to know them. Your professional image can easily be compromised by careless errors, or unattractively or inconsistently laid-out documents.

The *Word Options* dialog box (see Figure 2.17), which you can open by clicking on *Options* at the bottom of the *File* menu, allows you to customise or alter the program's default settings. Some organisations set certain defaults when providing employees with a computer or laptop, but many others can be activated to suit you.

The dialog box is divided into sections, and it is a good idea to work through each section to check that you have organised it correctly. The following are some useful options to check in the *Word Options* dialog box:

* The *General* section allows you to insert your name and initials so that when you use Track Changes or add comments while you are reviewing or writing a document, your additions can be identified by your initials or name. This is important when multiple people collaborate on a document. If no name or initials are included in the *General* section, any changes you make are simply identified as 'User'.

- If the *Language* section has not been set by an employer's IT department, it is essential to check the language options to ensure, for example, that the version of English that you need to use (South Africa, UK or US) has been enabled as an editing language.
- The *Proofing* section contains various options – depending on your version of Microsoft® Word™ – to assist you with reviewing, editing and proofing your work.

In the section *When correcting spelling in Microsoft Office programs*, find out which options are checked or unchecked.
Remove the tick from *Ignore words in UPPERCASE*. This box is checked by default, which means words in uppercase are not spellchecked.

It is also a good idea to remove the tick from the *Ignore words that contain numbers* box, so that the spellcheck will indicate any mistyping in this regard.

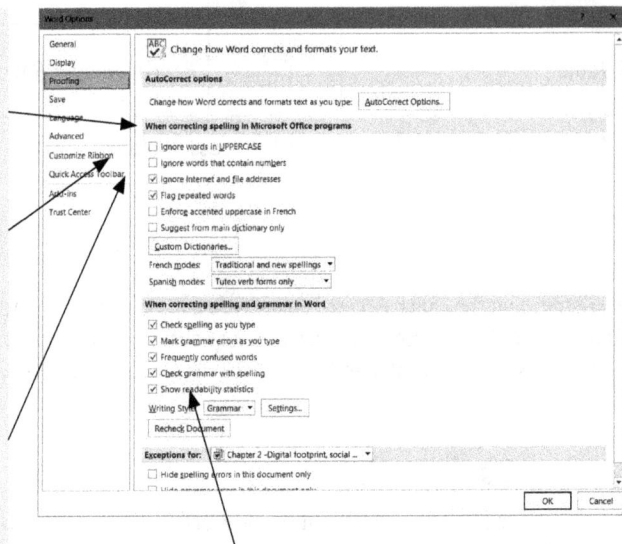

In the section *When correcting spelling and grammar in Word*, check all the options, including *Show readability statistics*.

Figure 2.17 The *Proofing* section of the *Word Options* dialog box

Readability statistics

The *Readability Statistics* dialog box (see Figure 2.18) only appears at the end of a spelling and grammar check. Readability statistics measure the readability of a text based on the length of words, sentences and paragraphs, how much of the passive voice is used, and so on. As an objective measure, it is unable to assess the value of your writing or how good it is, but you can learn a lot about how technically readable your writing is (for example in plain language terms), so it is useful to check these statistics.

In addition to the averages, two indices are offered in the statistics summary: Flesch Reading Ease and Flesch-Kincaid Grade Level. The easier score to understand is probably the Flesch-Kincaid Grade Level. It gives a score based on a school or university grade, indicating that someone with that level of education should be comfortable reading the document.

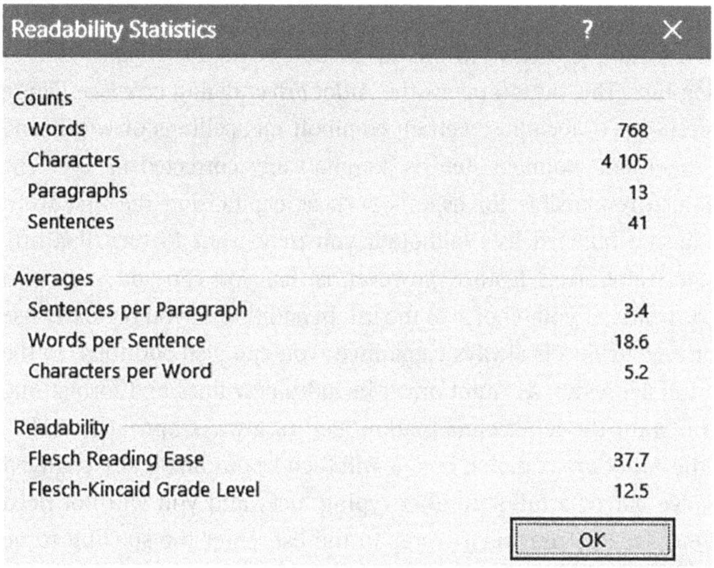

Readability Statistics	?	X

Counts

Words	768
Characters	4 105
Paragraphs	13
Sentences	41

Averages

Sentences per Paragraph	3.4
Words per Sentence	18.6
Characters per Word	5.2

Readability

Flesch Reading Ease	37.7
Flesch-Kincaid Grade Level	12.5

OK

Figure 2.18 Readability statistics

While many professional documents are aimed at readers with many qualifications, in the workplace it is not appropriate to pitch your writing at too high or too academic a level, not just because you cannot always be sure of your entire readership profile, but also because in a multilingual society, English acts as a lingua franca and for many people it is not a first language. This places the onus on writers to ensure that their writing is sufficiently plain and appropriate so as not to force readers to work too hard. (See Chapter 1 for advice on effective writing.)

How to check spelling and grammar

While it is tempting to correct spelling as you go, it is more efficient to wait until you are finished with a document or section and then perform a check. If you only want to check a section of your work, highlight the relevant section or pages before clicking on *Spelling and Grammar* in the *Proofing* section of the *Review* tab.

Before performing a spelling and grammar check on your work, select the entire document (press Ctrl + A) or the required section and then check what language is selected as the proofing language. You can do this by clicking on the correct section on the status bar or by using the *Language* command button on the *Review* tab. It is important to do this, as content pasted from other documents may be in a proofing language different to the one required for your document, such as US English, in which case the spelling and grammar check would not correctly identify all spellings that are classified as errors in your proofing language.

AutoCorrect

The *AutoCorrect Options* button is located in the top section of the *Proofing* section of the *Word Options* dialog box. This button opens the *AutoCorrect* dialog box (see Figure 2.19). AutoCorrect is designed to recognise certain common misspellings of words and automatically correct them. For example, 'teh' is automatically corrected to 'the'. The AutoCorrect feature is also responsible for aspects such as capitalising the first word in a sentence or capitalising bulleted lists (although you may want to turn this off). The major benefit of the AutoCorrect feature, however, is that you can add your own common misspellings or words of your choice to the list. In addition, if you regularly use long names, phrases or a word that is always capitalised, you can also add these to the list. You can even add full addresses, as AutoCorrect includes new lines and formatting.

For example, if you want the letter combination 'uct' to always appear as 'UCT', you can set this up in the *AutoCorrect* dialog box. It will then be automatically changed when you press the space bar or a full stop after typing 'uct', and you will not need to capitalise it each time. To add your own words to the list, enter the spelling to be changed in the *Replace* box (or highlight the misspelling before selecting *AutoCorrect Options*) and then add the word or phrase as you would like it to appear (including formatting or new lines) in the *With* box; then press *Add*. You can create your own code, for example 'uct' for 'UCT' and 'uuct' for the full form 'University of Cape Town'.

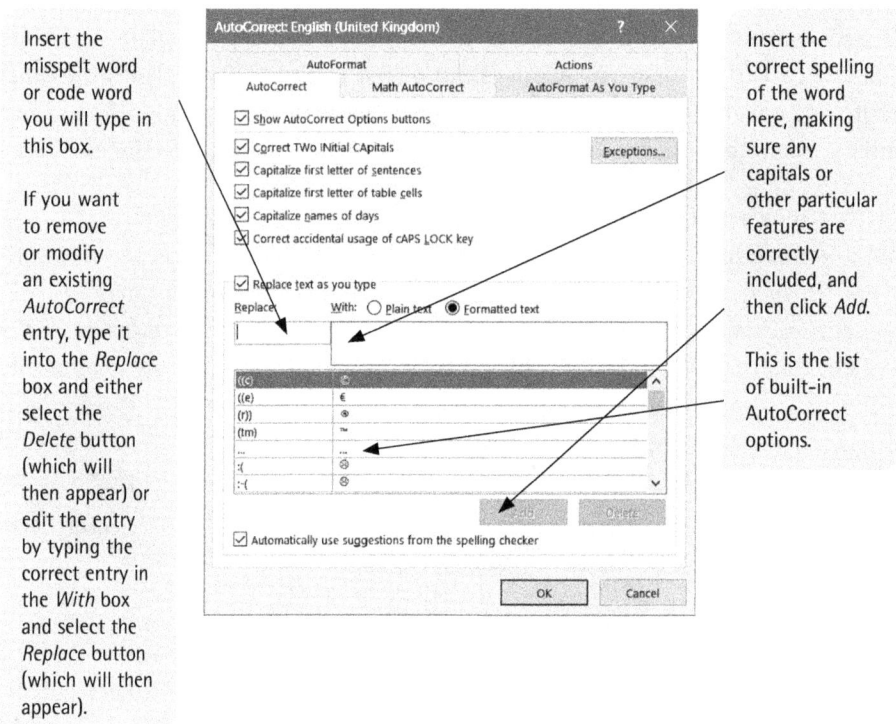

Figure 2.19 Entering items in the *AutoCorrect* dialog box

You may also want to add regularly used sentences, addresses or stock phrases or short paragraphs of boiler plate content (any text that is written or pasted into new contexts or applications with no or little editing or change to the original). To do this, highlight the required content, formatted as you want it to appear, and then when you click on the *AutoCorrect Options* button in the *Proofing* section of the *Word Options* dialog box, your highlighted text will already appear in the *With* box. All you now have to do is insert (in the *Replace* box) the letters or code that will trigger the automatic correction for this option, and press *Add*.

The built-in AutoCorrect options can be very frustrating in some cases. For example, if you regularly use letters enclosed in brackets for lists (such as in legal documents), you will find that when you type (c), the program corrects it to the copyright symbol: ©. To prevent this from happening, find (c) in the list of built-in AutoCorrect options and modify it, for example to ((c). In this way, you retain the option to have the copyright symbol appear when you need it.

AutoCorrect is also very useful in the case of names with a diacritic, such as an accent, on one of the letters, for example Irèna. Omitting the diacritic is equivalent to misspelling the name and can make a bad impression. Use the AutoCorrect feature as described in this section to avoid this.

Reviewing options

The *Review* tab contains useful features for when you are writing or editing your own or others' documents. The most important thing about working on documentation that others will use is that you must keep all comments and changes in one place.

How to track changes in a document

Microsoft® Word™ allows you to work on other people's documents and track any changes you make. Professionally, it is unacceptable to just change others' work without giving them a chance to see what has been changed. The Track Changes feature shows, among other things, insertions, deletions, moved text and formatting changes. It shows the changes in colours (a different one for each reviewer), accompanied by the reviewer's name or initials. The author can look at the changed document and accept or reject each alteration by right-clicking and selecting from the shortcut menu or by using the *Changes* section on the *Review* tab (see Figure 2.20).

Figure 2.20 The *Review* tab

Track Changes can be activated by clicking the *Track Changes* button in the *Tracking* section of the *Review* tab. When activated, the button appears highlighted or shaded – the colour depends on the version. The dropdown arrow on the button allows you to access the default *Track Changes Options* dialog box, where you can change the default options. For example, normally by default all deletions and formatting changes appear in the form of balloons alongside the document. If this does not happen, and the deletions appear as crossed-out text within the document, change it by choosing to show deleted text in balloons to the right of the document, as shown in Figure 2.21. This allows the reviewed text to be more easily read.

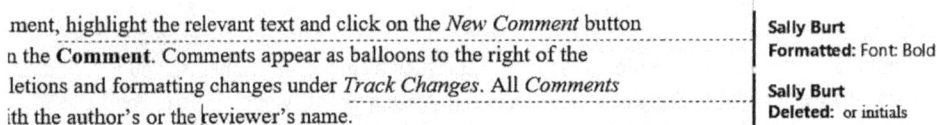

ment, highlight the relevant text and click on the *New Comment* button

n the **Comment**. Comments appear as balloons to the right of the

letions and formatting changes under *Track Changes*. All *Comments*

ith the author's or the reviewer's name.

Sally Burt
Formatted: Font: Bold

Sally Burt
Deleted: or initials

Figure 2.21 Deletions and formatting changes indicated in balloons alongside the document

The comments feature

To add a comment to a document, highlight the relevant text and click on the *New Comment* button in the *Comments* section on the *Review* tab. Then type your comment in the balloon that appears to the right of the document (in the same place as deletions and formatting changes done using the Track Changes feature). All comments are numbered and marked with the author's or the reviewer's name. To delete a comment, right-click on it and choose *Delete Comment* or use the *Delete* button in the *Comments* section on the *Review* tab.

The *Show Markup* option in the *Tracking* section of the *Review* tab allows the user to choose to see only some of the changes made. For example, formatting changes can be hidden, leaving only text insertions, deletions and comments showing. A document with extensive changes and comments can look very busy. Selecting *Simple Markup* from the dropdown menu just above the *Show Markup* option allows you to read a 'clean' document, although the changes can still be revealed or hidden as necessary for reference.

Use the *New Comment* feature even when you are not reviewing or working on a document collaboratively. Rather than stopping to write notes about changes needed or to look things up, add a comment to yourself noting what needs to be done, and continue writing. This is less disruptive to your thought flow. Furthermore, it ensures that a record of your thought process stays with the document, in the same way as reviewers' comments create a dialogue on the document itself. Each comment can then be deleted as it is dealt with.

Viewing options

How to view documents side by side

If you are reviewing different versions of a document and you do not want to use the *Compare* or the *Combine* (merge) option from the *Review* tab, the *View Side by Side* option (see Figure 2.22) on the *View* tab can be very useful. It shows both versions on the same screen, and the *Synchronous Scrolling* feature allows you to scroll through both documents at the same time. This command can be turned on or off, so you can work as suits your needs.

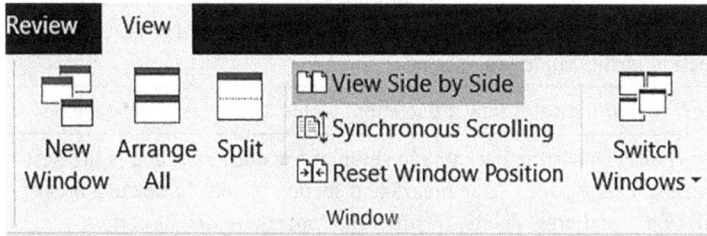

Figure 2.22 The *View Side by Side* option on the *View* tab

As content can be dragged from one document to another, it can be useful to have two completely different documents open side by side. If you drag using the left mouse button, the content moves; if you use the right mouse button to drag, a shortcut menu appears that allows you to select whether to move or copy. If you do move content across and you still need it in the source document, when you close the source document, you can select not to save the changes to retain the original content.

Views in Microsoft® Word™

Word has five main viewing modes, namely *Read Mode*, *Print Layout*, *Web Layout*, *Outline* and *Draft*. To access these views, you can either use the *View* tab on the ribbon or the shortcut buttons on the status bar at the bottom of the document (as indicated in Figure 2.23).

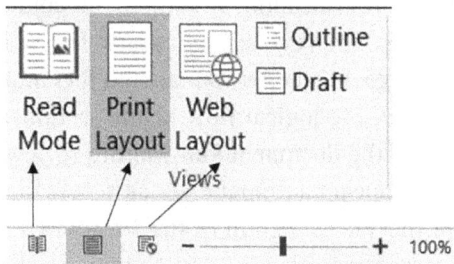

Figure 2.23 Views in Microsoft® Word™

Table 2.1 gives a synopsis of each of these views, after which *Outline* view is discussed in greater detail.

Table 2.1 A brief summary of the views in Microsoft® Word™

View	Description
Read Mode	*Read Mode* makes a document appear more like a book. It is important to note that the pages in full-screen reading view **do not necessarily correspond to the page numbers of the document**.
Print Layout	*Print Layout* is the default view, and it shows how the document will look when printed. However, it does not show where page and section breaks are unless the *Show/Hide Formatting* button (in the *Paragraph* section of the *Home* tab) is used.
Web Layout	*Web Layout* indicates how a document would appear as a webpage.
Draft view	*Draft* view shows the background setup of the document and is the best place to delete pages, page breaks and section breaks. To delete a break, click on it and press delete. Headers and footers, as well as certain pictures and diagrams, cannot be seen in *Draft* view.
Outline view	*Outline* view shows the document in the form of a hierarchy, like the *Navigation* pane, so you can review its organisation at a number of levels. However, unlike the *Navigation* pane, *Outline* view also allows whole sections and subsections to be moved around without copying and pasting.

Outline view

This feature is especially useful if the document contains complex numbering, as the numbering changes automatically.

Headings (or other styles you choose to create) are assigned a level by Microsoft® Word™, each of which can be expanded or collapsed:

- Heading 1: Outline Level 1
- Heading 2: Outline Level 2
- Heading 3: Outline Level 3
- Body text

You can plan a document in *Outline* view using your heading structure. You could write the whole document in this view, but it is not very appealing and it gives little idea of how the work will appear on the page. It is better to plan and then dip in and out of *Outline* view, to periodically check the logical flow of the sections. Once in *Outline* view, select how many levels of the document you want to review via the *Outlining* tab (see Figure 2.24), which appears automatically as a new tab on the ribbon when you select *Outline* from the *Views* section of the *View* tab.

These buttons promote or demote headings and text to another level.

The *Show Level* dropdown box is used to select the number of heading levels to be shown.

This closes *Outline* view and returns to the previous view of document.

| File | Outlining | Home | Insert | Draw | Design | Layout | References | Mailings | Review |

⟪ ← Body Text ▾ → ⟫

▲ ▼ ＋ －

⊕ Show Level:

☑ Show Text Formatting

☐ Show First Line Only

Outline Tools

Show Document   Collapse Subdocuments   Close Outline View

Master Document

Close

The arrows move selected sections up and down.

The +/– buttons expand and collapse levels.

This option shows the first line of each paragraph under the heading.

Use this to show or hide formatting.

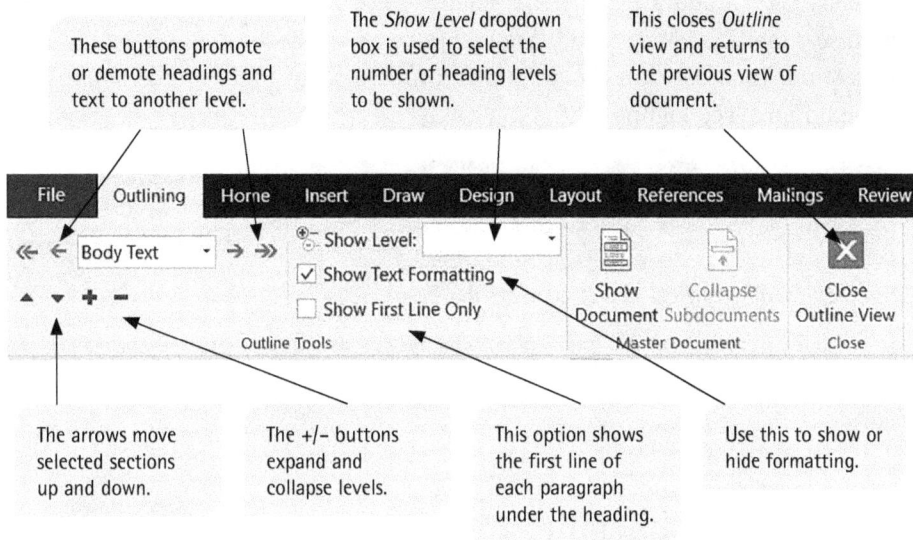

Figure 2.24 The *Outlining* tab

The document in Figure 2.25 is in *Outline* view, showing outline levels 1 and 2 only.

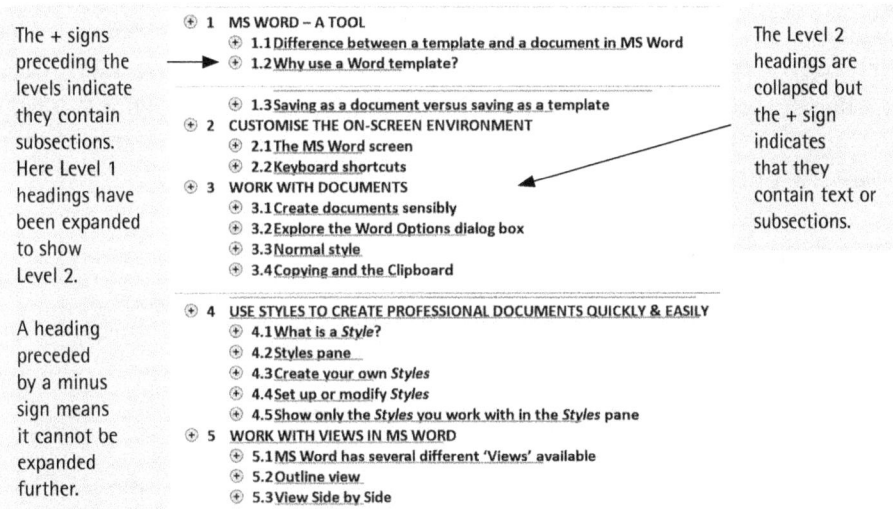

The + signs preceding the levels indicate they contain subsections. Here Level 1 headings have been expanded to show Level 2.

A heading preceded by a minus sign means it cannot be expanded further.

⊕ 1 MS WORD – A TOOL
  ⊕ 1.1 Difference between a template and a document in MS Word
  ⊕ 1.2 Why use a Word template?

  ⊕ 1.3 Saving as a document versus saving as a template
⊕ 2 CUSTOMISE THE ON-SCREEN ENVIRONMENT
  ⊕ 2.1 The MS Word screen
  ⊕ 2.2 Keyboard shortcuts
⊕ 3 WORK WITH DOCUMENTS
  ⊕ 3.1 Create documents sensibly
  ⊕ 3.2 Explore the Word Options dialog box
  ⊕ 3.3 Normal style
  ⊕ 3.4 Copying and the Clipboard

⊕ 4 USE STYLES TO CREATE PROFESSIONAL DOCUMENTS QUICKLY & EASILY
  ⊕ 4.1 What is a *Style*?
  ⊕ 4.2 Styles pane
  ⊕ 4.3 Create your own *Styles*
  ⊕ 4.4 Set up or modify *Styles*
  ⊕ 4.5 Show only the *Styles* you work with in the *Styles* pane
⊕ 5 WORK WITH VIEWS IN MS WORD
  ⊕ 5.1 MS Word has several different 'Views' available
  ⊕ 5.2 Outline view
  ⊕ 5.3 View Side by Side

The Level 2 headings are collapsed but the + sign indicates that they contain text or subsections.

Figure 2.25 An example of a document seen in *Outline* view

Breaks, headers and footers as ways to organise documents

Page and section breaks

Page breaks and section breaks have different functions, and both are useful. If specific information has to start on a new page, a page break should be used rather than pressing Enter until the top of a new page is reached. A page break ensures that the information always starts on a new page, regardless of what content is added above it. To add a page break, choose *Page Break* from the *Pages* section of the *Insert* tab (see Figure 2.26). You can also go to the *Layout* tab, to the *Page Setup* section. Then click on the dropdown arrow next to *Breaks* and choose *Page* from the options (see Figure 2.27).

Figure 2.26 Inserting a page break by using the *Insert* tab

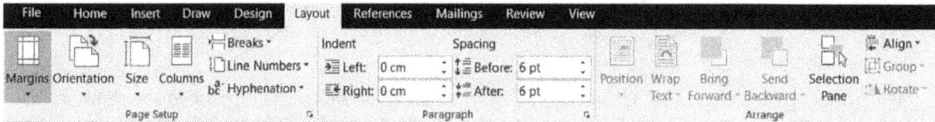

Figure 2.27 Inserting a page break by using the *Layout* tab

A page break only ensures that a new page is started. It is insufficient, however, to effect a change in the margins, headers and footers or page numbering. Page setup changes cannot be made page by page – for that, the document has to be divided into sections. Once a document has been divided into sections, instructions can be given to format a section differently to the previous or following sections.

To insert a section break, go to the *Page Setup* section of the *Layout* tab. Click on the arrow next to *Breaks* to open the dropdown menu (see Figure 2.28). There you will see various types of breaks. The most commonly used options are the following:

- *Next Page:* This type of section break starts a new section at the top of a new page. This is the most common type of break in business and academic documents, as many of the page layout changes required relate to entire pages as opposed to only part of a page; for example changing the page orientation to landscape, or inserting or making changes in the headers or footers.

- *Continuous:* This type of section break allows part of a page to have different margins, for example, or more than one column.

- *Column:* This type of break starts a new column. By default, the columns snake on in newspaper format. A column break thus forces a new column to start.

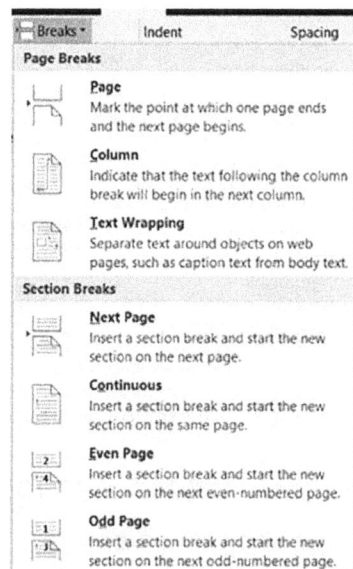

Figure 2.28 The dropdown menu for page breaks and section breaks in the *Layout* tab

You can also use Ctrl + Enter to insert a page break.

Headers and footers

Headers and footers are protected areas at the top and bottom of a document, set aside for certain items that must appear on each page of a document or section. Such items include:

- the date
- any fixed text (eg document name or chapter title, section of document, author, etc)
- logos and designs
- page numbers.

Headers and footers are linked to sections. Therefore, to change information in a header or footer, you need to create a new section. By default, headers or footers repeat what is in the previous header or footer, unless the link between the sections is broken. (See page 61 for information on how to break the links between sections.)

To create a header or footer, select the *Header* or the *Footer* button from the *Header & Footer* section on the *Insert* tab (see Figure 2.29). A dropdown menu appears, offering a number of pre-set options. If you do not want a pre-set option, select the *Edit Header* or the *Edit Footer* option.

To access an existing header or footer, double-click inside the header or footer area. Once you have clicked inside the header or footer, the remainder of the document will appear greyed out (as the header or footer normally appears). This means you can modify the contents of the header or footer. An additional tab will appear on the ribbon, called *Header & Footer Tools: Design* (see Figure 2.30). This offers a range of options. It disappears as soon as you exit the header or footer by clicking on the body of the document or by clicking on the *Close Header and Footer* button.

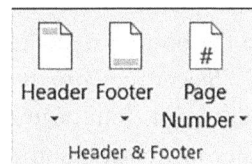

Figure 2.29 The *Header & Footer* section on the *Insert* tab

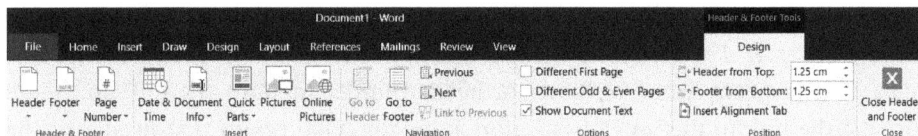

Figure 2.30 The *Header & Footer Tools: Design* tab

Page numbers

To insert page numbering, click on the *Page Number* button on the *Headers &*
Footer Tools: Design tab or on the *Insert* tab. This will bring up a shortcut menu
asking you where to insert the page number (see Figure 2.31). Each option reveals
a further level of built-in options via the fly-out menu arrows.

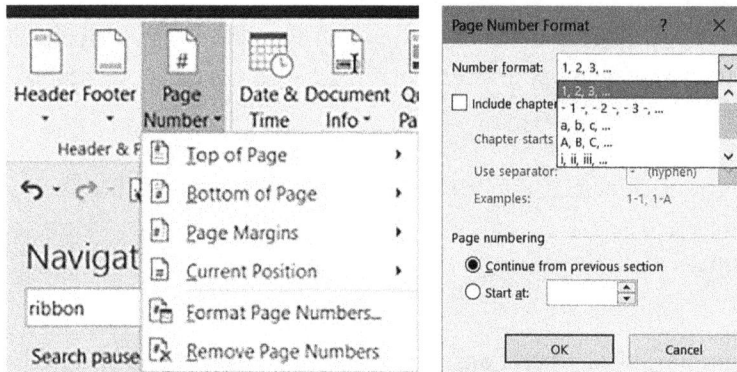

Figure 2.31 Page number formatting options

If you do not want a pre-set option, insert the page number via the *Current*
Position option (see Figure 2.31) and align it as required. Page numbers appear best
in the bottom right-hand corner of the page.

Select the *Format Page Numbers* option from the shortcut menu to modify the
alignment, font, size and style of the page number. If the page number inserted
does not correspond to the correct page number for the document (for example
because the title page has no page number and/or the preliminary pages have
roman numerals), click the radio button for the *Start at* option in the *Page Number*
Format dialog box (see Figure 2.31) and enter the correct page number.

How to break the link to a previous section

To change page numbering within a document, a new section has to be created,
because each footer or header is linked to the information in the previous section
by default unless instructed otherwise. If the page numbering format needs to
change, for example from Roman numerals to Arabic numerals, then the link to
the previous section must be broken.

To break the link, click on the *Link to Previous* button in the *Navigation* section
of the *Header & Footer Tools: Design* tab. Immediately, the *Same as Previous*
indicator disappears from the footer or header border to show the link no longer
exists. If the link to the previous section is broken, changes to that header or the
footer will not affect previous sections.

Headers link to other headers, and footers link to other footers, but not to each
other. If you break the link in the headers between two sections, the link between
the corresponding footers is not automatically broken as well.

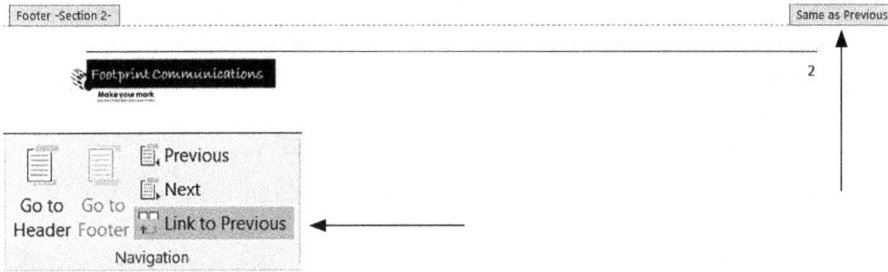

Figure 2.32 Breaking the link to a previous header or footer

If a new section is inserted, the page numbering may restart at 1 without you noticing. Always check the page numbering, section by section, when editing or proofreading the document and use the *Page Number Format* dialog box (Figure 2.31) to reset the numbering.

Automated features in Word

Word has several automated features, designed for efficiency. For example, in a report, it would be time-consuming and frustrating to have to keep updating the table of contents or the list of figures or tables each time content is added or deleted, or to keep correcting page numbers or figure or table numbers. The *References* tab (see Figure 2.33) allows you to access several of these automated features.

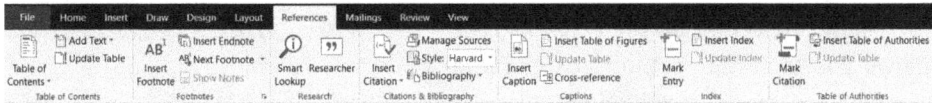

Figure 2.33 The *References* tab

Table of contents

You can insert a table of contents by using the *Table of Contents* button in the *Table of Contents* section of the *References* tab on the ribbon. Microsoft® Word™ has a range of built-in formats, but if you prefer to have the table of contents match the formatting of your document, you can organise it yourself via the *Table of Contents* dialog box. To open this dialog box, click on the *Table of Contents* button on the *References* tab and select *Custom Table of Contents* from the dropdown menu. Click on the *Options* button, which brings up the *Table of Contents Options* dialog box (see Figure 2.34). You can then select which styles you want pulled through to the table of contents, for example Heading 1, Heading 2 and Heading 3.

An automated table of contents updates automatically when you open a document or when you press F9 (or Function + F9) after making changes in the document. If a template has an automated table of contents set up, for example in a thesis or dissertation template, all you need to do is to right-click inside the table (or press F9, or Function + F9) at any time and select *Update Field*. The new headings and/ or page numbers will be picked up and added to the table of contents.

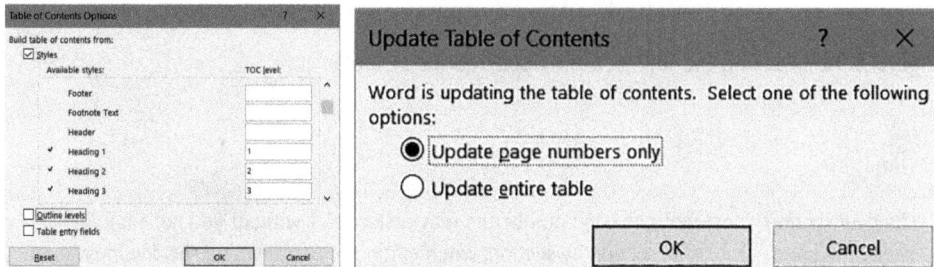

Figure 2.34 Working with a table of contents

Microsoft® Word™ uses styles and/or outline levels to build the table of contents. If you do not use styles consistently, it can affect the table of contents, as manually entered headings may be omitted.

Footnotes and endnotes

The *Footnotes* section on the *References* tab allows you to insert footnotes or endnotes in your document. The advantage of doing this is that the numbers automatically update if a new footnote or endnote is added earlier in the text. The number is inserted as a superscript number next to the selected entry and the footnote content appears at the bottom of the page, separated by a line from the normal content. If you need to switch from footnotes to endnotes, the mini-arrow at the bottom right-hand corner of the *Footnotes* section on the *References* tab opens the *Footnote and Endnote* dialog box (see Figure 2.35), which allows you to make the required changes and set preferences.

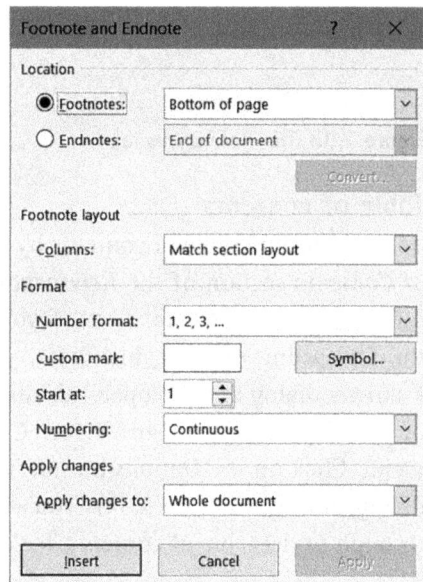

Figure 2.35 Working with footnotes and endnotes

Cross-references

Various fields can be cross-referenced, including headings, footnotes, captions, bookmarks and so on. To insert a cross-reference, type in your document the word 'section', 'paragraph' or whatever the case may be, as you would normally when referring to a particular part of a document. Then, rather than typing in the relevant number, click on the *Cross-reference* command in the *Captions* section of the *References* tab (or the *Links* section of the *Insert* tab) to bring up the *Cross-reference* dialog box (see Figure 2.36).

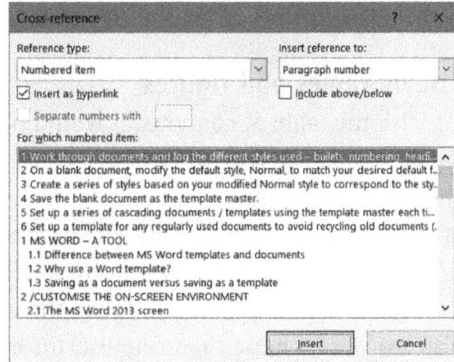

Figure 2.36 Inserting cross-references

This dialog box lists all the sections (numbered paragraphs, captions etc) in the document. Scroll down to find the number that corresponds to the required part of the document, for example 12 or 12.2. Select it and click on the *Insert* button in the dialog box. The number you select will be inserted into the document, next to its lead-in term. It will look like the surrounding text but when you select it, you will see that it has a grey background, indicating that the inserted number is a field rather than an absolute number. This allows it to be updated. From then on, if you move or add sections, the corresponding reference will be updated. If it does not update automatically, press Ctrl + A to select the whole document (or highlight a particular cross-reference), and press F9 (or Function + F9) to force the update.

Captions

Tables, figures, equations and so on are often given a number and a title or caption (descriptor), for easy reference. The caption feature adds the relevant number as a field, so that if another figure or table is added earlier in the document, the caption number will be updated automatically.

To insert a caption, launch the *Caption* dialog box (see Figure 2.37) via *Insert Caption* in the *Captions* section on the *References* tab. The default caption setting is *Figure*, but if you want to insert a table number and heading, click on the dropdown arrow by the *Label* option for alternatives. To add a new label (for example 'Plate' or 'Policy extract' as is

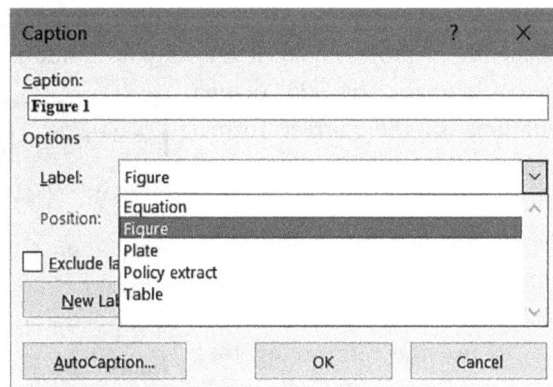

Figure 2.37 Inserting captions

63

shown in Figure 2.37), use the *New Label* button in the dialog box. The caption or heading can be added via the dialog box or later in the body of the document.

List of tables and figures

As with the table of contents, it would be a waste of time to insert a list of tables or figures manually. If all the tables, figures and so on have been correctly labelled using the automated caption feature (as described above), inserting the corresponding table is straightforward. Place your cursor where the table is to be and select *Insert Table of Figures* from the *Captions* section of the *References* tab. In the *Table of Figures* dialog box (see Figure 2.38), select the correct caption label to insert and click *OK*. You can insert more than one list, for example one for tables and one for figures.

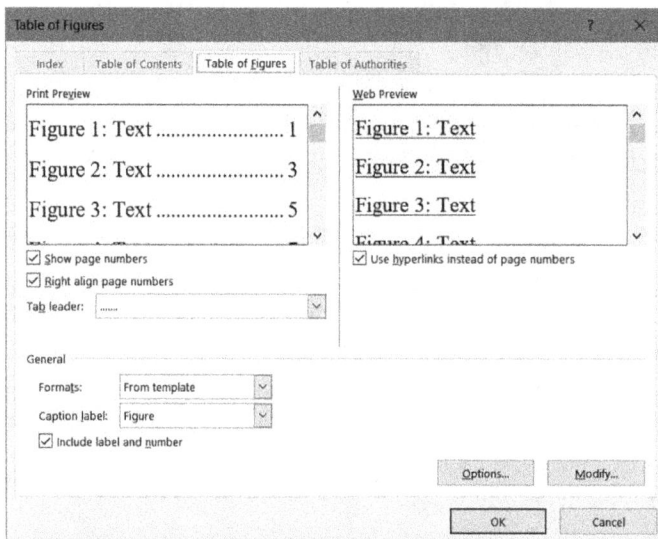

Figure 2.38 The *Table of Figures* dialog box

Referencing

Microsoft® Word™ has an in-built referencing tool which works very well for ordinary referencing activities in documents such as research reports, whether academic or professional. It allows you to add sources relevant to your document in a database, to add in-text citations in the correct format (for a wide range of standard referencing styles), and to insert an automated bibliography (list of references) in the correct format at the end of the document.

To use the referencing tool, go to the *Citations & Bibliography*

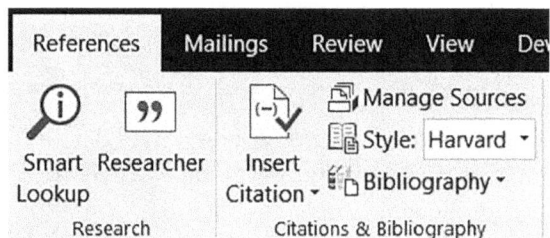

Figure 2.39 The *Citations & Bibliography* section of the *References* tab

section of the *References* tab (see Figure 2.39). Use the dropdown selection to choose the relevant style, for example Harvard. If the style you want is not there, most styles can be easily sourced from the Internet and added to Microsoft® Word™ to make them available for this tool.

A number of sites provide information and tutorials on how to add additional reference styles to Microsoft® Word™ for Windows or Mac (including how to set up a custom style, for more technically experienced users). These sites allow you to download a zip file of the bundled reference styles together with instructions on how to extract or install them into the correct place to make them available through Microsoft® Word's™ reference tool. For example, go to http://bibword.codeplex.com/wikipage?title=Styles&referringTitle=Home (Accessed 28 September 2016).

How to add a source

To add an in-text citation, click on the *Insert Citation* button in the *Citations & Bibliography* section of the *References* tab. If it is a new source, select *Add New Source* from the dropdown menu that appears, and it will take you to the *Create Source* dialogue box (see Figure 2.40). When you select the correct source type (book, journal article, etc) the dialog box presents the appropriate series of fields to be completed for the source type.

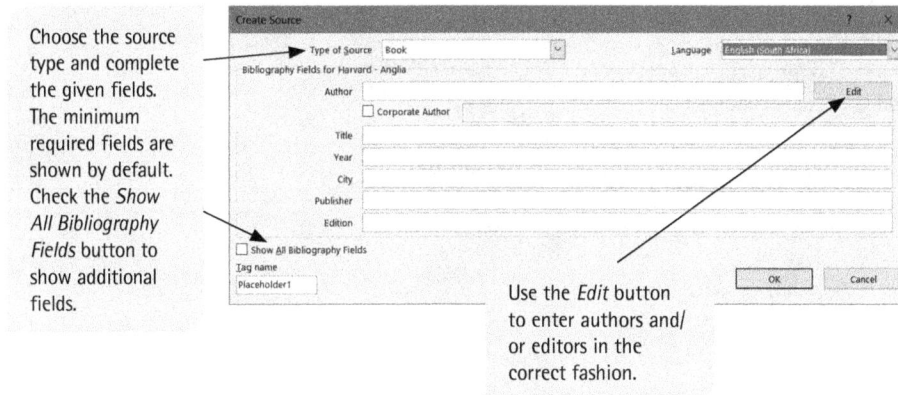

Choose the source type and complete the given fields. The minimum required fields are shown by default. Check the *Show All Bibliography Fields* button to show additional fields.

Use the *Edit* button to enter authors and/ or editors in the correct fashion.

Figure 2.40 The *Create Source* dialog box

How to insert a citation

Once sources have been added, they become available in a list for selection when the *Insert Citation* button is clicked. Place the cursor where the in-text citation is required and click on *Insert Citation*. Select a source from the list, as shown in Figure 2.41. The citation field will appear in the text – for example (English, 2017) – and the corresponding entry will be made in the bibliography, for example: English, J (ed). 2017. *Professional communication.* 4th ed. Cape Town: Juta.

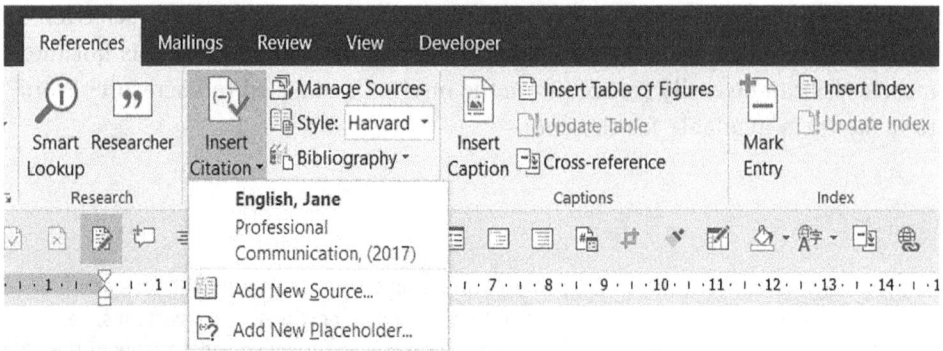

Figure 2.41 Inserting citations

How to edit or manage sources

To edit a source or to manage your list of sources, click on the *Manage Sources* button in the *Citations & Bibliography* section of the *References* tab. This takes you to the *Source Manager* dialog box (see Figure 2.42), which displays the master list of all the sources you have added on the left and the current list of sources relevant to the document you are working on to the right. Here you can transfer sources directly from the *Master List* to the *Current List* as well as delete or edit existing sources.

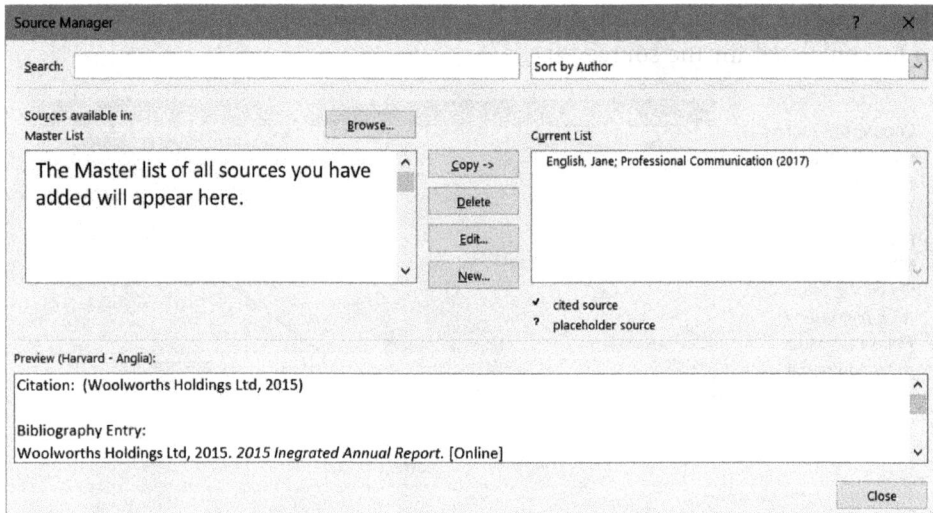

Figure 2.42 The *Source Manager* dialog box

How to edit an in-text citation

You may want to edit a citation in the text – for example to suppress the author name and just show the year or to add page numbers. Insert the citation as normal and then click on it. Select the dropdown arrow that appears to the right of the citation to bring up the *Edit Citation* dialog box, as shown in Figure 2.43.

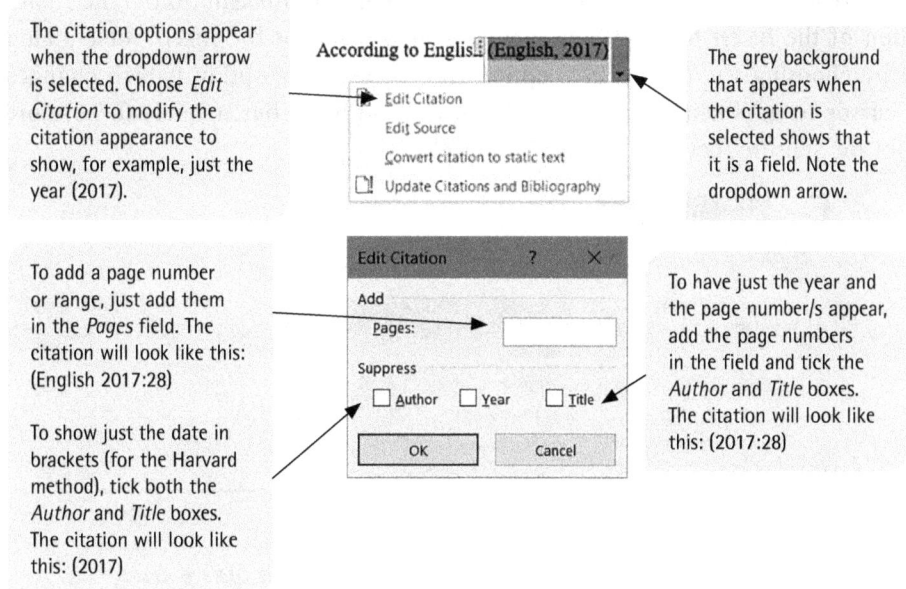

The citation options appear when the dropdown arrow is selected. Choose *Edit Citation* to modify the citation appearance to show, for example, just the year (2017).

According to Englis... (English, 2017)

Edit Citation
Edit Source
Convert citation to static text
Update Citations and Bibliography

The grey background that appears when the citation is selected shows that it is a field. Note the dropdown arrow.

To add a page number or range, just add them in the *Pages* field. The citation will look like this: (English 2017:28)

To show just the date in brackets (for the Harvard method), tick both the *Author* and *Title* boxes. The citation will look like this: (2017)

Edit Citation   ?   ✕
Add
Pages:
Suppress
☐ Author   ☐ Year   ☐ Title
OK   Cancel

To have just the year and the page number/s appear, add the page numbers in the field and tick the *Author* and *Title* boxes. The citation will look like this: (2017:28)

Figure 2.43 Editing a citation

The list of references or bibliography

To add a list of references or a bibliography at the end of the document, simply click on the *Bibliography* button in the *Citations & Bibliography* section of the *References* tab. The dropdown arrow opens a list with a series of built-in format options. However, the most sensible thing to do is to choose the *Insert Bibliography* option at the bottom of the list and format your list to match your document, for example using the standard body text style in use in the document. If a hanging indent is required, you can create a style for the bibliography or just select the references and quickly use the ruler at the top of the screen to create the hanging indent.

There are various versions of the Harvard style. Experiment and choose the one that matches the style of Harvard you require, for example (English, 2017, p. 28) or (English, 2017: 28).

See Chapter 12 for information on further online referencing tools for academic research.

Tables

While tables are often prepared in Microsoft® Excel™, formatting and working with the table can still be done after it is pasted into Microsoft® Word™. If it is a text table or a numeric table requiring only simple calculations, it is not necessary to use Microsoft® Excel™ first, as the formula function also operates in Microsoft® Word™.

Microsoft® Word™ tables are inserted by clicking the *Table* button in the *Tables* section of the *Insert* tab and then using either the grid or the *Insert Table* dialog box by choosing the *Insert Table* option. The *Draw Table* option (which changes the cursor to a 'pencil' or an 'eraser') can also be used, but it tends to be more useful for splitting columns and rows or cells.

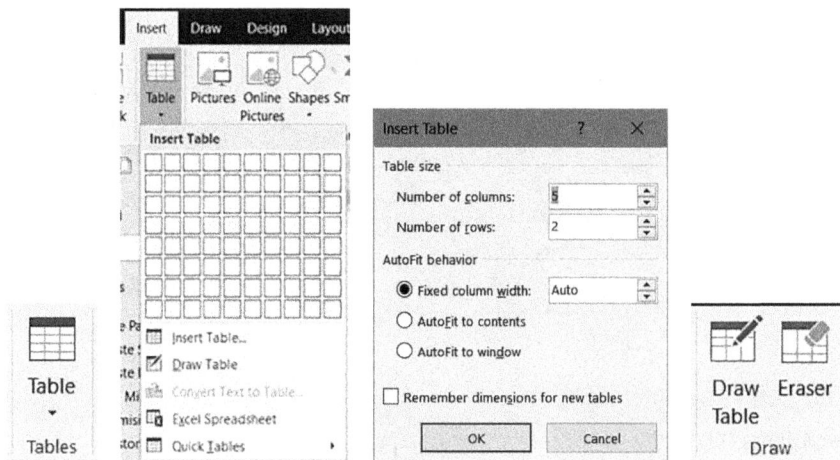

Figure 2.44 Inserting or drawing a table

To insert additional columns or rows, select an entire row or column, right-click and select *Insert,* either from the right-click menu or from the small context-sensitive floating toolbar that appears. Then choose what you wish to insert from the fly-out menu, for example a row above or below, or a column to the right or left. Alternatively, use the *Table Tools: Layout* tab, which appears when you insert or work in a table (see Figure 2.45). You can specify whether to insert a row above or below other rows and whether to insert a column to the left or to the right of other columns. Additionally, by pressing Tab while in the final cell, you can add a row to the bottom of the table.

To delete a table, use the *Delete* button on *Table Tools: Layout* tab. If you highlight or select the table and use the ordinary delete option, the contents of the table disappear, but the table remains.

Table Tools: Design and *Layout* tabs

These tabs (see Figure 2.45), which only appear when you are working in a table, allow you to determine the various table options and properties – most of which are fairly self-explanatory.

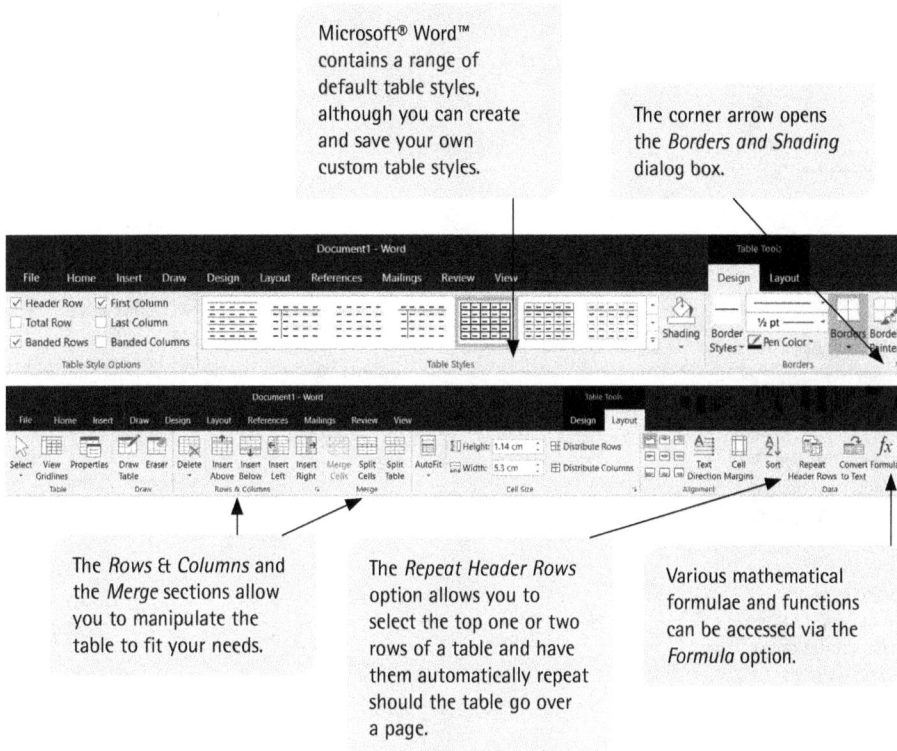

Microsoft® Word™ contains a range of default table styles, although you can create and save your own custom table styles.

The corner arrow opens the *Borders and Shading* dialog box.

The *Rows & Columns* and the *Merge* sections allow you to manipulate the table to fit your needs.

The *Repeat Header Rows* option allows you to select the top one or two rows of a table and have them automatically repeat should the table go over a page.

Various mathematical formulae and functions can be accessed via the *Formula* option.

Figure 2.45 The *Table Tools: Design* and *Layout* tabs

How to create a custom table style

The *Borders and Shading* options, which can also be accessed via a right-click shortcut menu, allow you to select line style, width and colour, with various shading options available from the third tab (the second tab contains the page border options). These options are necessary to create a professional look for your tables and, if necessary, to ensure that they match any corporate branding required. All tables within any one document should be formatted in a consistent style. The easiest way to ensure this is to create a custom table style.

Once you have a blank master template with all your paragraph or text styles set up – or any specific sub-templates such as a report template – create the table style to go with it. The custom table style does not appear in the *Styles* pane as your other created styles do. It appears as an option in the *Table Styles* section on the *Table Tools: Design* tab. The table styles are divided into *Custom, Plain Tables* and *Grid Tables*. Your new table style will appear in the *Custom* strip (see Figure 2.47).

To set up a table style, click on the *Table Styles* dropdown menu on the *Table Tools: Design* tab and select the *New Table Style* option below all the built-in table styles. The *Create New Style from Formatting* dialog box (see Figure 2.46) that appears allows you to specify the various options as you would like them to appear in your table.

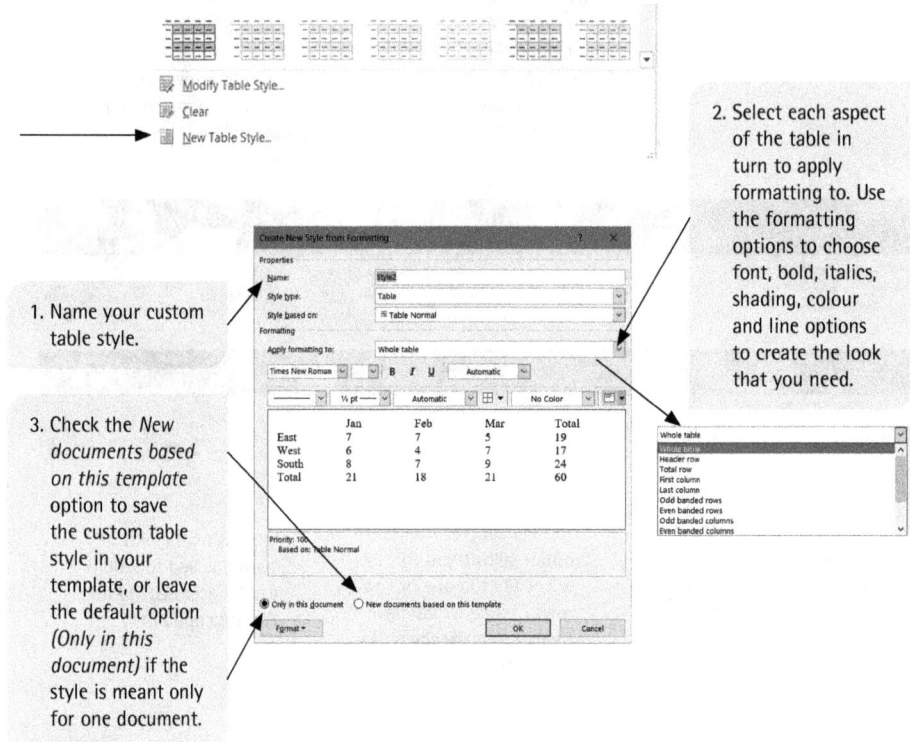

1. Name your custom table style.

2. Select each aspect of the table in turn to apply formatting to. Use the formatting options to choose font, bold, italics, shading, colour and line options to create the look that you need.

3. Check the *New documents based on this template* option to save the custom table style in your template, or leave the default option *(Only in this document)* if the style is meant only for one document.

Figure 2.46 Creating a custom table style

Alternatively, you can choose to modify an existing table style with your own colours and layout – it works in exactly the same way as modifying a paragraph style rather than creating one.

How to apply a custom table style

First, select the entire table. Next, click on the *Table Tools: Design* tab and select the *Table Styles* dropdown menu. Finally, click on the custom table style you need (see Figure 2.47). This will apply the style to the table you have selected.

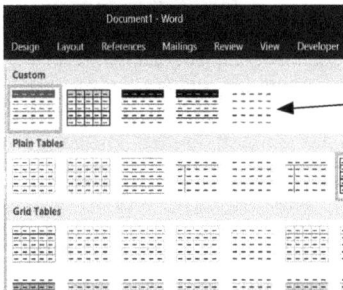

When you move the cursor over each custom table, its name will appear, although usually you will recognise it as the thumbnail reflects the design you set up.

Figure 2.47 Applying a custom table style

While you can specify many things when setting up a custom table style, it does not offer you the option to define the paragraph and line spacing. These are especially important for creating professional-looking tables. If you have set up your own paragraph or text styles, the text in the tables should be similar (but smaller) to reflect the overall look and feel of your styles.

Create your own paragraph or text style in the *Styles* pane, specifying, for example, that the font size should be one or two points smaller than the body text, that the line spacing should be single to 1.1 point, and that the paragraph spacing should be reduced to 3 points before and 3 points after. Most importantly, the text should be left aligned, to avoid the odd spacing and gaps created by justifying text in too narrow a column.

To apply the style, first select your table, and then click on your table text style in the *Styles* pane or *Styles* gallery. Only then go to the *Table Styles* section on the *Table Tools: Design* tab and select your custom style for the table.

Formulas in tables

Formulas in Microsoft® Word™ are not as sophisticated as in Microsoft® Excel™, but they can still be useful for straightforward calculations, as long as there is no manual formatting (manually inserted spaces, commas, etc) to prevent Microsoft® Word™ from recognising the digits as numbers.

To use the formula feature, enter numbers in the relevant table cells and then go to, for example, the 'Totals' cell. Click on the *Formula* button from the *Table Tools: Layout* tab to open the *Formula* dialog box, as shown in Figure 2.48.

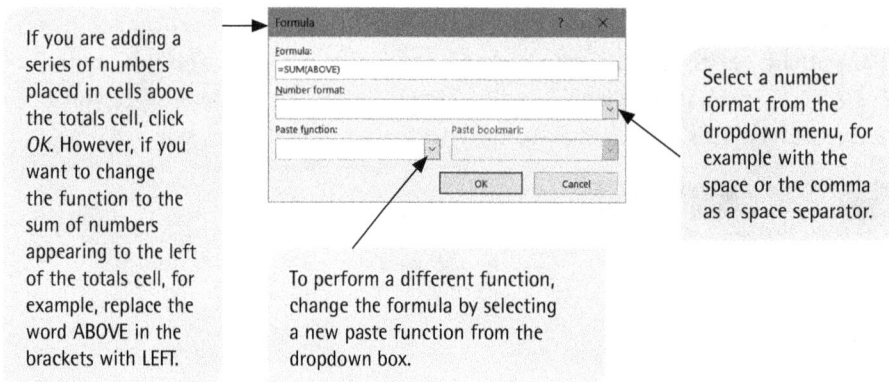

If you are adding a series of numbers placed in cells above the totals cell, click *OK*. However, if you want to change the function to the sum of numbers appearing to the left of the totals cell, for example, replace the word ABOVE in the brackets with LEFT.

To perform a different function, change the formula by selecting a new paste function from the dropdown box.

Select a number format from the dropdown menu, for example with the space or the comma as a space separator.

Figure 2.48 The *Formula* dialog box

Repeat header rows

Always use the *Repeat Header Rows* option from the *Data* section of the *Table Tools: Layout* tab (see Figure 2.45) in case your table runs over the page – it may not look as if it will at first, but should additional content be added above the table, it may cause the table to span more than one page. Select one or more rows at the top of the table. Click on the *Repeat Header Rows* button and the selected rows will be repeated at the top of each new page.

✓

Checklist for monitoring your online presence carefully and developing your skills

New communication platforms are being developed all the time. It is important therefore to be aware of which platforms you are active on and to learn to see yourself from the outside in – as a potential or even current employer would encounter you online. Use the following as a checklist to ensure you cultivate your online presence with care:

- Separate your personal and professional social media accounts and email.
- Keep your profiles on any online platform up to date.
- Be prudent and strategic about what you post and where.
- Be aware of new developments and features that will help you become more efficient and professional in your documentation and collaboration with others.

It is also important to keep up to date with new versions of software you use regularly such as Microsoft® Word™, Excel™ and PowerPoint™. Once you know the elements that you need to work with, for example the *Styles* pane or *Outline* view, even if the program features are moved or appear in a slightly different way, you will easily be able to navigate your way through new versions and take advantage of additional features.

Correspondence: mail to digital text

3

Whatever your profession or job, and whether you are a self-employed entrepreneur or an employee, you will need to write letters and emails. This correspondence may be informal and addressed to your colleagues, or it may be formal and addressed to people you do not know.

The purpose of an email, digital text or letter is usually to impart or request information. You need to choose the right format for your purpose. For example, you may write a text message if you need to get a message across in an informal way, but an email if your signature is needed. For many of us, an email is usually the first and most direct contact we have with others in the work environment, be they strangers or known to us. Faxes are still sent (mainly for business contracts), as they are legally binding documents. All of these messages create an audit trail which may be called up later.

Your message must reflect the image you wish to convey of yourself or of the company that you work for. You therefore need to use an appropriate style to reflect this and the relationship you have with the receiver. The less you know the receiver, the higher the degree of formality in style that is required. A clear and clean layout is best created through the company email format, with its logo and official signature.

This chapter covers ways for you to achieve efficient, direct correspondence with your employer, staff, client or customer. It looks at various aspects of correspondence or mail in all its forms, namely:

- levels of style and tone
- format, structure, planning and presentation
- types of correspondence – hard copy and electronic
- etiquette for digital correspondence.

3.1 Levels of style and tone

In correspondence, you need to establish a rapport with the person you are addressing in order to achieve your purpose, and so there is a personal element not found in other documents. It is your choice of vocabulary that conveys the feelings you have concerning the subject or towards the person you are addressing. While a workplace email is more personal than a report (for example, first names may be used), it must never be emotional. The appropriate tone in emails and letters is conveyed by a consultative, conversational style which is natural, courteous and tactful. It can be difficult to write a message which conveys extreme feelings of delight or anger and is still appropriately courteous and formal in tone, but it is important to learn the skills to do this.

Formal and informal tone

Which of the following phrases comes across as being more informal in tone?
- The manager asked the staff for their reasons for arriving late at work.
- The manager questioned the staff about unpunctuality at the start of the day.
- The boss wants to nail anyone who comes late.

In this example, the verb 'question' has unpleasant connotations of officialdom and authority, whereas 'ask' is a neutral verb. The third sentence is too informal. Its use of slang also leads to an accusatory tone.

Unnecessarily formal language and clichés (overused, trite expressions) can come across to the reader as arrogant. It is outdated to use vocabulary in a letter that you would not use when speaking. Use simple words and avoid unnecessary phrases. For example, one word can replace each of the phrases in the first column below:

Avoid	Prefer
Affix your signature	Sign
At a later date	Later
At this point in time	Currently

A great deal of jargon and many stock phrases, which give a pompous tone to a message, still appear in letter writing. However, occasional use of stock phrases (for example 'with our sincere apologies') can be appropriate and useful when you cannot think how to word what you wish to say. The danger is the overuse of clichés. Consider more natural, spoken phrases instead of those you learnt as part of letter writing convention. Here are more natural alternatives to examples of stock phrases or letter-writing clichés:

e9

Avoid	Prefer
We wish to acknowledge receipt of ...	We have received ...
Please be advised that the parcel ...	The parcel ...
Your letter of 26 February refers.	As stated in your letter (26/02) ...
Due to the fact that we require ...	We require ...
With reference to your request ...	Your request ...
The above matter refers	This matter ...

Consider the following two versions of the same letter to a client. The suggested version is still formal, but it has a more natural style than the original version.

e9

Original:	Suggestion:
We refer to a letter received on 1 June informing us of your change of address. We are unable to make any amendments to your account, as the instruction was not signed. Kindly sign the enclosed document and return it to our offices. A reply-paid envelope is enclosed for your convenience.	We have received your letter dated 1 June asking us to change your address. We were unable to make the changes, as the request was not signed. Please sign the enclosed letter and return it to us in the reply-paid envelope provided.
Should you have any queries, please contact our Client Services Department on our toll-free number.	You are welcome to contact our Client Services Department on our toll-free number if you have any queries.

The difference in degree of formality sets a different tone for each letter. A very formal style comes across as cold, and might create the impression that the writer is arrogant. A writer can unintentionally come across as uncaring through using long blocks of text, long paragraphs, long sentences and long words, as shown in the following passage from a letter refusing a request for a telephone line.

e9

Original:	Suggestion:
I regret, that the Survey Officer who is responsible for the preliminary investigation as to the technical possibility of installing a telephone at the address quoted by any applicant has reported that owing to a shortage of a spare set of wires to the underground cable (a pair of wires leading from a point near your house right back to the local exchange and thus a pair of wires essential for the provision of telephone services for you) it is a technical impossibility to install a telephone for you. (90 words; one sentence)	**Application for a telephone line to 35 Wadloes Road** I regret to inform you that a telephone cannot be installed at your home. The security officer responsible for investigating the possibility of new telephone wires undertook a preliminary investigation. There is a shortage of underground cables between your house and the post office. We will work at improving this situation as soon as possible. (55 words; four sentences)

Note the following flaws in the original letter:

- There is no subject line.
- The opening sentence does not give the main points of the message.
- The body of the message is poorly organised and is contained in one sentence.
- The message does not close with an expression of goodwill.

A courteous and tactful tone

Courtesy means being polite and respectful. A style that is too informal can come across as overfamiliar or disrespectful towards your reader. Writers of professional emails often have to be tactful. The danger of tactlessness is greatest in situations where the writer or the reader may be especially sensitive, for example in a:

- matter where there is disagreement
- matter requiring tact
- claim for damages
- refusal of a request.

A tactless writer uses words or phrases expressing suspicion, obligation and compulsion, or refers to the reader's inadequacies. To avoid being tactless, you should try to use words and phrases with neutral meanings. The following are neutral alternatives to replace phrases which have an accusatory tone:

Avoid	Prefer
You claim that ...	The suggestion is that ...
Your letter about the alleged loss of goods ...	Your letter about the misplacement of goods ...
You must have misunderstood our list of warnings.	Our list of warnings stated that ...

Although using the active voice is preferable, the passive voice may be used, as in the next example, to avoid tactlessness.

Avoid	Prefer
You failed to sign the tear-off slip.	The tear-off slip had not been signed.

3.2 Readability and structure

Readability

Any correspondence containing grammatical errors and spelling mistakes will make a bad impression on the reader and can be understood to indicate a lack of respect. Use the spelling and grammar checking facilities offered by your digital software to help check the accuracy of your writing. However, be aware that predictive text may suggest the wrong word.

Structure

The **subject line** is a critical item in both emails and letters. In the case of an email, it is the first item the recipients will read, and in a letter it defines the content and focuses the reader's attention on that content. In emails it also plays a role when you need to search for correspondence on certain topics. It is therefore important to change the email subject line to reflect the topic if the original subject has been abandoned and the email chain is now dealing with a new topic.

You need to structure the **body** of your message so that it is highly readable and accessible to the receiver. If a message is to be clear and readable, whether via email or hard copy, it needs to contain certain features, namely:

- a greeting that includes the reader's name, if known (eg Dear Ms Smith, not Dear Madam)
- an opening paragraph that says what the correspondence covers – even if it is in the form of a numbered or bulleted list. For an email that will be read on a small screen (such as a tablet or mobile phone) this is particularly important, as readers must know they need to continue scrolling down
- subheadings that emphasise the content of the paragraph
- short sentences with simple vocabulary
- a final paragraph that creates goodwill and indicates the action or reaction you want to the correspondence
- a closing salutation pitched at the correct level of formality, such as 'Yours sincerely', 'With kind regards', 'Best wishes' or 'Regards'. Keep informal language such as 'Ciao', 'Love' and 'xxx' for personal messages.

Electronic **signatures** may also be specified for staff within an organisation and may include a logo and typeface similar to the company letterhead. This standardises the company's image on all outgoing mail, conventional or electronic. Electronic signatures can be dropped into your emails manually or automatically. They usually include your full name, your title or position, the name of the company and your contact details, such as physical address, fax number and telephone number. Depending on your job, you may choose to give other information, such as your qualifications. Signatures may also reflect the activities of the organisation.

> Make sure your courtesy title is included in your signature if this is how you want people to address you. In addition, it is not always possible to know if a name belongs to a man or woman, and so the inclusion of the courtesy title can help your reader to know how to address you in return.

Style and purpose of message formats

Different formats are required for different types of messages (personal or less personal) and for the different contexts (within a company or beyond the company) in the workplace. Each of these formats has unique attributes and brings unique challenges.

There are challenges in managing digital messages such as email which do not apply to hard copy letters, the most serious one being the tone created through the level of language used. As writers, we move frequently between platforms, for instance from WhatsApp to email, and from private to business messages. As a result, we risk writing work messages using too familiar a tone. Table 3.1 summarises the different correspondence formats and their styles for a professional context.

Table 3.1 Different correspondence formats and their styles

Format	Readership and purpose	Style (vocabulary and grammar)	Risks
Digital messages: • Email • SMS • WhatsApp • Chat • Facebook messages • LinkedIn messages	**Readership:** • External and internal to the company • One-to-one or one-to-many. All these systems can broadcast to many but have controls which can be set. **Purposes:** • To establish rapport between sender and receiver • To have immediacy in sending the message and receiving a response • To ensure that the receivers (staff or clients) are receiving identical information	• Formal or informal, depending on the nature of the message and the relationship between the sender and the receiver • Allows for a conversational style, where appropriate, thanks to its immediacy and privacy (gained through the use of passwords) • First person	**Tone:** Often these approaches allow the writer to be too informal for work purposes, because of their common use for sending private messages and the use of abbreviations and emoticons. **Privacy:** You cannot control who sees your messages, as they may be forwarded without your knowledge. **Timing:** Messages reach the recipient immediately and must therefore be sent at appropriate times.
Letter	**Readership:** External to the company **Purposes:** • To establish rapport between the sender and receiver • To send and/or request information • To claim or to offer an adjustment to a claim	Formal or informal, depending on the nature of the message and the relationship between the sender and receiver	**Tone:** If unnecessary jargon is used, the tone will be too formal. Conversely, too informal a tone is a risk, as in the case of email as well.

$\longrightarrow$

Format	Readership and purpose	Style (vocabulary and grammar)	Risks
Fax (facsimile)	**Readership:** External to the company **Purposes:** • To provide material that is legally binding • To send information immediately	Formal, as faxes are used mainly for legally binding reasons	**Readability:** Poor scanning by a fax machine or printer will mean poor reproduction. Faxes must be typed. If a fax is hand-written, bold text and black ink must be used. **Privacy:** A fax often carries confidential material. As many printers are in shared offices, there is a risk of the fax being read by others.

Templates

Many companies and organisations have templates for regularly used company formats. Within the template, however, there may be variation in terms of items such as text size and heading style. Check if the company you are working for has requirements of this nature. Alternatively, you may download a template or create your own by using the document formatting options of your software. (Microsoft® Word™ provides a wide range of letter templates, which can be useful as a basis for your letter, adapting where appropriate. See Chapter 2 for more on templates and using Microsoft® Word™.)

The following example shows the block format used in professional letters where a **letterhead is pre-printed**. Such a letter is usually mailed as hard copy, but may also be scanned and sent as an attachment to an email.

e9

SOUTH AFRICAN MEDICAL MANUFACTURERS (PTY) LTD ————————— *Letterhead*

36 Vanguard Drive EPPING	Vanguardrylaan 36
PO Box 8	Posbus 8
Ph: +27 21 531 2430	Faks: +27 21 530 0762 ___ *Reference*

Ref/Verw: 2x703 ————— *Receiver's address*
30 October 20––

Mr T Jones
Old Oak Pharmacy ————— *Salutation (no full stops or commas in salutation or close)*
Bellville 7530

Dear Mr Jones ————— *Subject line*
Receipt of Goods: Order Number J/1165 —————
Thank you ....

.... ——— *Body*
We ....

Yours sincerely ————————————— *Complimentary close*
M BROWN
M BROWN ————————— *Typed name*
SALES MANAGER —————
———— *Position in company*

MB/tg ——— *Initials of sender and typist (when applicable)*

Encl ——

———— *Enclosures*

3.3 Types of emails and letters

The types of emails or letters you might have to write can be classified according to their purpose. For example, there are messages intended to:

- request or offer information
- introduce and accompany documents, such as curricula vitae, proposals and reports
- grant or refuse requests
- convey unwelcome information.

The following sections give examples and explanations of some common types of emails and letters.

Covering letter or email accompanying a document

If you are sending a report or proposal to a certain person, it should be accompanied by an introductory letter. This letter (or email) is also known as a letter of transmittal. (See Chapter 8 for more information on letters of transmittal.)

As with other letters, the subject line briefly introduces the subject and the first paragraph outlines the purpose of the document. The body paragraphs each usually contain one or two key points dealing with the preparation or content of the document: problems, resources, additional work, conclusions and recommendations. The final paragraph is a courtesy which encourages the reader to contact you about any queries.

Here is an example of a letter of transmittal which would accompany a report:

e9

Holsclaw and Moss Ltd
9669 Solomon Avenue
Pretoria 0002

16 June 20--

Ms Brooke DiNatale
Division Director
Holsclaw and Moss Ltd
Manufacturing Division
415 Industrial Way
Umbogintwini 4126
KwaZulu-Natal

Dear Brooke

Report on cracking of MV800
Accompanying this letter is the analytical report on the cracking problem of the MV800 that you asked me to investigate. The report examines the parts involved in the assembly and installation of the front bezel.

Results of the study
After examining the results of the studies on the problem and talking to the manufacturer of the panel trim, I have concluded that there are two causes for the cracking problem. The first cause is the shrinkage of the panel trim which occurs at the vendor plant. The second cause is that the equipment mounting rails in the CPU cabinet are set too low.

→

The report includes the illustrations and technical studies supporting the conclusions.

If you have any questions regarding this report, please feel free to discuss them with me at any time. I can be reached on 083 236 3345.

Yours sincerely

KA Barton

KA Barton
Process Engineering
KB:mm
Enclosure

The following is an example of a covering letter to accompany a proposal, sent by email:

e9

From: Jennifer Friedman jf@reimburse.co.za
To: jjs@jfs.co.za
Date sent: 1 November 20--
Subject: Proposal for JFS Benefits Programme
Priority: Urgent

Dear Mr Simpkins

PROPOSAL FOR JFS MANUFACTURING COMPANY

I appreciated our telephone conversation yesterday about the problems you are having with the benefits programme at JFS. Reimbursement Services proposes to design an employee benefits programme which fits the needs of JFS Manufacturing Company and costs less than the plan currently in use. The attached brief statement shows how Reimbursement Services can improve the package to benefit both you and your employees.

I have outlined below the specific services we offer and indicated our experience. I also provide a schedule of activities we would conduct for you.

Statement of problem
In today's market, healthcare costs are continually on the rise. As a result, employee benefit programmes are becoming more important to an organisation's efforts to retain the best employees.

Objective
By first understanding your needs in terms of a healthcare programme, we can develop one that will be most beneficial for JFS Manufacturing.

→

Procedure

We will:

- meet with either you or your benefits coordinator to ...
- collect information about JFS Manufacturing, including ...
- visit your firm monthly ...

Record of service

Reimbursement Services has successfully designed effective benefits programmes for over 100 South African firms. A list of names of clients will be provided on request.

Cost to JFS

Our suggestions for a more effective programme are free. You pay the normal cost of the plan to the insurance company, and we receive the usual agent's commission from the carrier.

Schedule

Week 1: Initial interview, collection of data and survey of insurance firms for information
Week 2: Analysis of results
Week 3: Presentation to JFS

Future action

Please email or telephone me if you have questions about the proposal. I look forward to working with you.

Yours sincerely

Jennifer Friedman

Benefits Counsellor

REIMBURSEMENT SERVICES
PO Box 74
Pietermaritzburg 3200
Tel: 033 167 1226
Cell: 083 554 4011

Attachment: Proposal

Letters of enquiry (request or complaint) and adjustment

One of the types of letters most frequently used is the kind asking for information – that is, a letter of enquiry – or requesting action, for example funding for study or a project.

A properly composed enquiry will make the recipient want to reply to you, and will make the task of answering your queries easier. A poorly written request may go unanswered, prompt an answer of little value or lead to a chain of letters going back and forth asking for clarification and additional information.

When you write to request something, whether it is to order an item or service, to invite someone to attend an event, to ask advice or to request information, consider the request from the reader's point of view. For example:

- How will your reader respond to your request?
- Will the reader feel positive or negative about your request?
- Will your reader be able to grant your request easily?

Anticipate questions that your reader may need to ask, and cover that information in your letter. The following sections are a guide as to what should go into a letter of enquiry or request.

First paragraph

Begin your opening paragraph with a clear statement of the purpose of the letter. Define the information wanted or the problem involved: what is wanted, who wants it and why it is wanted. Do not begin with an apology for writing the letter. This suggests to the reader a reason for refusing the request.

Body paragraphs

The opening paragraph should lead into a detailed explanation of the reason for the request. Your wording should be specific, and questions should be arranged so that they are easy to answer. A good technique is to use specific questions in the form of a list.

Final paragraph

Your final paragraph should contain an expression of appreciation, with a tactful suggestion for action.

The following letter of request is clear and will probably elicit an informative response:

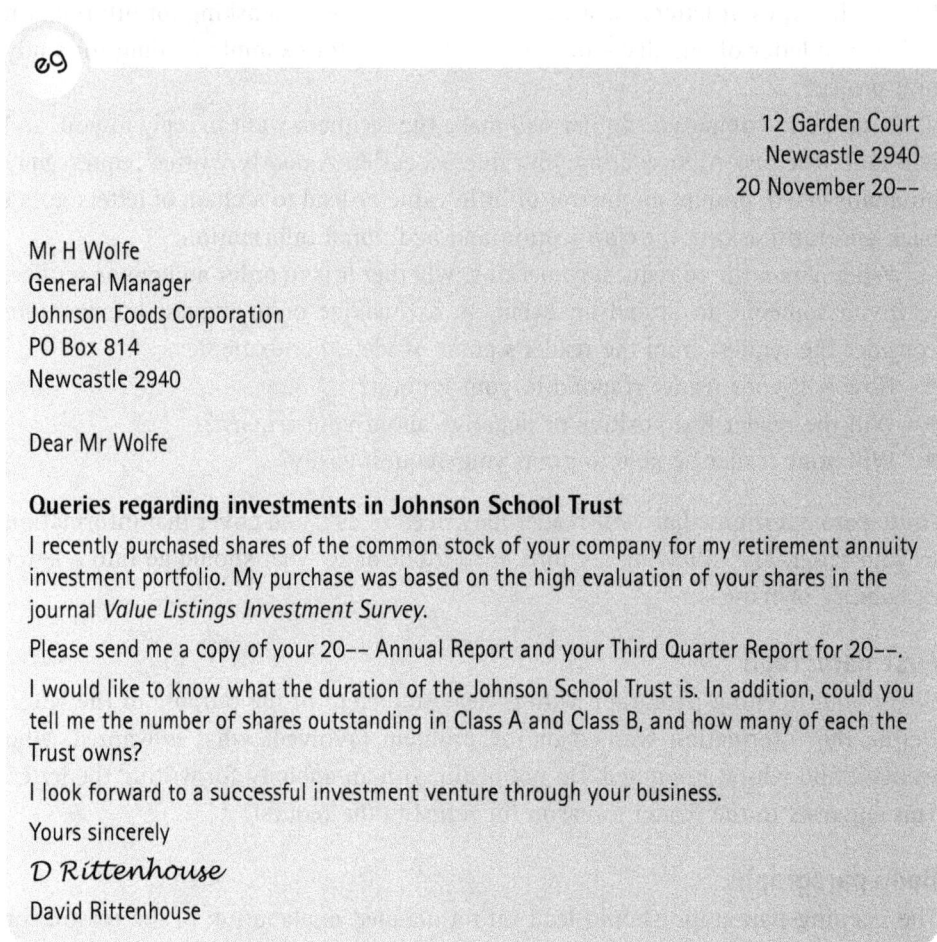

e9

12 Garden Court
Newcastle 2940
20 November 20--

Mr H Wolfe
General Manager
Johnson Foods Corporation
PO Box 814
Newcastle 2940

Dear Mr Wolfe

Queries regarding investments in Johnson School Trust

I recently purchased shares of the common stock of your company for my retirement annuity investment portfolio. My purchase was based on the high evaluation of your shares in the journal *Value Listings Investment Survey.*

Please send me a copy of your 20-- Annual Report and your Third Quarter Report for 20--.

I would like to know what the duration of the Johnson School Trust is. In addition, could you tell me the number of shares outstanding in Class A and Class B, and how many of each the Trust owns?

I look forward to a successful investment venture through your business.

Yours sincerely

D Rittenhouse

David Rittenhouse

Replies to requests

In replying to letters of enquiry, you may use the request to structure your response. If the request was a complaint, the reply is called a letter of adjustment. The following sections are guidelines for you to follow.

First paragraph

Begin by thanking the enquirer for the letter and restating the request. By restating the request, you are providing the enquirer with an opportunity to check that the message he or she sent was understood in the way it was intended. This is particularly important if the request was unclear or ambiguous.

Body paragraphs

Provide the complete and exact information requested, including whatever explanatory data may be helpful. Refer specifically to any sections within attachments that are pertinent.

If you cannot provide any part of the information wanted or do what is requested, this should be stated next. It should be accompanied by an expression of regret and an explanation of the reasons why the complete information cannot be given. Include any additional information that may be of value.

Final paragraph

End your reply by inviting the enquirer to request any additional help or information needed.

Here is an example of a reply to the previous example; that is, to the letter of request from David Rittenhouse.

e9

JOHNSON FOODS

Johnson Foods Corporation
PO Box 814
Newcastle 2940

30 November 20--
Mr David Rittenhouse
12 Garden Court
Newcastle 2940

Dear Mr Rittenhouse

An informative subject line gives an overview of the letter.

Queries regarding investments in Johnson School Trust

Thank you for your recent letter and for your interest in Johnson Foods Corporation. We always appreciate receiving comments and inquiries from our stockholders. Mr Wolfe has asked me to reply.

Short paragraphs

Enclosed are the 20-- Annual Report and the Third Quarter interim report as you requested.

In response to your question regarding the duration of the Johnson School Trust, it is perpetual. There are currently 74 907 932 shares of Common Stock and 15 278 404 shares of the Class B Common Stock outstanding. Of these, the Johnson School Trust holds 22 928 493 shares of the Common Stock and 15 153 003 shares of the Class B Common Stock.

The facts are clear and in a logical order.

Thank you again for your interest in Johnson Foods. We hope to offer you the best service we can, so please continue to contact us with any query you may have.

The final paragraph generates goodwill.

Yours sincerely

James A Edris

JAMES A EDRIS

Director
Investor Relations

Refusals of requests

Sometimes you have to refuse requests, and it requires a great deal of skill and tact to say 'no' without losing the goodwill of the enquirer. The response letter must contain a neutral subject line and the first paragraph should be neutral and act as a buffer, so that the reader is not unpleasantly surprised on opening the email or letter. You should also try to end on a neutral or, at best, a positive note.

An effective letter of refusal could consist of:
- an opening statement that makes the enquirer feel their request was welcome
- a review of the situation, with explanations of the circumstances or reasons
- the refusal of the request
- a suggestion of an alternative possible source where the enquirer may obtain the needed information or service
- a friendly close.

Table 3.2 shows some examples of the tone and style required and how the different elements of a refusal letter can be put together.

Table 3.2 Approaches to refusals

Example 1	Example 2
Neutral subject line	Neutral subject line
Buffer paragraph: Thank you for your enquiry about … . We are pleased that you wish to transfer your account to our company.	**Buffer paragraph:** Thank you for your letter and your CV. We appreciate your interest in joining our company.
Reason: In order to keep our premiums as low as possible, we are able to accept only a small number of new accounts.	**Regret:** Unfortunately, we do not have a position open that would match your qualifications.
Regret: Even though we would like to accept your account, we are not able to do so … .	**Reason:** We have found that our most successful managers have had experience in other countries.
Thanks: We do appreciate your considering our company.	**Thanks:** We wish you every success in your efforts to find a post.

Here is an example of a standard refusal of a request:

e9

SOUTHERN INFRARED SPECTROGRAPHICAL SOCIETY

15 IONA AVENUE
CARLETONVILLE 2499
UNITED STATES OF AMERICA

12 November 20--
Mr AZ Roberts
Technical Specialities
Louis Trichardt 0920

Dear Mr Roberts

Request for infrared spectra

Thank you for your letter enquiring about our spectra that were ——
described in the March 20-- issue of *Spectrographic Analysis*.

The writer refers to facts given by the sender, to clarify the subject.

The infrared spectra that you asked for are listed on our card system. Most of these cards are more than twelve years old, and are very outdated. We have a limited number of sets left. The Society has therefore decided to donate them to educational institutions on the basis of financial needs.

We regret that we cannot send you a set at the moment. However, if educational institutions do not want all the sets, we will gladly consider sending you one at a later date. ——

We have put your letter on file, and will contact you in six months' time.

Short sentences, friendly tone

Yours sincerely

AR SANDERS

AR SANDERS
MANAGER

Mail written to claim or complain

Claims and complaints are written about poor service and/or unsatisfactory products. Understandably, emails or letters with this purpose are often written in anger. Remember that your end purpose is not to admonish someone, but to straighten out the problem and obtain the satisfactory service or product that is due and that you need. State your case factually and objectively. Accusations and sarcasm will offend the reader and/or delay your obtaining an appropriate adjustment. It is in your interests to write courteously.

You can include the following elements in a claim letter:

- Give a clear explanation of the situation or of what has gone wrong. Full details should be provided for the identification of the defective product or service, together with any information that may help the recipient check the matter.

- State the loss or inconvenience resulting from the mistake or defect.
- Motivate the recipient to take the desired action by appealing to his or her sense of fair play, honesty or pride.
- Indicate what you consider a fair adjustment to be.

The following is an example of a letter of complaint where the writer has let her anger cloud the message. The letter will make the recipient feel defensive and will therefore be less likely to achieve the outcome desired. Note the sarcastic tone created by quoting selected single words from the original ('allege'), using pompous expressions ('therefor'), including slang ('dogsbodies') and using punctuation for emphasis (exclamation marks and question marks). Later in the letter, the writer's tone is insulting ('Your ... is completely absurd'). Finally, there is no attempt to guide the recipient to the next stage of a successful close to this business.

e9

Messrs C McKenzie, C&D Quantity Surveyors

Messrs C McKenzie
C&D Quantity Surveyors
PO Box 10
Epping Industria 7475
27.03.20--

Johnson Brothers Design
Overly Stadium
Claremont 7700

Dear Sirs

Re: Tinston Towers

We are in receipt of your letter of the 26th March. Your first paragraph states that we 'allege' certain items are 'unproved'. We do not 'allege' this. They are unproven in terms of the contract and it is your duty, not ours, to get written authority therefor.

We are, in terms of our appointment and in terms of the contract, only the quantity surveyors and not the architects, builder's clerks or general dogsbodies!

We prepared your claims and have further also had to beg many times for receipt accounts, invoices and labour sheets. You now intimate that these are permanently mislaid (??) on the site, to wit: 'proven by a physical check on the site'.

Your second paragraph is also completely absurd, as:
- you state that you 'are unable to accept any account drawn up'
- you state that the items were 'accepted by (you) in toto without close (??) examination'
- you would like 'it back so as to re-examine it'.

→

Which of these do you actually intend?

You further state that you have requested that 'this contract be referred to arbitration'. This is something new to our experience and implies that no part of the contract is now in standing. If so, what is the standing of the quantity surveyors (ourselves) now?

Finally, the final account is available here for 'scrutiny', 're-examination', etc as you may wish. Therefore, it is not necessary to write in this connection.

We also wish to point out that substantial errors were not found in the 'rates' but in the extensions which were not finally checked and of which we informed you before handing you the final account.

Yours faithfully

J Dunbar

Janine Dunbar for C McKenzie

Next follows a letter of complaint where the writer has followed the pointers for an effective request for the redress of an unhappy situation. The writer gives details about the product and service and explains what redress is required. The tone is courteous throughout, appeals to the recipient's sense of fair play and refers to a continuing positive business relationship.

e9

Material Specialities (Pty) Ltd

36 St George's Street
Cape Town 8000
www.matspec.co.za
20 September 20--

Mr C Luthuli
Manager
Jacque's Leather Accessories
38 Twining Building
Jeppe Street
Johannesburg 2001

Dear Mr Luthuli

Incorrect quality of leather supplied: Order no 125

On 23 August we ordered 10 m of your FINE QUALITY leather at R158 per metre. However, when the order arrived, we found that you had sent us 10 m of your EXTRA FINE QUALITY leather at R204 per metre. We are writing to ask if you would credit our account for half the cost of the EXTRA FINE QUALITY leather.

→

Our reasons are as follows:
- We received the leather from you one month after the order, instead of the usual 10 days. We were wondering if there had been an error in the order.
- When the leather arrived, it was of the wrong quality.
- You charged us an amount not commensurate with our order.

We had a deadline to meet for one of our clients and so had no alternative but to use this leather for the chairs on order. Our quotations for this job were based on the cost of the FINE QUALITY leather at R158 per metre. We had no way of making up the R46 per metre difference and therefore lost money on the job.

We have had a long and favourable business association. We therefore believe that you will view the situation as we do, and will agree to credit our account with the amount in question: R460.

Yours sincerely

A Hassam

A Hassam

Company Accountant

Mail offering or refusing adjustment

Adjustment emails or letters are replies to claims or complaints. Whether the adjustment is to be granted in full, partially or not at all, the sender wants to keep the complainant as a customer. Creating the appropriate tone is thus essential.

Granting an adjustment

If the adjustment is granted, the letter could include the following elements:
- Thank the reader for calling attention to the difficulty or problem.
- Immediately tell the reader that steps have been taken or will be taken to remedy the problem, and that the loss or damage will be made good.
- If necessary, review or explain the facts about the problem.
- In some situations, there are certain steps the recipient needs to take to expedite the adjustment. Explain these and request that the recipient take the necessary steps.
- Grant the adjustment ungrudgingly. Voice your desire to maintain good relations with the customer and express appreciation for their business.

Here is an example of an adjustment granted:

e9

Jacque's Leather Accessories

Jacque's Leather Accessories
38 Twining Building
Jeppe Street
Johannesburg 2001
www.jacquesleather.com
27 September 20--

Mr A Hassam
Company Accountant
Material Specialities (Pty) Ltd
36 St George's Street
Cape Town 8000

Dear Mr Hassam

Order no 125: Adjustment of account for leather supplied

We are sorry about the inconvenience you describe in your letter of 20 September and are concerned about your loss of money on the job. We are, therefore, pleased to credit your account with R460.

We cannot understand the unusual delay in the delivery of the leather and are making internal enquiries. We fully appreciate the deadline that you had to meet and regret that you had to use the more expensive leather.

Jacque's Leather Accessories looks forward to receiving further orders from you and we assure you that they will be executed efficiently. Please contact us immediately with any queries regarding orders.

Yours sincerely,

C Luthuli

Charlton Luthuli

Manager
Jacque's Leather Accessories

Refusing an adjustment

When you must refuse an adjustment, you still want to keep the business relationship positive. Start on a positive note. The following elements could be included:

- Thank the reader for calling attention to the problem or difficulty.
- Review the facts surrounding the claim from the point of view of your decision.

- Partially grant or refuse the adjustment.
- Explain the reason for your decision.
- Close positively to rebuild the business relationship.

When replying to a request for an adjustment, avoid words or expressions that suggest that the person requesting the adjustment is behaving in any of these ways:

e9

Careless:	You failed to include the essential details.
	You overlooked the tear-off slip.
Lying:	You claim we did not ...
	You say we enclosed the account ...
Ignorant:	We cannot see how you missed the instruction.
	We are at a loss to know why you omitted payment.

3.4 Etiquette for digital correspondence

Mobile technology has many advantages, and both professional and personal messaging can have many positive outcomes. Sending messages across digital platforms (eg SMS or WhatsApp) is convenient, but it poses a risk. It is a challenge to remember to use the right style for the message. The informal tone you use in personal emails, SMSs and on your Facebook page is not appropriate for a workplace email. It is easy to make the mistake of writing an inappropriately informal work-related SMS if you normally text for social reasons.

It is also easy to become too informal, even overfamiliar, in an email. The trend to use first names, a colloquial style and a casual closing salutation can mean that the appropriate register for the business relationship is not created. No matter what kind of relationship you have with the recipient and/or subject matter, an email is still a written document that can be stored and read by other readers. Spelling errors, weak grammar, slang and careless writing will make a poor impression. Furthermore, your message may be exposed to others without your knowledge, as the recipient can forward the message or reply with others in the blind carbon copy (Bcc) field. For these reasons, it is best to separate your work email from your private email address, so that you do not confuse your approach to correspondence. Another reason to do this is that the company that holds the email server will always have access to all your email.

Many people today receive and read correspondence on small screens. Emails and IMs are increasingly read in situations where the reader is short of time or is partially distracted by the environment (such as a site, meeting place, home, etc). This must be considered as a factor in making your digital message readable. If the message cannot be read in the space of one or two screens, the message requires an overview, subheadings and, if pertinent, numbering.

The style most often used for digital communication is consultative, with the frequent use of first names instead of surnames, and a conversational tone. The trend in email is not to write in capital letters, since these are regarded as shouting at your readers. Use only lower case letters for passages of text. Write short sentences in short paragraphs separated by line spaces. If you have to impart information on a number of different topics, either use subheadings or, preferably, write separate emails with appropriate subject lines.

Here is an example of an informal email.

e9

To... (Nigel van der Pith) supervan@iafrica.com

Cc...

Subject: Items to discuss on Wednesday

From: Evan Morris <elegant@mweb.co.za>
To: Nigel van der Pith <supervan@iafrica.com>
Date: 12 December 20– – 10:19
Subject: Items to discuss on Wednesday

Nigel

I agree with Sid's ideas about steps to approach Juddson's, and especially the matter of the labour report.

Looking at the distribution of labour, I feel we need a consultant to advise us to make sure that we follow the best policy. You had some good ideas on this – could you put them forward for the agenda? The more comprehensive, the better. The items I have put together quickly for the meeting are:

1. Labour report to Juddson's
2. Briefing/summary from labour law consultant
3. Times of shifts of works section
4. Budget for the expanded canteen
5. Leave requests

Add yours and send the list back to me. June mentioned meeting a bit earlier. I am happy. Please let me know what you decide.

Thanks

Evan

The format of address and addresses is set by the software.

Lack of formal salutation 'Dear' makes the style abrupt. This is acceptable in regular correspondence, but not for less regular correspondence.

The speed of email means it can serve as a conversation. In this case the email implies that it is part of a number of emails passing between the writers.

Informal close acceptable for regular correspondents, but not for less familiar ones.

Here is an example of an email that is so sloppily written as to be unclear:

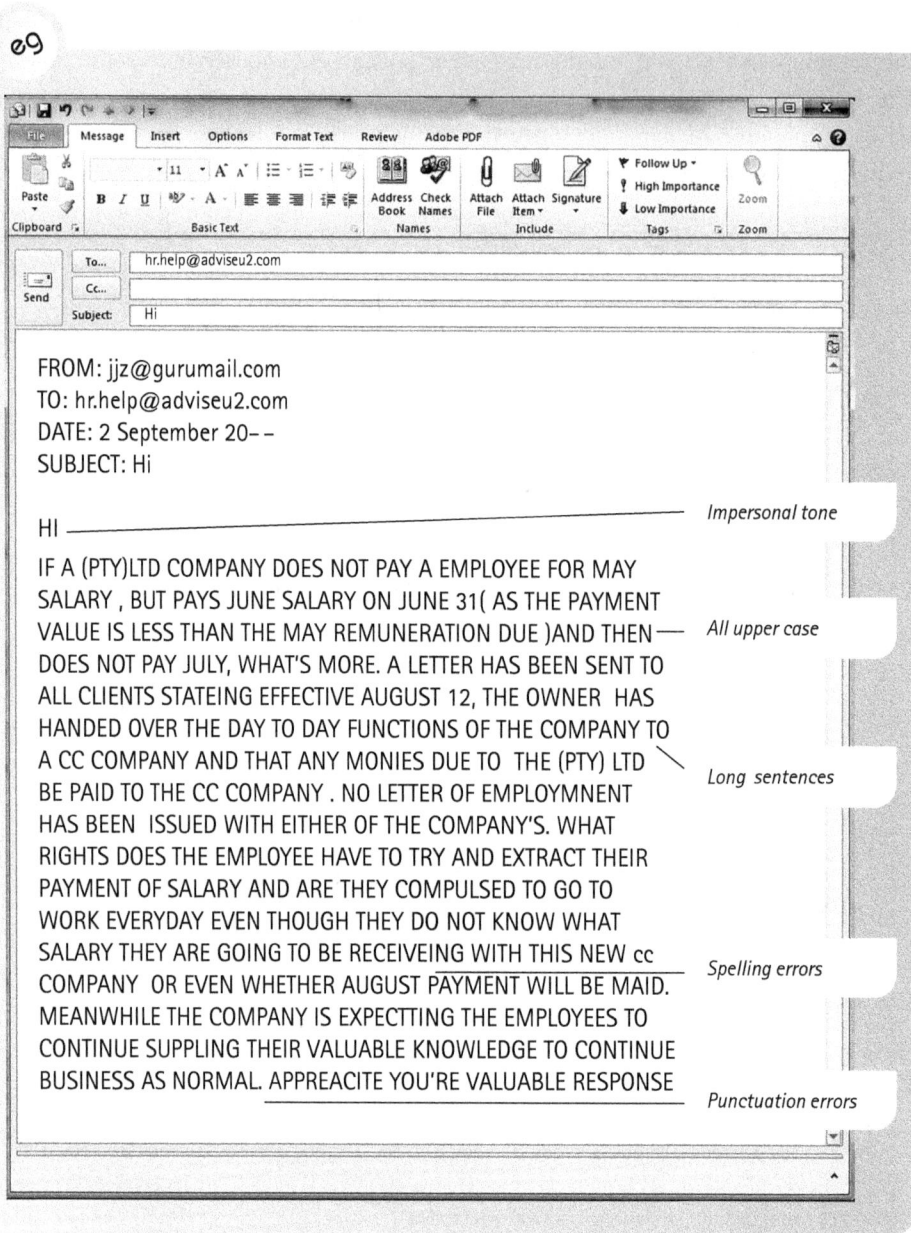

e9

To... hr.help@adviseu2.com
Cc...
Subject: Hi

FROM: jjz@gurumail.com
TO: hr.help@adviseu2.com
DATE: 2 September 20– –
SUBJECT: Hi

HI ——————————————————————— *Impersonal tone*

IF A (PTY)LTD COMPANY DOES NOT PAY A EMPLOYEE FOR MAY
SALARY , BUT PAYS JUNE SALARY ON JUNE 31(AS THE PAYMENT
VALUE IS LESS THAN THE MAY REMUNERATION DUE)AND THEN —— *All upper case*
DOES NOT PAY JULY, WHAT'S MORE. A LETTER HAS BEEN SENT TO
ALL CLIENTS STATEING EFFECTIVE AUGUST 12, THE OWNER HAS
HANDED OVER THE DAY TO DAY FUNCTIONS OF THE COMPANY TO
A CC COMPANY AND THAT ANY MONIES DUE TO THE (PTY) LTD
BE PAID TO THE CC COMPANY . NO LETTER OF EMPLOYMNENT *Long sentences*
HAS BEEN ISSUED WITH EITHER OF THE COMPANY'S. WHAT
RIGHTS DOES THE EMPLOYEE HAVE TO TRY AND EXTRACT THEIR
PAYMENT OF SALARY AND ARE THEY COMPULSED TO GO TO
WORK EVERYDAY EVEN THOUGH THEY DO NOT KNOW WHAT
SALARY THEY ARE GOING TO BE RECEIVEING WITH THIS NEW cc
COMPANY OR EVEN WHETHER AUGUST PAYMENT WILL BE MAID. *Spelling errors*
MEANWHILE THE COMPANY IS EXPECTTING THE EMPLOYEES TO
CONTINUE SUPPLING THEIR VALUABLE KNOWLEDGE TO CONTINUE
BUSINESS AS NORMAL. APPREACITE YOU'RE VALUABLE RESPONSE
Punctuation errors

3.5 How to manage email

Email etiquette

The following are some etiquette guidelines for working with email:

- When you send an email, the recipient receives your name and email address automatically. However, you need to include all other useful information.
- The first impression the reader has of your email is the subject line. The subject line should summarise the content of the email. It is helpful to maintain a thread on a single topic; avoid creating one thread containing emails on different topics. This means that if the content of the message changes, you need to create a new subject line for the email.
- When sending an email to more than one recipient, consider whether the secondary recipients should be in the Cc address line or the Bcc address line. Only include those who need to receive the mail. Needless copying in wastes recipients' time, as they have to clear their inboxes of emails that are not relevant to them. The Bcc function prevents recipients' addresses from being seen by the other recipients. Thus, it is a good option for a mass message where you do not want to publicise the addresses of the recipients, for example an invitation to an event. However, it can be used inappropriately to avoid transparency in communication. Also keep in mind that what you write in an email may not remain confidential if the recipient decides to forward your email or replies to you and includes others in the reply. Be mindful of others' and your own confidentiality in your use of email.
- Do not reply to email unless you need to. For example, do not reply 'Great' or 'Agree' if you were not asked for an opinion – you will simply be cluttering other people's inboxes.
- As most readers receive mail immediately on their mobile devices, it is courteous to send mail at appropriate times, eg in working hours. There is software available to help you manage the sending of emails, which is useful if you work after hours but only want your email to leave your outbox within working hours.
- If you are writing in anger or on a difficult topic, take the precaution of sending the email to yourself first. Open the email as a reader and you will get a different impression of it than you had as a sender. You may then edit the email before forwarding it to the person to be addressed.

You also need to manage your emails carefully if you want to be as efficient as possible:

- Manage your email inbox; do not let emails manage you and your time. Use the functions provided to have mail filed directly into folders or to have it colour-coded according to importance or subject.
- Delete all junk mail before opening it.

- Scan emails for viruses before opening them and only read emails that are applicable to you.
- Ask to be taken off lists if you are receiving mail that is either not relevant to you or is inappropriate for your working day.
- Deal with mail according to its importance.

Faxes

Faxes are still required in legal transactions for the transfer of original signatures. Faxes are usually documents scanned and sent as email attachments. In the transfer of an original faxed message, the print can become less legible. When presenting a message to be faxed, do the following:

- Use a typeface with a minimum point size of 12.
- If writing by hand, use a black pen, and print.
- Place the addressee's fax number and your own at the top of the first page. This is very important, lest the fax go to the wrong number. The receiver at the wrong number can resend it.
- Include the recipient's name and/or department in the address section. Many offices have a shared fax machine for a number of users, and the fax needs to reach the correct person/s.
- Indicate on every page the number of pages the fax runs to (eg 1 of 5 pages, 2 of 5 pages, etc).

Microsoft® Word™ also provides online access to a wide range of fax templates.

✓

Checklist for well-organised and persuasive correspondence

In order for your message to lead to the outcome you desire, it must be readable. Use the following checklist when you prepare a message:

- Follow the etiquette for the particular format.
- Make sure your message reflects the company's or your professional image.
- Use a suitable, up-to-date format with a topical subject line.
- Use a heading system and/or a numbering system, if appropriate.
- Open the message with an appropriate salutation that contains the recipient's name.
- In the body of the message, give the facts in a clear and logical order, with the main points properly organised and emphasised.
- Use the style and tone that suit the situation.
- Write the message coherently, so that the reader can follow the argument from sentence to sentence and from paragraph to paragraph.
- End the message with a closing paragraph that generates goodwill, regardless of the content of the message.
- If appropriate, include a clear call to action or an indication of the next steps to be taken.

Curricula vitae, application letters and interviews

4

Today employers expect an applicant to have the necessary knowledge and skills and for this knowledge to be reflected in the applicant's curriculum vitae (CV), covering letter and in the interview, if granted. (The term résumé is also used to refer to a CV, but more often in the USA.) If you are applying for a job, you need to have researched the job and/or company and to have tailored your application accordingly. And, if you are given an interview, you need to have the knowledge to ask pertinent questions. You need to know that the prospective employer will also check on your digital footprint to find out about you – and they may find things which you are not including in your CV (see Chapter 2). Your application must be tailored to the recipient and not to yourself. Therefore, you should not have only a single CV or letter or approach to being interviewed; rather, you need to style each item according to the person or institution on the receiving end.

This chapter addresses these areas and is divided into three main sections, namely:
- types of CVs for employment and further study
- letters of application for employment and study
- interviews.

Once you have worked through this chapter, you will be able to:
- choose the appropriate type of CV
- select pertinent material from your education and work experience to provide an informative CV tailored to a job or company
- write a letter of application
- tailor a CV and letter of application for an academic position or funding
- prepare for an interview for employment.

4.1 Types of curricula vitae

In an increasingly competitive job market, CVs have had to become not only a record of your experience, but also a selling document that will promote you ahead of other applicants. While you may have a general, brief CV attached to your LinkedIn profile, for example, the CV that you use to apply for a job needs to be edited with that position in mind. The recommended length of a concise CV is two pages. Every full CV of more than two pages should be accompanied by a one-page summary. In the summary, you should provide:

- your essential personal details
- information about your qualifications
- information about your experience
- a personal profile that summarises your developed abilities, key selling points, future plans and career goals.

For your records, prepare and keep a full CV as a portmanteau which holds all the information about you and your career. From this, you can select and adapt information for each application, so that you highlight the skills you have that are pertinent to that particular job. This is also a more time-efficient approach if you are sending out many applications.

Traditionally, personal information was included in CVs, but it has become the practice more recently to include only critical information (ie your name and email address). It is not required that you disclose your age, race, gender, marital status or history of salary.

A recent trend is to include a photograph of yourself with your CV and, if applicable, examples of your work. You may do this to personalise your CV, but only in a situation where you feel that it is appropriate. Some companies may not wish for a photograph to be included. If you choose to do so, include a photograph that is professional and of high resolution.

Microsoft® Word™ has a number of CV templates. Alternatively, you can download a CV template from the Internet or format your own. However, as with all templates, exercise caution before using a generic one, as the template may not be conducive to presenting information in the best way for that particular application. If you have an agency, compile your CV and work with them to ensure that they do not unnecessarily expand the layout of your CV. You do not want to devote a page to personal details which tell the reader nothing about your aptitudes. Details about your skills, knowledge and talents should appear on the first page.

Traditional or chronological curriculum vitae

The traditional method of presenting a CV is to list your personal details (limited), education, experience, activities, interests and references. The trend today is to give your most recent education and experience first. If relevant, your family details, bursary commitments and travel experience may be mentioned. The chronological approach works well if your progress has been consistent, there are not too many gaps and the recruiter is in a more conservative field, such as a legal practice.

Your CV may be accompanied by scanned certified copies of documents (for example school and/or qualification certificates) and testimonials. **If you decide not to mail these, have them at hand for the interview.**

Ensure that the first page of your CV is rich in information and opens with a personal statement or aim. However, if you describe a personal quality (eg hard-working), substantiate this with evidence (eg 'I simultaneously studied full time and worked part time'). Do not try to be everything, and do not claim skills that you do not possess. Furthermore, do not have introductory pages bearing only your name or personal details. It is a nuisance for the reader to have to scroll down the pages and is wasteful of paper should it be printed.

Here are some examples of chronologically presented CVs, with the most recent activities and qualifications given first. These examples are of a first-year student (Janelle Canham), a recent graduate (Christopher Molteno) and two experienced professionals (Joseph Axel and Tapiwa Tevera). Note the various options for presentation offered by the different formats. Note too that each CV opens with a personal statement which defines the applicant.

eg

Janelle Canham Email: canjaxxxx@myuct.ac.za Phone: 012 XXX 2870 • Cell: 071 XXX 3467	**CV**

Personal profile

I am currently a full-time chemical engineering student; however, I have a keen interest in the business and financial sectors. I am hard-working, ambitious and adaptive: these skills I exercise daily by balancing my studies and extra-curricular activities. My studies in chemical engineering have given me tools to prepare me well for the work environment. I have taken the initiative to develop my own skills in programming and computers.

Experience

Sasol Chemical Engineer: Job shadow   **2015, January**
- Worked in a team on optimising plant efficiency. Various methods were formulated and tested.
- Analysed process simulation with prior programming knowledge. Developed these skills further, while gaining a new skill, namely that of problem diagnosis.

Telkom: Vacation work as a personal assistant   **2014, June**
- Greeted and served clients and guests of Telkom. Practised interpersonal skills.
- Responsible person for organising meeting logistics (planning suitable date, time and venue) as well as recording meeting minutes. Honed valuable organisational skills in a professional environment.

→

Volunteer tutor: Bona Lesedi Secondary School   **2013–2014**

- Tutored Mathematics, Physical Science and English to matric learners from Bona Lesedi Secondary School. Teaching forced me to solidify my personal understanding of the concepts I taught.
- Hosted workshops teaching students time management, stress management and study methods and skills. This trained me to communicate effectively in order to convey lessons to the students.

Education

Chemical Engineering: University of Cape Town   **2015–present**

I am currently studying toward a Bachelor of Science in the field of Chemical Engineering. I hope to use my qualification in the future to better society in South Africa.

2015:   Recipient of Sasol bursary

2015–2016:   Member of Engineers Without Borders society

Pretoria Girls' High School: Pretoria, Gauteng   **2010–2014**

Completed my secondary education, achieving eight subject distinctions.

2014:   IEB and NSC subject distinctions in Mathematics, Xhosa, English, Afrikaans, Information Technology, Physical Science and Life Orientation

2012–2014:   Achieved academic honours for three consecutive years

2014:   Prefect, house prefect, and voted prefect of the year

2013–2014:   Won the University of Pretoria's programming challenge

Sport, culture and service

2013–2014:   Provincial chess team for two consecutive years

2013–2014:   Merit for choir

2010–2014:   Provincial merit for water polo

2014:   Sporting honours in squash

2014:   Serviceman's award for community service

Skills

Computing skills

- Programming languages: Delphi, Java, C++ and HTML (for web design)
- Proficient in Microsoft® Word™, Excel™ and PowerPoint™
- Skills gained in IT and extracurricular courses applied practically during part-time work at Telkom

Laboratory skills

- Practised working in laboratory environments through chemistry and chemical engineering lab work.
- Further developed laboratory skills while job shadowing at a Sasol plant, as these were an essential tool.

→

Oral communication
- Languages: Fluent in Xhosa and English; proficient in Afrikaans; conversational Shona
- Experienced in communicating lessons through work as a volunteer tutor
- Public speaking (Xhosa and English) practised as a prefect during sporting and other school events

Leadership and teamwork
- Able to develop and further my leadership skills during my time as a prefect in 2014
- Teamwork was vital in playing provincial water polo, and singing in the Pretoria Girls' High School choir
- Developed through school and chemical engineering; and practised during vacation work, determining solutions to operating problems and performance efficiency

Time management and organisational skills
- Developed through balancing academic, sporting, cultural and leadership roles during high school
- Further developed as a personal assistant at Telkom

Referees

Mr Kobus Smit
Headmaster, Pretoria Girls' High School
Email: kobuskxxx@xxx.com

Mrs Reshada Naidoo
Academic Head, Pretoria Girls' High School
Email: reshada.naidoo@xxx.com

e9

Christopher Molteno

Email@gmail.com | (0)787 xxx xxxx

Personal statement

Having studied chemical engineering in South Africa, I have chosen to pursue a career path that will allow me to couple this technical background with my interest and ability in business. I have run both a private business and a charitable organisation, but am looking for a career opportunity that will allow me to continue learning and improving my skills. I come from a large family and consequently I have excellent negotiation skills and a diplomatic disposition, which I have put to very good effect in my current position. I seldom experience conflict with colleagues and work well in a team. During my extensive gap year travels and in my present job, which involves international travel, I have developed a high degree of independence, initiative and a strong work ethic. I have well-honed communication skills, have presented to large audiences and written well-received important reports for my employers, the public and government offices.

→

Professional experience

Enviro Green Agencies: London, 2016 — Contracted from January 1st

Innovation Engineer — Responsible for the project management of a funding process that included the preparation and submission of research grants and the launching of a financial mechanism. Successfully defended the company's right to its concession in Namibia to the extent that it was offered a one-year extension on its licence. Completed technical projects, including mapping of oil deposits, preparation of technical public relations literature and research grant applications.

Work based in the UK but included extensive travel to Namibia, South Africa and Botswana

Centre for Biological Engineering Research (Ceber): University of Cape Town, 2015

Researcher — Investigation of the behaviour of sulphate-reducing bacteria (intended for the remediation of acid rock drainage) on different physical growth supports for use in continuous reactors.

Skills acquired: Academic research and paper writing, biological laboratory work with anaerobic cultures

Clariant: Heufeld, Bavaria, 2014–2015

Research Intern, R&D department of Clariant Chemicals, Heufeld — Responsible for the commissioning of a drying test unit and initial drying tests on barium-based adsorbent. Successfully commissioned the test rig and provided recommendations for its future use.

Skills acquired: Business etiquette, project management and laboratory work protocol with hazardous materials

Education and achievements

University of Cape Town: Cape Town, 2012–2015

Bachelor of Science degree (1st class Hon) in Chemical Engineering (for full academic results, see academic transcript)

2015 — Winner of the Chevron Prize for the best chemical engineering design

2014 & 2015 — Chairperson of Habitat for Humanity, UCT charter (a charitable society with approximately 250 members)

2013 — Awarded a six-month exchange at the University of Merced, California

2012 & 2014 — Two inclusions on the UCT Dean's List for academic excellence

2012 — Invitation to the Golden Key society (top 15% of students)

2012 — A university entrance scholarship

Bishops Diocesan College: Cape Town, 2006–2010

National senior certificate matric pass (BD) with distinction

All eight subjects above 80%, including 96% for Mathematics

2010 — Member of the Ten Club for the top ten academics

2010 — Awarded full colours during high school for leadership

2010 — Awarded a Golden President's Award by the South African president and the British High Commissioner

→

2008 – Winner of the Royal Society of Science essay competition on possible sources of power in South Africa (Molteno, C. 2008. How best to meet South Africa's future energy requirements. Transactions of the Royal Society of South Africa. 63(2): 189.)

2008 – Awarded a three-month exchange to Orchard College in Curico, Chile

SACS Junior School: Cape Town, 1999–2005
Prefect

Additional skills

Communication

Am a confident public speaker, having been requested to speak to large audiences on multiple occasions through school and university leadership positions.

Presented to the Technical Advisory Committee of NamCor, Namibia, and successfully defended my company's right to its exploration concession.

Gave a training course on communication to underprivileged children for the University of Cape Town's outreach programme.

Possess basic spoken and written Afrikaans and French.

IT/computer literacy
Proficient in all Microsoft® Office™ programs, including Visio™ and Project™.

Proficient in using process simulation programs, including COCO and Aspen Plus.

Talented at webpage design using WordPress, having designed websites for three private companies and a consultant.

Teamwork and leadership
Was a member of and then head of the committee that led Habitat for Humanity, UCT.

Was the pastoral head of the Grade 8s during the final year of school.

Worked in the research team at Clariant (Heufeld, Germany).

Self-reliance
Travelled alone for a year after school across Western and Eastern Europe, Britain and South East Asia. Continue to travel at every opportunity and have now visited nearly 40 countries.

Sport and interests
Rowing: Member of Bishops 1st VIII (2010). Rowed for university during annual Boatrace event (2013 & 2014). Member of London Rowing Club (2016 & 2017).

Running: Enthusiastic runner, having competed in a number of half marathons. Personal best time of 90 minutes.

Horse riding: Experienced rider.

Wave skiing, skiing and hiking: adept and enthusiastic.

Vocational work

Parking business: Cape Town, 2000–2015
Head of a parking business which sells parking space on family property during Newlands Rugby Stadium rugby matches. Park and move the vehicles. Parking capacity of 32 cars. Ongoing business with regular and long-term customers.

Skills acquired: People skills, negotiation skills, driving and parking skills with any car

→

Villa Renovations: Antibes, 2011

Team member — Worked in a team renovating a villa in Antibes. Work was cleaning, painting and small scale demolition.

Skills acquired: Ability to operate building tools such as a jackhammer

Riverford Organic Vegetable Farm: Normandy, 2011

Worked as a **farm hand** on a large vegetable farm. Worked involved picking, planting and packaging of vegetables.

Yacht deckhand: Between Cannes, France and San Remo, Italy, 2011

Temporary deckhand for luxury yachts in harbour. Work involved cleaning and polishing. Worked on the yachts: Where Dreams Never End, Melina, Julia and Luna.

e9

JOSEPH AXEL

ID no: 820xxxxxx084

Address:
120 xxxxx xxxxx
1xx xxxx Road
Sea Point
Cape Town
8005

Email:
joseph.axel@xxxx.com

Phone:
(C) 082 xxx 99xx
(H) 0xx 433 xxxx

PERSONAL PROFILE

I am an energetic, ambitious individual, whose maturity and responsibility have developed over time. I have a passion for research and analysis, especially in South African current affairs. My communication and interpersonal skills are excellent.

KEY ACHIEVEMENTS

- Chaired Cape Town Rotary Conference (2014 and 2015)
- Elected onto the Board of the South African Media Society (2013)
- Presented with the Trinity Exhibition Award for the highest distinction mark for the Advanced Classical Music Certificate in South Africa (2012)
- Awarded the Ford Foundation Scholarship to study abroad for one semester in Washington, DC (2010)

KEY SKILLS

- Excellent interpersonal and leadership skills
- Extensive experience in facilitating small-group work
- Strong written and verbal communication skills
- Supportive, positive team member
- Highly IT proficient, including Microsoft® Word™ and Excel™, Internet-based research and social networking

→

EDUCATION

2016–Present	**Financial Management; Business Research and Analysis Certificates**
	GetSmarter and University of Cape Town (UCT)

2013–2015   **Master's in Justice and Transformation**
UCT

2010–2011   **Bachelor of Arts (Honours) in Political Studies**
University of the Witwatersrand (Wits)

2006– 2009   **Bachelor of Arts**
Wits
- Major subjects: Politics and International Relations
- Undergraduate Law background

2005   **Crawford College, Sandton**

PROFESSIONAL EXPERIENCE

2014–2016   **South African Media Awareness Organisation**
- **Head of Media and Public Affairs**
- Lobbied national, regional and local government
- Managed various social media platforms
- Created and maintained relationships with all forms of media
- Researched and created policies regarding key areas of concern

2013–2014   **Gold Communications**
- **Consultant** for various companies requiring reputation management

2013   **University of Cape Town**
- **Tutor** for second-year Public Policy and Administration (PPA) students

2010–2012   **MixitFM**
- **Radio presenter and producer** for a daily talk show on current affairs, as well as a weekly talk show on environmental affairs
- Required to research interesting and current topics
- Interviewed relevant leaders and professionals

2011   **Open Society Initiative of Southern Africa (OSISA)**
- **Education intern**
- Responsible for website development
- Processed grants for partners
- Developed database for programme partners, networks and contacts in the southern African region

2010   **University of the Witwatersrand**
- **Tutor** for first-year Political Studies students

→

VOLUNTEER EXPERIENCE

2012–Present (Cape Town)
- National Executive for South African Rotary Organisation. Chaired the 2014 and 2015 Cape Town Rotary Conferences, and created the programme for the 2012 Johannesburg Rotary Conference/2013 Cape Town Rotary Conference, an international event for 550 delegates.

2010 (Washington DC, USA)
- Volunteered at Dreams for Kids (DC), engaged with at-risk and disabled youth in the greater DC area.

2009 (Johannesburg)
- Observed South African National and Provincial Elections for the South African Media Society.

2006–2009
- Was a member of youth movement, Ace Kidz. Created informal educational material for children aged 11–17 and young adults. Chaired the Johannesburg branch from 2008 to 2009. Ran successful summer camps for specific age groups in 2008 and 2009.

REFERENCES

Mike Clelland
Gold Communications
David Smithson
South African Media Society

- mike@xxxxx.co.za
  xxx 632 xxxxx
- dxxx@gmail.com
  083 xxx 6050

e9

TAPIWA TEVERA

Flat xxx xxxx Court
45 xxxxx Square
xxxx Road
Rondebosch, 7700

Cell: 079 xxx xxxxx
Email: xxxx@xxx.com
Passport number: XXXXXX
Nationality: Zimbabwe

WORK EXPERIENCE

April 2015 – present: Lead Buyer, Johnson & Johnson
- Support, build and execute B-BBEE Enterprise and Supplier Development & Diversity Strategy
- Manage all the import/export activity of raw materials and packaging components
- Manage all purchasing activities within inbound supply chain
- Ensure payment of suppliers in accordance with agreed payment terms

→

January 2016 – March 2016: Interim Lead Buyer, Johnson & Johnson
- Provision of procurement support to Cape Town plant and ownership of supplier relationship management initiatives
- Worked with sourcing managers to quickly resolve supply-related issues (eg delivery delays, pricing discrepancies)
- Continuation and completion of projects led/managed by previous lead buyer

January 2014 – March 2015: Sourcing Specialist, Johnson & Johnson
- Optimised chemicals supply to market strategy in order to achieve cost savings and to eliminate poor performing suppliers
- Worked with sourcing managers and local plants (Cape Town and East London) to establish 100% compliance with business awards (Quality, Price, Quantity, Lead times)

PROFESSIONAL QUALIFICATIONS

May 2016 – present: Diploma in Procurement and Supply, Chartered Institute of Procurement & Supply (CIPS)

EDUCATION

2011–2014: Master of Science in Engineering (Materials Engineering) (by dissertation), UCT
- Thesis topic: Assessment of Corrosion Behaviour of Zinc Coated Steel Using a Salt Spray Chamber

2010: Bachelor of Science (Honours) in Materials Science, UCT

2005–2009: Bachelor of Science in Chemical, Molecular and Cellular Sciences, UCT
- Majors: Biotechnology and Microbiology
- Sabbatical in 2008 due to ill health. Returned to complete.

2004: Advanced Level Certificate, St Georges College, Harare, Zimbabwe

ACHIEVEMENTS AND AWARDS

2011–present: Guest Examiner for fourth-year Engineering Entrepreneurial Course, UCT
- Selected for role after obtaining top mark in Professional Communication Studies postgraduate course

2010: UCT Student Leadership Award
- Most Outstanding UCT Student Leader in a Postgraduate Faculty Council: Engineering and the Built Environment (EBE)

2010, 2007: Ackerman Family Foundation Leadership Award Recipient
- Award sponsored by the Ackerman Family to recognise and perpetuate excellence and achievement in student leadership at UCT

July 2007: 19th All African Student Leaders Conference, Windhoek, Namibia
- Selected as member of a five-person delegation that represented student leaders from UCT

2005: Clarinus Village Fresher of the Year Award Recipient
- Award recognises the significant contributions of a first-year student to the residence in the areas of service and leadership

→

LEADERSHIP POSITIONS

2011: Chairperson of the EBE Postgraduate Students' Council
- Led the development of a website project for the council, in order to better inform students of the activities of the council
- Introduced the Dean's Postgraduate Students' Forum to promote interaction between the students and management

2010: President of the Zimbabwe Students' Society
- Raised approximately R10 000 in sponsorship
- Promoted awareness among students on the situation in Zimbabwe through a public lecture

2010: Chairperson of the Kolbe Catholic Society
- Increased membership through an effective advertising drive during orientation week
- Organised successful events that addressed spiritual growth and development which saw increased student participation

2010: Student Representative of the Bachelor of Science (Honours) in Materials Science Programme
- Collaborated with professors and lectures about course work material
- Set test and exam dates through consultation with students and academic staff (there is greater flexibility for this at postgraduate level)

2007: Elected Head Student of the Woolsack Residence

2007: Secretary of the Undergraduate Science Students' Council

2006: Head Student of Clarinus Village Residence

TEMPORARY EMPLOYMENT

February 2011 – December 2012: Administrator Temporary Assistant (part-time): EBE Faculty Office, UCT
- Registered students for courses using Oracle's PeopleSoft Enterprise application
- Performed filing duties on a regular basis to update student records

May 2011 – December 2012: Hospitality Waiter (part-time): Event Life Blend, Cape Town
- Carried out waitron duties at corporate events
- Training included understanding the importance of being well groomed and the development of effective ways of communicating with guests in both crisis and non-crisis situations

November 2007 – January 2008: Vacation Subwarden: The Woolsack Residence, UCT
- Responsible for the daily running of the residence during the vacation period
- Ensured that the rules of the residence were adhered to, for example security procedures for students entering and leaving the residence

SKILLS
- **Languages:** Fluent in English and Shona, basic French
- **Communication:** Effective oral communication skills developed through delivering speeches, Microsoft® PowerPoint™ presentations and through Professional Communication Studies course

$\longrightarrow$

- **Leadership and teamwork:** Derive fulfilment from leadership roles, constantly embracing and promoting the ethos of achievement through teamwork
- **Stress and time management:** Successful in managing academic, leadership and employment responsibilities
- **Learning and teaching capacity:** Ability to embrace new learning opportunities through exposure to positions of leadership and employment which are subsequently passed on to others

REFEREES

Ms Moira Smith: Executive Director, Student Affairs, UCT

Telephone: 021 650 xxxx

Email: xxx@uct.ac.za

Professor Gervaise Brown: Director, Centre for Engineering, UCT

Telephone: 021 650 xxxx

Email: gerxxx@uct.ac.za

Non-traditional or functional curricula vitae

A CV can also be arranged to highlight your best points, as opposed to giving information chronologically. This approach is useful if you have no conventional work experience – for example if you are a new school leaver – or if you wish to downplay long gaps in study or employment. Both theoretical (study) and practical (work experience) details are organised under headings which describe your talents and skills. This method also defines the fields in which you wish to continue developing. Furthermore, you will be describing qualities that are unique to you.

The following examples of non-traditional CVs show information presented according to functions. They open with a summary directed at the developed abilities of the person and their goals, followed by the full CV. For some positions, particularly those in the creative fields of arts and design, an infographic CV is appropriate. The additional advantage of the latter is that they may be loaded onto platforms such as Instagram or shared via Twitter and Facebook. The other platform for a digital CV is to have a website, such as one created through WordPress or Wix.com. These are discussed in Chapter 13.

e9

Flora Burt

Cape Town, South Africa
Tel: 072 xxx xxxx

Email: Fxxx@xx.co.za
Nationality: South African

PERSONAL PROFILE

I am a hard-working and dependable person, skills I practised as deputy head of various portfolios at school. These positions have helped me develop my leadership skills. I am ambitious and outgoing; I enjoy travel, adventure and interacting with people of various cultural backgrounds. I consider myself a people person and hope to work with young people while travelling on a gap year.

EXPERIENCE

SRC — Deputy Head of Student Representative Council (SRC) at Springfield Convent

Purpose	To facilitate engagement between students and management at Springfield
Summary	The SRC is a body of students representing each class and grade in the high school. Weekly meetings with student representatives are chaired by the head and deputy head; in these meetings students air any complaints and ideas, which are then put forward to management in weekly meetings. Furthermore, the SRC supports staff in all major events and is involved with a charity, Dignity Dreams, and its initiatives. These meetings and events were opportunities to exercise and strengthen my leadership skills.

Borneo Expedition — World Challenge Youth Leadership Expedition

Purpose	World Challenge expeditions allow students to develop leadership and teamwork skills, as well as confidence and self-esteem, and their capacities for building a global society.
Summary	The 16-day expedition to Borneo included a two-day jungle trek, a hike up Mount Kinabalu (4095.2 m) and a community outreach project to build a small road in Long Pasia, a rural village in Borneo. I was responsible for personal budgeting, accommodation, transport and food. Additionally, each group member was responsible for certain areas and individuals took turns to lead the group.

French Tour — School tour to France with several participating South African schools

Purpose	To improve French language skills and experience the culture of France
Summary	I attended classes at the International French language school, and experienced the cultural values of France. I learned the value of being immersed in a culture as a tool to understand people's perspectives and learn new languages.

→

LEADERSHIP	
Deputy Head: Swimming	Deputy head of a major sport in the portfolio. Responsibilities included managing training sessions, organising weekly interschool galas and events.
Sport Portfolio Committee	This committee is for the heads and deputy heads of each sport. The Sport Portfolio Committee organises, manages and runs the various sports, as well as encouraging support of and involvement in all sports and at all events.

ACADEMIC RECORD	2002–2015: Springfield Junior and High School, Cape Town
Matric subjects	English, Maths, Science (including physics & chemistry), History, French, Afrikaans, Life Orientation
Full academic colours	2014: Cumulative average of over 85% every year
Academic scroll	2011–2014: Over 85% average in each year of high school
Olympiads	2013–2014: English Olympiad entrant; bronze award in 2014
	2010–2013: Entrant in SAMO Junior and Senior Maths Olympiads
	2012: Entrant in Senior Maths Olympiads
Award for Excellence	2011–2013: Excellence in Mathematics
Silver award for Science Expo	2012: Achieved between 80–85% in Grade 9 Science Expo Competition
Xhosa prize	2011: Top achieving student in Xhosa third language in Grade 8

SPORT	2011–2015
Netball	U14A/U15A/U16A (captain) & Springfield First Team
	• 2013: Burger Trophy for Service to Netball in Grade 10
	• 2011: U14 Netball Trophy in Grade 8
Swimming	2013: Team swimming – Roscoe Cup for Swimming in Grade 10
Water polo	U14A/U15A/U16A/Second team

SKILLS/EXTRA-CURRICULAR	
Juno study skills	2014: A two-day course learning study skills and techniques
Toastmasters	Certificate of achievement: six-week course on public speaking
Computer literacy	Proficient in Microsoft® Word™, Excel™ and PowerPoint™
Scuba diving	2013: PADI Basic Diving Course in KwaZulu-Natal, South Africa

→

REFERENCES		
Name	Ms F Ackermann	Ms B Houghton
Organisation	Springfield High School	Springfield High school
Relationship	Afrikaans teacher (2012–2015)	Head
Contact:	xxxxx@springfieldschool.co.za	xxxxx@springfieldschool.co.za

e9

Andile Vuyo Xola

Contact number: + 27 (0)79 xxx 32xx

Email: xolaandile@xxx.com

ID: xxxxxxxxxx

Since successfully completing my BA Honours in Brand Communications, graduating in 2010, I have added experience to theory and built on the skills I previously developed working in higher education. I have held various positions, ranging from student advisor to marketing and alumni relations. I am experienced at engaging and interacting with a broad range of stakeholders, including students, academics, alumni and service providers in both the private and public sectors. I have acquired a diverse range of skills and an understanding of etiquette in serving the various institutions.

I have excellent verbal and written communication skills. I take pride in serving my employer and building strong and successful brands for the organisations I have been associated with. I am a sociable and approachable person with the ability to self-motivate and to build and maintain strong relationships with internal and external stakeholders.

I look forward to new challenges and to applying my skills in new contexts.

EDUCATION

2010	BA Honours in Brand Leadership, Brand Communications School
2008	ND Marketing Management, Cape Peninsula University of Technology (CPUT)

Short courses

2012	Certificate in Public Relations, CPUT (four months)
2011	UCT Business Writing and Legal Documents, GetSmarter (10 weeks)
2011	Applied Writing Skills and Processes Masters Course (one week)

→

SKILL SETS

Project management

- Managing and implementing new and existing projects for alumni
- Ensuring time lines for projects, such as events, surveys and new project developments
- Managing and reporting on the annual budget
- Evaluating projects at regular intervals and milestones to assess impact

Client relationship management

- Initiating, building, engaging and managing strong and meaningful relationships with alumni and students
- Managing alumni relationships (existing alumni affinity groups and chapters as well as establishing new ones), looking to add mutual value in line with good practice
- Researching and developing suitable benefits and programmes for both alumni and students (and any engaged stakeholders)
- Approaching successful alumni for planned talks or other events, and building strategic relations in line with strategic goals and brand

Marketing and communications

- Working closely with the Communications Department to ensure timely, relevant and accurate communications to alumni via email, newsletters and other publications and media
- Planning and implementing a clear marketing strategy for both students and alumni, by reviewing different ways to engage students, alumni and businesses in line with the overall strategy
- Managing briefings with agencies, and negotiating and supervising strict time lines
- Contributing and overseeing the website, making sure it is updated with relevant information
- Contributing articles and ideas for the annual alumni magazine and the alumni and student newsletter
- Managing the development of marketing material with service providers

Brand management

- Building a unique brand for alumni and students within the global branding mandate
- Re-branding the student association to clarify and make its offering more meaningful
- Supporting students in brand activation programmes through plans integrated via the brand strategy
- Managing the advertising for various programmes via print, radio and posters
- Understanding the value and reputation attached to a brand, and the consequent need to protect, nurture and develop it

Stakeholder relations

- Identifying strategic partners and managing and engaging in collaborations with internal stakeholders — from working with Head Office to other departments and faculties
- Working and maintaining close relationships with external stakeholders — sponsors, partners and service providers, which range from affluent alumni and business owners to retailers
- Working with various government departments on projects and policy
- Overseeing the development and execution of sponsorship budgets and agreements

→

Data management

- Managing and overseeing the continuous updating of the database with the ability to sort data intelligently when necessary — including segmenting the data into key constituency groups and other groups that may be relevant for a particular project

Reporting and writing

- Writing quarterly and yearly reports on various projects
- Writing business letters, professional emails and minutes
- Analysing data and writing up research projects

Professionalism

- Aptitude for working hard under pressure and to tight deadlines
- Working effectively, both independently and in a team
- Good communication, management and leadership skills
- Ability to foster good relations and trust
- Good presentation and public speaking skills
- Innovative, creative and solution-orientated thinker
- Capacity to take initiative and follow through
- Self-motivated to continue my professional education through study and acquiring new skills and broadening my experience base

EMPLOYMENT HISTORY

November 2010 to April 2015 — Development and Alumni Department

Alumni Relations Officer

Essentially, as Alumni Relations Officer, I was responsible for overseeing, researching, developing and managing all aspects relating to alumni and ongoing engagement. My role included planning, organising and managing events locally, nationally and internationally; communicating with alumni and other relevant stakeholders and service providers regarding events, general queries and other news; and developing our database, value-add services and engagement opportunities to ensure the organisation remains in line with relevant international practice in relation to alumni, mutually beneficial relations with stakeholders and philanthropic giving. I worked both independently and as part of a broader team in line with the Development and Alumni strategy and brand. My role also included servicing the Alumni Advisory Board and co-ordinating the Special Interest groups.

March 2010 to October 2010 — Brand Communications School
Assistant Marketing Manager (part-time school)
My role as Assistant Marketing Manager included managing and running the regional part-time school, conducting necessary market research to ensure world-class positioning, developing regional marketing and sales strategies in line with the national strategy, planning and organising events, and overseeing the general school administration.

January 2009 to February 2010 — Brand Communications School
Marketing Co-ordinator (Contact Navigator)
I worked closely with the National Marketing Manager in the roll-out of the national marketing strategy to market and promote full-time courses. This included managing the admissions process, delivering presentations to schools and universities and attending career fairs and exhibitions. It also meant presenting weekly reports, managing regional events and updating the database.

$\longrightarrow$

April 2008 to January 2009 — Brand Communications School
Admin Assistant (part-time photography)
This position was largely administrative and focused on co-ordinating applications, running the courses, assisting lecturers with general administration, and reporting on numbers.

October 2005 to March 2008 — Graduate School of Marketing
Student Advisor

As a Student Advisor, I was the first point of call to provide advisory services to students in line with the prospectus. I co-ordinated student applications and registration, maintained the library to ensure relevant learning material was available, updated the database and assisted with the co-ordination of training and graduation.

June 2005 to September 2005 — Ethical Leadership Project
Project co-ordinator
This project was run by an interim board which I was responsible for supporting through administration, co-ordinating travel, taking minutes, and general office administration and processes.

Referees
Ms Maureen Erasmus
Individual Giving Manager
Development and Alumni Department
Tel: xxx 347 xxxx; Cell: 076 xxx xx36
Email: maureen.erasmus@xxx.co.za

Mr Marco van Niekerk
Brand Strategy Manager
Brand Communications School
Tel: 011 xxx 8089; **Cell:** xxx 656 xxxx
Email: Marco@xxxx.com

Ms Lianne Markam
Communications Officer
Development and Alumni Department
Cell: 074 xxx xxxx
Email: Lianne.xxx@xxxx.co.za

Infographic curricula vitae

The following is an example of an infographic CV which is appropriate for those working in design and arts. However, it would not be appropriate for someone working in a traditional profession such as an accountant or doctor. This graphic was created first with a hand drawn sketch and then drawn in Adobe Illustrator.

e9

Paul English Industrial Designer

Statistics

12 years — Experience as an Industrial Designer.
54 feet — Largest product that I have been involved with.
140 mm — Smallest product that I have been involved with.
18 products — Number of successful products.
9 countries — Number of countries where my products have been sold.
135 000 units — Total amount of Avocado Prep Tools sold to date.

1 First successful yacht launch
2 New model of yacht successfully launched
GOOD DESIGN Australian Design Award for kitchen tongs
red dot design award International Design Award for Avocado Prep tool.

Work Experience

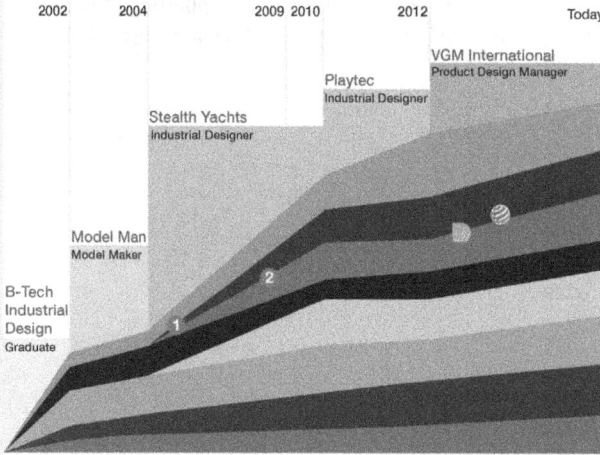

2002   2004   2009   2010   2012   Today

VGM International
Product Design Manager

Playtec
Industrial Designer

Stealth Yachts
Industrial Designer

Model Man
Model Maker

B-Tech Industrial Design Graduate

Cape Town   Sydney

3D Cad/Surface Modeling
Product Development
Freehand Design Illustration
Prototyping
Concept Realisation/Imagination
Problem Solving
Computer Rendering
Project Management

Ai Adobe Illustrator
Ps Adobe Photoshop

3S SOLIDWORKS

Rhinoceros
AUTOCAD

Office Microsoft

Interests

Camping
Trail Running
Snowboarding   Rock Climbing
Surfing
Travel **Drawing**
Ocean Swimming

✉ paul@mail.com   ☐ 0123456789   in paul.linkedin.com

Academic curricula vitae

Applicants to university or research positions in all fields, for funding or for further study, need to include areas of information pertinent to academia. Essential to most applications will be research experience, conference presentations and publications, as shown in the example that follows. For lecturing positions, teaching experience is required. Just as LinkedIn profiles are influential for those working in commerce and industry, so having a profile on Academia.edu and ResearchGate.net is essential for those in academia. These sites track citations and significantly contribute to academics' publications being more accessible and read more widely.

Sinead English

Current address: Department of Zoology, University of Cambridge, CB2 3EJ

Email: sineadenglish@xxx.net   *Website:* sineadenglish.xxxx.com

EDUCATION

2006–2010	**Clare College, University of Cambridge**
	PhD in Zoology (Behavioural Ecology)
	Thesis: *Individual variation in co-operative behaviour in meerkats*
2004–2005	**New College, University of Oxford**
	MSc in Biology – Distinction
2001–2004	**Clare College, University of Cambridge**
	BA (Hons) Natural Sciences – First Class

EMPLOYMENT

2015–present	**Royal Society Dorothy Hodgkin Fellow**
	Department of Zoology, University of Cambridge
	Conflict in the womb: The evolutionary consequences of viviparity
2014–2015	**Visiting Research Fellow at the Department of Zoology, University of Cambridge**
	Research Associate at the Department of Zoology, University of Oxford
	Freelance consultant on WHO/TDR project (part-time 60% from May 2015)
	Maternal investment and climate change in wild tsetse flies
2012–2015	**European Union FP7 Postdoctoral Research Associate**
	Edward Grey Institute, Department of Zoology, University of Oxford
	(Parental leave: October 2013 – April 2014; part-time 80% from October 2014)
	Developmental determinants of ageing and lifespan

→

2009–2012	**NERC Postdoctoral Research Associate & Clare College Research Associate**
	Large Animal Research Group, Department of Zoology, University of Cambridge
	Adaptive suppression of growth in co-operative meerkats

GRANTS & AWARDS

Oct 2015	Royal Society Dorothy Hodgkin Fellowship, £460k inc £56k research expenses
July 2015	Elizabeth Hannah Jenkinson Fund, £2 110
April 2015	ASAB Research Grant, £5 790
Dec 2014	University of Oxford Returning Carers Fund & Lockey Award, £1 960
April 2009	ASAB Honourable mention for talk at Easter ASAB conference, Cardiff
2006–09	NERC Studentship for PhD at University of Cambridge
2004–05	BBSRC Studentship for MSc in Biology, University of Oxford
June 2004	Royal Society Summer Studentship, University of Cambridge

INVITED WORKSHOP PRESENTATIONS

Sep 2015	International workshop: Early life developmental effects: unifying evolutionary and biomedical perspectives. Falmouth, UK
Jul 2015	Capacity Building Workshop for the TDR/IDRC Initiative on Climate Change and Health. Geneva, Switzerland
Mar 2015	Pre-conference Symposium: Evolutionary developmental biology: Current debates. European Human Behaviour and Evolution Association 2015. Helsinki, Finland

INVITED INSTITUTIONAL SEMINARS

May 2016	Institute of Evolutionary Biology and Environmental Studies, University of Zurich
Apr 2016	Department of Evolution, Ecology and Behaviour, University of Liverpool
Mar 2016	Department of Psychology, University of Exeter
Mar 2015	Centre for Ecology and Conservation, University of Exeter
Feb 2015	Department of Zoology, University of Cambridge
Mar 2012	Clare College, University of Cambridge
June 2011	Institute for Evolutionary Biology, University of Edinburgh
May 2011	Madingley Sub-department of Animal Behaviour, University of Cambridge
May 2011	Department of Behavioural Ecology, University of Bern

CONFERENCE PRESENTATIONS

Aug 2013	European Society for Evolutionary Biology, Lisbon, Portugal
Aug 2013	International Ethology Congress, Newcastle, UK
Jan 2013	Edward Grey Institute annual conference, Oxford, UK

→

Nov 2012	London Evolutionary Research Network annual meeting, London, UK
Sept 2012	Plasticity and non-genetic inheritance workshop, University of Oxford
Apr 2011	Social Decision Making: Bridging Economics and Evolutionary Biology, Ascona, CH
Mar 2010	Clare College Research Symposium, Cambridge, UK
April 2009	Easter ASAB Meeting, Cardiff, UK
Aug 2008	12th International Behavioral Ecology Congress, Ithaca, USA

TEACHING

Research	Supervised 11 final-year Cambridge University undergraduate projects (2008–2012): analysing long-term meerkat data (seven students) and a dataset of wild tsetse flies (four students)
Tutorials	Supervised 46 students for 15 colleges at Cambridge University (2008–2012) in second- and third-year Natural Sciences (Zoology) courses (Behavioural Ecology, Ecological Genetics and Population Dynamics); and 15 students for six colleges at Oxford University (2012–2013) in Evolutionary Ecology of Animals course
Statistics	Demonstrator for statistics practicals (final-year undergraduate and postgraduate students), organised statistics practicals for Part II Zoology field course (Cambridge)
Outreach	Presented lecture to the Cambridge Natural History Society; co-organised workshop for Young Zoologists Club at the University Museum of Zoology (Cambridge); wrote popular science article for online magazine *The Conversation*

OTHER PROFESSIONAL RESPONSIBILITIES

Peer review	Reviews editor for *Frontiers in Ecology and Evolution*
	Reviewed grants for French National Research Agency (ANR)
	Reviewed journal articles for *Animal Behaviour, Behaviour, Behavioral Ecology, Ethology, Behavioural Processes, Biology Letters, Ecology, Ecology Letters, Frontiers in Ecology and Evolution, Functional Ecology, Journal of Evolutionary Biology, Journal of Zoology, Philosophical Transactions of the Royal Society B, PLoS Computational Biology, Proceedings of the Royal Society B.*
Workshops	Co-organising symposium: 'From parents to peers: The consequences of information use for evolution, development and social behaviour' (ISBE Conference, Exeter, August 2016) and 'Origin and role of epigenetic information transmission in evolution' at Mathematical Models in Ecology and Evolution (Paris, July 2015). Organised an international workshop for 40 participants on modelling plasticity and non-genetic inheritance (Oxford, September 2012). Co-organised annual meeting ('Co-operation in mongooses') at (Cambridge, 2009–2011)
Societies	British Ecological Society, Association for the Study of Animal Behaviour

→

SELECTED PUBLICATIONS

Total output: 27 peer-reviewed publications; total citations: 372; h-index: 11

1. Huchard, E., S. English, M.B.V. Bell, N. Thavarajah, T.H. Clutton-Brock. 2016. Competitive growth in a cooperative mammal. *Nature* 533, 532–534.

2. English, S., H. Cowen, E. Garnett, J.W. Hargrove. Maternal effects on offspring size in a natural population of the viviparous tsetse fly. *Ecological Entomology*, in press.

3. English, S., T.W. Fawcett, A.D. Higginson, P.C. Trimmer, T. Uller. Adaptive use of information during growth can explain long-term effects of early-life experiences. *American Naturalist.* 2016. 187, 620–632.

4. English, S., L.E. Browning, N.J. Raihani. Developmental plasticity and social specialization in cooperative societies. *Animal Behaviour.* 2016. 106, 37–42.

5. English, S., I. Pen, N. Shea, T. Uller. Non-genetic inheritance in plants and animals. *PLoS One.* 2015. 10(1): e0116996.

6. Uller, T., S. Nakagawa, S. English. Weak evidence for anticipatory parental effects in plants and animals. *Journal of Evolutionary Biology.* 2013. 26(10), 2161–2170.

7. English, S., A.W. Bateman and T.H. Clutton-Brock. Lifetime growth in wild meerkats: Incorporating life history and environmental factors into a standard growth model. *Oecologia.* 2012. 169(1): 143–153.

8. English, S., S. Nakagawa and T.H. Clutton-Brock. Consistent individual differences in co-operative behaviour in meerkats (*Suricata suricatta*). *Journal of Evolutionary Biology.* 2010. 23(8): 1597–1604.

4.2 Letters or emails of application or covering letters

A letter of application accompanying your CV may be the most important letter you will ever write, as it is often the deciding factor in whether or not you are granted an interview for a job. While the CV will convey your details to your prospective employer, the personal emphasis, style and tone of the covering letter will persuade him or her to grant you an interview. This is your opportunity to state that what you bring is unique to you and to describe the benefit your employer would derive by hiring you and not another candidate.

It is preferable to use the person's name, if you have it – it can be well worth doing some research to find out the relevant name. It is increasingly common to include the first and surname in the salutation (eg Dear Evelyn Fiyo). This is convenient when the gender of the person being addressed is not recognisable from the name. If the title is known (eg Mr, Ms, Dr, Prof), then only the surname is required (eg Dear Rev Fiyo).

Do not send supporting documents (eg transcriptions of academic results and reference letters) until they are requested – only mention that they are available on request. Should you be mailing hard copy, send certified copies of the originals, not the originals.

Structure of a covering letter

The covering letter should contain:

- your email address
- your telephone and/or mobile phone number
- date (the day on which you plan to post it)
- addressee's title, initials and name
- addressee's designation
- name of the department
- name of the organisation
- organisation's full postal address, with postal code.

The followings sections discuss information which could be included in the body of the letter.

First paragraph

This paragraph gives the reason for contact (a bursary application, job application, request for information, etc). Make this as powerful an opening as possible:

- State the position, job, bursary or programme you are applying for and how you heard about it. If you are responding to an advertisement, give details.
- Give details of how you were referred to the organisation, for example name a personal contact.
- Refer the reader to documents enclosed in support of your application (CV, application form, certificates, etc).

Body paragraphs

These motivate your application or requests and highlight what recommends you:

- Explain how your skills, qualifications and experience would benefit the organisation or programme.
- Describe the benefit to the employer, company or bursar of employing you (and not another candidate).
- Describe the benefit to your future and career development to be derived from the bursary, vacation job or whatever the case may be.
- If you are answering an advertisement, identify the attributes and work experience the advertiser is looking for and give examples of how you meet each requirement.

Final paragraph

Write a positive conclusion and then a statement that encourages the reader to act:

- Indicate, if relevant, that you would like a personal interview and that you are available at the reader's convenience.
- Finish with a positive statement that encourages the reader to act on your letter.

Complimentary close

Start the complimentary close with 'Yours sincerely' if the letter is addressed to a person by name, or 'Yours faithfully' if the person's name is not mentioned in the salutation (for example 'Dear Sir/Madam'). Then add your signature, and type or print your name underneath the signature, whatever is appropriate.

The following is an example of an application letter to an engineering recruitment agency, requesting the agency to find a job for the writer.

e9

xx xxxx Street
Rondebosch 7700
Work: (021) xxx xx88
Home: (021) 689xxxxx
Email: xxxjborman@xxx.net
Date: 19 May 20--

Mr Jerry Dlamini
Manager
Dlamini Employment Enterprises
PO Box 22
Bellville 7532

Dear Mr Dlamini

APPLICATION FOR A JOB SEARCH —————————— *An effective subject line*

I wish to request your recruitment firm to accomplish an effective search for a position in environmental engineering. I heard about your company through the managing director of Mitteka Industries, Mr David Silovitek, who suggested I contact you. My objective is to join an engineering services firm specialising in remedial investigations and feasibility studies.

The opening paragraph gives the reason for contact and an overview of the letter.

Academic background and experience

My background, stemming from vacation work and research for my thesis, includes:
- experience in formation evaluations
- stratigraphic profiling
- borehole geophysical surveys ——————————
- groundwater analysis
- data acquisition and processing.

Bullet lists give the reader a short overview

My environmental knowledge and experience include:
- storage, transportation and surveying of radioactive sources
- handling, storage and transportation of explosives and explosive materials
- familiarity with RCRA, CERCLA, SARS, TSCA, NRC, ATF, DOT and similar regulations and regulating agencies

→

- scientific analysis of borehole geophysical data and the application of interpretation to describe hydrogeologic conditions
- market development activities, including client studies and market assessments
- preparation and presentation to senior management.

Please review my background in the attached curriculum vitae. I would appreciate an interview with you. I can be reached at (021) xxx xx88 during working hours. Alternatively, I will contact you in two weeks' time.

Yours sincerely

J Borman

Joseph Borman

Attachment: Curriculum vitae

> *The last paragraph refers the reader to supporting documents. The concise closing paragraph indicates future action to be taken.*

This is an example of a letter responding to an advertisement:

e9

Yusif Hassiem Jaffer
xxx xxxx Drive
Crawford 7764
9 February 20--

Mr John Eldon
Manager, Human Resources: HDI
19 South Road
Mowbray 7700

Dear Mr Eldon

Position of Trainer/Facilitator: Human Development Institute

Please accept this letter and curriculum vitae. I am sending them in response to your newspaper advertisement in the Argus of 8/2/20-- for the position of trainer/facilitator with HDI.

> *Good analysis of recipient's needs*

> *This is an unconventional method of organising information. The effect is immediate and dynamic.*

You require:	I offer:
• excellent interactive training skills	a well-used, excellent combination of counselling, education and business skills emphasising experiential participation
• highly developed group facilitation skills	over 15 years in counselling, training and teaching very effectively using diverse, potent facilitation or processing skills

→

- a dynamic, expressive personality   an energetic, personable, articulate, good-humoured, balanced professional character

- four to eight years' experience in corporate training and facilitation   three years' experience in training and facilitation at universities, and three years' private practice

- BA, master's preferred   two master's degrees: Counselling and Education Administration (including MBA courses: organisational behaviour, management)

I believe that I am well qualified for the trainer/facilitator position, and would like to offer your company my skills. I will call you next week to see if you will be available to meet me to discuss my application.

Yours sincerely

Y Jaffer

Yusif Jaffer

Attachment

Here is an example of an application for an academic position:

e9

Sinead English	**Email:** xx23x@xxx.ac.uk
Large Animal Research Group	Tel: 01223 336xx
Department of Zoology	

12 September 20--

Dear Dr Wei-Yu

I am writing in support of my application for the position of Postdoctoral Researcher in Evolutionary Biology (Vacancy ID xxx), as advertised on the Evoldir mailing list. I believe that my relevant research experience on related topics in meerkats, combined with an aptitude for applying statistical models and an enthusiasm to learn new theoretical approaches, makes me a highly eligible candidate for this position.

I have extensive experience working on evolutionary theory and questions pertaining to the development of life-history strategies within species. In my current position as a postdoctoral research associate at the University of Cambridge, I have been afforded the flexibility to target my research toward my own primary interests, which involve exploring the link between early environment, developmental trajectories and life-history decisions. As a species where individuals either follow a strategy of remaining a subordinate or becoming a dominant breeder, with marked differences in lifespan and reproductive success, meerkats are an ideal system to explore such questions. These interests were formulated during my doctoral work on the same study system, in which I investigated the extent to which individual variation in helping is plastic or consistent over time.

During my academic career thus far, I have acquired skills in mathematical modelling, particularly in the application of statistical models to vast, long-term data sets. I have recently developed a predictive model of growth in meerkats, incorporating life history and environmental parameters into a standard growth model. This model implemented novel techniques not previously used in growth research [....] an analytical model looking at the link between group size and reproductive skew, and an empirical test of this model on the *Polistes* wasp system.

Having described my collaboration network, I hope I have demonstrated my teamwork and collaboration skills. Other aspects of my current job description give further insight into this: for the past two years, I have co-organised the annual 'Co-operation in birds and mammals' meeting in Cambridge, attended by about 40 researchers. Good time management has been essential to my job, which requires balancing research, teaching and project management, with regular interactions with the team at the field in South Africa. I have presented my research at several international conferences and invited seminars.

In summary, I have a strong empirical background coupled with mathematical aptitude, and would bring my skills and sincere enthusiasm for the topics to be investigated to this position. I hope you consider my application in this light. Regardless of the outcome of my application, I shall certainly follow the work of this project with great interest, as I strongly feel that developmental plasticity is one of the most exciting topics in evolutionary biology today.

Yours sincerely

S English

Sinead English

Presentation and formatting

Before submitting your covering letter, CV and supporting documents (if you choose to or are required to submit supporting documents), proofread them carefully and ensure that your formatting is consistent.

It is preferable to email or submit your documents in PDF format so that the information cannot be changed and to ensure that the template appears on other screens and prints in a way that is true to your design. To convert a Microsoft® Word™ document to a PDF file, use the *Save As* command and, in the *Save As* dialog box, choose the file format for PFD in the *Save as type* dropdown box.

4.3 Interviews for job or funding applications

With a comprehensive CV and covering letter, you hope to be granted an interview. For a commercial position, employers look at interpersonal skills which cannot be conveyed in documents. So, they will seek analytical skills in logical answers, problem-solving skills in carefully considered solutions, and overall communication skills in the articulacy and clarity of your response. From the questions you pose, they will hear whether you have intent to lead and be involved, and whether you have a strong interest in their industry and business.

In your responses, you must take the opportunity to showcase the experience you refer to in your CV. For example, you may have headed a sports team. It is a one-line mention in the CV, but in the interview, you can describe an incident which happened while you were in this role and which shows the leadership or teamwork skills you used. If you were involved in a critical project, prepare additional relevant material to quote, such as statistics of the project, with money spent or saved. If you cannot give the facts, do not fabricate them; rather say that you do not have them at hand but can send them on later.

The interview will involve some closed questions which are easy to answer, as they require little more than a 'yes' or 'no' (for example: 'Would you be prepared to work in Alaska?'). Be prepared, however, for the interviewer to ask open questions, such as these:

- Tell me about yourself.
- What are the highlights in your CV?
- What are your strengths and weaknesses?
- Give an example of a situation that tested your leadership ability/tolerance/ analytical skills.
- Tell me about a time you had to do something in the line of your work that you didn't enjoy.

You may also be asked leading or multiple questions. These are harder to answer. The leading question is there to trip you up – to force you into a corner. Take time before you answer so that you give the answer you want to give. You may buy time in an interview by first commenting on the question (eg 'Thank you for raising that. It was a difficult time in my job, but the experience proved useful'). Then bring your answer to focus on the areas you want to project.

If the interviewer asks a few questions in one, rephrase and unpack the questions one by one before replying; this also buys you time for considering your responses.

The underlying common factor in all these aspects of job search is sincerity. If you have prepared each item so that it truly reflects you and your skills, this will come across. A reader or listener can quickly discern when someone is not genuine. Thus, do not cover up areas you are asked about: be truthful and give full descriptions.

In order to be successful at an interview, you need to go through three stages: your preparation, the interview and your follow-up.

Before the interview

To prepare, research the organisation, person (if applicable) and subject matter. By asking questions that show evidence of this research, you will indicate your interest. Ensure you are wearing appropriate clothing and that you have worked out the travel time to the location so that you will be neither late nor too early. Do not wear something which is new and to which you are unaccustomed, since you may not feel comfortable in the outfit. An uncomfortable outfit may also leave you feeling unsettled and awkward during your interview. For example, women should not wear very high heels unless they are accustomed to walking in them, as their body language could come across as uncertain should they be unsteady in their shoes.

Have a practice session, or a mock interview, with a family member or a friend and have that person ask you difficult questions. Start the mock interview from the moment you enter the room. Film this and observe how you come across.

During the interview

Body language and appearance are reputed to account for one-third of the impact one makes in an interview. While you convey facts through the content of your answers, your character and your attitude come across via your tone of voice and the level of confidence conveyed in your body language. It is conveying the appropriate attitude that will earn you credibility in the eyes of the interviewer. Make direct eye contact and have a firm handshake.

Take time to answer fully – a short silence will show you to be a thinking person who values both the question and the interviewer. In answering a question, you may use the topic to include other positive points or concrete experience. For example, if asked about an experience in which you led a team, you may also include in the description how you managed conflict in the team and settled a difficult issue harmoniously.

Check yourself for mannerisms or gestures which reveal nervousness or insecurity. For example, do not gaze out of the window, fiddle with your 'phone (have it switched off – and if you have forgotten, turn it off should it ring), play with jewellery or touch your hair. Sit in a relaxed but composed way while waiting for the next question and use the time to check on interesting, additional contributions you can make. Appear confident but not overly relaxed: do not lean back in the chair or cross your legs, and do not use slang or inappropriate vocabulary. If asked about your former peers, colleagues or employers, never say anything negative.

The STAR approach is an approach to conducting an interview in which you will be asked questions based on your competencies, as opposed to your past activities. This helps you explain in a fluent way something that may be quite vague. The STAR acronym stands for the following:

- **Situation:** Briefly describe the situation you were in, in terms of the qualities the employer is seeking – such as problem solving or leadership – and give concrete examples.
- **Task:** Explain the role you were in and the responsibilities you carried in relation to the performance of the team.

- **Action:** Outline what you did as an individual and how you did it. Include your reasons, if useful.
- **Results:** Wrap up the incident by accounting for the outcomes of your actions. Describe if your actions meant that the expectations of the project were met; be truthful about where outcomes were not achieved.

Closing the interview and folllow-up

Thank the interviewer and make it clear that, whatever the outcome, you have appreciated the opportunity to learn more about the position. If necessary, make notes of anything you may have to follow through with – this will give you an opportunity to ask for a business card. Leave the interview room with the same self-assured manner with which you entered it. Within the next two days, write a thank-you email. If you do not hear at all from the organisation or person (and you were not told that there would be no response), it is appropriate for you to call to ask about the status of your application.

✓

Checklist for a well-organised and persuasive CV, letter of application and interview

Before submitting your CV and letter of application and/or attending a job selection interview, confirm that you have paid attention to the items in this checklist:
- Use a current and readable format for the CV and letters of application.
- Use an appropriately formal tone and style that convey sincerity.
- Make sure your skills, knowledge and experience are relevant to the position reflected in the document.
- Proofread the written documents. Remember that a small typographical error could cause your application to be discarded without consideration.
- Create PDF versions of the documents for submission.
- Advise your referees.
- Do research into the company and the logistics of attending an interview.
- Select clothing appropriate for the interview.
- Rehearse or have a practice run for the interview.

Managing teams, negotiating, working ethically

5

The aim of this chapter is to outline the interpersonal and spoken communication tools you need as a manager in order for you to participate in or lead effective meetings, be they face to face or virtual. As a manager you will need to manage groups and teams. Part of this involves knowing how to build a team, the stages a team goes through in its functioning and the roles its members play. This chapter will help you analyse the type of leader you are or need to be. It considers the impact different styles of leadership have on the team and the task – the latter often being one of problem solving.

Your leadership style defines how you negotiate to win. In negotiation, there are three main approaches: joint problem solving, pure bargaining or a combination of these. The timing of presenting information is critical in a negotiation – whether it is done before, during or after the negotiation process.

As a manager, you are responsible not only for your own decisions and actions; you also act on behalf of your company. Thus, you need to ensure that you appreciate and act within the ethical codes of your profession and of your society. It is not merely a case of thinking, 'What is best for me or my company, right now or for the next ten years?' It also means thinking, 'What is best for my community, my country and my planet, right now and for the next two hundred years?' Our present actions define our future lives, and while it is comfortable and easy to live for today and the profits of today, our consciences should guide us as to what is best for ourselves, the greater community and the greater world – not just today, but after tomorrow as well.

This chapter describes teams and team building, leadership and negotiation, and the role of ethics in the professional and corporate workplace, including the guides offered by professions and by government decrees. By the end of this chapter, you will know how to:

- build effective teams
- recognise the qualities of a good member of a team
- understand process and task roles in a team
- recognise styles of leadership
- solve problems
- negotiate and persuade

- use the stages in a negotiation
- incorporate ethics in the workplace.

5.1 Building effective teams

Groups and teams are not the same item. A group is a collection of people defined by a similar characteristic – such as a class of learners or a gathering of holidaymakers on a tour – but with no interdependency nor any need to work together. A group becomes a team when the members acquire a shared purpose; that is, when they have the aim of achieving a certain outcome and need each other to achieve it, such as a class working together to raise funds for their graduation ball or a tour group climbing Mount Kilimanjaro with the intention that every member manages it.

Characteristics and life cycles of teams

An effective team is one which has a shared purpose and a definable membership. This commitment to shared goals and membership means it is conscious of itself as a defined team or group. The individual members of a successful team will be:

- involved with other team members
- willing to interact in a unified way
- interdependent in the satisfaction of their needs
- willing to abide by the group's decisions.

However, having strong commitment to the team overall does not mean the individuals are repressed. Successful team members have high morale and also:

- contribute to the group without commands or pressure
- discuss questions with lots of give and take
- use disagreements to clear the air
- keep their sense of humour.

With these attributes, a well-functioning team is able to move the required task forward in an organised way. The team's functioning will also be influenced by what stage of its life cycle it is going through. A team is likely to go through a number of phases in its development, as shown in Table 5.1.

Table 5.1 Phases of development of a team and its members (adapted from Truckman, 1965, in Tubbs and Moss, 2008)

Phase	Description
Phase 1: Form	Members break the ice and begin to establish a common basis for functioning. The initial tension is called 'primary tension'.
Phase 2: Storm	Conflicts occur in the group as individuals assert their dominance.

→

Phase	Description
Phase 3: Norm	Members of the team resolve their conflicts for the good of the common task. They share information and work to achieve the team's purpose.
Phase 4: Perform	The team members achieve consensus and maximum productivity.
Phase 5: Mourn	The task has been completed and the team no longer has a purpose. Members feel regret at the disbanding of the group.

Source: Adapted from Truckman 1965 – in Tubbs and Moss 2008

Process and task roles in groups

Individuals in a team usually develop different roles in that team according to their personalities, their knowledge and skills, and their commitment to the task. Most team members will attend to both the ways in which they perform their task (task roles) and to the ways in which they work together (process roles). Some members will be more inclined to play one role over the other; however, balance between roles is important. While task roles are needed to solve problems and achieve the task, process roles are essential in maintaining relationships and interpersonal functions between the members, as indicated in Table 5.2.

Table 5.2 Roles played by individual members of a team

Task roles	Process roles
initiating new ideas or approaches	hearing people out
seeking information	drawing in quiet members of the group
giving information and opinions	acknowledging members' viewpoints
clarifying to help others understand	encouraging members of the group
elaborating	mediating conflict
co-ordinating information	gate-keeping, ensuring everyone is heard
defining the progress of discussion	setting standards that are agreed on
testing if the group is ready for discussion	following the general viewpoint
summarising past discussion	relieving tension

Source: Adapted from Tubbs

As can be seen from the items in Table 5.2, activities which support the task, such as elaborating on a point and helping others to understand, require the support of process roles, such as hearing people out and encouraging members of the group. The team that inhibits its members may find it can never achieve a task if the key to it lies with the withdrawn member. Equally, task and process roles are better enabled if all members of a team adhere to core good behaviours, such as being punctual and not eating or using mobile 'phones during workshops or meetings.

5.2 Styles of leadership

A factor which makes an impact on the team and its character, purpose and life cycle, is its leadership. The inter-relationship between the leader and members of the group, or the leader member exchange (LMX), underlies the development of the roles each person plays in the team. Likewise, the nature of the team may influence the leadership style which it develops or accepts. Leadership falls into three main types: autocratic, laissez-faire and democratic.

Autocratic leadership

An autocratic leader dominates the team and pays little attention to the needs and suggestions of the team members in making decisions. The leader may tend to railroad; that is, push his or her own ideas over those of others. If the team elects such a leader, it is usually because of the person's charismatic and driven personality. In cases where the appointment is by another party and has nothing to do with the team, the autocratic leader may be quiet and reserved.

If this type of leader has been given authority from a higher level, he or she may not be interested in the process or the people, but only in achieving the outcome stipulated by his or her superiors. In this situation discussion and, therefore, cohesiveness are limited, as the leader shows a lack of interest in colleagues. The working group can make suggestions, but these will be of little or no importance to the autocratic leader. The members of the team may become dispirited, which will affect the climate in the group. Its cohesiveness and participation may become minimal. This would create a chain reaction, in that the lack of cohesiveness would result in a lack of ideas, which would lessen the chances of the best solution being selected.

There are times, such as a crisis, when autocratic leadership has its place. In case of a fire, for example, most people would rather be led decisively and without discussion to the nearest exit. On the other hand, in instances where group involvement is needed to ensure buy-in for the decision, autocratic leadership is ineffectual, as the group is unable to contribute. In these cases, democratic leadership would be the preferred option.

Laissez-faire leadership

Laissez-faire means 'to let go' and describes a nominal and ineffectual leadership, where the members of the group are allowed to do as they wish and their decisions and actions are not necessarily channelled in accordance with the objectives. As the leader has little interest or makes no impact, there may be cohesiveness in the group, but there will be a lack of discipline. Thus, the process will likely suffer from protracted discussions, poor evaluation of decisions and the non-completion of tasks. These factors will negatively affect cohesiveness and outcomes.

Democratic leadership

Democratic leaders are the most productive, as they involve the team extensively and thus draw the most contributions from it. The democratic leader also shows enthusiasm for the task and tries to involve all the members in the execution of the task. This type of leader listens to the team members' suggestions and takes their opinions into account, which bodes well for a cohesive, supportive and contributory climate in the group. Productivity is good and, although time may be lost in the process (for example in long discussions), these teams usually achieve their purpose and complete the task.

In order for a climate of support to be created, all team members must feel that their contributions are of value and that they are not at risk of personal criticism. In working on a task, the leader should manage the team and encourage active participation through listening and shared contribution until a satisfactory decision is made. In the case where some members of the team still do not agree with the decision, these members should also be encouraged to present their views and be acknowledged.

The following are some of the qualities that define a democratic leader:

Own behaviour

- Does not dominate discussion; shares responsibility
- Is open-minded, not defensive of own ideas
- Listens attentively and empathically
- Encourages a friendly, co-operative and democratic atmosphere
- Shows respect to others
- Shows appreciation and is responsive
- Is natural, honest and sincere

Attitude to team

- Does not control or manipulate
- Allows as much interaction as possible
- Can allow different points of view even if they offend some members
- Allows members freedom to suggest 'wild' ideas
- Promotes mutual approach; avoids competitiveness
- Avoids dogmatic attitudes; is flexible
- Does not take sides
- Maintains appropriate distance from team

5.3 Techniques for solving problems

A common purpose of a team is to solve problems – either an existing problem or one that is predicted to occur. Thus the team members' energies may be directed towards analysing current evidence or projecting possibilities. For both activities, the real problem, not the perceived one, needs to be defined and any criteria to be applied must be set.

One plan or agenda that offers a universal problem-solving technique is a six-stage plan that was first developed by John Dewey (Tubbs & Moss, 2008) and as shown in Table 5.3. The different skills and roles required of the team members are also evident in this plan. As individuals differ in their talents, it is obvious that a team using this method will cover more of these activities than an individual. This translates into the synergy that teamwork produces.

Table 5.3 Dewey's six stages for problem solving

No	Stage	Activity
1.	**Define the problem.** The apparent problem may not be the real one. Drill down to the real problem and its scope.	Analytical
2.	**State your objectives** to solve the problem. You may need to define the criteria which will govern the solution.	Analytical
3.	**Formulate alternative strategies** for achieving these objectives through one or more approaches: research, experimentation and brainstorming.	Creative
4.	**Evaluate each strategy** in terms of your objectives.	Evaluative
5.	**Select the strategy** that best meets your objectives or that solves the problem and meets the criteria, if any exist.	Evaluative
6.	**Evaluate the success** of the problem-solving exercise and/or consider the success of the solution once implemented.	Evaluative

Source: Adapted from Tubbs & Moss 2008

An effective exercise for taking the personalities out of a conflict situation in order to resolve problems is De Bono's Six Thinking Hats. It can be found online at http://www.debonogroup.com/six_thinking_hats.php.

5.4 Negotiation and persuasion

The common denominator between persuasion and negotiation is influence. Persuasion is communication designed to influence others by modifying their beliefs, values or attitudes. Negotiation is communication with the intent to influence others to modify their decisions and actions.

Negotiation may be used to solve a problem, but it usually goes beyond the fact to the personalities involved. Many people shy away from negotiating because of the confrontational nature of facing conflict. However, with good negotiation skills you can resolve conflicting interests through a process that involves persuasion, perhaps compromise and, on occasion, hard bargaining with joint problem solving. Competition and co-operation are both necessary facets of negotiation, but they need to be kept in balance. To regard all disputes as possible to solve without negotiation is naïve, while concentrating on the competitive aspect of negotiation may also lead to no cohesive close.

Approaches to negotiation

The negotiation process includes a number of distinct sub-processes, the most common being joint problem solving and pure bargaining. These two processes are antithetical and lead to actions which can interfere with one another. Trade-offs are inevitable. Those involved have to decide which sacrifices are necessary to reach their goals. For example, a threat to walk out may strengthen the pure bargaining position and improve the negotiator's internal political situation, but such action will inhibit joint problem solving and create unfavourable attitudes among the other parties.

A core requirement for maintaining the appropriate climate for all successful negotiation is that interests and facts be under focus, not positions and personalities. Thus, the people involved must be separated from the problem.

Joint problem solving

Joint problem solving refers to common interests and is a co-operative activity. It is based on trust and open communication, which allow you to define and solve your mutual problems. However, while joint problem solving can be a win-win situation, it may have to be a variable-sum game. If you can solve joint problems, both sides gain. For example, if labour and management can find a better way to handle grievances, both sides gain. Price negotiations offer few opportunities for joint problem solving, but most negotiations include issues on which the parties' interests are at least partially parallel.

Follow these steps prior to joint problem solving:
- Identify issues with clearly co-operative elements.
- Check for agreement on the definition of issues.
- If possible, take co-operative issues out of the central negotiations.
- Work first on the primarily co-operative issues.
- Honestly communicate your goal.
- Encourage the other party to do the same.

Do the following during joint problem-solving negotiations:
- Clarify and honestly communicate the similarities and differences between both parties' goals.
- Honestly discuss differences in priorities.
- Listen respectfully.
- Make sure your openness is reciprocated.
- Propose many alternatives.
- Select the alternative that is the best combination of objective quality and acceptability to both parties.
- Go slowly on mixed issues.

Pure bargaining

Pure bargaining is a win-lose or zero-sum game. Each gain for one side is balanced by an equal loss for the other. Price negotiations are almost entirely pure bargaining, because losses for one party equal gains for another. For example, if you are to receive R10 000 more, your opponent has to receive R10 000 less. Since your interests directly conflict, pure bargaining is always competitive and based on power. You cannot convince most people to lose for your gain, but you may be able to force them to do so.

Pure bargaining versus joint problem solving

Joint problem solving and pure bargaining are the two most important sub-processes in negotiations. They set the tone for the entire negotiation. Some negotiations consist entirely of pure bargaining, and in others, some issues should be approached as joint problems. In certain negotiations, the two sub-processes are mixed together. One of the most difficult tasks for a negotiator is to decide when to bargain competitively and when to co-operate on mutual problems.

Pure bargaining is based on power. Joint problem solving is based on trust, and without that trust neither party will communicate honestly, nor will they take action which might give away an advantage. Thus, pure bargaining requires manipulative communication while joint problem solving requires open communication. Unfortunately, even when both parties want to co-operate to solve joint problems, pure bargaining usually dominates the negotiations. Power is more tangible and less fragile than trust. Power creates a feeling of security, while trust always involves some risks. The other party may take advantage of the weakness you create when you try to problem-solve.

Since pure bargaining and joint problem solving require essentially incompatible tactics, you must be able to select the right approach. Sometimes you need only one approach for an entire negotiation. However, in many negotiations you need to use pure bargaining tactics on some issues, and joint problem-solving tactics on others. Of course, it is not an either/or matter. You rarely move all the way to either extreme. On some issues, emphasise problem solving; on others bargain as hard as you can, but only if you are in the more powerful position.

Stages in negotiation

Negotiation meetings have the same requirements as all other meetings: for the meeting to be successful, you need to:
- plan carefully before the meeting
- use good interpersonal skills to manage the process during the meeting
- engage in effective post-meeting summary and analysis.

Before the negotiations

Set your priorities. In multiple-issue negotiations, decide which issues are most important to you. Then decide how much you will trade off on minor issues to achieve the outcome you want on the major issues. Plan your and your team's strategy and establish whether all members are clear about the role they are to play.

Decide upon the arguments you will use to convince the other party of the logic of your argument. Plan the approach to presenting these arguments so that you can explore or take positive action on issues with joint problem solving without greatly weakening a pure bargaining position.

During the negotiations

Continuously revise your estimates of the other party. Follow your planned negotiation strategy unless the other party behaves contrary to your expectations. If this happens, analyse the change in behaviour and make new plans. The purpose of this analysis and planning is to get away from relying exclusively on intuition.

In interacting with the other party, it is more productive to offer as many alternatives to agreement as you can, so that the best option can be reached. Communicate clearly and clarify differences and agreements, but guard against exposing all your tactics. Good communication practice is important, such as:

- listening respectfully
- talking to and not at people
- being responsive to non-verbal cues.

From time to time, stop and analyse what has happened. A useful strategy is to call a break for the team to caucus. This gives the team the opportunity to regroup, to discuss in private the stage the negotiation has reached and to plan the strategy from this point onwards. The leader can summarise the progress to date and propose forward action. The team members can share information, test their understanding and ask questions to confirm their knowledge. If there is conflict and emotions have been triggered in the discussion, it gives the participants time to calm down and to better manage the situation.

After the negotiations

The outcome of the negotiations will determine the process following the negotiation. Consult the minutes or notes taken during the discussion and analyse what occurred. Consider if there was agreement and resolution of all disagreements and what future action was decided on. Have a post mortem of your own team's role. Consider whether your team followed the plan, presented logical arguments supported by fact and operated as a cohesive whole.

If the process followed an unexpected direction, consider the probable causes for the behaviour of the other party. Assess the strengths and weaknesses of your team or organisation. From the conclusions you draw, decide how to negotiate with the other party in future.

Roles in the negotiating team

There are a number of roles in a negotiating team which different members may play. One person can fulfil more than one role. Some roles conflict with each other. For example, you cannot be both tough and friendly, and it is difficult to analyse either behavioural or objective data when, as spokesperson for the group, you must reply quickly to the other party's comments.

The important roles in negotiating teams are the chief negotiator, spokesperson and social observer or analyst of information:

- The **chief negotiator** holds the team together, assigns activities and has the ultimate authority on all issues. The chief negotiator is not necessarily the spokesperson.
- The **spokesperson** does most of the talking, but may have relatively little authority. The choice of spokesperson should be based on the situation. For example, if joint problem-solving tactics seem appropriate, the spokesperson should be a friendly, rational problem solver. If most issues require pure bargaining and there appears to be a small bargaining range, a forceful spokesperson would be the better choice. If the issues require technical expertise, the team needs the credibility of a technically knowledgeable spokesperson.
- **Social observers** are acute to verbal and non-verbal cues. They often have quiet and sensitive personalities.

Other roles are those played in all meetings by different members of the group, from those who are more task-orientated to those who are more maintenance-orientated. Both types of roles have value, but both need to be kept in check.

5.5 Ethics at work

This section is concerned with professional ethics, as required of those in the workplace. Professional or corporate ethics are those defined by one's profession or the company one works for, and with which all involved must be compliant. Ethics is a set of guiding principles or values that supersede the formal rules and structures governing professional activity. These guiding principles are aimed at ensuring best practice within a profession. Best practice includes the best interests and safety of the profession and the public that the professional serves.

Ethics: From the person to society

Human beings are fundamentally impelled to do what is best for themselves, when given the choice. It may be assumed that all people have an implicit knowledge of the difference between right and wrong, and good and evil. However, what is good or best for one person is often not best for others. Society, which is made up of separate individuals all contending for their own space and to satisfy their own needs, tends to degenerate rapidly towards a state of anarchy, no matter the context or the circumstance, when its central authority has been removed. This is the state of nature. Literature has attempted over the millennia to study and depict the discord that arises when human beings find themselves in the same location, fighting over the same land, food, water, air and potential partners. The solution that we have adopted over the millennia has been to institute laws and regulations, imposed by a higher authority, with the fear of punishment used as an enforcing tool.

Every community, or civil society, has developed its own sets of rules to avoid anarchy and discord. They govern themselves through various codes or sets of rules, including:

- **law**: enforced through punishment, such as fines, jail or the death sentence
- **religion**: enforced through excommunication or the fear of hell
- **morality**: enforced through fear of social shame or alienation.

A civil society thus depends on its laws and its powers of authority in order to ensure peace, stability and harmony, which are necessary for the survival of all, not just of the fittest.

But rules and laws only reach so far — not every situation can be foreseen or regulated. In the workplace, for instance, regulations governing the treatment of workers and trading partners have been slow to develop since the Industrial Revolution and the onset of capitalism. However, these regulations have gradually increased in strength over the past century and decades, to arrive at the current far-reaching legislation governing safety in the workplace, equity and fair or unfair dismissal, to name but a few.

Law and ethics are separate concepts, but have the same or similar endpoints or aims: justice and fairness. Where laws have not been developed or promulgated, ethics tries to operate. It is not just the workplace that has shown a growing need for ethical conduct and regulation, but also all those affected by the actions and activities of businesses. Capitalism has long been perceived as grasping and ruthless in its drive to make profits — and this drive has long given rise to detrimental consequences for those affected directly or indirectly by its activities. The conscientious efforts of movements (such as Greenpeace, to name just one) working for healthier environments, and against the destruction caused by industries polluting rivers, land and the air, have led to greater legislation governing these actions. This is an example of ethics leading to the establishment of law. International bodies now govern the activities of businesses, and while they may not always be able to punish these firms through the law, they can restrict trade with those that defy laid-down conventions and standards. Where societies would once excommunicate individuals who transgressed laws or norms, the business world now excludes companies that defy their regulations or norms, by barring trade with them.

It is clear that without codes of ethics and set procedures for enforcing them, it is difficult to regulate enterprises and the individuals that populate them. We can see ethics and regulations as pertaining to three levels within the sphere of work:

1. At the **individual level**, ethics are applied to day-to-day decisions on one's own behaviour.

2. At the **professional level**, professionals put power and materials to work for the benefit of humankind, providing ways to improve people's quality of life. Professionals often enjoy high social status, respect and titles, high remuneration, self-regulation and the freedom to choose clients. Professionals therefore have a great responsibility towards society, as they hold its well-being in their hands. And so, the relationship between professionals and society is one of trust. But as trust is not always enough, and self-regulation is not always sufficient, external regulations are required: codes of conduct that determine how professionals should behave within their particular contexts.

3. At the **corporate level**, ethics are applied to corporate governance; balanced and integrated economic, social and environmental performance (referred to as triple bottom-line reporting); workers' rights; the right to strike; the ethical status of comparable worth in the marketplace; and what constitutes bribery and whistleblowing, among other things. Recent decades have seen the ethical behaviour of companies come under the spotlight after numerous international disasters caused by unethical practices, particularly in the production of chemicals or the movement of oil. Through corporate governance, countries have sought to contain the behaviour of companies engaged in activities with risk. The good governance of a company is evident in the way it manages its relations towards its shareholders, the public, the environment and its employees, ensuring that these relations are always ethical and for the greater good (De George, 2015).

Theoretical views of ethics

An ethical person has a set of values by which they live and which are shared by the group they function in. An ethical person also lives by a set of values which is universally accepted by society. In essence, ethics is about right and wrong actions, and making decisions for the good of the majority. Ethics therefore refers to the issue of 'how to act'. There are various schools of thought regarding ethics, and differing views of what is ethical:

- **Utilitarian** theories promote the greatest amount of good for the greatest number.

- **Negative utilitarianism** (NU) promotes the least amount of evil or harm, or preventing the greatest amount of suffering for the greatest number. Proponents of NU argue that this is a more effective ethical formula, since, they contend, the greatest harms are more consequential than the greatest goods.
- **Deontological ethics** or **deontology** (Greek: δέον [*deon*], meaning 'obligation' or 'duty') is an approach that focuses on the rightness or wrongness of actions themselves, as opposed to the rightness or wrongness of the consequences of those actions.
- The **ethics of care** is a normative ethical theory that emphasises the importance of relationships.

There are many schools of thought besides these, and with all these differing and opposing theories and ideas, decisions on ethical behaviour can potentially be difficult to make.

Ethics at work

There are varying levels of ethics in the professional sphere, namely (De George, 2015):

- **governance:** regulation, corporate governance committees, auditing, etc
- **global business ethics:** cross-cultural issues that arise in countries such as China and India
- **ethical culture:** loyalty, honesty, strategic planning, human resources, etc
- **leadership:** executive compensation, the tone at the top, the role of the CEO in ethics, etc
- **corporate social responsibility:** sustainability, stakeholder theory, the triple bottom line, etc
- **workplace issues:** labour and employment practices, monitoring, work–life balance, etc
- **product and brand:** consumer safety, reputation, intellectual property and strategic marketing
- **corporate wrongdoing:** corruption, bribery, scandals, whistleblowing, etc.

Ethical theories have developed as people attempt to develop a satisfactory theory by which to regulate action at work. Ethics at work govern professional dealings – the relationship between the enterprise or the individual and/or the community or the public. Governments and professions often use codes of conduct or ethical principles to guide them, such as the Constitution of the Republic of South Africa, (1996) and the code of conduct of the Engineering Council of South Africa (ECSA) for the engineering profession. ECSA, for example, legislates and enforces the standards of practice and the code of conduct for engineers registered as members.

It covers nine spheres of engineering: electrical, mechanical, metallurgical, civil, aeronautical, agricultural, chemical, industrial and mining. Other professions have similar codes by which their members are bound.

While the above codes may not be sufficient to ensure justice and fairness in all situations, a lack of codes of ethics or codes of conduct has led to serious miscarriages of justice and corrupt practices in the past. Ethics therefore moves between the individual level and the corporate level.

The important point is that ethics is **not an after-thought** in a profession – it is integral to it, as Figure 5.1 shows. For example, in the Emerging Technologies and Ethical Issues in Engineering workshop in Washington, DC, it was said that 'ethics is not peripheral to, or an add-on to, engineering. It is integral to the practice of engineering, part of engineering problem solving. Safety and guarding against avoidable harm are built into engineering; they are the principles that underlie engineering codes and standards' (Weil, 2003).

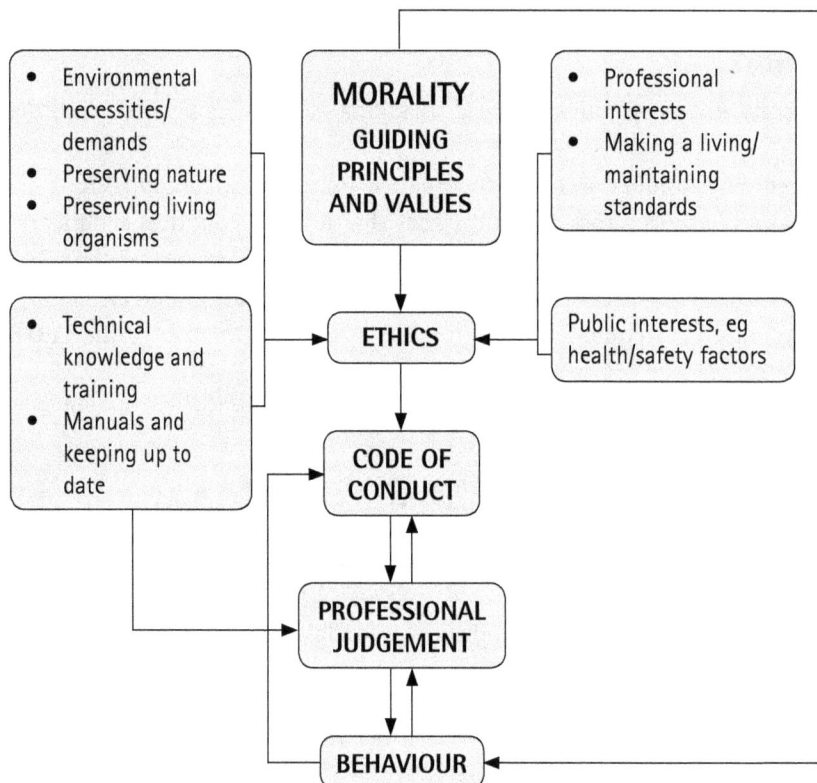

Figure 5.1 A flow chart showing integration of ethics in professions

Corporate governance in South Africa

In 1994, the King Report on Corporate Governance (King I) was published by the King Committee on Corporate Governance, headed by former High Court judge Mervyn King. The first of its kind in South Africa, it incorporated a Code of Corporate Practices and Conduct. It was aimed at promoting the highest standards of corporate governance in South Africa. With time, the code has been developed to meet the current needs: King II (2002), King III (2009) and King IV (2017) have gone beyond the focus on companies to those they deal with and those who govern them to include the greater fiscal and social environment.

Ethics therefore apply to many levels. It moves between the public and the private domain, the corporate and the community, as well as the employee and the company. It has origins in law, religion and morality but is specific to groups and communities. It is concerned with rights and duties: predominantly, the rights of the public, and the duties of the enterprise towards the public it serves, and which supports it.

In the South African context, corporate ethical practice has various nuances, namely:
* **legal factors:** the Constitution, the Bill of Rights
* **corporate social responsibility:** since the King III Report
* **cultural factors:** African social values, eg ubuntu
* **historical factors:** the need to redress the inequities of the past through the development of human capital.

This brief summary in Figure 5.2 of the regulatory and legislative framework affecting South African companies charts how legislation attempts to ensure a fair and just environment for business to operate in. Nevertheless, however good the legislative framework, issues of professional and corporate ethics will continue to challenge us.

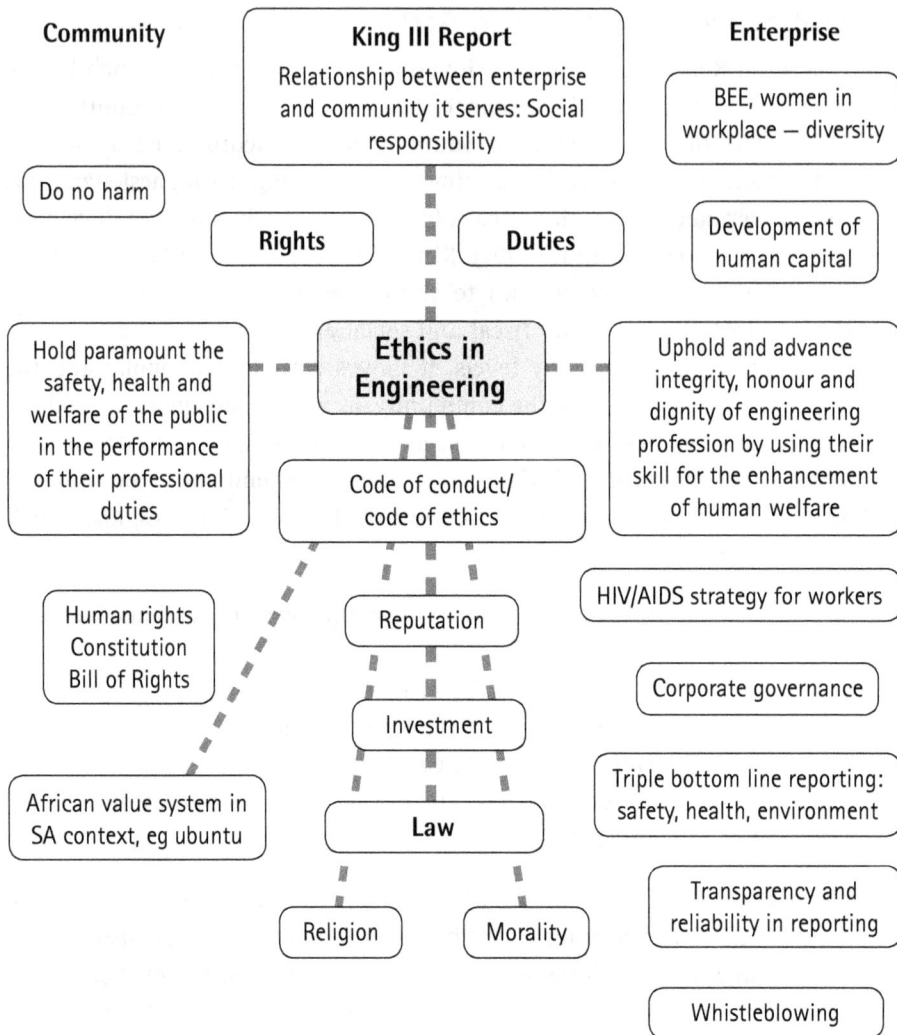

Figure 5.2 Flow chart describing ethics in the engineering profession

Conflicts of interest

Competing interests make an impact on decisions. These competing claims give rise to a conflict of interest, where the requirement to act ethically is challenged by competing priorities and conflicting choices. For example, a professional's undertaking to conduct a safety inspection on site at a particular time may conflict with his or her personal obligation as a parent to care for a sick child.

Conflicts of interest can be identified in various spheres, namely:

- professional or corporate
- personal, family or gender-related
- religious or cultural
- environmental
- financial.

Within a professional environment, it is generally accepted that professional interests take precedence over other interests. There are, however, situations where the conflict may appear irreconcilable.

Furthermore, an action that is **legally** permissible is not necessarily **morally** or **ethically** permissible. Suppose an engineer discovers that the company he or she works for is emitting a substance into the atmosphere which is not regulated by the Environmental Protection Agency (EPA). Suppose further that the engineer reads scientific literature that indicates that the substance causes respiratory and potentially more serious health problems. Should the engineer reveal this information to the EPA? An ethical code is likely to answer this dilemma by insisting that the professional has an obligation to ensure that people are not harmed. Not reporting it may be unethical. Whatever your views on this matter, the fact that emitting the substance is legally permissible does not necessarily mean it is morally permissible to do so. This does not settle the question as to what the engineer should do; however, most ethical codes require that the professional's actions comply with accepted moral standards.

✓

Checklist for effective managers

As a committed manager, you will be seen to be credible if you are able to manage and develop teams, solve problems and negotiate towards a satisfactory outcome. An effective manager will:
- develop the skills of team members
- develop their own leadership skills
- guide a team through problem solving
- manage the negotiation process through its different stages
- work according to an ethical code which is informed by the law, morality, culture and professional knowledge
- assess what is right and wrong in professional behaviour.

6 Meetings, agendas and minutes

Meetings are a critical part of doing business. While meetings may have varied formats and purposes, the essential principles and etiquette remain the same. At the end of this chapter you will be familiar with the processes and practices that surround well-planned, well-run and well-recorded meetings.

Whether you are leading, participating in or servicing a meeting (taking minutes), you need good written and spoken communication skills in various areas, namely:
- the justification for meetings
- negotiating the various stages of meetings
- initiating meetings, with clear agendas
- processing meetings efficiently according to their agendas
- ensuring efficient outcomes based on comprehensive minutes and tables of action.

In this chapter, you will learn about:
- the value and purpose of holding meetings
- the different stages of meetings and the preparation required for each stage
- the purpose, organisation and style of successful agendas
- the purpose, organisation and style of professional and efficient minutes, including the benefits of preparing a table of action.

6.1 Reasons to hold meetings and take minutes

Meetings are primarily required to make decisions, such as decisions required to move business or projects forward or decisions required by official bodies and committees in fulfilment of their mandates. Minutes record the discussion and the decisions made at a meeting and provide a convenient review for those who attended as well as for those who did not. Minutes also give continuity to a process, as the minutes of the previous meeting are referred to and approved, and a plan for a subsequent meeting or any particular action required is considered.

As soon as an organisation, body or grouping has to account for its finances and how it operates, it is likely to have a committee or a meeting group defined by its set of rules, sometimes referred to as its constitution or terms of reference, to ensure business is carried out and recorded properly and with transparency.

A constitution should clearly describe the purpose and operation of a committee – essentially how it is to function, which includes its membership, the chair, all decision-making and communication lines, its terms of office, its quorum (a minimum number of members who must be present to conduct business or make legitimate decisions) and the general conduct in meetings, among other things. Standing or permanent committees tend to be governed by a constitution, whereas limited-term groups that have a specific task, particularly one to be completed within a finite timeframe such as working parties or project teams, tend to be governed by terms of reference, which include some but not all of the elements required in a formal constitution. For example, a terms of reference may well not prescribe a quorum or meeting frequency, as these will be determined by the group.

Different professions and businesses record minutes or take notes at meetings in their own way. However, there is a common core to minutes. In certain cases, minutes are the legally binding official records of a meeting and carry weight. If they are to be only notes, it is important to call them an *aide memoire*, or notes.

6.2 Different stages of meetings

While there is a well-understood process for getting through the business of a meeting, it is usually up to the chair or the person running the meeting to outline the conduct of the meeting; for example who may speak and when, as well as how decisions will be made. Standard meeting procedure is ultimately based on parliamentary procedure – a set of rules for conduct at meetings that allows everyone to be heard and to make decisions. Any divergence from standard meeting protocol needs to be made clear before starting the meeting.

Many organisations, clubs and other groups use or refer to *Robert's Rules of Order* (newly revised) (available at http://www.robertsrules.org) as their guideline for conducting meetings and making decisions as a group to ensure everyone understands how business will be done. Many use these guidelines, essentially based on parliamentary procedure, as the basis for their constitutions or terms of reference. Indeed, some define specific rules for the committees in question and defer to *Roberts's Rules* for all other procedural issues.

Excepting board meetings or annual general meetings, which need to adhere to the relevant governance requirements and where minutes are legally binding, many business and project meetings are less formal in their procedures. However, to be efficient, all meetings need to follow a process to ensure they are productive, purposeful and done within the allocated time. Efficient meetings are distinguished by good preparation, efficient execution and comprehensive recording and follow-up: before, during and after. The two key roles in the process are the chair and the minute taker, or secretary to the meeting. While the same person may on occasion fulfil both roles, it is generally advisable to separate the roles to allow them to be an effective double act, especially during the meeting itself.

Figure 6.1 outlines the core features of the three phases. While emphasis is often placed on the minutes and the difficulties associated with recording the discussion and outcomes accurately, this stress can be considerably alleviated by shifting the emphasis more heavily towards the preparation phase, in particular the drawing up of the agenda.

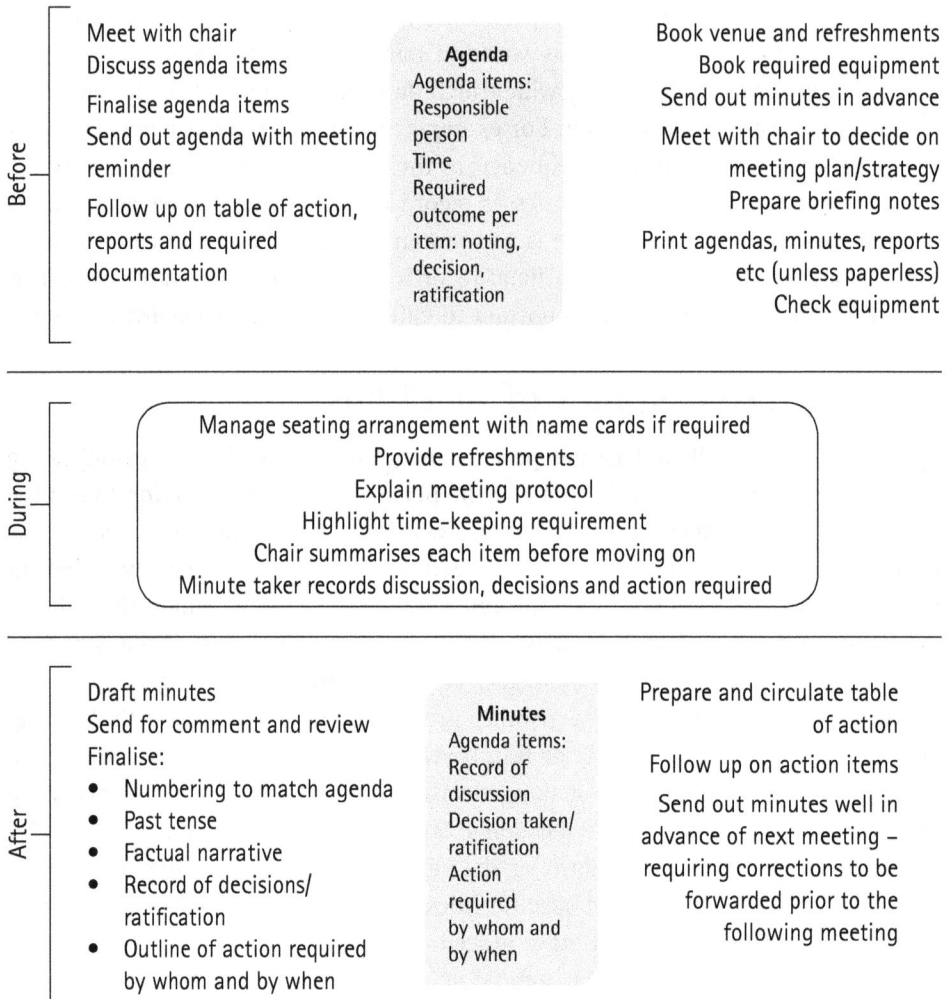

Before

Meet with chair
Discuss agenda items
Finalise agenda items
Send out agenda with meeting reminder
Follow up on table of action, reports and required documentation

Agenda
Agenda items:
Responsible person
Time
Required outcome per item: noting, decision, ratification

Book venue and refreshments
Book required equipment
Send out minutes in advance
Meet with chair to decide on meeting plan/strategy
Prepare briefing notes
Print agendas, minutes, reports etc (unless paperless)
Check equipment

During

Manage seating arrangement with name cards if required
Provide refreshments
Explain meeting protocol
Highlight time-keeping requirement
Chair summarises each item before moving on
Minute taker records discussion, decisions and action required

After

Draft minutes
Send for comment and review
Finalise:
- Numbering to match agenda
- Past tense
- Factual narrative
- Record of decisions/ratification
- Outline of action required by whom and by when

Minutes
Agenda items:
Record of discussion
Decision taken/ratification
Action required by whom and by when

Prepare and circulate table of action
Follow up on action items
Send out minutes well in advance of next meeting – requiring corrections to be forwarded prior to the following meeting

Figure 6.1 Activities involved in the three phases of meetings

Before the meeting

The planning in advance of the meeting can be divided into three categories, namely:
1. confirming the agenda and supporting documents
2. housekeeping
3. administration.

Confirming the agenda

The chair or person convening the meeting may set up the agenda without outside input, but more usually the chair will consult with those who are to attend the meeting, either at the previous meeting or through a call for items to be included. Many departmental or official committees will have standing items that appear on each agenda, with everything else being classified as new business.

If agenda items are called for, the process must be managed carefully and as strictly as possible, with non-negotiable deadlines for matters to be included. Items should not be raised unexpectedly on the day or brought up under umbrella terms such as 'Any Other Business' (AOB) or 'General' – these tend to be placed at the end of the agenda and operate as black holes in relation to time taken up. From time to time, urgent matters may well arise within too short a time to be officially included on the agenda; these can be managed under the heading 'Matters of Urgency'. This should, however, be used as sparingly as possible, because it is impossible to plan a meeting properly if there is no clarity about the extent of the business needing to be covered. Poor agenda discipline can lead to meetings running grossly over time, which is frustrating for everyone attending – in these cases people frequently resort to checking emails and so on, thereby not giving their full attention to the business under discussion. Furthermore, as many meetings have a fixed time limit - determined, for example, by room availability or subsequent appointments – items towards the end of the agenda tend to end up being rolled over to the next meeting time and again.

Once the agenda outline has been agreed upon, it needs to be turned into a working agenda for maximum efficiency before it is circulated. (For more on working agendas, see the discussion on pages 165–170.)

Housekeeping

Part of the planning for a meeting includes setting or confirming the date and time. In the case of regular meetings, the date is often scheduled at the previous meeting or even at the beginning of a year or business cycle. It is, however, usually necessary to confirm the meeting time in advance, which can often be done in conjunction with sending out the agenda or the minutes of the previous meeting.

Other housekeeping issues include checking and arranging the venue and seating, setting up minute taking and ensuring that the appropriate equipment (for example a recorder, laptop or data projector) is in place and working. Data projectors or equivalent can be useful for projecting agendas or minutes during meetings to enable live updates or to create a paperless environment for the meeting.

If the meeting is a virtual meeting or involves some members attending via video- or teleconference, Skype or other group platform, all communication media need to be verified well in advance and sufficient time must be allowed for everybody to log into the meeting.

Administration

As meetings usually take place to enable decision making, all documentation relating to meetings should be filed and stored in a set location and eventually archived. In non-digital environments, agendas, minutes and associated documentation are often printed and pasted into a meeting book or placed in a physical file. In a digital environment, documentation storage needs to be carefully managed. It is all too easy for a minute taker to simply store the documents on a local hard drive. There are several potential issues here: the hard drive could be damaged or even lost, and the files themselves could be misplaced or spread across several locations, particularly with a change of minute taker – at worst, confidential material could fall into the wrong hands.

A meeting protocol should be set up that outlines how and where committee or meeting documentation is stored in order to create an accessible and transparent audit trail, particularly if the minutes contain legally binding decisions. Such a protocol should include guidelines such as the ones listed in Table 6.1.

Table 6.1 Guidelines on documentation for meeting protocol

Aspect	Guideline
File naming conventions	The convention must identify the type of document, the meeting or committee it relates to and the date, for example HRComAgenda_210716, HRComMinutes_210716 or HRComTOA_210716.
File storage location	A designated folder should ideally be set up in a location accessible to any relevant individuals, either on a network drive or via a cloud storage facility.
Access control	Minutes often contain sensitive or confidential information and therefore access needs to be carefully controlled by: • limiting access to the folder itself, for example via SharePoint or an equivalent role-based access platform • using password-protected documents.
Back-up and archiving procedures	Even if the documents are stored in the cloud, if the organisation's documents are not regularly backed up as a matter of course, they should be manually backed up, preferably to an off-site facility or location, or via hard copy print-outs. Some documentation needs to be kept for specified amounts of time according to whether it is governance-related or has legal, financial or other specific status. After this period of time, it is still advisable to make sure the records are archived properly.

The minutes of the previous meeting need to be sent out in advance of the meeting. As with the agenda, this process needs to be managed strictly so as not to waste time during the meeting. When the minutes are sent out, they need to be accompanied by a deadline for queries or corrections so that these can be resolved prior to the meeting. This job is usually handled by the person taking the minutes or whomever is responsible for the administration of the meeting. Further to sending out the minutes electronically, they sometimes need to be printed prior to the meeting.

In addition to the document protocols, preparation for a meeting involves ensuring that any reports or annexures are attached to the agenda and are circulated in advance of the meeting to allow people to prepare properly. If documents are only introduced at the meeting, valuable time is taken up by people reading and processing the documents. This job is usually done by the person taking the minutes or servicing the committee or meeting as the secretary. If the meeting has revolving minute takers, the administration role will need to be allocated to a designated person to ensure continuity and follow-up.

Furthermore, if you are taking the minutes, it is extremely helpful to have been able to review documentation in advance, as it helps you predict and understand the potential discussion and outcomes of the meeting. It can also be useful to contact the person responsible for a report or other document due to be reviewed at the meeting to ascertain the key points to be put forward. You can then use this information to begin to prepopulate the minutes, which will make the taking down of what is put forward at the actual meeting less onerous and stressful.

If a table of action (see pages 180–181)) has been circulated following the previous meeting, it is important to follow up in advance of the meeting to check on progress in relation to the action items. This can also help you prepopulate the minutes, as you will be more aware of what is likely to be reported in advance on the various agenda items.

Paperless meetings

More and more meetings are becoming – or aiming to become – paperless. If this is the case, it needs to be clear that everyone attending is responsible for bringing a device on which the agenda, minutes and associated meeting documentation can be read and noted on, or that they are responsible for printing and bringing their own hard copies. Many meetings still require the previous set of minutes to be printed for each member, but will allow reports and so on to be viewed electronically in advance, especially if they are long, with perhaps only a summary available at the meeting. (Note that if a summary needs to be prepared, this must be organised in advance.) At the very least, a hard copy of the previous meeting's minutes should be printed for the chair to sign and date, to formalise (or legalise) the record of that meeting.

The only downside of paperless meetings is the temptation for people to be distracted by emails or messages during the meeting.

During the meeting

In creating an agenda, the chair formalises the procedure for the meeting as well as providing the framework for the minutes. (The role and management of the agenda and minutes are discussed later in this chapter, from page 157 onwards). The following sections discuss the processes that need to be engaged in during the meeting itself.

Opening the meeting

The following steps should be followed at the beginning of the meeting:

1. The chair opens the meeting, which involves outlining the reason for the meeting and defining any limitations (such as time and protocols) that need to be set.

2. If the meeting is to be recorded by the official minute taker, this is usually mentioned. In some cases – for example bid evaluation and adjudication committees in formal tender procedures – it is a legal requirement that a meeting be recorded as well as minutes be taken. Should anyone else wish to record the meeting, for example at a board meeting, that person would usually need to get permission from the board.

3. If there are guests who are not part of the meeting membership, they must be welcomed and introduced. Absentee apologies are acknowledged and in certain cases proxies are acknowledged and recognised. In some cases, people who are absent but who have not sent apologies also need to be noted, to ensure that a quorum is present should any official decisions or votes need to be taken. (Every committee should have a set of rules outlining its purpose and function, its required membership and any special rules, including what constitutes a quorum. Should decisions be made without a quorum present, any such decisions would not be legally binding and could thus be challenged.)

4. In many cases, an attendance register will need to be signed to confirm those present, particularly for official or board meetings to legitimise any decisions taken – a record of who attends board meetings usually appears in a company's annual report.

5. Before the meeting gets going, it is useful for the chair to confirm the agenda. If any matters of urgency arise, the chair can then decide whether it is appropriate to deal with them at the current meeting or whether they need to be deferred to a later or specially convened meeting. Most meetings have tight programmes, and new items cannot always be accommodated given the urgency of other agenda items.

6. Once the agenda has been confirmed, the minutes of the previous meeting are approved. This should be a formality, as any queries or corrections relating to the minutes should already have been forwarded and dealt with when the minutes were sent out for comment. Once these preliminary matters have been dealt with, the meeting gets underway with the business of the day.

Controlling the process during the meeting

Having initiated the meeting, the chair must ensure that those involved make suggestions and/or comments and do not sit silently. This requires that the chair create a positive climate where everyone feels sufficiently confident to contribute. A chair who creates a positive climate will convey enthusiasm without dominating the discussion, and will facilitate discussion and the exchange of ideas without critical evaluation of whoever is presenting the ideas. As dominating the discussion and early critical evaluation may inhibit quieter members of the group from presenting their ideas, it is essential for the chair to control discussion.

The most important controlling function of the chair is to ensure that the agenda is followed. While free speech may be encouraged, if a member dominates and labours a point, the chair must move the discussion on to avoid time being wasted and the agenda not being covered.

A two-tier technique that can be used to assist with timekeeping involves allocating time slots to each item on the agenda. Not only does time allocation make the person presenting the report or point for discussion aware of how much time is available, it also allows the minute taker to monitor the time and bring it to the chair's attention. The chair can then bring the discussion to a close and enable the meeting to move on. Should an item not be completed, the chair must decide whether to allocate additional time or to reschedule the discussion for a later meeting or forum.

Summarising and evaluating during the meeting

All meetings – even informal ones – should have a secretary or a member responsible for taking notes or minutes. All decisions need to be noted and kept on record as part of the audit trail. The formality of the notes or minutes may vary, but the record must be clearly referable and decisions actionable. Should anything be raised at the meeting that should not be minuted, this should be brought to everyone's attention during the meeting. It may be helpful for the minute taker, particularly if he or she is unfamiliar with everyone attending the meeting, to have a plan of the meeting table with the names of people indicated at the places where they are sitting.

The discussion in a meeting rarely takes place in chronological order or even according to a logical flow. To ensure that an accurate record can be taken of a discussion, the chair should therefore pause the meeting at appropriate moments (for example at the end of each agenda item or important decision) to summarise and restate key points. This ensures clarity for all, not least the minute taker. Such a summary helps the group review the matter under discussion and assists the participants to understand the facts and any action expected of them. This in turn promotes co-operation in future meetings.

At the end of the meeting, the chair should confirm the conclusion and – if not already predetermined – confirm a date for the next meeting.

After the meeting

The secretary or minute taker needs to ensure that all relevant and necessary information is included in the minutes, for example:

- the relevant department
- the name of the working group
- the names and details of attendees and of those who sent apologies
- the type of meeting (daily, weekly, monthly or special)
- the purpose of the meeting
- the times the meeting began and ended.

Notes or minutes should be emailed or sent as hard copy to participants within a week of the meeting if possible, although in most cases the chair will review the minutes before they are sent out for comment. It is important that the participants read how the meeting was recorded while they still have good recall of the discussion.

Although the minutes contain a record of the action required, it is useful to pull out a separate table of action to be circulated as soon as possible – even directly via email – to ensure that everyone has a record of what is required, by whom and by when. This is particularly relevant for people who were unable to attend the meeting, as they should be alerted as soon as possible of any action required – perhaps sooner than when the minutes can be sent out. This is important, even if participants take their own notes, as it confirms what was decided in the meeting should there be any confusion as to responsibilities. (See pages 180–181 for more on an action table.)

The accepted minutes of the previous meeting must be signed and filed appropriately as soon as possible so that they are easily locatable. Anything confidential should be marked as access restricted to designated people.

A flow chart of the activities that fall within a meeting is given in Figure 6.2.

Read/check meeting rule and purpose

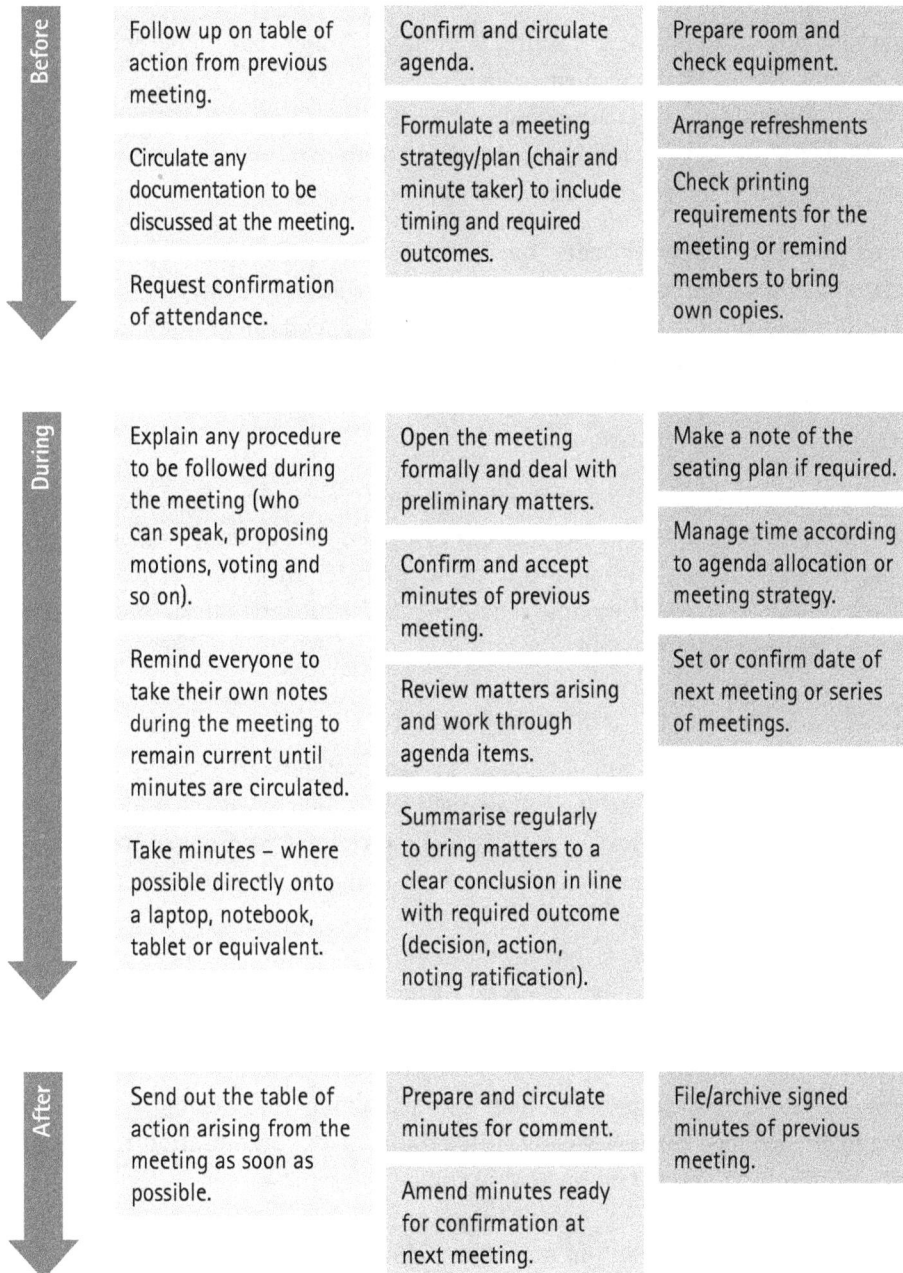

Before			
	Follow up on table of action from previous meeting.	Confirm and circulate agenda.	Prepare room and check equipment.
	Circulate any documentation to be discussed at the meeting.	Formulate a meeting strategy/plan (chair and minute taker) to include timing and required outcomes.	Arrange refreshments
	Request confirmation of attendance.		Check printing requirements for the meeting or remind members to bring own copies.

During			
	Explain any procedure to be followed during the meeting (who can speak, proposing motions, voting and so on).	Open the meeting formally and deal with preliminary matters.	Make a note of the seating plan if required.
	Remind everyone to take their own notes during the meeting to remain current until minutes are circulated.	Confirm and accept minutes of previous meeting.	Manage time according to agenda allocation or meeting strategy.
	Take minutes – where possible directly onto a laptop, notebook, tablet or equivalent.	Review matters arising and work through agenda items.	Set or confirm date of next meeting or series of meetings.
		Summarise regularly to bring matters to a clear conclusion in line with required outcome (decision, action, noting ratification).	

After			
	Send out the table of action arising from the meeting as soon as possible.	Prepare and circulate minutes for comment.	File/archive signed minutes of previous meeting.
		Amend minutes ready for confirmation at next meeting.	

Figure 6.2 Flowchart of meeting activities

6.3 Agendas: Purpose, organisation and style

A good agenda ensures that a meeting is productive and that the attendees' time is positively spent. As mentioned earlier, agendas should be circulated prior to the meeting to inform those attending of the meeting's purpose, the topics under discussion, the attendants' role and whether any preparation is required in order to make a useful and well-informed contribution.

Agendas come in many formats, but the most useful is what is known as a **working agenda**. This contains useful guidance for attendees on:

- the purpose and the required outcome for each agenda item (for example for noting, for decision, for ratification and so on)
- the person responsible for each item
- the proposed time allocations.

The agenda is usually sent via email with a request for confirmation of attendance of the meeting. As a general rule, it needs to be sent out at least two days ahead of the meeting to give participants time to prepare. However, in many cases, committees will have specified time requirements for the circulation of documents built into their terms of reference.

Agendas: what to do and what not to do

The less information given on an agenda, the less well prepared attendees will be, resulting more often than not in less productive outcomes. For the allocated time to be sufficient, the chair must make a realistic prediction and not try to cram an unreasonable number of items onto an agenda or allocate too little time for items requiring thought and discussion.

Agendas should follow a template, designed according to the needs of the company or group. Furthermore, each set of meeting minutes and agenda should be consistent and follow the same format and pattern of numbering. A clear, professional and consistent layout helps participants know where to look for important items. If the organisation or group holding the meeting has a logo, it should be included on the agenda. In addition, if the organisation has a style guide, all meeting documentation should follow the same format in terms of font size, style, layout and so on. Not all fonts are the same size or have the same characteristics, so if there are no guidelines, choose a professional font and stick to it. (See Chapter 1 for information on readability and different fonts, and see Chapter 2 for information on setting up templates and using styles.)

The example below demonstrates a skeleton agenda, with an indication of the potential pitfalls that accompany such an agenda.

e9

Witbooi & Khangala Civils

H&S Division
AGENDA

No end time is provided, making it difficult for attendees to plan their time.

Date: 4 April 20--   **Time:** 14:00   **Location:** Meeting room 4

The names of those attending (together with job roles/titles) should have been included.

The purpose of the meeting has been omitted. The purpose of the meeting should always be included, not just to focus the meeting but also for providing an audit trail of meetings held.

These subheadings identify the projects to be covered, but give little indication of what will be covered or who will be presenting.

The next item does not clarify if the same projects are to be covered as in point 4.

The minutes will include the way forward for each item under discussion, making this agenda line redundant.

1   **Welcome and apologies**
2   **Matters of importance**
3   **Training**
4   **Feedback**
    • Project W&K64008
    • Project W&K39014
    • Project W&K 66203
5   **Quarterly reports from projects**
6   **Other H&S matters**
7   **AOB**
8   **Way forward**
9   **Date of next meeting**
10 **Closure**

'Importance' is a relative term and gives no indication of what will be discussed.

'Training', 'Feedback' and 'Other H&S matters' are generic terms. They are vague and give attendees little idea of what will be covered.

'AOB' or other catch-all headings (eg 'General', 'Miscellaneous') should not be included, as all agenda items should be planned. Allowing members to bring up unplanned items can lead to a lack of discipline during the meeting and a lack of control over the length of the meeting.

This item is not required, as the date of the next meeting signals closure.

Please confirm your attendance

No date is given by when attendance must be confirmed. It also does not specify to whom notification of attendance should be given.

Standard agenda items

There is no such thing as a correct or incorrect agenda. Ultimately, an agenda needs to serve the purpose of the type of meeting it is prepared for. However, certain agenda items are useful, as they contribute to creating a regular and easily recognisable format for the meeting to follow. It is important that all agenda item headings indicate the content to be covered, even in the case of standard items. As shown in the example above, generic or formulaic headings do not help participants prepare adequately for the meeting. Table 6.2 give details of standard items that should be included in an agenda.

Table 6.2 Standard agenda items

Category	Agenda items	Description
Organisational items	Meeting title, time, date and location	• The agenda must clearly specify the type of meeting, which usually also identifies the purpose of that meeting, for example a quarterly board meeting or a weekly project update meeting. • The date and location should be clearly marked on the agenda. • The time of the meeting should include an end time as well as a start time, to indicate to participants how much time they will have to set aside for the meeting.
	List of participants	• The participants should be listed individually, either with or without courtesy titles. An abbreviation of the initials and surname should be given after each name to indicate how that person will be referred to as the responsible person in the agenda or later in the minutes. • The chair of the meeting needs to be identified clearly, as well as the minute taker. If the minute taker or secretary is not also a member of the committee, it is usual to identify him or her as 'In attendance' or as the 'Servicing officer'. • Any guests attending the meeting who are not part of the committee or who do not regularly attend meetings should be identified as 'In attendance' or 'Guest'. • Any proxies attending the meeting should also be indicated as such.

→

Category	Agenda items	Description
	Housekeeping arrangements	• The agenda should clearly indicate by when and to whom confirmation of attendance should be sent. • Information relating to whether refreshments will be provided should be included, especially if the meeting is long or taking place over a lunch period. • It is useful for the agenda to include a note on whether printed agendas, minutes, reports and so on will be provided or whether participants should print their own or bring a device on which they can view required information.
Preliminary matters	**Welcome and apologies**	Members are welcomed, apologies are noted and any guests are introduced and given context.
	Confirmation of agenda	This is optional and can be used as an alternative to 'Matters of Urgency'. If a matter has arisen too late to be included on the agenda, the chair can decide whether it is important enough and whether sufficient time is available to cover it without compromising the rest of the meeting's business.
	Minutes of previous meeting	This item is an important legality and binds members of the meeting, committee or board to what has been recorded.
Matters arising	**Matter arising** **Matter arising ...**	• Matters arising are matters that need to be followed up from the previous meeting, for example any action items or feedback on progress requiring further decisions. • This should not become a catch-up session on all action items from the previous meeting — these should have been followed up on independently. If too much is covered here, it prevents the meeting moving on to matters on the agenda proper. • It is important that the items are separated, each with its own heading, so that matters can be tracked through meetings if necessary. It can be useful, therefore, to include reference to the agenda item being referred to in the item heading.

→

Category	Agenda items	Description
Standing items	**Standing item** **Standing item ...**	• Standing items are matters that come up and need to be discussed or reported on at every meeting. For some meetings, almost all items will effectively be standing items, for example board meetings where various subcommittees or business areas table regular reports. In such cases, there may be only one or two new items of business, which means that standing items do not need to be marked out. • As these are recurrent items, the attendees should be able to deal with them efficiently and quickly. • Again, each item should have its own title. • As with matters arising, care needs to be taken not to take up too much time with standing items if the agenda contains significant new items.
New items	**New item** **New item ...**	• Each item for the agenda needs a separate heading and, if required, clear subheadings to clarify exactly what is to be discussed under that item. • It may happen that there are no new items for a particular meeting, in which case this section can be omitted.
Closing matters	**Items for next meeting**	• In some cases, part of the meeting closure contains a brief discussion about items to be included on the agenda for the following meeting. This does not prevent items being called for at a later date. • This is a useful mechanism, especially if there has not been time to deal with any matter in sufficient depth or if it has been ascertained that further information is required to progress the matter.
	Date and location of next meeting	Even if the date of the next meeting has already been set, it is a good idea to close the meeting by confirming the date and time with members present, as a formality.

Agenda numbering

While numbering on an agenda is not essential, it can be helpful, especially for extensive agendas with various subheadings. The most important issue is that an agenda and its corresponding set of minutes have matching numbering. Occasions arise when a new item is included in the agenda at the meeting itself. If this occurs, when the agenda is confirmed the numbering of the new item must be established either as an additional subsection or an item at the end of the agenda, so as not to disrupt the existing numbering system.

The exact format of the numbering system is unimportant as long as it matches in the agenda and the minutes. It could be a multilevel decimal numbering system, as in the examples that follow. Alternatively, letters and small Roman numerals could be used: (a), (i) and so on. If numbering and bullets are used in combination, each bulleted item must still be a clear subheading. If no numbering is used at all – just headings and potentially bullets – each main heading must be used in the minutes to ensure easy reference. It is not necessary to number the paragraphs in the minutes if the agenda items have clear headings and subheadings.

The following example shows how different variations of a numbering system can be used effectively in an agenda.

e9

AGENDA

PRELIMINARY MATTERS ─────────┐

1 Welcome and apologies

2 Confirmation of agenda

3 Minutes of previous meeting dated xxxx

MATTERS ARISING

In this example, unnumbered organiser headings have been used to separate the different sections of the agenda.

4 Matter arising

4.1 Subheading if required (example)

4.2 Subheading if required (example)

5 Matter arising

6 Matter arising

STANDING ITEMS

7 Standing item

7.1 Subheading if required (example)

7.2 Subheading if required (example)

8 Standing item

NEW ITEMS

9 New item

9.1 Subheading if required (example)

9.2 Subheading if required (example)

The advantage is that the numbering system only has to go to the second level.

10 New item

CLOSING MATTERS

11 Items for next meeting

12 Date & location of next meeting

AGENDA

1 **PRELIMINARY MATTERS** ─────┐

1.1 **Welcome and apologies**

1.2 **Confirmation of agenda**

1.3 **Minutes of previous meeting dated xxxx**

In this example, the organiser headings separating the different agenda sections are numbered.

2 **MATTERS ARISING**

2.1 **Matter arising**

2.1.1 Subheading if required (example)

2.1.2 Subheading if required (example)

Each heading becomes a subheading, so a third level of numbering is required, which can get a bit busy and overcomplicated.

2.2 **Matter arising**

2.3 **Matter arising**

3 **STANDING ITEMS**

3.1 **Standing item**

3.1.1 Subheading if required (example)

3.1.2 Subheading if required (example)

3.2 **Standing item**

4 **NEW ITEMS**

4.1 **New item**

4.1.1 Subheading if required (example)

4.1.2 Subheading if required (example)

4.2 **New item**

5 **CLOSING MATTERS**

5.1 **Items for next meeting**

5.2 **Date and location of next meeting**

Some organisations find it useful to include a number for the meeting together with the agenda item number in order to track how often an item has been rolled over from a previous meeting or to identify when an item was first raised. This is particularly useful for project meetings, as there are likely to be a limited number of meetings over the life of the project. For example, in the numbering system shown below, item 1.3.2 would deal with point 2 of section 3, first raised at meeting no 1.

e9

		DESCRIPTION	ACTION	DEADLINE
9.	**2**	**MATTERS ARISING**		
6.	2.1	**Drawings issued**	BN	
		Revised drawings were issued and the drawing register will be updated accordingly and attached to these minutes.		
3.	2.2	**Environmental management plan**	GG	11 06/08/20--
		No further progress on acceptance.		
		MEASUREMENT	BN	13 12/12/20--
		12 The next measurement date is 25 November 20--. Following this payment certificate, a complete re-measurement of the project will be carried out.		

In meeting no 9, under 2. Matters Arising.

Drawings issued relates back to an item arising from meeting no 6.

Environmental management plan relates back to a matter arising from meeting no 3.

Working agendas

An agenda is essentially a framework for running a meeting and, at its most basic, a list of items to be covered. However, for a meeting where a lot of business has to be discussed, best practice would be to develop a working agenda. A working agenda has two main advantages:

1. It allows meeting attendees to prepare properly.
2. It allows the minute taker to be well prepared for the meeting, which alleviates much of the burden of taking the minutes during the meeting.

Most working agendas involve a brief description of why each agenda item has been included and what outcome will be required; for example whether the item is for noting, for decision, for ratification or for action. These agendas also usually include a column indicating the responsible participant, a column indicating the time allocated for the agenda item and, if required, a column indicating any relevant annexes and reports to be consulted during the meeting.

What follows is an example of a simple, working agenda with just the responsible person and time included. It is clearly a regularly held operational meeting.

e9

HSG Health & Safety Group
Agenda: Monthly meeting

The difference in type gives definition to the page.

Chair: Thomas Phums Mzizi (TPM)

Participants: Jacques Dyer (JD), Jaco du Toit (JDT), Lisa George (LG), Lilly Kelvin (LK), Rashid Ally (RA), Simphiwe Marnus (SM)

Secretary/minute taker: Matafita Khoza (MK)

Details of who is to participate, with abbreviated initials.

Date: 14 August 20--   **Time:** 9h30–11h00   Place: Staff Centre 3

	Item	RP	Time
1.	Welcome and apologies	TPM	2 mins
2.	Minutes of last meeting	TPM	3 mins
3.	Incomplete projects • Workplace inspections • Site-specific training	TPM, LG	15 mins
4.	Past inspections • Factory floors • Recreational block	JDT, MK	15 mins
5.	Employee feedback on training	MK	10 mins
6.	Equipment budget • Current • Projected	LG, RA	15 mins
7.	Planned projects	JD	20 mins
8.	Year-end function	TPM	5 mins
9.	Next meeting: 28 August 20--	TPM	5 mins

This column indicates the person or persons responsible for preparing and presenting the agenda item.

The minutes of the previous meeting need to be approved by the chair and confirmed as such to the committee/meeting.

This indicates the approximate time allocated to the item.

Every section is specific, with no opportunity for random items under generic headings such as 'Other' or 'AOB'.

While visible gridlines may be useful while preparing a document, it is cleaner for the reader if the grid is hidden before it is sent out.

More extensive working agendas may also include extracts of reports to be presented or key information based on which a decision may need to be made. The previous example shows a basic working agenda, while the following example illustrates a more extensive working agenda including specific information required for decision making during the meeting.

e9

JC Hospital Trust Investment Committee

Date: Tuesday, 21 May 20–– **Time:** 14h00 to 16h00   **Location:** Ashanti boardroom

Committee members	In attendance
Ms N Hassen (NH) – Chair	Mr G Bartzen (GB) – Executive
Dr JD Griffin (JG)	Director – Pride Investments
Mr T Kaira (TK)	Dr C Nelson (CN) – Hospital
Mr A Skatulla (AS)	Administrator
Ms B Petersen (BP)	Mr D Steele (DS) – Committee
	Secretary

A clear outline of meeting details and who is due to attend the meeting

The line draws attention to the start of the agenda proper.

	AGENDA	RP	Time	Attachment
1.	Welcome and apologies	NH	14h00	
2.	Confirmation of the minutes of the meeting held on 23 November 20––	NH	14h05	Attachment A
3.	Performance of the Cash Term Deposit Portfolio		14h15	

The highlighting indicates the columns for the responsible person (RP), the time each item will begin, and any relevant attachments per item.

Mr G Bartzen from Pride Investments will present to the meeting on the Cash Term Deposit portfolio over the past quarter, with the key figures included below.

Extract of key figures for the committee's attention. The change in font indicates it as information.

For noting

Income has been distributed to the Term Deposit Portfolio for the first quarter as follows:

Month	Average call rate % (provided by SBSA)	Return on funds invested %	Income distributed %
January 20––	5.00	5.84	5.75
February 20––	5.00	5.84	5.75
March 20––	5.00	5.87	5.75
Average for half year	5.00	5.85	5.75

The committee is reminded that returns achieved are calculated on a rolling six-monthly basis and the distributions are rounded down to the quarter percentile below this figure.

4.	**Distribution of income to hospital funds**	**JG**	**14h45**	**Attachment B**

Based on the performance of the JC Hospital No 2 Portfolio for 20--, the Committee agrees to distribute realised profits of R2.79 million or 3.45% (2015 – 3.93%) and income earned of R1.82 million or 5.3% (2015 – 6.64%) to the individual funds.

For ratification

5.	**Investment strategy for the year ahead**		**15h00**	**Attachment C**

Mr G Bartzen from Pride Investments will present the JC Hospital investment strategy for the year ahead.

Questions will be taken

Decision required

6.	**Meeting dates for 20--**	**NH**	**15h55**

The proposed Tuesday meeting dates are as follows:

23 August 20--; 22 November 20--; 27 February 20--; 22 May 20--

Decision required

Clearly indicated parameters for confirming attendance

Please confirm attendance by no later than 15 May 20--, to Dan Steele at dan.steele@JCHT.org.za

On occasion, if a committee has a terms of reference, it may also be included on the agenda as a reminder of the parameters of the committee's or working group's function.

In order to avoid having to send an email with a number of attachments to be read alongside the agenda (for example related reports, accounts, contracts and so on) it is useful to embed the associated documents within the agenda itself. The document can be any type of Microsoft® Office™ file or another similar document, or a PDF. When the recipients open the agenda, they can double-click on the icons and the related documents will open. See the example that follows.

eg

5. Investment strategy for the year ahead

Mr G Bartzen from Pride Investments will present the JC Hospital investment strategy for the year ahead.

Questions will be taken

Decision required

Do the following to embed a document or file into Microsoft® Word™:

1. In the document, click where you want the file to be inserted.
2. Go to the *Insert* tab on the ribbon.
3. In the *Text* section, click the dropdown arrow next to *Object* and select *Object* to open the *Object* dialog box.
4. Go to the *Create from File* tab and click on *Browse*.
5. Select the required file. The file location will appear in the *Object* dialog box.
6. Check the box *Display as icon*.
7. Click *OK*.

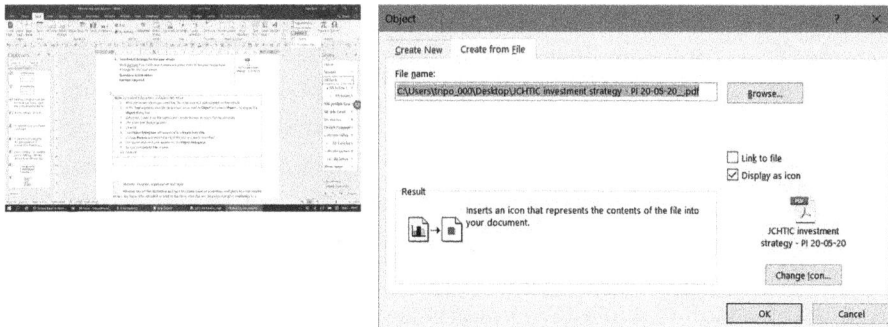

Figure 6.3 Embedding a file as an object in an agenda

6.4 Minutes: purpose, organisation and style

The minutes are a record of the discussions and any decisions made at a meeting, and provide a convenient review for those who attended as well as for those who did not. Minutes also give continuity to a process, since the minutes of the previous meeting are referred to and approved and a plan for a subsequent meeting or any particular action required is considered.

Different professions and businesses record minutes or take notes at meetings in their own way. However, there is a common core to minutes. In certain cases, minutes are the legally binding official records of a meeting and carry weight. As mentioned before, if they are to be only notes, it is important to call them an *aide memoire* or meeting notes.

Minutes: what to do and what not to do

When you take minutes, remember that it is a formal document. You therefore need to adhere to the following guidelines:

- Follow the **agenda**, which should have been circulated before the meeting. The agenda is the agreed plan for the meeting. Even if an item is added into the agenda at the start of the meeting, it cannot disturb the initial numbering system. The numbering of the agenda and minutes must match.
- Use a **template** with columns for the different items, designed according to the needs of the company, group or organisation.
- Note down the **date, time, place, organisation, type of meeting, attendants, apologies** and **chairperson**. Be sure to note whether a **quorum** is present for meetings that will require that level of decision making.
- Include the start and finish **times** as well as the **date** of the next meeting.
- **Summarise** information rather than taking it down verbatim.
- Write down all **decisions** made (also known as 'motions' in more formal meetings) and the names of those who proposed them, if appropriate.
- Record the names of the **proposer** and the **seconder**, where a decision has required them.
- Record any **action** required following the decision and the person who will be responsible for the action.

Below is an example of a set of minutes for a meeting recording the progress on a contract project:

e9

Minutes of Handover of Khami Site 1

Contract No. 22

Regravel of Sisulu Drive

Meeting held on 17 January 20– –, at Johan Kobus Consultants, Johannesburg

These minutes are structured according to the specific professional requirements of the company.

NOTE: These minutes serve as a legal record of decisions and events at the meeting.

SUMMARY OF CONTRACT DETAILS

EMPLOYER	CONSULTING ENGINEER	CONTRACTOR
Department of Transport and Public Works Contracts Engineer: **Sidney Chobe**	Johan Kobus Consultants Engineer: **Samantha Howard**	Lion Construction Contracts Manager: **Felix Pienaar**
Braamfontein Regional Office Private Bag X2 Braamfontein Cell: 083 3928567 Tel: 011 239 0556 Email: schobe@ pgwc.gov.za	Johan Kobus Consultants (Pty) Ltd PO Box 4589 Durban Cell: 071 9900456 Tel: 031 237 7880 Email: samh@ kobuskonsult.co.za	Lion Construction PO Box 7689 Humansdorp, 6300 Cell: 073 3345644 Tel: 041 372 1850 Email: felix. pienaar@lion.co.za
File Ref no: 13/5/1/2/2-833	File Ref no: 14945/ WR/400/...	File Ref no: ...

The template uses even spacing and uniform headings and patterns of information.

The contract details are placed up front, as they inform the entire meeting the minutes are from.

→

Original Tender Amount	R1 568 890
Estimated Final Contract Amount	
Contract Commencement Date	8 August 20--
Contract Period (Months)	14 (including special non-working days)
Original Contract Completion Date	8 October 20--
Extension of Time Awarded (days)	0
Extended Contract Completion Date	0
Current Status (days ahead/behind)	4 days ahead
Current Anticipated Completion Date	8 October 20--
Contract Participation Goals (Target value/ Achieved)	
Civil Subcontractors	R1 917 992.96 / R 0.00
Suppliers & Manufacturers	R1 573 745.60 / R 0.00
Local Labour	R1 917 992.96 / R 0.00

Next site meeting: 30 April 20-- at 9:30 at the Site Office in Khami

Action

The highlighting of the 'Action' column makes for easy differentiation from the minutes proper.

1. WELCOME

The chairperson and acting Engineer on the contract, Ms Samantha Howard, introduced herself and welcomed all present.

2. ATTENDANCE AND APOLOGIES

	Representing	Name	Initial
Present	Employer:	Sidney Chobe	SC
	Consulting Engineer:	Samantha Howard	SH
	Employer:	Felix Pienaar	FP
	H&S Representative:	Len Waqu	LW
Apologies	Consulting Engineer Assistant:	Anita Peters	AP

The use of terms such as 'employer' and 'engineer' make the minutes objective and keep the focus on the task, not the individual.

Action

3.   ACCEPTANCE OF PREVIOUS MINUTES

3.1 Acceptance

The minutes of the previous meeting were approved, with all corrections having been noted and amendments made prior to the meeting. The chairperson duly signed the minutes.

The section headings in capitals and the minor headings printed in bold text make the minutes easily skimmable and readable.

3.2 Distribution

The minutes of all site meetings are distributed electronically in PDF format according to the attached distribution list.

SC/SH/FP

4.   SITE AND ENVIRONMENT

4.1 Access to site

The Engineer said that although Khami Site was accessible, the Site would only be handed to the Contractor on the date of commencement of development.

4.2 Offices and laboratory

Signpost headings highlight the different aspects of the agenda item.

Offices
The Engineer confirmed that she would require an office for the Engineer's Representative (ER) and her assistant (AER), as well as a conference facility large enough to accommodate up to eight personnel for Site Meetings. The Contractor is expected to provide services for the Engineer's Site personnel, as agreed with the ER and as allowed in the Bill of Quantities.

The style is formal: full sentences and appropriate vocabulary, with no slang or unnecessary jargon.

Laboratory
No laboratory building will be required, because the Engineer and the Contractor, should they agree to opt for a combined or shared laboratory, will use an existing site laboratory in Khami.

4.3 Signage relating to Employer and Consultant

The Engineer said three Contract Name Boards (in English, Xhosa and Afrikaans) would be erected at the main entrance to the site by 01 October 20--.

SH/AP
01/10/20--

5.   HEALTH AND SAFETY REPORT

5.1 H&S representative

The Engineer confirmed that Safe Working Practice cc, represented by Len Waqu, had been approved in principle to be appointed as H&S Agent/Representative on behalf of the Employer.

LW

→

	Action
The Engineer said that the H&S Representative's responsibility was to ensure the Contractor complied with the Act and Regulations on behalf of the Employer. She would not interfere with the H&S Representative's actions.	AP

5.2 Traffic safety

N/A at this stage.

Numbering allows for easy reference to different agenda items.

6. FUTURE MEETINGS

The next meeting will be held on **30 April, 20–– at 9h30**, at Khami Site Office.
Subsequent meetings have been provisionally scheduled for the following dates:
30 June; 30 August; 30 October.

Employer: _____   Date: _____
Engineer: _____   Date: _____
Contractor: _____   Date: _____

For meetings where decisions, proposals and so forth have to be recorded – for example board or committee meetings – it is useful for the proposal to be clearly stated in the minutes together with a record of the relevant discussion. Any decision or action required is then clearly outlined at the bottom of each item for easy reference.

The following example shows an agenda item with a clear outline of what will be discussed. This allows all participants to prepare in advance.

3. Management structure and protocols for GHG unit

The committee will discuss the following items for agreement and/or action:
- Documentation sign-off
- Minute taking and recording
- Staff meetings.

The following example shows the corresponding minutes, which include a record of the discussion:

ℰ9

3. Management structure and protocols for GHG unit

BM (Chair) led the committee in a discussion on the necessary protocols required both in terms of authority and practicality in relation to documentation sign-off, minute taking and recording, and staff meetings. The committee agreed to the following, with no questions or objections being raised:

> *Each item under discussion is dealt with separately after a brief summary.*

- If the unit head is unavailable, LD will sign off documentation as unit deputy director.
- Minutes will be taken for all meetings; audio recording will not be mandatory but at the discretion of the minute taker.
- Full staff meetings will take place on the first Tuesday of every month, with a rotating minute taker. MM will draw up a rota before the next meeting for agreement.
- Staff meetings will take place as scheduled even if the chair (BM) is unavailable. LG or someone else will be appointed to chair the relevant meeting.

> *Clear outline of decisions made and any action required (including by whom and by when)*

Decision: All the above points were agreed to.
Action: MM to draw up a rota of minute takers before the next meeting.

The minutes shown in the following example lack structure, essential information and an indication of responsibility. The text is dense and lacks readability. These minutes would not serve the company well, and would not be clear to anyone who had not attended the meeting or who was reading them after a time lag.

ℰ9

Minutes: Meeting 23 JULY 20--, 10am

Welcome

> *Inadequate information: No full names or contact details are given, only initials.*

1.1 HM welcomed all to the preliminary strategy planning meeting for the health and safety initiative.

1.2 Attendance: HM (chair), NR, EAG, MS & LE (H&R committee), SN (minutes)

> *There is no separate summary of actions/decisions, or action column for initials of those responsible for undertaking tasks.*

1.3 Apologies: VY

Response from H&S visit

HM gave an overview of the Health and Safety officer's comments on the building. His comments were discussed and noted. The company needs to be more mindful of H&S and put systems in place.

→

Personnel

Participants were given spreadsheets giving venues and times of H&S lectures. More to come.

Overview of 2 different courses (1 x week; 2 x week)

The timetables of the 'short' and 'long' courses were discussed and noted by all. Note attendees need to come in suitable clothing.

> There is a lack of definition or detail. For example, the difference between a long and a short course is not given.

How to manage H&S course for accreditation

A   Written assignments will not be marked by the trainer, but looked over. The session attendees will mark the assignments during the session. The assignments will then be taken in and the marks recorded.

B   The strategy's submission date for improved H&S is 12 August 20--.

C   A mock emergency situation will be organised, which will be staged while staff are on the course to see how they handle things.

> The passive voice is vague, as it provides no reference as to who will ensure the mock emergency takes place.

MS repeated what he said last year: that he has been concerned for some time about the fact that attendees can pass the course even though in practice at work, the fundamentals are shaky — especially CPR. With a pass mark of 50%, those who scrape through inevitably have significant gaps in their knowledge. (A known problem in training is that many people are not good at transferring knowledge from courses to reality.) He has thus developed a basic skills test that focuses on basics, such as emergency treatment following an accident.

> The comments of one person (MS) are described in detail, but there is no reflection of other discussion at the meeting.

Future meetings

Future staff meetings will start promptly at 9.15.

Admin issues:

- Staff are requested to acknowledge emails if prompted to in the subject line.
- Staff have been issued with boots and hard hats.
- Telephone lists have been emailed for posting on office noticeboards.
- Those requesting a special menu for office fun night must tell Sue.
- The stores section is looking for more office space for equipment.

> The illogical ordering of items under 'Admin issues' make for difficult comprehension (menus for fun night and office space are not part of this meeting's content).

Any other business

There being no other business, the meeting closed at 11h46.

> The date of the next meeting is not given.

The following points indicate further weaknesses with the minutes above:

- No discernible **template** or **ordered layout** has been used:
    ▸ The numbering is inconsistent (decimal numbers, letters and bullets are used at random).
    ▸ Inadequate spaces between sections makes it harder to read, with a lack of white space overall.
    ▸ The Comic Sans typeface is too casual. It is more suited to a social invitation than a formal document.
- The **discourse structure and style** are weak:
    ▸ Clarity is lacking because of poor discourse structure and casual style.
    ▸ Vague expressions are used, such as 'more mindful' and 'more to come'. What is meant by these terms?
- The minutes are **short on detail**: For example, while those who attended may be fully aware of what is meant by 'suitable clothing', it would not be clear to an outsider or someone not present at the original discussion.
- There is no clear indication of **who will do what and by when**.

Action minutes and tables of action

Action minutes

As minutes are required for a wide range of meetings, it is not surprising that minute styles can also vary. Some meetings may only require action minutes, as more of an operational and running record of decisions and of who is doing what than a legal requirement. Below is a template of a table that can be used to draw up action minutes. This can then either inform a full set of minutes or be used as is as a set of minutes.

Company logo

MINUTES OF XXXX COMMITTEE

10 April 20-- Location: xx Time: 14h30–16h00

Minutes of xxx Committee
10 April 20-- Location: xx Time: 14h30

Attendees: [Have complete list written here and drag or cut and paste those sending apologies to adjacent column]

Absent:

Apologies:

In attendance:

Agenda item	Decisions	Action to be taken	Date	RP
1 Agenda item and number (eg Welcome & apologies)				
A record of the discussion/key comments can be entered here, with a framework if necessary added in advance.	•	•		
	•	•		
2				
	•	•		
	•	•		
3				
	•	•		
		•		
4				
	•	•		
	•	•		

Date & time of next meeting:

Location:

If all regular or required members are included on the template, it is easy just to drag across those sending apologies in advance of the meeting, or in the meeting if required.

Some meetings, for example board meetings, officially record those who are absent (ie those who have not sent apologies). It allows an audit to be easily done on which board members are fulfilling their obligations.

The shading allows agenda items to be clearly visible in the table.

The table in this example is designed to be used in the meeting (using a device such as a laptop, notepad or similar) and is most successful if prepopulated as far as possible, as with other minutes drawn from meetings guided by working agendas. If proper preparation is done, very little that happens in a meeting will be a complete surprise. Furthermore, using a structure such as this aids the minute taker to extract and categorise what is being discussed and decided as the meeting progresses, which in turn makes it easier to construct a clear narrative around the discussion.

Input to the table may be done in point form during the meeting, and it should take very little to edit these points into clear, plain and professional minutes that are readily actionable and referable. In addition, the right-hand columns act as a table of action to clearly show what has been decided and who needs to do what and by when. It is critical that everyone is clear about who needs to do what. It is surprisingly easy to make a decision about what needs to be done without assigning a responsible person or deciding on a deadline.

A table of action

Since minutes can take some time to prepare and approve before being distributed for comment, it is helpful to those attending the meeting – and even more so to those who were unable to – if a summary or table of action can be distributed by email as soon as possible after the meeting. It can either be an attachment or pasted directly into the email. The table of action should simply document any decisions made and any actions required, preferably in table form for easy reference. While members attending meetings are usually advised to take their own notes and act accordingly, it is preferable to still send out a table of action to ensure there are no gaps relating to what is required and by whom.

e9

> The 'Comment' column may be used by the minute taker or person tracking the table of action. It allows a dialogue to be created around the action table, either when the action items are followed up in between meetings or for the responsible person to communicate regarding progress or problems that have arisen.

Table of action

Meeting of: _____ Held on: _____

Agenda item	Action required	RP	Date	Comment
4.3 Refurbishment of kitchen at GDS Secondary School	• Site visit to review existing equipment for possible re-use • Draw up draft specifications for approval at next meeting prior to obtaining quotes from service providers	NM	14/06/20__	

> This column highlights the responsible person, for easy reference.

Style for minutes

Minutes should be written in plain language, using clear short sentences and accessible language. If extensive jargon or technical language is required, it is useful to include a brief glossary in both the agenda and the minutes.

Minutes are written in the **past tense** and in reported speech. They are written in the third person and often refer to a position rather than a name. Never record verbatim direct speech.

e9

The Contractor confirmed a finish time ...

The Engineer requested more plant ...

Many people believe the passive voice is more formal and therefore more suitable for a formal set of minutes. This is not the case. Where possible, write in the active voice; only use the passive voice where necessary. For example, the following passive sentence does not indicate who is responsible for submission of the programme, nor on whose instruction. As a result, the sentence is vague and weak:

ℰℐ

A revised programme must be submitted to the Employer before the next meeting, as instructed.

The same sentence written in the active voice provides a concise record of who gave the instruction and who is responsible for carrying it out:

ℰℐ

The Engineer instructed the Contractor to submit a revised programme to the Employer before the next meeting.

In meetings where decisions are made by a committee or by vote, it is important not to assign individual responsibility for the decision: it is a committee decision. It is still not appropriate, however, to use the passive voice to hide the agent of the decision, as in the example below, because it in fact fails to assign responsibility at all, even to the committee. The questions remain: Who was it decided by? Where was it found?

ℰℐ

It was decided that ...
It was found that ...

It is better to indicate the subject of the sentence:

ℰℐ

The committee decided that ...
The report revealed that ...

The list below gives examples of useful vocabulary to use when moving from direct to reported speech:

Direct/verbatim speech	Indirect/reported speech
Now	Then/at the time
This	That
These	Those
Here	There
Today	That day
Tomorrow	The next day/the following day
Yesterday	The previous day
Last night	The previous night
Last week	The previous week
Next week	The following week
Thus	So

English has many forms of the past tense. The following are examples of how tenses can be used in different situations in a meeting and how they should be recorded in the minutes.

℮9

Scenario 1: At the fourth meeting, the Contractor asks for a copy of Drawing A.

Wording in minutes: The Contractor *asked* for a copy of Drawing A.

Comment: Note the use of the *simple past tense* to minute an action that occurred at a meeting in progress.

℮9

Scenario 2: At the fourth meeting, the Contractor asked for a copy of Drawing A. It is now the fifth meeting and he still does not have the drawing.

Wording in minutes: The Contractor *said* that the copy of Drawing A, which he *had requested* at the fourth meeting, *had not yet been produced.*

Comment: Note the use of two tenses for actions occurring at different times: the *simple past tense* to minute what the Contractor said at the fifth (current) meeting, and the *past perfect tense* to minute an action that had occurred, or not, at some time before the fifth (current) meeting.

In minutes, the *past perfect tense* does not occur in isolation: it is always accompanied by the simple past tense. In other words, the past perfect tense always refers to the earlier of two (or more) actions in the past.

e9

Scenario 3: The Contractor, during the sixth meeting, asks to receive a new set of drawings in two months' time.

Wording in minutes: The Contractor *said* that he *would* need a new set of drawings in two months' time.

Comment: *'Would'* replaces *'will'* to indicate an action that is to be completed at some time in the future.

See Chapter 1 for more information on an effective writing style.

✓

Checklist for effective meetings

Be proactive in your approach to meetings. Whether you are part of the planning or responsible for running meetings, taking a proactive approach helps dramatically. The more you are aware of what people need in order to be able to contribute meaningfully at meetings, the more smoothly and productively the meetings will run. Putting the work in before the meeting reduces the load during and after the meeting.

Use the following checklist before, during and after meetings:
- Make sure you know the rules and purpose relating to all meetings you attend.
- Check what needs to be done before, during and after the meeting and, if necessary, prepare a meeting timetable and strategy.
- Develop templates for agendas, minutes and tables of action related to your meetings.
- Use a working agenda to ensure everyone attending the meeting is aware of what will be covered and what outcomes are required.
- Write your minutes as soon after the meeting as possible.
- Use clear, short sentences and accessible language when writing minutes. Write in the past tense, in reported speech and, where possible, in the active voice.
- Extract a table of action to send out after the meeting to remind everyone of what needs to be done and to help monitor progress.

7   Business proposals and business plans

For anyone planning a new venture or starting a business, a good proposal and an effective business plan are essential. You may have a good idea for a product or service, but you need to look at it from the perspective of a future market or a funder, as most businesses – traditional and start-ups – need support at the beginning. Alternatively, you or your company may be putting in a bid in response to an advertised request to tender, commonly known as a request for a proposal (RfP). Both ventures require a proposal or business plan. You can create your own or you may be given a template as part of the RfP process.

A proposal is a persuasive message used in business and industry to generate work. A proposal writer tries to persuade his or her readers (potential funders, contractors or procurers) to take action or to accept the action that the writer has proposed. For all proposals, you must consider the extent of detailed factual data needed for your projections to be feasible. In the case of applying to a potential funder, you need to provide information to persuade the funder to make a donation (should your organisation be a non-profit organisation) or to provide equity for a commercial venture.

When you respond to an RfP, you will see that the sections for completion are indicated and points are awarded for each section. It is the points system that enables the agency or company procuring the work to compare the tenders and award the contract to the most suitable bidder. If no indication is given by the client of what the business plan must incorporate, you need to decide on a format.

Proposals have a wider application than business plans. Proposals do not necessarily deal with the starting up of a company. Instead, they focus on a wide variety of future actions. Business plans, on the other hand, are used for start-ups or expansions. A business plan may also be used to support a change in direction for which financial forecasts are required. All types of business plans include a detailed budget.

This chapter covers:
- business proposals as persuasive documents
- different types of business proposals: requested and non-requested
- the sections of a business proposal (with examples)
- business plans as a form of raising finance

- how to do develop a business plan
- how to write the sections of a business plan (with examples).

After reading this chapter, you will be able to:
- write a persuasive proposal for a new funder
- prepare a detailed business plan for a new venture or an expanding business.

7.1 Business proposals as persuasive documents

The persuasive power of a proposal rests strongly on facts, proposed actions and justification. Justification is necessary to persuade the reader that the proposed actions are feasible. The likelihood of success is stressed and the feasibility of the proposed actions can be used to persuade the reader that the costs of the proposed actions are valid.

When you write a proposal, you need to stress what the reader will gain from accepting it. First, you need to define your objectives and research the necessary facts. (See Figure 7.1 for suggested areas to be defined and researched before the proposal can be written.) Facts on their own, however, are not necessarily sufficiently persuasive. You will need to emphasise what makes your proposal unique: justify it in terms of what it may offer society, business and, most of all, the client. Persuade the reader that your skills and the skill set of your team are exceptional.

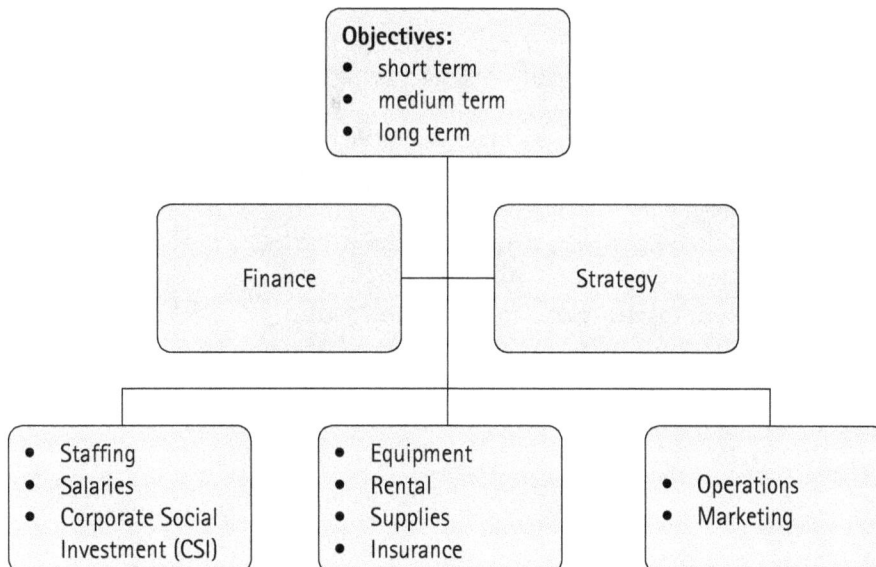

Objectives:
- short term
- medium term
- long term

Finance

Strategy

- Staffing
- Salaries
- Corporate Social Investment (CSI)

- Equipment
- Rental
- Supplies
- Insurance

- Operations
- Marketing

Figure 7.1 Suggestions for brainstorming business proposals

7.2 Different types of proposals

There are two kinds of proposals: requested and non-requested.

Requested proposals

A requested proposal is prepared in response to instructions from a client. These instructions are the client's terms of reference (also called a brief or RfP), and they tell you exactly what is wanted. Not all clients phrase their requests well, so it is in your interests to present a full proposal in response, even if the request is vague.

The two examples of advertisements for proposals that follow indicate the variety in RfPs. The first example gives little indication of what is wanted in the proposal, while the second example gives precise guidelines. However, a good proposal will do as much to influence the authority tendering the work in the first example as the authority in the second example.

e9

BREDASDORP MUNICIPALITY

CONTRACT NO: 1T-231

CALL FOR PROPOSALS

TO HOST A DRAG RACING EVENT IN BREDASDORP

The Overberg District Municipality hereby calls for proposals to host a drag racing event in Monk Road between Queen Street and Garden Road. Proposals will only be considered for acceptance if they conform in all respects with the requirements of Sport-Motor-South Africa (SMSA) and if the applicant bears all costs associated with the event, including the labour costs of the City such as law enforcement, fire services, etc. Of these, the most favourable offer to Council will then be chosen.

Proposals must be marked 'Racing Proposal', and delivered to the 2nd Floor, Council Building, Main Street, Bredasdorp, on or before 11:00 on 2003-02-20--.

For any enquiries, please contact Josie Smith on 072 435 7668.

J Smith

J Smith,

Manager

City Council

℮9

TRANSPORT EDUCATION AND TRAINING AUTHORITY

The Transport Education and Training authority (TETA) was established in terms of the Skills Development Act, 97 of 1998. The purpose of TETA is, inter alia, the development and implementation of a sector skills plan within the framework of the National Skills Development Strategy; it aims to promote learnerships, check the quality assurance of training providers and programmes, and to manage levy income and disbursements within the transport sector.

CALL FOR PROPOSALS TO CONDUCT PROFESSIONAL DRIVER AND DEFENSIVE DRIVING SKILLS TRAINING — NSF STRATEGIC PROJECT

Proposals are invited from interested training provider companies to conduct professional and defensive driving skills training for the taxi industry.

The TETA is embarking on a national programme to enhance sustainability and increase growth prospects and competitiveness of small businesses in the taxi industry. Through integration with the National Road Safety Strategy, the impact will result in a decrease in the rate of road accidents.

It has become clear that a great number of our drivers require professional defensive driving skills. The industry has attested to a need to carry out the transportation skills development exercise around specific SAQA-registered unit standards. In line with collaborative arrangements, 20 drivers from each province (180 in total) will be trained through this project.

Upon completion of the project, the participants will:
- be able to observe and adhere to road signs, safety rules and regulations
- be in a position to react to incidents in a responsible manner
- be able to handle customers with care
- be able to interact with other road users
- understand their roles as drivers charged with the lives of commuters and society at large.

The provider must ensure that, upon completion, participants earn credits in line with the NQF standards and TETA requirements towards an Advanced Professional Driving qualification.

The programme will be provincially based. The actual delivery of the project will run for not more than six weeks after the conclusion of the contract (final certification or granting of credits may fall outside this timeframe).

The following must be submitted:
- Proposal (outlining the process, costs, milestones, etc)
- Proof of accreditation or proof that an application for accreditation has been made with an etqa
- Résumés of project staff
- Authorised copy of company registration
- References
- Tax clearance certificate.

→

Terms of reference documents and further information can be obtained by contacting
Ms Refilwe Ndaba, TETA NSF Project Management Unit, TETA, 1st floor, Transport
Towers, Main Road, Johannesburg. Tel: (011) 751 6780

Proposals must be handed in by 24 January 20--. Pending assessment of your proposal,
you may be invited to make a presentation to the Selection Committee between 10 and 14
February 20--. Exact times and venues will be communicated by 28 January 20--.

NB: If you have not heard from us by 28 February 20--, please consider your submission as
unsuccessful.

Non-requested proposals

You might, perhaps as a member of a group of experts, decide to draw up your
own proposal. In this case you would not have any terms of reference and would
not know your potential client's objectives. You would therefore have to do your
own research. There are various analytical tools to assist you in defining what is
to go into your proposal and to use for brainstorming the topics. For example,
you could use:

- a **SWOT analysis** (Strengths, Weaknesses, Opportunities and Threats) to
  brainstorm what your position is in relation to your competitors
- a **PESTLE analysis** (Political, Economic, Social, Technological, Environmental
  and Legal) to brainstorm the norms and rules within which you will
  be functioning (this is sometimes abbreviated to PEST, omitting the
  environmental and legal elements)
- **Porter's five forces** to focus on the industry you will be entering and the
  forces that will place pressure on your proposed business.

Porter's model determines competition level in an industry using five forces.
These competitive forces concentrate on:

- rivalry within the industry
- threat of new entrants
- threat of substitutes
- bargaining power of suppliers
- bargaining power of buyers.

The collective strength of these five forces determines the nature of the
competitiveness in an industry. It varies from intense to moderate and affects
profitability. An industry is often dominated by one of these forces.

A change in any of these variables can create an opportunity or pose a
threat to an organisation. The organisation can prepare itself for changes in
the environment by scanning that environment; changing its strategy; and/or
restructuring to become more flexible and adaptable.

7.3   Write the sections of a business proposal

Before writing up the sections of a proposal, it is important to have a clear overview of the proposal. Dewey's six stages of problem solving will assist you in conceptualising your project and defining ways of presenting it to a potential funder or client. Dewey's six stages of problem solving are the following (Barkley, Cross & Major, 2005):

1. Identify and define the real problem, not the apparent problem.
2. Consider all objectives and criteria.
3. Identify solutions.
4. Test feasible solutions and estimate the resources needed.
5. Select the best option, reassess and measure the outcomes.
6. Implement the chosen solution to the problem.

As fixed-format documents, proposals have clearly defined sections, each with a specific role to play. The recommended sections of a proposal are explained in the sections that follow, with examples where applicable.

Note that this is like a menu, and you must select the relevant sections to suit your specific needs. Additional sections for a non-requested proposal are set out on page 198.

The title page
This should create a good first impression. It should contain:
- a full title, stating the proposed action
- a line stating who the proposal was prepared for (if possible, give names and job titles)
- a line stating who the proposal was prepared by (give names and job titles)
- the dates (give the date when the proposal was requested and the date when it is due)
- index words (to enable a person to find this proposal in an electronic storage system).

The terms of reference (if no RfP template provided)
These are the instructions that the client gives you. If there is a formal RfP, a template will be provided. If not, you will need to formalise the terms of reference. To do this, you need to state:
- who instructed you
- when you were instructed
- why you were instructed
- exactly what you have been asked to do (ie the client's objectives)
- when you have to submit your proposal.

Always ask for your terms of reference in writing. If you are not sure about the instructions, always negotiate with your client until all parties are satisfied with them. In some cases, it is appropriate for the terms of reference to be signed.

The client's objectives (requested proposals only)

These record what the client would like to achieve as a result of the proposed action. If you know the client's objectives, state them in full in this section of your proposal. If the clients have not yet given you their objectives, negotiate with them until you are able to record their objectives. In the following example – an extract from a proposal – the client's objectives are stated in full.

e9

ii

BHP SOUTH AFRICA

Client's objectives

The client, namely the Department of Mineral and Energy Affairs, intends to justify the exploitation of the Hondeklipbaai natural gas field in terms of its benefit to the South African economy and the possible impact on the environment. The department plans to assess the manufacturing of an alternative, clean fuel from the natural gas. There are three reasons why this has become a priority:

- South Africa's reliance on coal and oil can no longer be justified due to the increasing fuel price and the long-term shortage of these fossil fuels.
- The West Coast of South Africa is an underdeveloped area and would benefit, in terms of job creation, from industrial development. Furthermore, it is in South Africa's interests to keep pace with internationally emerging technology in the field of alternative fuel production.
- Increasing pollution in urban areas has made the search for a cleaner fuel necessary.

Summary

Make sure that you place your summary after the terms of reference and client's objectives. This section summarises the full proposal. It may contain illustrations such as tables, line graphs, pie charts and bar graphs. It may also include details about the cost of the proposed action.

Note that opinions differ as to whether you should include the costs in your summary. Some experts argue that the proposal should psychologically prepare the reader for the costs. Others argue that costs are so important that they should be placed in the summary. You will have to decide on this important point yourself.

Make your summary highly readable. Use subheadings, bullet lists, short sentences and a variety of paragraph lengths. The summary should be good enough to replace the whole proposal for the busy reader. It should be 5–10% of the word count of the entire proposal. The following example shows an abridged form of the summary of a business proposal.

iii

BHP SOUTH AFRICA

Summary

This proposal is a response to the request from the Department of Mineral and Energy Affairs for tenders to exploit the vast resource of natural gas at Hondeklipbaai. South Africa's increasing dependence on rapidly depleting coal and oil reserves, coupled with the need to seek more environmentally friendly fuel sources, has made the government reconsider its earlier decision not to exploit the gas field. Any proposed project would need to benefit both the local communities and the country at large on both an environmental and sociological scale.

The first sentence should state what the proposal covers.

The proposal

Broken Hill Proprietary Limited (BHP) aims to exploit this natural resource by constructing a plant at Hondeklipbaai to produce methanol from natural gas. This detailed proposal describes the work already performed, and provides a comprehensive schedule of proposed activities necessary to complete this project. BHP is a world leader in the field of methanol synthesis, with many years' experience in this field. In addition, in 20-- BHP constructed a plant in Melbourne, Australia, that is very similar to the proposed Hondeklipbaai plant. Throughout this proposal, the Melbourne plant will be used as a basis for technical, economic and environmental reviews.

Methanol production

Although there are other possible uses for natural gas, as a result of global experience in this field BHP has concluded that methanol production is the most viable usage. Importantly, methanol is more environmentally friendly than other hydrocarbons such as petrol and diesel.

It is important to summarise the justification for the proposal. The writers have done this well.

Benefits to be gained from the proposal

BHP believes this proposed plant would be beneficial to South Africa for the following reasons:

- The production of methanol will decrease South Africa's reliance on depleting fossil fuels such as coal and oil.
- Methanol is a cleaner alternative to conventional fuel sources and therefore has environmental advantages.
- BHP is ideally suited to construct such a plant. The experience gained in building and running the similar, successful Melbourne operation is invaluable ...

Table of contents

This section lists the headings in the proposal up to the second level. It gives the page number for each heading and subheading.

Note that the table of contents shown in the following example does not include all the sections which are recommended for a proposal.

e9

BHP SOUTH AFRICA

Table of contents

→

The justification is a very important section of the proposal. It is used to persuade the reader to accept the proposal.

Tables and figures

Tables and figures are listed separately. If both are contained in the proposal, the section is headed 'List of illustrations'.

Glossary

The glossary is like a special dictionary for the proposal. Define all technical words, as well as difficult words if necessary. Use alphabetical order.

List of symbols and acronyms

If you use any special symbols or acronyms (groups of first letters of words), you must define them. Use alphabetical order if possible. If not, use an order that will be clear to the reader.

The body of the proposal

The main sections of the body of a standard proposal are as follows:

1. **Introduction**
    1.1 The need for the proposed action
    1.2 Background to the proposal
    1.3 Description of the problem(s) to be solved
    1.4 Purposes of the proposal
    1.5 Procedure used to gather information
    1.6 Description of the layout of the proposal
2. **Procedure used to gather information**

This section should contain some or all of the listed subsections, with numbered headings.

If this is a long description, make it Section 2, as shown below.

This is very important if the proposal is complex.

→

3. **Detailed proposal**

   3.1   Detailed proposed action

   3.2   Boundaries of the proposed action

   3.3   Scope of the proposed action

   3.4   Limitations of the proposed action

   3.5   Breakdown of tasks to be performed

   3.6   Environmental impact assessment (EIA)

   3.7   Detailed costs

   3.8   Method of payment

4. **Justification**

5. **Urge to action**

> *This section sets out the proposed action in detail. Include some, or all, of the subsections shown, with numbered headings.*

The example that follows is a short series of extracts from the body of a proposal concerning BHP South Africa. Note that not all the sections are reflected (sections 1, 2, 3 and 6 are omitted), so the numbering does not appear consecutive.

e9

8

BHP SOUTH AFRICA

4. Proposed schedule for project

4.1 Detailed engineering

Detailing the proposed project involves finalising all relevant drawings (piping and instrumentation diagrams, process flow diagrams). The layout and exact locations of the plant must also be decided, along with the specifications of the process units. For example, the type of methanol converter technology must be specified, as well as its size and duties.

> *Note how the writers have effectively stressed future action.*

The detailed engineering stage also includes building and commissioning a pilot plant of the process. Pilot plants are very useful in quantifying the effect that various process conditions have on the plant. For example, the effect that a different natural gas grade would have on the process could quickly be determined using a pilot plant. The pilot plant of the BHP process will be designed, built and commissioned by the end of the detailed engineering phase.

[Sections 4.2 and 4.3 are not reproduced here.]

9

4.4 Full production

This stage involves the steady increase in production rate of the plant. During this increase, the behaviour and performance of the plant will be studied for future reference. The staff and operators will receive final training in anticipation of maximum production rates.

→

Table 4.1 gives the detailed schedule of BHP's proposed actions. The table refers to what has already been done and to what the group proposes to do.

> *Note the reference to the table. This reference prepares the reader for the table.*

Table 4.1 Schedule of BHP's proposed actions

Time	Process	
Completed See page xx.	**Conceptual engineering:** • Preliminary economic evaluation • Product research and development • Human resource studies • Preliminary process flow diagram (PFD) • Preliminary mass balance • Initial location options • Initial stages of environmental impact assessment (EIA) • Discussions with the interested and affected parties (I&APs)	✓
Completed	**Basic engineering:** • Final PFDs • Specifications for units • Mass and energy balances • Control philosophy defined • Waste treatment process defined	✓
1st to 6th month	**Detailed engineering:** • Complete EIA • Final piping and instrumentation diagrams (P&IDs) • Detailed plant layout • Full equipment specifications • Exact location decided • Pilot plant construction begins	
7th to 12th month	**Detailed engineering continues:** • Pilot plant start-up • Recruitment and training of key staff **Procurement:** • Receive and evaluate tenders • Place orders • Receive and store materials and equipment	
13th to 36th month	**Construction:** • Natural gas pipeline construction begins • Earthworks and roads built • Buildings and structures completed • Equipment fabrication and installation • Recruitment and training of operators and other staff • Electronics and instrumentation completed • Insulation and painting	

> *Note the ticks (✓) in the right-hand column to show what has already been done. This is an effective summary table.*

> *Note the effective time scale proposed.*

→

| 37th to 40th month | **Commissioning:**
• Check compliance and design
• Final testing of the natural gas pipeline
• Detailed training of operators and staff
• Start-up to 50% of full production capacity | |
| 41st to 42nd month | **Full production:**
• Final training ends
• Ramp plant to 100% production capacity | |

11

5. Environmental impact assessment (EIA)

5.1 Background

As part of the primary design activity, it was necessary to establish whether the proposed development is not only technically realisable, but also socially and environmentally acceptable. The Environmental Conservation Act, 73 of 1989, which has been further developed under the Environmental Impact Assessment Regulations 2010 (Government Gazette 544, 2010), requires that any proposed development must prevent pollution, promote conservation and secure ecologically sustainable development. These requirements are evaluated in an EIA.

Note the reference to the relevant environmental legislation. This establishes the group's credibility.

Justification

Your justification is the persuasive part of your proposal. Use this section to persuade your readers of:

• the feasibility of your proposed solutions to their problems
• the benefits of accepting your proposed actions.

This is an important section if you have prepared a long and detailed proposal. Use this section to create a positive last impression. Remember to keep this section short, to the point and persuasively worded. The following example shows the justification section from the same report used earlier.

e9

17

7. Justification

This proposal has the following advantages:

7.1 BHP's experience

BHP's role in the field of methanol synthesis gives the company access to the necessary technical expertise to produce methanol efficiently from natural gas.

In addition, BHP has achieved great success with its Melbourne-based methanol plant. The Hondeklipbaai plant will be based on this successful venture.

7.2 Methanol as a product

Methanol is environmentally clean and, as internal combustion technology develops, it is likely to be the successor to gasoline. Amongst all possible products from natural gas, methanol is the most viable and useful in the 21st century. Methanol will help South Africa to become less reliant on shrinking petroleum reserves.

7.3 Economic viability

By virtue of having performed a complete cost estimate for the process, BHP is certain the project will be profitable and financially beneficial for the people of South Africa. The project has an expected rate of return of 20.4%, which is higher than all standard investments.

7.4 Development of a historically poor area

BHP acknowledges its social responsibility by working closely with communities and committing a percentage of profits to local development. BHP intends to stimulate growth in the area and to provide equal opportunity employment. BHP has demonstrated this commitment by preparing to invest expertise and capital in this project.

7.5 International recognition

A successful venture, such as is proposed here, will lead to further international recognition of South Africa as an emerging industrial nation. This will have positive economic and social benefits for the country as a whole.

The above-mentioned benefits demonstrate beyond doubt that government approval of the proposed BHP methanol _____ plant at Hondeklipbaai would be the most appropriate course of action.

Note the use of persuasive language.

References

List all the sources that you have used. These could include books, encyclopaedias, reports, theses, journal articles, opinions from interviews, online references and other research sources. See Chapter 12 for instructions on managing citations and referencing.

Appendices

In this section, include your results from detailed research, including computer printouts, detailed calculations and tables, examples of research questionnaires and typed versions of interviews.

Extra information for non-requested proposals

When you write a non-requested proposal, include some, or all, of the following descriptive and supporting material to help persuade your reader(s) to accept your proposal. You will need to prepare:

- references from previous clients
- references to an earlier association with the reader(s)
- a description of previous experience with projects
- short CVs of staff, as well as their qualifications
- the company's organisation chart
- a statement of the financial condition of the company
- a description of employment practices, including employment equity, Black Economic Empowerment (BEE) and corporate governance
- a general description of company policies
- a description of where the company is located
- descriptive, promotional and advertising literature.

7.4 Business plans as a form of raising finance

Proposals and business plans are related. Both are used to generate work or raise finances for a new project. Business plans, however, are directed more at raising finance for new businesses or expanding current businesses. Proposals and business plans are both persuasive messages. They use facts, or projections based on facts, as the basis for persuasion. Both may include justification sections that seek to persuade the reader to accept the proposed action or to arrange to provide finance. However, a business plan always includes a detailed budget.

Your final business plan will need to contain the following sections:

- A list of goals
- Steps to be taken to reach those goals
- Planned completion dates
- Priorities
- Finances required (budget).

As mentioned previously, a business plan is an essential tool for raising money. It stresses the functional planning that gives the applicant the credibility needed to get financial support. The plan outlines the goals of the proposed company and analyses potential markets as well as customers. It describes a course of action to be taken, highlights business opportunities and points out the potential of the business from a prospective investor's point of view. Money can be raised in the form of equity or a loan, or a combination of equity and a loan.

An exit strategy is essential for raising equity. It is not a sign of defeat but of pragmatism and foresight, and adds credibility to your plan. Consider when and how the potential investor could exit or when or how all of the initial stakeholders could exit (eg listing the company as a public company).

7.5 How to develop a business plan

Planning a potential business is a process that consists of various stages:

1. **Brainstorm** to pin down your business objectives in detail. At the same time you should prepare your vision or mission statement, in which you describe the purpose of your business and what you plan to achieve.

2. **Consider your short-, medium- and long-term goals.** Most importantly, decide on your intended market and determine its size. You must thoroughly research your proposed market so that you understand any opportunities and threats. Make sure you know who the competition is. Find out as much as you can about your target market, your customers and their priorities, as this will inform your planning process. Many people at this stage make use of business planning tools such as a SWOT analysis, where they analyse the strengths, weaknesses, opportunities and threats facing their business. This allows them to anticipate the challenges ahead more effectively while also identifying the key strengths of their business.

3. **Draw up a strategic plan establishing your goals and objectives.** When you set out your business objectives, you must be very clear as to what your business is about and what you plan to achieve over a specific time span. Critical here is to plan the budget: cash needed in and expenditure. There are various financial modelling tools to assist with this. It is also vital to have a clear timeline in your head, even at this early stage of your planning.

4. Then work out an **operational plan**, describing in detail how you intend to ensure the success of the strategic plan.

5. Finally, you should draw up a **detailed business plan**, describing exactly how you intend to ensure the success of the strategic plan and covering every aspect of the business. This is discussed in greater detail in the following section.

Your business plan should not just explain what your intended business proposes to do; it should also explain what is special or unique about your product or service. It should establish your credibility by giving reasons why you are well qualified to make the most of the business opportunity.

As part of your planning, do the following:
- Establish your priorities and identify problems that could get in your way.
- Anticipate any future technological advances and draw up proposals to exploit them.
- Analyse the competition: their strengths and how you will better them.
- List all the benefits as well as any disadvantages of your proposed product

or service. Stress unique features and competitive strengths and how these should make market penetration easier. For this you may want to explore the SWOT analytical tool.

- Define your level of performance and the quality you expect. Set standards by which to measure your progress.
- Set goals to manage uncertainties and reduce your risks. However, ensure that your goals are specific, measurable, time-related and attainable.
- Having set the goals, describe the action necessary to realise each goal (as described in Figure 7.2) and plan target dates for accomplishing each goal.
- It is also important to develop detailed marketing, sales and financial plans. This will be discussed in the next sections.

STAGE 1

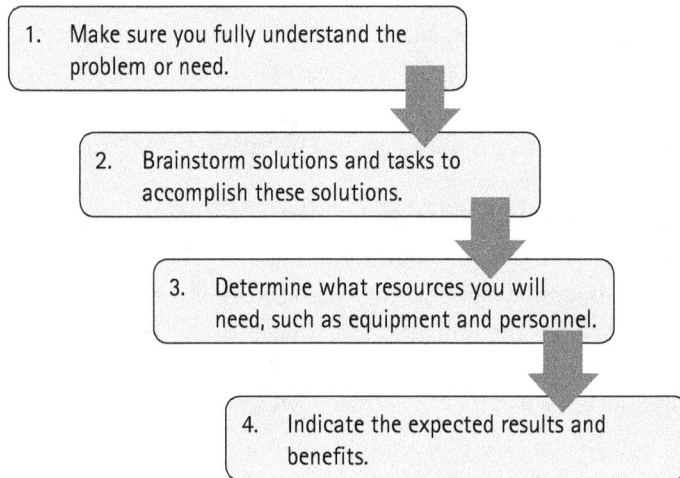

STAGE 2

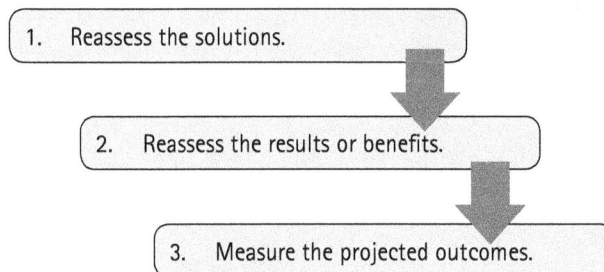

Figure 7.2 Goal setting for a business plan

When using any of the analytical tools, such as SWOT or PESTLE analyses, do not merely identify the issues and leave them in your plan; identify what you can do to, for example, overcome any weaknesses or threats identified. This will show readers that you have not only identified issues but proposed action to mitigate or manage them. It is also worth considering omitting the analysis tools from your plans and proposals and just including the outcomes or your responses to the analyses. The analytical grids can be reserved for internal purposes.

You will also need to plan:

- the registration of your company
- the dates when your staff need to be in place
- where you will source your materials.

Marketing and sales plan

Your marketing plan should be based on your research into the market and the competition; and the sales programme must support and complement your marketing plan. Once you have a marketing and sales plan, you must plan a production programme that will ensure delivery on your stated plans and objectives. A basis for this is the four Ps: price, place, promotion and product. By studying the market according to each of these aspects, you may be sure you have considered all exigencies, as detailed in Figure 7.3.

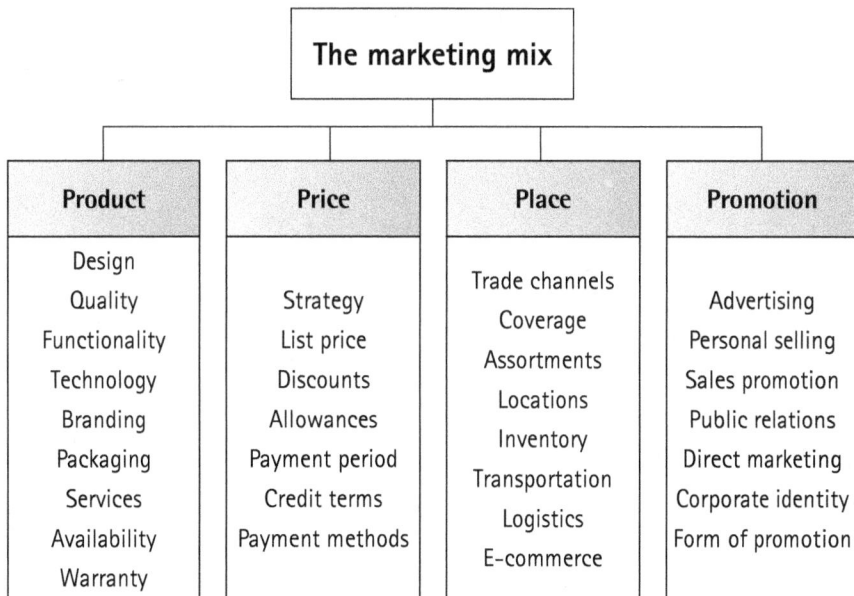

The marketing mix			
Product	**Price**	**Place**	**Promotion**
Design		Trade channels	
Quality	Strategy	Coverage	Advertising
Functionality	List price	Assortments	Personal selling
Technology	Discounts	Locations	Sales promotion
Branding	Allowances	Inventory	Public relations
Packaging	Payment period	Transportation	Direct marketing
Services	Credit terms	Logistics	Corporate identity
Availability	Payment methods	E-commerce	Form of promotion
Warranty			

Figure 7.3 Marketing considered in terms of the four Ps
Source: Von Brocke 2012

Financial plan

Your financial statement should include details regarding:

- cashflow
- the cost of acquiring equipment, if relevant
- rental costs
- salaries and wages
- the costs of obtaining supplies
- travel expenses and contingency funds.

There are many financial modelling programs available for planning finances. Microsoft® Excel™ also has many tools that will assist you.

7.6 Write the sections of a business plan

When you assemble your final document, keep in mind that a business plan must forcefully persuade prospective investors to take a risk.

Each section of a business plan is described in detail here. For some sections, extracts from a real business plan are given as examples. Some of these sections have been abridged.

The title page

This page should include:

- a clear title, giving the plan a focus
- a line stating whom the plan was prepared for (names and job titles)
- a line stating whom the plan was prepared by (names and job titles)
- the date
- key words or index words.

e9

Telephone Handset and Mobile Recycling

	A business plan ———
Prepared for:	ABC Bank
	Risk Finance Division
Prepared by:	Michelle Dyers, MBA
	Nancy Ncomo, MBA
	15 January 20--
	CONFIDENTIAL

The authors make it clear from the beginning that this is a business plan.

Note the use of key words. These are also called index words or search words.

Key words: handset, mobile, recycling, second-hand, foreign sales, investment

A summary

This should include content regarding the:

- **subject** or **purpose** of the proposed business activities (one or two brief sentences)
- **function or product description** (about half a page or one-third of the length of the content on this topic in the proposal)
- **innovation and credibility** of the venture and the reasons why your business or you and your team are unique and thus financially attractive (about half a page or one third of the length of the content on this topic in the proposal)
- **justification,** including further selling points, such as corporate social investment (CSI), exceptional staff or meeting government drives for inclusion of personnel (about half a page or one third of the proposal)
- what an investor or authorising company **can expect to gain** for its support and legal requirements (brief references, if appropriate).

e9

Summary

Trading as Telephone Handset and Mobile Recycling, we propose to set up a business to recycle handsets/mobiles that householders and businesses no longer want. Our business plan describes how we propose to do this.

> Note the use of the personal pronoun 'we'. This direct, personal style is acceptable in a business plan or a proposal. The authors could also have used an impersonal style to make their plan more formal.

Background to the business plan

We estimate that South Africans will buy 1 000 000 new 'phones in 20--. As a result, there will be about 750 000 old, unwanted handsets/mobiles, 90% of which will be in good working order. These handsets/mobiles will either be stored in back rooms or be thrown away.

> The authors have placed this important statement in a frame to attract attention to it.

We expect this trend to continue as advances in technology and styling cause increasing numbers of South Africans to replace their handsets/mobiles.

Telephone Handset and Mobile Recycling will be aimed at foreign buyers

Telephone Handset and Mobile Recycling will be a highly profitable channel for selling old 'phones to markets in Africa, Asia and South America for domestic and industrial uses.

We believe that our plan will persuade South Africans to trade in their unwanted handsets/ mobiles rather than throw them away.

→

Proposed method of operating

We propose the following simple method:

1. Representatives from Telephone Handset and Mobile Recycling will contact Telkom, as well as all offices and shops selling new 'phones.

2. Customers who buy new handsets/mobiles will be told that they will receive R50 off their new 'phones if they hand in an old one in any condition. Telephone Telephone Handset and Mobile Recycling will pay the agent the trade-in price (ie R50) for every second-hand telephone collected.

Our extensive market research has shown us that telephone suppliers are very willing to absorb a R50 per sale expense, as they are able to recoup the R50 by collecting second-hand handsets/mobiles from their clients.

Note the use of full headings to guide the reader.

Note the numbered steps to explain the procedure.

Telephone recycling procedure

*   Telephone Handset and Mobile Recycling will clean and repair all handsets/mobiles received. These will then be sold to foreign markets in lots of 50.
*   All 'phones beyond repair will be dismantled for spares.
*   Our market research (see Appendix 1) has shown us that there is a large and expanding market for handsets/ mobiles in the price range of R150 to R300 per unit.

The writers have carefully explained their procedure. This attention to detail is important for persuading the readers of their ability.

This gives the writers credibility.

Finance requested: R600 000

As a result of our market research, we propose to start our business with a starting capital of R900 000. We have already raised R300 000 of our own. Therefore we are requesting R600 000.

We seek twelve investment units of R50 000 each to make up the R600 000. Each unit will earn 6% of the company's net profit per year. A loan of R600 000 would give a total investment interest in the company of 67%. We, as principals, propose to keep a 33% share in the profits.

Note the use of figures and percentages here.

The following example shows a summary that uses a graphic.

e9

INTELLIPLUG™

MAKING HOME AUTOMATION EASY

Smart home automation devices are fairly expensive and therefore inaccessible to many consumers. With this in mind, IntelliPlug (Pty) Ltd introduces the IntelliPlug. A simple, affordable home automation solution which enables a user to control multiple power plug outlets through the use of a smartphone application. The business plan for the IntelliPlug as proposed by IntelliPlug (Pty) Ltd is summarised below.

Product Description

The IntelliPlug is a wireless automation device which is made up of a customised multi-plug outlet and an Arduino microcontroller. Appliances can be plugged into the IntelliPlug and be wirelessly controlled via a computer or smartphone application. The Arduino serves as the control unit providing smart wireless functionality to allow users to connect to their IntelliPlug and control appliances from any location via the Internet.

The Arduino will be pre-loaded with default IntelliPlug software to provide basic appliance control functionality to schedule appliances to turn on and off as well as monitor energy consumption of appliances. However, since Arduinos are compatible with open source software, more ambitious users can modify the software to enable more advanced IntelliPlug automation functionality.

Marketing Plan

The IntelliPlug is a versatile device that can double as a home automation device and an educational tool in the field of software and electronics. Thus there is a market for the IntelliPlug amongst home owners, electronics hobbyists and university students. There is also a market for future partnerships with energy utilities such as Eskom with regard to domestic energy saving initiatives.

Marketing strategies will be put in place to establish and grow a customer base. These strategies will include official product launches, multimedia advertising (social media, technology magazines, radio and newspapers), promotions, free software upgrades, dedicated customer services and product quality and safety guarantees.

Business Operations

IntelliPlug (Pty) Ltd will be headed by an executive board of qualified engineers of various specialisations. An additional seat on the board will be available should an external investor want a place on the executive board.

Over the course of the first five years of operation, six additional staff members will be employed to facilitate the running of the business.

The business will operate out of a warehouse located in Epping, Cape Town. A technical workshop will be set up in the warehouse wherein the assembly, performance testing and packaging of the IntelliPlugs will take place.

$\rightarrow$

IntelliPlugs will be sold to customers via an online webstore and through selected retail stores. Courier delivery options will be available on the webstore for customers who want the product delivered to them.

Financial Overview

IntelliPlug (Pty) Ltd will require a total of R900 000 as start-up capital funds. R600 000 of this total is going to be funded through investment from the IntelliPlug founders and a bank loan. This leaves a R300 000 deficit which will be required from an external investor, who will receive a 40% share of ownership in return.

Figure 1 shows the projected annual net profit over the initial five-year period of operations based on an initial selling price of R1 150 for the IntelliPlug.

It can be seen in Figure 1 that the business is projected to become profitable within three years of operation. Dividends will be paid out as of year 3, with a total of R1 100 000 in dividends being paid out to the external investor by the end of year 5. This total will further increase over subsequent years of operation.

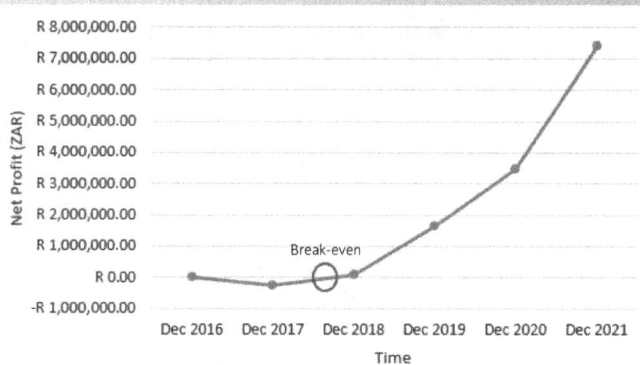

Figure 1: Projected annual net profit over 5 years

Justification

The IntelliPlug is an affordable South African product which will provide many people with access to modern wireless home automation technology. The versatility of the IntelliPlug's features, along with the flexibility to expand the product concept in the future, will give it a firm edge over its competitors. IntelliPlug (Pty) Ltd.'s executive board consists of a strong team of qualified engineers who are dedicated to ensuring that the IntelliPlug is a high-quality, cutting-edge product. Therefore, the IntelliPlug will be a highly successful and rewarding endeavour.

A description of the basic business idea

In this section, make sure you do the following:

- Present your vision and mission statement, objectives and goals.
- Explain your concept and justify why it is worth supporting.
- Describe each part of the process or describe the processes involved in the concept.
- Describe how your product or concept compares with that of your competitors.

- Show why your product will be more profitable: cash forecast and equity and/or financial needs
- Include an exit plan for the long term or earlier, in case the venture is not successful.

The following example is an abridged extract from a business plan.

1. Description of the business concept

Recycling is a growing industry in South Africa. It will continue to grow in the future, as South Africans become more sensitive to the environment. For example, glass recycling has grown into a multimillion-rand business, with average profits of between 12% and 14%. Paper and cardboard recycling is also increasing in importance, with a turnover of R45 million in 20--.

This background to the business plan prepares the reader for the plan.

Note the use of preparatory detail to get the reader thinking about the business opportunity.

The concept of telephone recycling offers South Africans an exciting challenge. Rather than throwing away their unwanted 'phones, they could take them in for a R50 discount.

A consumer report of 20-- estimates that South Africans are storing up to 750 000 old 'phones. Most of these will be thrown away because there is no market for them.

South Africans are now buying new handsets/mobiles in record numbers. Sales of new handsets/mobiles are expected to increase by 25% over the next ten years.

Proposed products or services

In this section, describe the products and services that your business concept will generate. Use illustrations to sell your product or services.

2. Telephone Handset and Mobile Recycling products and services

Telephone Handset and Mobile Recycling will sign contracts with all major outlets to pay R50 per 'phone handed in. We will pick up all used handsets/mobiles from the outlets' distribution points. We will also pay the transport for lots of 100 used handsets/mobiles sent to us.

Major sections of the plan are introduced with first-level numbers. Each new section should start on a new page.

Management team

Describe the personnel, skill sets and experience required and how this team matches the requirements. Give their qualifications and work history (CVs) and, if relevant, photographs of the members of the team.

The marketing and sales plan

Cover the following points in the section discussing your marketing and sales plan:

- Describe your potential market (how many potential customers there are, where you will find them, why they buy, how much they spend and what they like). State specifically who is likely to buy your products or services, and why.
- Give a detailed account of your marketing strategies. Back up your assertions with specific marketing and demographic information.
- Give a forecast of sales by unit.
- Stress your competitive edge in the market. Describe competitors in the market and their strategies, and stress what benefits your business will offer over the competition.

e9

3. Marketing plan

Telephone Recycling proposes to market its services in five ways:

3.1 Prospectuses for decision makers

We will approach all decision makers in telephone service centres and shops selling telephones. In addition, each centre and shop will receive a professionally prepared prospectus and proposal.

Note the use of subheadings to guide the reader through each stage of the plan.

3.2 Contracted partners

All telephone service centres and shops will receive follow-up visits. We will sign a contract with each one.

3.3 Advertising in foreign trade journals

We will advertise in foreign trade journals and magazines to alert foreign buyers to our new source of used handsets/mobiles. We will use any interest shown by foreign buyers to encourage South African sources to sign contracts with us.

3.4 Nationwide advertising

As soon as we have signed contracts with a number of service centres and shops, we will begin a nationwide publicity campaign. We propose to do this through a digital strategy: website, SEO, social media and broadcast and print media advertisements. This campaign will encourage South Africans to trade in their used 'phones.

3.5 The use of salespeople in foreign countries

As soon as we have signed enough contracts and have a stock of 700 000 'phones, we will pay a group of commissioned sales staff in selected foreign countries. Their job will be to find buyers of second-hand handsets/mobiles.

The proposed organisation

In this section, describe what kind of organisation you propose to establish to produce your products or services:

- Define how you propose to manage and run your company.
- Describe your staff, their qualifications and experience.
- Describe your administrative and record-keeping systems.
- Show that the efficient and intelligent management of your company will maximise your profits.

Legal requirements

Describe any legal requirements for setting up your business.

Proposed company location

State where you wish to locate your company and supply the necessary maps.

Company's finances

In this section, include details about your financial plan:

- Set out the reasons why you need the specific amount of money.
- Describe how profits and potential losses will be treated with regard to investors.
- Forecast your cash flow and project your likely profits.
- Provide a break-even analysis.
- Forecast your return on sales, return on assets and return on investments.
- State your start-up costs and at what stages you will need the money. Stress what you are seeking from investors.
- State your legal costs.
- State your costs, for example for staff, premises, insurance, office equipment and supplies.
- Describe the investors' degree of liability for your company operations and the terms of their financial participation in company profits.

e9

4.   Financial plan

4.1 Capital outlay — start-up costs

We plan to use R900 000 in the first year. This will be used as follows:

- R200 000: Staff salaries for two technicians and one secretary. (As principals, we have undertaken not to draw salaries for the first year.)

  Note the breakdown of costs to show the level of financial planning.

- R200 000: Rent for warehouse and office, payments for office furniture, leasing of two vans, other overheads, printing and advertising.
- R250 000: Paying for second-hand handsets/mobiles.
- R250 000: Running the company, including travelling.

4.2 Projected income and profit

The following projected income and profit for the next three years are based on an estimated 60% profit on each 'phone after repairs and transport.

The prices below are based on an average price of R200 per 'phone.

Table 1: Projected income and profit for first three years

Year	Units sold	Gross income	Gross profit	Expected net profit after costs of 40%
First year	10 000	R2 000 000	R1 500 000	R900 000
Second year	22 000	R4 400 000	R3 300 000	R1 980 000
Third year	30 000	R6 000 000	R4 500 000	R2 700 000

These projections show that an investor holding a 6% share of the net profit could expect the following from the R50 000 investment unit:

- R54 000 in the first year
- R118 800 in the second year
- R162 000 in the third year.

> *Note the continual use of detailed planning and estimates. The writers have continued their persuasive arguments.*

Justification and statement of requirement

At the end of the document, refocus on exactly what you want:

- Once again, stress the specifics of what you are offering, how much it will cost and what return investors are likely to get.
- Stress your mission.
- Emphasise your likely competitive edge.
- Emphasise your key to success.
- Explain why your business is likely to be financially attractive.

e9

5. Details of our request

We are seeking R600 000 divided into units of R50 000. We will be happy to send copies of our contractual Limited Partnership Agreement to anyone interested in investing in one or more units.

For anyone who decides to invest, we request payment by bank-guaranteed cheque payable to Telephone Handset and Mobile Recycling (Pty) Ltd. Individual investors may own up to four units. The company seeks to place a total value of twelve units with investors.

✔

Checklist for persuasive business proposals and business plans

For your message to lead to the desired outcome, it must be both persuasive and readable. Review the points below to confirm that your proposal or plan achieves what it sets out to do. While there is a considerable overlap between proposals and plans, the points have been listed separately.

Business proposals:
- Consider whether your proposal is requested or non-requested and whether you have addressed the necessary aspects.
- Review the key features of the proposal: the basic idea, the market, any relevant social or legal requirements, and your pricing, costs and potential profit.
- Critically assess your analysis and check you have followed a sound process.
- Review the structure of your proposal, ensuring that all the appropriate sections are not only included but also presented clearly to give the client or potential client a clear understanding of the concept and its unique factor.
- Finally, take a step back and assess whether the idea is well justified and its presentation persuasive.

Business plans:
- Identify the critical information that needs to be presented in your plan to show you have thought it through comprehensively. This includes:
  - the core business idea, product or service
  - the intended management or leadership team and required personnel
  - a rigorous assessment of the competition
  - the target market with the proposed marketing and sales plan
  - the projected financial plan
  - an outline any of legal requirements.
- Assess whether you have provided sufficient evidence to support any of the claims you make.
- Organise the plan to make sure that different levels of readers can find what is relevant to them.
- Finally, encapsulate your aims and approach in a well-considered vision and mission statement.

8   Report writing

Report writing is a part of every professional job, even jobs that are practical in nature, as various types of reports serve many different functions. For numerous professions, such as accounting, business or engineering, reports are a core activity. For example, an accountant may write month-end reports, a businessperson feasibility reports, and an engineer may write design and progress or interim reports. There are many programs used for report writing, for example Google Docs, DropBox, InSync and Microsoft® OneDrive™, as it is often a collaborative activity.

For detailed advice on the style for reports, see Chapter 1; for using and creating templates, see Chapter 2; and for researching material, see Chapter 13.

When you need to write a report, you will have to think about the following questions:
- What is the best length for a summary in relation to the whole report?
- What is a clear and readable format and layout in which to present your information?
- What are the names of the sections of a standard report?
- Do the headings, subheadings and table of contents tell the story of your report?
- What information should be put into graphic form?
- What is the best style for report writing: point form or full sentences? Should you use the active or the passive voice?
- When is it appropriate to write in the first person (eg 'I/we found ...') and when should you write in the third person (eg 'The findings showed ...')?

Read through this chapter to find the answers to the above questions. After you have done this, you will understand:
- the nature of reports
- types of reports
- writing techniques to aid readability: the language and style of reports
- the sections of a fixed-format evaluative report (illustrated with examples taken from a formal, professional report).

8.1 Nature of reports

Reports are fixed-format messages that give the results of investigations or record the facts that have been established. A report also records the conclusions a writer has drawn from the facts and sets out recommended actions based on these conclusions.

Any writer who recommends actions has to ensure that these actions are feasible and can be put into practice. You have to show that your conclusions have been logically and carefully drawn from the detailed factual record. You do this by including a discussion section in which you interpret the facts, show their significance in terms of your purposes and prepare the reader for your conclusions. Furthermore, the facts, conclusions and recommendations should speak to and address the aims set up at the beginning of the report. Recommendations must be based on the conclusions you have drawn. Figure 8.1 shows the continuity between parts of the report.

Figure 8.1 Flow of ideas and facts in a report

Relationship of reports to other documents

Reports are related to many other kinds of written messages – at college, university and in business and industry. In terms of format, style and approach, reports are related to theses, business proposals, business plans, minutes, instructions and technical descriptions.

All these messages are also classified as fixed-format documents. These texts have to be highly readable, even though many of them include technical information and mathematical calculations. The technical information can be conveyed through tables, graphs, annotated photographs and diagrams. Readers expect these messages to be written in a clear, formal, impersonal style. Readers expect to find specific sections in these documents, with numbered headings and subheadings. Companies are increasingly devising templates to aid writers with the layout of documents such as reports, plans and minutes.

Readers of reports

You may have no control over who reads your reports. Many reports are circulated in companies; they may be sent with the blind carbon copy (Bcc) function selected and filed for future readers. While for the most part you write for a defined readership, your reports may be read years later by strangers who know little about the conditions prevailing at the time the report was written. This means that reports may have to be written with various different readers in mind, some of whom may not be experts in that field.

Furthermore, reports are often written for a range of readers, all of whom have different needs. These readers are not of equal importance in terms of power, status and the need to read the report. Write your report with the following three levels of reader in mind:

1. **Main reader:** Your main reader is the decision maker. This person has to approve the report and is likely to pay a great deal of attention to the **summary** (containing the objectives), **conclusions** and **recommendations**. By creating a clear thread of information that leads the reader through these sections, you will emphasise the relevance of your recommendations.

2. **Second-level readers:** Your report may cover more than one subject or section of an organisation. The main reader may need to consult subject experts or department heads before deciding on your recommendations. These people are the second-level readers. For these readers you should emphasise **specific parts within the results section** that are relevant to them. You may, for example, cover the specific needs of the human resources, finance, information systems and marketing departments in a company.

3. **Third-level readers:** Once your main reader has decided on a course of action based on your report, other readers will have to implement your recommendations. They are the third-level readers. They will need to read the detailed sections of your report in which you specify exactly what has to be done. For these readers you need to emphasise your detailed **findings, conclusions, recommendations** and **appendices**.

You should also be able to classify your readers as follows:
- **Expert readers** have detailed knowledge of your field.
- **Mixed readers** are a group of which some are experts and some are not.
- **Non-specialist readers** are intelligent and experienced readers who are not experts in your field. They will generally be in a management position. They may have to use your report for making a decision.
- **Technical readers** are experienced technicians who have to implement your recommendations. They are experts in the practical aspects of the work, but may not be familiar with your theoretical approaches.

Reports as permanent records

Your report will become part of the company's permanent records. Make your report easily accessible by doing the following:
- Include **key words** on your title page to enable your readers to search for your work.
- Give the report a relevant **title** that covers the key points in the report.
- Write a very clear **summary** that is easy to read. This summary should be sufficiently comprehensive that it could replace the original report for busy readers.

- Use comprehensive, accurate **headings** and **subheadings** to help your reader gain a quick overview of the report within the table of contents.

8.2 Writing techniques for reports

Techniques to improve readability

Use all or some of the following techniques to improve readability (also see Chapter 1):

- Make sure your text is organised well, with an effective **numbering** system.
- Use pertinent **headings** that reflect the content. Avoid one-word headings which do not allow for meaning. For example, the heading 'Techniques to improve readability' describes the content of this section precisely, whereas a heading such as 'Readability' would not.
- Vary the **font sizes** within a font for headings to attract attention and define the hierarchy of the content. But remember: be consistent!
- Write in clear, **simple language** that is easy to understand.
- Define all **technical terms,** either in a glossary at the beginning or in footnotes at the bottom of each page.
- Use **bullet lists** for lists of items.
- Write short **paragraphs** and **sentences.**
- Use a line **spacing** of 1.15.
- Make sure you use **white space** generously.
- Put diverse or comparative information in **tables** with bold print or frames for emphasis.

You can achieve clarity of presentation through using a document template which has set styles. For each type of regular report you write, it is worth setting up a template. Most computer programs contain a range of pre-set templates and many others can be downloaded off the Internet. Be aware, however, that the majority of downloadable templates were set up with a specific purpose in mind and may not, on closer examination, be appropriate for the content and context of your report. You may find it more useful to define and format your own template to suit your needs. Furthermore, a downloaded template is unlikely to conform to your organisation's house style or brand, or your personal style of documentation. When readers can recognise a well-presented and organised style of documentation they associate with a credible writer, they tend to give it more attention. See Chapter 2 for more information on templates.

Plan for a logical sequence of ideas (discourse structure)

Plan your report carefully. Use the following steps to arrange your facts and arguments in a logical order that your reader can follow:

1. **Record all your research.** This step could be mind-mapped.
2. **Organise the material under the appropriate major sections of a report.** At this stage your information is not yet in a logical order within sections. It is arranged in broad categories. For example, your methodology would be in one section, your findings in another.
3. **Arrange the information in each section in a logical order.** You can do this by creating a topic outline, which is a numbered outline with headings. (See Chapter 1 for more on a topic outline.)

By reading your headings, a reader should be able to understand the contents of your report and follow the logical development of your thoughts. An effective topic outline will ensure that your report has unity, coherence and the right emphasis, which creates a structured argument or discourse structure. (Also read Chapter 1 for more information on unity, coherence and emphasis.)

Unity

When you organise your report, ensure that **one main theme** flows through your work. If you are covering a number of topics in a report, ensure that each topic also has one unifying theme.

If you write a number of paragraphs in your findings, make sure that each one is unified. Each paragraph should have a **topic sentence.** This sentence expresses the main idea in the paragraph, and the rest of the paragraph expands on this idea. The topic sentence is usually the first sentence in a paragraph. However, sometimes an introductory sentence precedes the topic sentence.

Coherence

Coherence refers to the **linking of one paragraph to another.** Coherence is achieved by the use of a well-organised multiple-decimal numbering system, apt headings, sign-posting, cross-referencing and conjunctions – all of which link one sentence to the next. When you are writing paragraphs, make sure you use words that show continuity. Words such as 'however', 'consequently' and 'therefore' maintain the thread of your argument and help the reader to follow it. Phrases such as 'the first point' or 'for example' also act as signposts for the reader.

Consider the following techniques to achieve coherence:
- Arrange the items in lists **in order of importance.**
- Repeat **key nouns.**
- Repeat **key verbs.**
- Use the **pronouns** 'it', 'this', 'those', 'these' and 'they' as reference words.

- Use **co-ordinating conjunctions**, such as 'and', 'but', 'or' and 'nor'. These join sentences, phrases or words of equal value in order to help the reader follow the idea.
- Use **subordinating conjunctions**, such as 'although', 'since', 'as', 'if', 'when', 'where' and 'while'. These words join parts of sentences of unequal value. For example, they join a subordinate clause to a main clause, as in: 'We will be successful (main clause) if we analyse the process step by step (subordinate clause).' (See Table 1.2 in Chapter 1 for a comprehensive list of these linking words and their functions.)

Achieving the right emphasis

The reader of a report needs to find out immediately what the most important parts are. Emphasis can be achieved in a report in the same way as it has been achieved in the short passages in this chapter; that is, by:

- using a fitting **title** that contains the key points in your report
- including a precise **summary** at the beginning
- placing the **most important points** at the beginning of the sections, in bold or contained in tables
- using **key sentences** and **terms** at the beginning of paragraphs.

Language and style of reports

The level of language (formal but not too formal), tone (impersonal), voice (active rather than passive) and vocabulary (concrete rather than abstract) are important for the readability and credibility of your report.

Readers of reports and other messages in business and industry are often multicultural and multilingual and may have limited proficiency in English. Write clearly and simply, and define all technical terminology. To judge whether your writing will be clearly understood by your intended reader, use your word processor's tools to check the spelling and grammar and the readability index of your writing.

Using readability statistics in Microsoft® Word™

The readability index is a measure of the vocabulary used and length of sentences; it describes how easy or difficult it is to read a piece of text. Follow these steps to use the readability statistics feature in Microsoft® Word™:

1. In the *Word Options* dialogue box (accessible by clicking on the *File* tab on the ribbon and then clicking on *Options*), select the *Proofing* section.

2. In the *When correcting spelling in Microsoft Office programs* section, review which options are checked or unchecked:

→

a. Remove the tick from *Ignore words in UPPERCASE*. This box is checked by default, which means that words in all upper case are not spellchecked. If you remove the tick, Microsoft® Word™ performs a spellcheck on all words, even those in upper case.

b. Remove the tick from *Ignore words that contain numbers*. If you have accidentally typed a number in a word, it will not show as an error unless this box is unchecked.

3. In the section *When correcting spelling and grammar in Word*, add a tick to the box *Show readability statistics*. If this readability statistics box is checked, a summary box will appear after you have performed a full spellcheck, either on a section of your writing or on the entire document.

The readability statistics only measure readability based on the length of words, sentences and paragraphs, and how much passive voice is used. Nevertheless, it is a useful guide against which to measure your writing.

Two indices are offered in the statistics summary (see Figure 8.2): the Flesch Reading Ease score and the Flesch-Kincaid Grade Level. The easiest score to use is the Flesch-Kincaid Grade Level; it gives a score based on a notional school or university grade, meaning that someone with that level of education should be comfortable reading the document. However, the fact that in South Africa English is not a first language for many readers should be taken into account when you consider a reasonable Flesch Reading Ease score. A writer should not force a reader to work unnecessarily hard — especially in a second (or third, fourth etc) language, even if the reader is highly qualified.

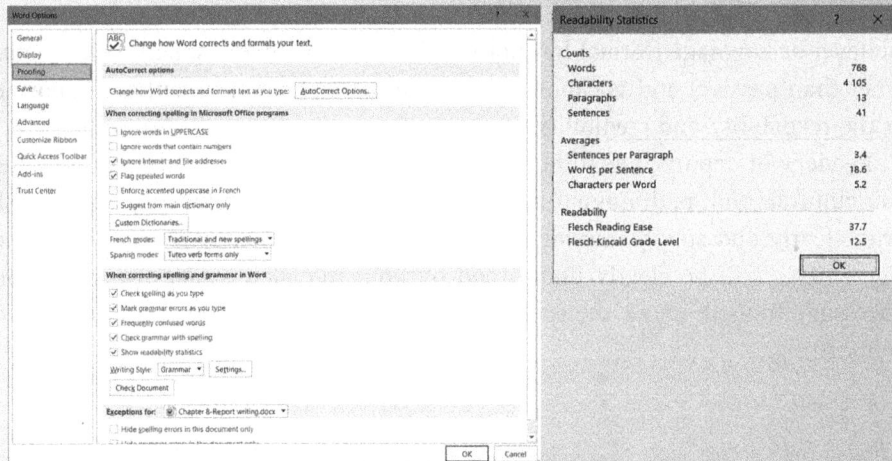

Figure 8.2 Using readability statistics in Microsoft® Word™

You can also set your computer to automatically correct language use. It is recommended you set the language option to 'English (South Africa)'. This will influence the spellcheck and grammar options. South Africa follows UK spelling (eg 'colour'), not US spelling (eg 'color') which is the default of Microsoft®.

Writing in a formal style, but not too formal

Depending on your audience, a clear, formal style is best. However, this does not imply that your style should be so formal that it becomes unreadable and too technical. For examples of formal and informal writing, refer to chapters 1 and 3.

Writing in an impersonal, active style

In some professions, such as engineering, a formal report or thesis must be written in an impersonal style. This means that you would not use the pronouns 'I', 'we' or 'you'. Rather, stress the facts, conclusions and recommendations. You have two choices, namely:

1. an impersonal active style:

> *The writer*　　　　*prepared*　　　　*the report.*
> *(actor)*　　　　　*(action)*　　　　*(acted on)*
> *The writer hypothesises that ...*

2. an impersonal passive style:

> *The report*　　　　*was prepared*　　　　*by the writer.*
> *(acted on)*　　　　*(action)*　　　　*(actor)*
> *It was hypothesised that ...*

However, in fields such as social science and many businesses, it is becoming more and more common to use the pronoun 'we' in reports and dissertations when referring to the company or organisation. It is seen as part of taking responsibility for the actions and views expressed and locating yourself within the research process.

Writing in a concrete style

Give facts and figures in your reports and theses. Avoid vague words such as 'frequently', 'regularly', 'often' or 'many' when exact details are called for. Instead, give exact figures or percentages. Stress precise action in your recommendations, and use specific words. Look at the following examples:

℮9

✗ Instead of writing	✓ Write
Frequently	Every day at 10h00
Often	90% of the time
Many	10 out of 12 people
The bridge is very high.	The bridge is 200 m above the river.
Sufficient data was collected.	Data from three surveys of 100 data points each was collected.
A minimum error	An error of 2%

℮9

Generic	Less generic	More specific
Four-door sedan motorcar	Petrol-driven four-door sedan	Mazda 626 four-door manual sedan with front-wheel drive

8.3 Types of reports

As the purpose of writing a report varies, your approach to writing your specific type of report should be tailored to its purpose. The different types of reports you may be required to write can be divided into two categories:

1. **Informative reports:** Some reports, for example interim reports or reports on visits to factories, may be purely informative. They simply give the facts of the situation. Informative reports include scientific research reports, technical reports and progress or interim reports.

2. **Evaluative reports:** Other reports include facts and evaluation of these facts, with recommendations for action. Evaluative reports include investigation, feasibility and summary reports.

Write the sections of informative reports

Informative reports, such as scientific reports on experimental work, stress facts. They are written in a neutral style with the aim of informing a reader. For example, if you report monthly on the progress of a project, this progress or interim report will give the facts, backed up with tables and figures such as line graphs, to show how the project has progressed. In this type of report, you would use some or most of the features listed below. Subsequent reports would only detail new or modified information, reporting on new or changed methodologies, experimental results and any conclusions.

An informative report consists of the following sections:

- **Preliminary pages (with page numbers indicated by Roman numerals: i, ii, iii, ix, etc):**
  - Title page
  - Terms of reference (the instructions or brief given by your manager or client)
  - Summary (one page or up to 10% of the full page count)
  - Table of contents
  - List of illustrations (tables and figures that occur in the body of the report)
  - Glossary (terms your reader might not know)
  - List of symbols (also known as 'Nomenclature')
  - List of abbreviations

- **Main body (with page numbering indicated by Arabic numerals: 1, 2, 3, etc):**
  - Introduction (covering the motivation for the scientific pursuit, its purpose and the definition of the problem)
  - Theory relevant to the topic (the scientific basis or established fact of the subject matter as well as the background information necessary to understand the research or report)
  - Literature review (previous work done by other scholars on the subject matter)
  - Methodology (a description of the approach that was used)
  - Findings/Results (an objective delivery of facts and figures)
  - Discussion of findings
  - Conclusions (drawn from the findings and the discussion)
  - Recommendations for further research

- **Additional sections (but carrying importance):**
  - Glossary (if not given within the preliminary section)
  - List of references
  - Bibliography
  - Appendices

Technical reports

A technical report is one type of informative report. If you were asked to visit a site or a factory, you would concentrate on describing exactly what you saw. You could back up your descriptions and statements with photographs. You could also use diagrams and sketches.

Your technical report would include all the normal sections of a report, as described above, as well as various additional features, namely:

- the use of technical terms that lay readers would not understand
- detailed mathematical calculations
- technical diagrams
- a variety of tables and figures
- technical descriptions
- a reference list
- detailed appendices.

Write the sections of evaluative reports

While informative reports stress the facts, evaluative reports stress the implications to be drawn from the facts. Evaluative reports therefore include facts and an evaluation of these facts, with recommendations for action. In these reports you rely much more on a set of criteria to help you draw appropriate conclusions from the results you have gathered. As mentioned before, evaluative reports include investigation, feasibility and summary reports.

The sections for most evaluative reports are as follows:

- Title page
- Terms of reference (instructions or brief given by your manager or client; this may also fall within the introduction)
- Summary (one page or up to 10% of the full page count)
- Table of contents
- List of illustrations (tables and figures that occur in the body of the report)
- Glossary (terms your reader may not know)
- List of symbols (also known as 'Nomenclature')
- Introduction (covering the motivation for the investigation, purposes of the project, definition of the problem and, in feasibility reports, criteria)
- Procedure used to gather information (method of investigation; this may also fall within the introduction)
- Findings (an objective delivery of facts and figures)
- Discussion of findings (optional)
- Conclusions (drawn from the findings and the discussion; and, for feasibility reports, from the criteria)
- Recommendations (suggested future actions arising from the conclusions)
- Reference list
- Appendices

Investigation reports

In investigation reports, your terms of reference instruct you to investigate a problem and report back on your findings. The terms of reference also define for whom and for what reason the report is written; this information defines the shape of the report.

Feasibility reports

For a feasibility report, you are expected to report on whether or not a project is possible. You could also be asked to examine a range of options, conclude which option is the best according to a set of criteria and then recommend which option should be selected. You may be asked to apply a set of criteria when weighing up the findings and drawing conclusions. Examples of such criteria may be:
- the time scale needed for each option
- the cost of each option
- the effectiveness of each option in meeting the client's needs
- the availability of spare parts and services.

8.4 Letters of transmittal

Many reports have a letter or email of transmittal attached at the beginning. Its purpose is to introduce the report to the reader and establish goodwill. As it is correspondence, it is written in a more personal style, which helps the writer to establish the right tone before presenting the formal and factual report. Often reports are sent online, via email. In this case an email can serve as the letter of transmittal to introduce the attached document (which is normally in PDF format).

> It is advisable to send finalised attached documents in PDF format rather than Microsoft® Word™ format, as it means that no one is able to change or edit anything in the report.

Apart from generating goodwill, your letter or email of transmission could include details regarding:
- how your report **fulfils the expectations** of your reader, as expressed in the terms of reference
- your **main conclusions** and **recommendations**
- the **problems** you found during your investigation
- the **limitations** that were imposed on you, for example budgetary or time constraints
- how **helpful** any organisation, groups or individuals were
- the **personal insights** you gained from your investigation
- how **successful** or **unsuccessful** you think the study was
- any **further action** that you think is necessary.

8.5 Example of an evaluative report

What follows here are the sections of an actual report. Some of the findings have been abridged for convenience. Each section is discussed in detail, with notes pointing out relevant features or characteristics.

Preliminary pages

Title and title page

Your title should attract attention. A good title is like a short summary. It should cover the main ideas in the report and use key words that help the reader to concentrate on what the report contains. It should be printed in bold in a large font size.

e9

Report on communication issues that impact on foremen in Excalibur Construction (Pty) Ltd

Prepared for: ——————

Mr Geoff Naidoo

Managing Director

Excalibur Construction (Pty) Ltd

> *Give the name and title of the recipient. Give his or her position in the company.*

Prepared by: ——————

Ms Lyn Dewar

Consultant in Change and Development

> *State the name and title of the writer and his or her position.*

Key words: foremen, construction, contract managers, communication

April 20--

> *Submission date of report*

> *Use key words to help your reader find your report in an electronic database.*

Acknowledgements

Some reports include a short acknowledgement section at the beginning to thank people who have helped the writer. Some writers prefer to put this at the end of the preliminary section, or at the end of the report.

e9

ACKNOWLEDGEMENTS

The writer wishes to thank the following people for their encouragement and support during this research project:

Prof H Bosch

Mr J Ndube

The writer also owes a debt of gratitude to Excalibur Construction (Pty) Ltd for its financial support and for allowing her to conduct research there for two months.

The terms of reference or brief

The terms of reference are the instructions or brief given to the writer. They tell you what you are expected to do. Terms of reference should contain information regarding:

- who issued the instructions
- when these instructions were given
- why these instructions were given
- exactly what the writer is expected to do
- when the report has to be finished and handed in.

The instructions should be listed in point form, following a concise introduction. These instructions give you the essential guidelines for doing your research and then presenting your report. Vague or badly worded instructions will certainly lead to a poor report; generally, however, those briefing you will blame you for their incompetence. Ensure, therefore, that you negotiate your terms of reference until they are clear. Make sure that they are in writing, so that you can check them carefully. If you are instructed to do a feasibility report, make sure that you are given criteria to enable you to draw conclusions.

Sometimes you may wish to write a report without being instructed. If you do this, make sure that you identify clearly the purposes of your investigation and the purposes of your report in your introduction.

e9

i

TERMS OF REFERENCE

Note that Roman numbering is used for the preliminary pages.

In March 20--, Geoff Naidoo, Managing Director of Excalibur Construction (Pty) Ltd, initiated this intervention. The need for it arose as a result of outcomes from the team-building exercise held at Kromrivier in 20--, which was attended by directors and managers from all the branches.

Give the date when the report was requested. State who requested the report. Give a brief reason why the report was requested.

Mr Naidoo's specific instructions were the following:

1. Interview contracts managers and foremen in all branches of Excalibur Construction.

List the instructions given to you. These should be as complete as possible. Give the hand-in date for the report.

2. Establish, by means of these interviews, what the main communication issues and problems are among the foremen in Excalibur.

3. Compile a report detailing these problems.

4. Draw conclusions on the causes of any communication breakdowns reported.

5. Make recommendations for appropriate courses of action.

6. Submit the report in time for the directors to have read it before their board meeting in Cape Town on 15 April 20--.

The summary

The ability to summarise messages is a key ability in professional writing. The summary is the most widely read item in a report. Every report longer than eight typed pages should start with a summary, which should be so concise and clear that it can replace the original report for the busy reader.

A summary may include key illustrations and references may be cited in the summary. As it is often read as a single item independent of the full document or report, it must include sources and references as footnotes and not refer to the reference list in the full report.

Your summary should include:
- what the report is about (purpose and objectives taken from the terms of reference)
- the background to the investigation
- the main purpose of report
- a brief outline of the procedure
- the main findings (very briefly, as the emphasis is on the next two sections)
- the main conclusions
- the main recommendations.

Remember that a summary has flexibility, and you can change the order relative to the full-length report to suit the purpose and proposed readership. You can emphasise certain sections, such as conclusions and recommendations, and leave out others.

For different documents, different terms can be used to refer to a summary. For example, these terms include:
- **abstract**: used in academic documents such as conference papers; an abstract is often limited to 100–300 words
- **summary**: the most common expression
- **synopsis**: used for academic theses
- **executive summary**: commonly used in commerce.

The length of a summary
If you are summarising a long report, aim to reduce it to 5–10% of the length of the original. For example, a company submitting a tender document of 60 or more pages would submit a summary of four to six pages. Many companies and organisations, however, prefer one typed page, which is about 400 words. Always ask your readers what length they require.

The readability of a summary
Summaries must be highly readable. Use some, or all, of the following features to help your readers:
- Layout:
  - Subheadings
  - Bullet lists
  - Bold print for important statements
- Style:
  - Clear and simple language, as for the report
  - Short paragraphs
  - Average sentence length of 15–25 words
- Additional information:
  - Summary illustrations
  - Photographs
  - Exact figures

The procedure for writing a summary
The summary is written last, after completion of the report. It is a summary of the document; it is not an article on the topic of the report. Include some content for each section of the report in the summary. However, note that the summary will give different weighting to the sections from the full report. For example, 50% of the length of the summary may be dedicated to the conclusions and recommendations, as they are critical items. A summary may or may not include subheadings, graphics and tables.

e9

ii

SUMMARY

This report concerns communication issues that have emerged as areas for concern, as far as they specifically affect foremen in Excalibur.

Background to the investigation

The need for this intervention arose out of decisions taken at the team-building exercise at Kromrivier, held in 20––.

iii

At this event, directors and managers felt that, because the foremen are a powerful link in the Excalibur system, attention should be given to issues that seem to cause difficulty in delivering quality work on time. Communication was identified as the main problem.

Procedure used

The information for this report was gathered by means of private interviews with foremen and small-group interviews with contract managers in the Western and Eastern Cape offices of Excalibur.

Please note that the main purpose of this report is to examine communication issues that impact on foremen. Other areas for concern in the company arose during the interviews, but these were not recorded and have not been included in the report. The omission of other issues is in keeping with the specific brief given by Geoff Naidoo.

Results of the investigation

The findings revealed systems and structures that operate on sites, and between sites and offices. In addition, the variety of styles, backgrounds and experience among foremen and contract managers which are part of the systems were analysed.

Conclusions

From the results the following conclusions were reached. Flexibility within the systems and structures of Excalibur was found to be essential. However, the findings showed that there is inadequate orientation to work and events, and a lack of well-formulated systems for site management. In addition, foremen's meetings are not held frequently enough, which contributes to the inadequate flow of information.

Thus, the report concludes that technical and managerial skills are lacking in the company. This is the reason why Excalibur is not able to maintain its competitive edge.

→

Recommendations

The recommendations for action to be taken to upgrade the systems and communication structures in Excalibur Construction are that the company should:

- ensure that the experience of foremen and contract managers is used to full advantage in the company
- set up appropriate decision-making systems and support structures to ensure good communication
- run courses to train staff to be creative and flexible in their approach to their work
- run courses in technical and managerial skills.

Table of contents

A table of contents (also abbreviated as ToC) is a list of the main headings and subheadings in your report, as well as the page numbers on which these sections start.

Do not create a table of contents yourself; rather have your word-processing software create it automatically from the headings, subheadings and page numbers in your report. Here it is important to use a template and built-in headings so that the table of contents can be automatically created and updated (see Chapter 2 for details on how to do this in Microsoft® Word™). Remember to set up your template – or choose one from your word processor or off the Internet – so that it gives you the right sequence of headings and numbering. When you need to change a heading or page number, do so in the report and then update the table of contents field accordingly. All changes will be made instantly.

In the table of contents, each heading will carry the corresponding decimal number and give the page number it falls on. Record the headings in your text down to the third level. Different establishments choose the number of levels of headings to be used in their documents and reflected in the table of contents. A common choice for long documents is three or four levels in the text but only two levels in the table of contents. Short documents may reflect all levels in the table of contents. The headings should use the same wording as in your report, and be in the same font as in the report. For page numbers, set up your template to number the preliminary pages with Roman numerals (i, ii, iii, iv etc) and the balance of the document with Arabic numerals (1, 2, 3, 4 etc). It will then appear like this in your table of contents as well. There are many options for different heading levels, such as the style used in the example of the ToC on the next page.

Table of contents

Main headings should be written in capitals.

Include this section if appropriate.

The subsections are indented.

The subsections in this example are indented, but this is not a requirement. The template can be set to not indent any subsections

List of illustrations

A combination of tables and figures is called a list of illustrations. This serves as a list of all the illustrations in your report, with their titles and page numbers. It is not necessary to list illustrations if there are fewer than three. Divide your list of illustrations into figures and tables, and a list of equations, if applicable. If you have tables only, this section would be called a 'list of tables'; likewise, if you only have figures, the heading is 'list of figures', etc. Ensure the titles and captions are descriptive, as shown in the example.

The list of illustrations should be created by using a template, so that it can be automated. For detail as to how to do this, see Chapter 2.

_e9_

> List your tables separately from your figures.

> The term 'figure' covers all illustrations except tables.

The glossary

This is a special dictionary for your report. It will include technical terms but also regular terms which are used to convey a certain meaning in your report. Glossaries are becoming essential, as more documents are read globally and by readers for whom English is not a first language or who do not have knowledge of the technical language of the subject matter or company. Words should be listed in alphabetical order, as shown in the example below. Write simple definitions for the terms – use language that the readers will understand. If necessary, give examples.

_e9_

vii
GLOSSARY

Autocratic leadership:	This type of leadership does not allow subordinates any say in how a company is run.
Benign paternalism:	This approach to leadership implies that the leader directs others, acting as if he or she were a caring parent.
BIFSA:	Building Industries Federation of South Africa

List of Symbols or acronyms

If you have used any symbols in your report that have specific meanings, list and define them. If necessary, give examples. List all your acronyms (groups of initial letters of words, for example CEO) and show what they stand for. Note that the plural of an acronym takes only an 's', not an apostrophe and an 's'. For example, BMWs is the correct form of the plural, while BMW's is incorrect.

Body of the report

The introduction

The introduction prepares your reader for the rest of the report. It sets the scene so that your reader:

- knows why the report was written
- understands the problems investigated
- knows the purposes of your report
- understands how you have organised your report.

Note that the summary and the introduction are not the same. A summary is a reduced version of the whole report. Your introduction, on the other hand, gives background information that leads into the main report. Your background information tells the reader why the report is necessary.

Follow these guidelines for structuring an effective introduction:

- Use numbered subheadings. These help your reader to follow the flow of information quickly.
- You may include a subsection *Purposes of the investigation* (for example to describe, analyse, compare). When you word this section, remember that it is not the report that has undertaken the investigation – you have!

eg

Do not write:

   This report investigates ... X

   This report analyses ... X

Instead, write:

   This report concerns an investigation ...

   This report records an experiment ...

- You may include a subsection *Procedure used to gather information* in your introduction. Describe your procedure in broad terms in the introduction and then expand on it in a separate section.
- It is not mandatory to include literature review and/or theory sections in the introduction, but this may be required for scientific reports.

e9

1

1. INTRODUCTION

1.1 Subject of and Motivation for Report

This report describes the communication issues that have emerged as areas for concern as far as they specifically affect the foremen in Excalibur. It is believed that communication problems are the reason Excalibur Construction is not able to maintain a competitive edge.

Remember to use Arabic numerals for the pages from here onwards.

The first sentence states what the report is about.

1.2 Background to Investigation

In 20-- a team-building exercise was held at Kromrivier, Eastern Cape, attended by directors and managers ...

The background to the report sets the scene for the reader.

1.3 Objectives of Report

The objectives of this report are therefore to:
- describe communication issues ...
- draw conclusions on the extent to which the communication issues that surfaced ...
- recommend strategies for further action.

The objectives deal with the reasons for writing the report.

2

Page numbers are given as from the original document but are not sequential as the pages of the document are not all printed.

1.4 Limitations and Scope of Investigation

Although other issues emerged during the interviews, the focus of this investigation is limited to matters that affect the role and functions of the foremen only. For the most part, the issues that emerged are common to all branches of the company. Where there are marked differences between the regions, these have been noted.

Limitations tell the reader what factors influenced the report, eg time, cost, etc. The scope of the report gives the boundaries of the report: what it covers and does not cover.

1.5 Plan of Development

The report begins with a brief description of the methods of investigation before describing the current contextual factors for the building industry in South Africa. It then focuses on the systematic factors within Excalibur that have a bearing on the investigation. Attention is then paid to specific communication events and issues that influence the role and functions of foremen. Conclusions are then drawn on the basis of these findings and, finally, recommendations are made based on these conclusions.

The plan of development tells the reader how you have organised your report. It is an important section, especially if you have a complex structure in your report. It is also important if you have organised your report in an unusual way.

Method of investigation

The introduction usually has a paragraph describing the method followed in the investigation. However, if the content on the method of investigation is lengthy, it might warrant a separate section, as illustrated in the following example. This section can also be called *Methodology, materials and methods* or *Research approach*.

Divide this section into numbered subheadings. Describe in detail how you gathered your information or set up experimental apparatus, where relevant. Take care to record exactly how you gathered your information. This section is very useful to future researchers.

Describing how the material in the findings was accessed gives credibility to the work; however, the sources must not dictate the presentation of the findings. You may interview a number of people and describe them in the methodology (it may or may not be appropriate to give their details) but, thereafter, you should not focus on them, but rather on the information they gave.

For some work concerning people, ethical approval according to the professional code of ethics of the field of study must be obtained before the research can be undertaken. Confidentiality of sources is required by many organisations.

e9

3

2.   METHOD OF INVESTIGATION

2.1 Interviews with Foremen

Hour-long private interviews were held with 12 foremen in Cape Town and 8 foremen in Port Elizabeth and East London. These interviews were semi-structured. A copy of the focus questions appears in Appendix A.

The numbers one to nine are written as words in text, and from 10 up the numbers are written as digits. However, where more than one number – some under 10 and some above 10 – occur close to each other, as in this case, all are written as digits.

2.2 Interviews with Contracts Managers

Contracts managers in Cape Town (three) and Port Elizabeth (five) were interviewed as two separate focus groups. A copy of the questions addressed appears in Appendix B. The interviewees were invited to use English or their home language, whichever they felt more comfortable using.

Findings

This section covers the factual section of your report. It records the results of your investigation or describes your factual progress if you are writing an interim report. While the facts or findings may come from different sources, such as questionnaires or interviews, journals, books and/or websites, this section is not organised according to these sources. Sources are acknowledged through citation and referencing, but are unimportant to the arrangement of the data. The data is arranged according to the objectives of the report and topics of factual material.

Findings or results sections must be highly readable. To ensure that your findings are easy to read, use features such as:

- a multiple-decimal **numbering system**
- **clear, specific headings** to prepare your reader for what follows – use headings of more than one word that give useful information about the facts to follow, and avoid headings that contain the word 'findings' or 'results'
- **bulleted lists** to attract attention – preferably with not more than six items
- **well-integrated illustrations** such as tables, line graphs, bar graphs and pie charts.

Achieving coherence in your findings

Make sure that you present your facts in a clear and logical order. Help your reader by having an opening paragraph that explains how you have organised your facts. Each section of factual information should lead logically to the next. Use a numbering system that emphasises the coherent relationship of headings to one another.

If necessary, write a one-sentence link between one section and another. For example: 'This section has covered the principles of strategic environmental assessment (SEA) in South Africa. Section 4 covers the key elements of an SEA process.'

Integrating illustrations

Make sure that you integrate your illustrations into your findings. Introduce each illustration before you present it to the reader for examination. Tell the reader what to expect, and then present the illustration. Use highlighting and arrows to show the reader where to look. Do not assume that your reader will understand your illustration at first glance. Once your reader has seen the illustration, analyse it. Explain to the reader how to interpret it.

Make sure that every illustration has a very clear title. The title of a table may be placed above the table, but increasingly the trend is to place it below the table. Figure titles are given below figures. Provide a descriptive caption, particularly if a source needs to be referenced. Write the caption separately from the title you insert – in this way it will not be automatically drawn into the list of illustrations.

For more information on templates for illustrations and graphics, see Chapter 10.

Discussion of findings/results (optional)

In this optional section, you analyse the significance of your findings. It may be combined with the results section or given separately. For example, the findings section may principally consist of tables and diagrams with brief textual references. This discussion section would then expand on the tables and diagrams. This section should lead your reader into the conclusion, where you will express your views on the facts that you have given, interpret them and show their significance.

The example that follows is the findings section from the sample report. The findings, conclusions and recommendations have been abridged for practical reasons. Thus the sections do not reflect the full table of contents – sections 4 and 5 are not included here.

e9

13

6.   COMMUNICATION ISSUES AND EVENTS THAT AFFECT FOREMEN IN EXCALIBUR

6.1   Induction into the Company

Induction of new foremen into the company is reported to be inconsistent. Foremen who have recently been appointed report very different experiences. These experiences relate to being inducted to the company as an employee, as well as being inducted to the daily work on site both through theoretical input and practical tuition.

> *Note the clear, specific heading. Headings used in the findings section of a report should be neutral and factual.*

6.1.1   *Induction as an employee*

Induction to the company by Mr Geoff Naidoo – in the form of extensive theoretical and historical background, and formal introduction to colleagues in the office – was given to 30% of the sample (six foremen). The theoretical input did not include receiving the company foremen's manual. Of the sample, 10% (two foremen) described being given only practical time to be on site before being given a site of their own, in addition to the company induction. This group was in Cape Town.

> *Numbering systems can go to 4 places (eg 1.2.5.4) but it is not recommended. Preferably number your headings to the third level, as shown here. If you wish to subdivide further, use (a), (b), (c), etc. Fifth-level subdivisions should have Roman numerals: (i), (ii), (iii), etc.*

14

6.1.2   *Induction to site*

Findings in the Eastern Cape were that no guided experience in practical work is given and that there is no clear, collective system for completion of tasks (60% of the sample, or 12 foremen).

> *The numbered subheadings help to guide the reader down the page.*

Further findings in this region were that no new recruits (40% of the full sample) were given any form of induction.

Figure 1 below sums up the foremen's experience of induction into the company. The pie chart shows three categories:

1.   Formal induction only (30%)

2.   Mentoring by another foreman in addition to induction (10%)

3.   No induction (60%)

→

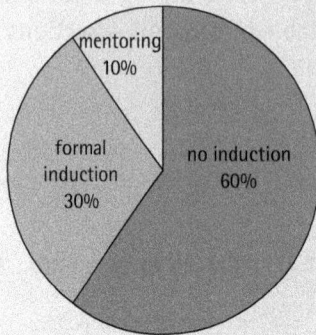

When you prepare a pie chart, start at 12 o'clock. Move clockwise, starting with the largest slice. Note that the percentages have been included.

Use a range of illustrations such as tables, pie charts, bar graphs and diagrams. Always integrate your illustrations into your text, as described.

Figure 1 Procedures for induction of foremen into the company

This figure illustrates that 60% of newly appointed foremen were ...

15

6.2   Contact between Contracts Managers and Foremen

6.2.1   *Verbal and face-to-face contact*

Daily contact is maintained by telephone ...

Site visits by the contracts manager are not always daily ...

Often matters discussed at these times are immediate and specific. Descriptions of these topics were as ...

6.2.2   *Written communication*

Site diaries, requisition books and site whiteboards are to be updated on a daily basis. Findings for these items were that updating happens at random: after a few days or weekly. Much depends on ...

Minutes taken at site meetings are given to foremen. Minutes were recorded as coming no earlier than 10 days after the meeting and up to a month late.

16

6.3   Pre-start Meetings

Meetings prior to the start of a new contract vary in content and purpose. At these meetings the contracts manager hands over the plans and gives the location of the site ...

In 5% of these meetings an opportunity is used to carefully orientate the foremen to the possible idiosyncrasies of the job: ... what the boundaries of their authority are.

Note the use of factual language here.

Without exception, foremen saw this omission as a critical cause of stress. Those who do ...

Of the foremen, 75% stated that this contributes to a feeling of safety, personal self-esteem and a sense of being part of a meaningful professional relationship.

6.4   Post-completion Meetings

Of the sample, 100% stated that these meetings do not take place. Comments described the need for meetings to provide valuable learning opportunities and to turn meetings into a way of avoiding mistakes in the future.

→

Figure 2 shows the level of foremen's satisfaction with four types of meetings. Their level of satisfaction is expressed as a percentage of total satisfaction.

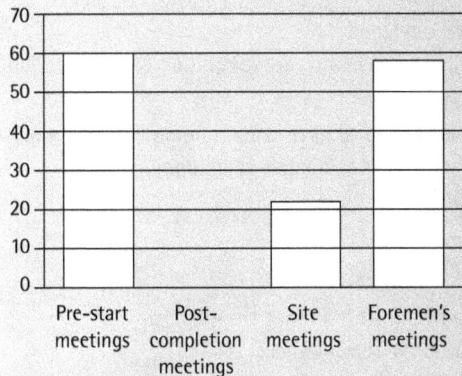

Figure 2 Summary of levels of satisfaction expressed at four types of meeting

Note that the level of satisfaction at site meetings is low. Only 22% ...

17

6.5   Site Management

6.5.1 *Subcontractors and their labour*

Some subcontractors fail to appoint a supervisor of their labour on site. When this happens, a foreman finds himself ...

6.5.2 *Excalibur labour and contract labour*

The way foremen described their interactions with site labour varied widely. Some have daily pre-start meetings and/or a pre-start meeting at the start of the contract to give them a broad overview of the duration of the work ...

Some nominate a charge hand. Others allow their labour to choose their own. Some appoint a charge hand for the duration of that contract, after which ...

Descriptions (see Appendix A) indicated that having a charge hand on site is arbitrary.

6.5.3 *Site office management*

It has already been mentioned in 6.2.2 above that there are inconsistencies in the documentation systems used on site.

> *In order to ensure that the section is highly readable, use a range of reading aids, such as numbered headings and subheadings, white space and bullet lists where necessary.*

18

6.6   Foremen's Meetings

Despite the fact that meetings have been scheduled over time in the Cape Town office, they are not held regularly ...

When they were held, the following facts were evident:

- The meetings do not have a pre-meeting, circulated agenda. As a result, the purpose of the meeting ...

Of the sample, 25% have only had experience on small sites and all these foremen revealed anxiety about not being able to cope if they were suddenly transferred to a bigger site.

Short paragraphs and continued use of white space result in easy readability.

It also emerged that it was not only foremen who needed training, but charge hands too. These also needed to have a clearer definition of their role on site.

With the growing demands on them, foremen also need to have skills training in leadership. Examples are participation in meetings, being part of a team and understanding the full meaning of being a critical link in the Excalibur chain.

...

6.9   Performance Appraisals

There are noteworthy and critical skills for appraising staff so that the exercise becomes not only a mutual opportunity for assessing performance ...

Conclusions

Conclusions are the implications drawn from the facts. They are the insights gained from the investigations. Most of all, they are the interpretation or evaluation of the findings according to the objectives. Therefore, conclusions do not end a report. The general use of the word 'conclusion' to mean 'ending' does not apply here. Rather, the interpretation of results, leading to conclusions, prepares the reader for your recommendations. You might, for example, conclude that one course of action is more likely to be effective than another. At this stage no new information must be added. Also note that the style here is more emotive; it is more related to opinion writing than to factual writing.

Criteria as a means to draw conclusions

If you are weighing up the effectiveness of a range of equipment for a particular job, for example, you could weigh up each item against a set of criteria. You then conclude which item of equipment best meets your needs.

Logical reasoning

Make sure that you take your reader through clear, logical steps. Stress the implications for your reader at every stage. Make sure that you show your reader how each line of argument is related to and follows from another. Use connecting words such as 'but', 'however', 'although' and 'nevertheless' to guide your arguments. Make sure that you do not introduce any new ideas at this stage – all conclusions must be drawn from facts in the report.

Arrange your conclusions

Use numbered subheadings for your conclusions. Head each conclusion with a subheading that describes that conclusion. Where possible, list your conclusions in order of importance, or according to your set of criteria.

e9

19

7. CONCLUSIONS

Based on the foregoing information, the following ————
conclusions have been drawn.

Note the use of a linking phrase at the beginning of this sentence.

7.1 Flexibility within Systems and Structures Essential

Flexibility is a virtue in any organisation, particularly when the context keeps changing. However, this needs to be present in direct and overt proportion to the quantity and quality of communication that occurs. In the absence of information and clear systems and structures, freedom quickly translates into isolation and fragmentation and an absence of total meaning in the work people do.

Because slavish attention to systems can crush initiative and creativity, it is critical to combine clear, meaningful boundaries within which people can work, while simultaneously making flexibility not only possible but desirable.

Note the use of numbered subheadings. Each subheading should state the main conclusion for that subsection.

...

21

7.6 Orientation to Work and Events Lacking

In the absence of clear orientation and boundaries relating to authority and work expectations, such as induction into the company ...

23

Given that work associations constantly change, there is a ——
need to constantly adapt to individual idiosyncrasies and styles. This can result in miscommunication, which increases stress and can lead to costly mismanagement of time and labour.

The obvious anxiety surrounding the interviews for this report bears testimony to the importance of informing staff not only of the fact that events are to take place, but also the reason for them.

Connecting words such as 'because', 'therefore', 'given', 'moreover', etc help to build your argument. On the other hand, connecting words such as 'but', 'however' and 'although' indicate changes in the flow of your argument.

7.7 Inadequate Systems for Site Management

Given that much depends on the style of the foreman, his training and the nature and complexity of the site, it is clear that systems for managing the site tend to be ad hoc and not overtly linked to agreed best practices.

The interviews revealed a wide range of ideas and systems, not only between branches, but within branches.

Lack of time is a constraint. Therefore, to increase effectiveness and efficiency on site and between site and office ... basic structures need to be agreed upon ... useful information is likely to fall through the cracks.

→

22

7.8 Insufficient Foremen's Meetings

A valuable opportunity is lost for building relationships, celebrating wins, learning from mistakes ... because meetings are held so infrequently.

Individually, foremen have a wealth of experience. Without a forum for pooling that, their expertise lives and dies with them.

It may well be that the perceived lack of participation may be due to a lack of experience in being in meetings, a lack of maturity and a sense of wanting to continue to 'do things my own way'...

7.9 Poor Flow of Information

No one has control over the meaning that individuals ascribe to the information they receive; therefore it is essential that information be as unambiguous and timely as possible. Moreover, in the absence of information, people make up their own. It becomes their 'truth' and is often unshakable ... Furthermore, in the absence of trustworthy and regular official information, the grapevine flourishes.

Therefore, it cannot be stressed enough that attention needs to be given to ... with the same purpose: to support and sustain life functions.

Recommendations

Your recommendations follow the terms of reference. They show how the purposes of the investigation can be met. They stress the exact action to be taken as a result of your findings and conclusions.

e9

23

8. RECOMMENDATIONS

On the basis of the above conclusions, the following recommendations are made:

8.1 Establish Basic Systems

Determine basic systems and structures for Excalibur in respect of:

- site management
- orientation to work – inductions, pre-site meetings
- information flow – office notice boards, whiteboard on site
- appointment of a personnel officer.

Appoint task teams to explore each of these and then present them to the rest of the decision makers ...

> Note the use of action headings with an imperative at the beginning of each heading. These headings are used to attract the reader's attention. The imperative should focus on the action.

8.2 Start Uniform Induction Process

Institute a formal and uniform induction process into the company for new recruits.

...

→

25

8.6 Clarify Foremen's Function and Role

Establish clear boundaries and expectations governing the foremen's function and role. Hold regular and structured foremen's meetings.

8.7 Provide Training Workshops

Consider separate two-day training workshops for foremen and contracts managers, at which there will be an opportunity to explore general and specific issues surrounding work, while also building effective professional relationships.

8.8 Ensure Uniform Performance Appraisals

Ensure that performance appraisals are conducted uniformly with purpose, structure and regularity.

End matter

References and/or bibliography

For details on how to manage referencing, see Chapter 12.

Appendices

Your appendices contain extra, detailed information that is too complex to be placed in your report. Make sure that you refer in your report to the material in the appendices. However, very few readers are likely to read appendices. Make sure, therefore, that you place your important items in the main sections of the report. Use letters, for example Appendix A, B and C, to distinguish your appendices from the rest of your report.

Examples of material which would be included in the appendices are:
- computer printouts that would make your report too bulky
- complex and detailed tables
- detailed mathematical calculations, especially intermediate calculations
- examples of questionnaires
- illustrations such as full-page photographs and diagrams
- examples of contract letters, letters of appointment and other correspondence
- transcriptions of recorded dialogue
- detailed plans.

e9

APPENDIX A: GUIDELINES FOR INTERVIEWS WITH EXCALIBUR FOREMEN

1. Orientation: My role (as the interviewer), the context of these interviews and the link with Excalibur's five-year plan

2. Perception concerning Excalibur's culture and value system

3. Perceptions about the foremen's work function:
    - servicing internal and external 'clients'
    - being a link in the Excalibur chain
    - projecting the Excalibur image
    - administering people, the site and plant

4. Perceptions about how the foremen are perceived by management

5. Perceptions about big-picture issues or consequences:
    - productivity cycles
    - cash flow
    - waste and inefficiency

6. Perceived barriers to effective/efficient performance:
    - flow of information
    - discipline
    - cross-cultural issues
    - contextual factors: social, political
    - subcontractors

7. Suggestions for improvement in interpersonal skills needed by foremen

Besides for the appendices themselves, make sure you do the following:
- Summarise detailed tables and other detailed results that you have placed in your appendices. Place these summaries in your report where they are more likely to be read.
- Refer to your appendices in your report. Explain their significance to your readers and tell your readers where to look in the appendices to find important information.

✓

Checklist for a well-organised report

When you write a report, use the following checklist to ensure that your report is organised as suggested in this chapter:

- Keep to the facts in the findings.
- Remain impartial in the presentation of the facts.
- Give enough facts that can be confirmed and are therefore convincing.
- Show the difference between fact and opinion, keeping in mind that other people's opinions will be presented as facts if you place them in the findings.
- Use a formal, referential style.
- Eliminate subjective wording from the findings.
- Draw conclusions that meet the objectives and are based on the facts given in the results.
- Link the sentences with appropriate connectors to conclude the argument clearly.
- Use imperative (action) language in the recommendations.
- Reference all sources cited.
- Include supporting documentation in the appendices.

9   Presentation skills

There are many options for disseminating information – from email to cloud sharing, from Skype conference calls to creating video clips. And yet, most professionals, businesspeople and academic practitioners still prefer to interact with a presenter in person, in real time.

Giving presentations is an activity which is at the core of most professional jobs, and it can be critical to advancing your career. Yet, many of us are nervous about speaking to colleagues and clients or to the public. In trying to overcome their nerves, some presenters use incorrect methods, such as writing out the entire speech and reading it to the audience or learning it by heart.

This chapter will cover the skills and methods required in order to give an effective presentation:

- In preparation for the presentation, you need to be able to:
  - ▶ analyse the audience
  - ▶ select and organise information
  - ▶ support the speech by writing out key phrases only
  - ▶ plan paired and group presentations
  - ▶ practise, practise, practise.
- During the presentation, you need to be able to:
  - ▶ maintain a positive attitude
  - ▶ establish a rapport with the audience and gain credibility as a speaker
  - ▶ speak with expression and projection
  - ▶ display appropriate non-verbal cues such as posture and gestures
  - ▶ handle visual aids and presentation software and hardware
  - ▶ dress appropriately.
- At the end of the presentation, you need to be able to:
  - ▶ handle the question-and-answer (Q&A) session
  - ▶ close within the time allocated
  - ▶ troubleshoot to overcome barriers to giving effective presentations.

9.1 Before the presentation

Analyse the audience

Think about your audience. Find out everything you can about them. Attempt to identify with the audience and consider what needs to be covered in order for them to understand your objectives. Having this knowledge will enable you to select the correct vocabulary, the correct examples and the appropriate approach to meet the audience's needs and expectations. To do this, consider the following about your audience:

- What is the extent of their knowledge of the topic?
- What is their attitude towards the topic?
- What are their needs? Why will they be listening?
- What are their backgrounds (eg education, norms and values)?

Select and organise information

Having analysed your audience and their needs carefully, you can select and organise the information and so plan the talk to meet those needs.

There are **four steps** you must go through when planning your talk:

1. Consider your topic and the reason for covering it.
2. Jot down ideas or themes from your topic.
3. Select information carefully and plan the body of the talk.
4. Once you have done a mind map of the body of the talk, plan the introduction and conclusion.

Step 1: Consider your topic and the reason for covering it

If you do not know enough about the subject, first read about the topic to broaden your knowledge. Every talk should have some objective as its outcome. There are always definite, tangible outcomes in a successful presentation, even if only to inform people in order to add to or change their point of view. Given your topic and audience, ask yourself, 'What do I want my audience to think or do?' By answering this question you will arrive at the reason for your talk. At the end of your talk, the audience must know why they were listening to you and what they should do with the information you have given them. This purpose statement is the only sentence you should write out in full for your talk. The rest of the content must be planned through mind maps and visuals.

Step 2: Jot down ideas or themes from your topic

Brainstorm and jot down all the ideas you have about the topic – perhaps your knowledge, perhaps research you have undertaken. Do not restrict your ideas at this stage. You might be tempted to censor an idea by thinking that it is on the fringes of your topic or not relevant, but write it down nevertheless. It could turn out to be a major point when you start planning your talk.

Step 3: Select information carefully and plan the body of the talk

If you have a clear purpose and a definite audience in mind, it will be simple to select all the information (from your brainstormed list of ideas) that the audience will need to hear in order to persuade them of your point of view; that is, to achieve your purpose. If you are giving a five-minute presentation, for example, you will only be able to discuss about three major ideas from your brainstormed list.

Once you have selected the main ideas, do the following:
1. Under each of these main topics, write down supporting examples and points.
2. Choose a major point or two that you wish to illustrate with a visual.
3. Plan the body of the presentation, taking into account unity, coherence and emphasis, as discussed below.

As explained in Chapter 1, there are three major principles you must bear in mind when delivering any message, whether it is oral or written. They are unity, coherence and emphasis.

Unity

Unity means that the whole message deals with a single topic and there are no unrelated ideas in your talk. Check this by making sure that your major points relate to your objective. Your topic will then be unified. Next, check that the supporting ideas under each major point correctly expand that point and relate specifically to it. If they do, the ideas and major points will be unified.

Coherence

Coherence refers to the logical development of ideas. When you practise your talk out loud, practise using transition words and phrases to help the audience follow your ideas and your thinking. Transitions are words or phrases that connect one major section to the next. For example, you might say, 'Two major ideas are associated with this concept. The first one I have mentioned is the most important. On the other hand ...' or 'Consequently ...' or 'As a result of this ...' See the list of transitional words and phrases on page 12 in Chapter 1 – this list also applies to a spoken delivery.

The three squares in Figure 9.1 represent the main points in the body of a talk. The arrows in the figure point both ways. This illustrates that the transition should indicate what has gone before and suggest what comes next.

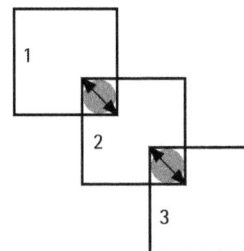

Figure 9.1 The structure of a coherent presentation

Emphasis

This is the principle most often misused. Emphasis means that the most important points are stressed in various ways. You could mention them first, and you would certainly emphasise them in your conclusion and by means of the transitions that you use; for example, 'The major point I wish to make is ...'

However, the most important form of emphasis is achieved by the careful use of visual aids. Your whole talk should be planned around how you would use visual aids to enhance your points. Sections you want to emphasise and that you want your audience to remember should be illustrated with a suitable graphic or image.

Step 4: Plan the introduction and conclusion

The introduction and conclusion are the sections of the talk where you make the most impact, so they need to be planned and prepared thoroughly.

Your **introduction** should include:

- a clear statement of purpose
- some background information on your topic
- an overview of your topic.

Do not begin with a joke. Unless you are a master of ceremonies in a situation where jokes are acceptable, they are nearly always out of place. Jokes do not necessarily relax an audience, as they usually create the wrong atmosphere, and you might alienate your audience. However, if you open with a story, image or quotation which is pertinent, interesting and funny, then at least those who do not find it amusing will still find it relevant.

Your **conclusion** should include:

- a clear link to your objectives
- a reinforcement of your major points.

End on a note of finality. There must be no new facts in the conclusion. Consider rounding off with a quotation or image that carries your message, but do not introduce a new theme. Do not end weakly by saying, 'Are there any questions?' That question does not have anything to do with your topic. Stop speaking. If you remain silent and wait for members of the audience to ask questions, you create far more impact. (See page xx for ways to deal with questions after your presentation.)

Support your speech with key phrases

Note cards with key phrases can be reassuring and may increase your self-confidence. Use them while they are of help; once you are more experienced as a presenter you will probably no longer need note cards. Guard against using slides with a lot of text as cue cards. These are not effective as visuals for your audience.

Many people are afraid that if they do not write out their whole talk they will forget what they have to say. This is a needless fear. You might be tempted to write out your whole talk and memorise it, but this is problematic, as written language differs from spoken language in various ways:

- Written and spoken sentences are different in many aspects. Written sentences are constructed in the passive voice more often than spoken sentences are and have a higher level of formality. For example, we often write '... and thus', but we never say it.
- Written sentences are often long and we often need to read the whole sentence before we can make sense of it. Sometimes we even need to re-read it. For example, a written sentence of more than 25 words is difficult to read – we often have to start rereading the sentence from the beginning before we have read to the end, as we cannot immediately grasp the meaning of the sentence. On the other hand, we are taught to speak in short phrases and therefore people battle to understand long spoken sentences.

If you work from a full written text and read it out loud, it will have a negative effect on your delivery. Table 9.1 lists the advantages of using key phrases rather than a full text.

Table 9.1 The advantages of using notes with key phrases only

Disadvantages of writing out the speech in full	Advantages of using key phrases
Your speech will be laboured, tedious and lacking in emphasis. This will make it difficult to listen to and understand, and the audience will become bored.	Your speech will be easy to listen to and follow. The audience will remain involved.
You will try to memorise your talk, or you will inevitably memorise some phrases or sentences. This will rob your speech of spontaneity.	Your speech will always sound spontaneous. You can moderate your delivery, vocabulary and pace.
If you forget what you need to say during your presentation, you will have to search through masses of text to find your place. It will be difficult to re-establish fluency and coherence, causing you to lose credibility with your audience – let alone losing confidence in yourself.	If you forget something, it will be easy to find your place by glancing at a few notes if you need to. It will also be easy to add a transition phrase and continue talking, without anyone realising you have forgotten anything.
Your concentration will be directed inward, on the paper and not on the ideas you are trying to convey. This means your pace will become quicker and your voice monotonous.	Your concentration will be directed outward. You will be focusing on ideas, not on trying to remember text. Variety, correct stress and enthusiasm will result. You will make an impact on your audience.

It is clearly much better to write out key phrases to assist you while you deliver your talk. Preparing your speech by writing out key phrases requires as much preparation time as writing out a speech in full, but it prevents the order and coherence of the presentation from being compromised and it enables you to retain flexibility in your responses to the audience.

For conference presentations, the same requirements apply as for other presentations: the presenter should select material appropriate to the time allocated and speak naturally. It is tempting for an academic to read the script of an academic paper, as it has been crafted with such precision. The result is that the presenter reads as fast as possible and renders the research even more difficult to follow.

Paired and group presentations

Teamwork, and thus paired and group presentations, are much more evident in the workplace these days. Collaboration on projects requires that the presentation be unified and coherent.

There are no rules about how to share a presentation between two or more speakers. However, each speaker should speak for approximately the same amount of time and the change-over of speakers should happen at points where there are logical breaks in your talk, to ensure the correct emphasis. A master of ceremonies (MC) speaker is one who introduces and closes the presentation, and they may function as the link between speakers.

Do not divide the presentation into many small sections, because the overall impression you create will be a jerky, poorly emphasised one. All the speakers must plan the sharing of the content to ensure that the audience's overall impression is of a coherent, well-linked, well-emphasised presentation.

Each section of your presentation must stand on its own as a complete unit. It should therefore have a sentence or two as an introduction, where you give an overview of what you are going to talk about.

Make sure that when you hand over to your partner or the next team speaker, you link your section coherently to what your partner will be saying. Your partner should follow the same procedure. For example, the second speaker, presenting the first major finding of the group report, might start his or her talk as follows:

e9

'You have heard [*name of speaker*] describe the methods we used to obtain our results. They led to our first major finding. I will deal with that. I will tell you how this result was inconclusive.'

This transition phrase links to the previous speaker, thereby maintaining coherency.

In the above example, the speaker states the purpose of the talk and gives an overview leading into the body of the talk. At the end of the section, the speaker might say:

℮9

'So, as you have heard, we had major problems getting conclusive evidence for our market research. And now [*name of next presenter*] will tell you what the consequences of this were for our clients.'

Summary of the main point

Coherent link to next speaker

The final speaker should conclude the group's presentation by summarising the contributions and linking them to the major objectives given in the first speaker's introduction. This ensures overall unity. If it is a report you are presenting, you end with the recommendations. Check that they develop from the major conclusions preceding the recommendations and that they achieve the objectives which were discussed at the beginning of your presentation. If it is a proposal, it will end with a strong justification for the proposal and a call to action.

Timing is of the essence in a paired or group presentation. Make sure that when you practise out loud, you present your ideas within the time allotted to you. Table 9.2 gives a plan as well as the suggested timing for a group of six speakers presenting a business proposal within 25–30 minutes.

Table 9.2 Possible plan for a group presentation for six speakers

Order of speakers	Section of presentation covered	Transition to the next speaker	Timing
Master of ceremonies (MC) or Speaker 1	The first speaker: • introduces him- or herself and the partner or team • gives the objectives of the talk, report or proposal • explains how the talk will be unpacked — who will cover what and why • gives any relevant information, eg limitations or housekeeping.	Hands over to the next speaker	Approximately three minutes

→

Order of speakers	Section of presentation covered	Transition to the next speaker	Timing
Speakers 2, 3 and 4	Each of these speakers: • delivers an introduction, stating the purpose or objective of his or her section • delivers his or her section of the talk, with pertinent visuals. Visuals and models must be used in application, not for the sake of theory.	• Makes reference to the previous speaker • Creates a coherent link to the next speaker • Hands over to the next speaker	Approximately five minutes per speaker
Speaker 5	This speaker delivers the: • main conclusions • recommendations, if applicable • justification, if applicable.	• Makes references to the previous speakers • Hands over to the next speaker	Approximately five minutes
Speaker 6 or MC	The final speaker: • refocuses on key issues • opens the question period. • thanks the audience and invites them to refreshments if applicable.	Makes references to previous speakers	Approximately two minutes

Practise, practise, practise

Using a few key phrases as support, you now need to practise your speech out loud. Practising your speech is very important, especially if you are nervous and if the outcome of your presentation is critical (eg a presentation of research at a conference as opposed to an informal speech telling your peers or colleagues about your research).

In order for a talk to be fluent, coherent and correctly timed, it needs to be verbalised prior to being presented to an audience. The reason for this is that we think about four or five times faster than we talk, and therefore it will always take longer to verbalise our ideas than to just run through them mentally. Practising out loud thus ensures that **your timing will be correct**. The first time you rehearse your talk out loud, you might take two or three times as long as the allotted time for your talk. Furthermore, by rehearsing the talk out loud, you will become more fluent and the correct vocabulary will come to mind more easily. You will also hear whether the points you are making are sequential. If not, you can easily adjust your talk to ensure that what you are saying is coherent – it is no problem to change the order of a few phrases or words on your note cards or on your computer.

Practise with your visual aids, as handling the hardware and software makes demands on time. Finally, use a smartphone or camera to film yourself. Play back the footage and observe how you come across, making allowances for the fact you are rehearsing a presentation to be given in person, not as a trained presenter on screen. However, it is likely you will find yourself presenting or being interviewed digitally at some point, for example via Skype, so it is advisable to have a sense of how you come across on this platform.

9.2   During the presentation

Maintain a positive attitude

Our thoughts and feelings influence our behaviour. If you are nervous about giving a presentation, what are you saying to yourself as you think about it? If you think to yourself, 'This is going to be awful, I hate standing up and giving a talk in front of people I don't know,' you are likely to present poorly. However, you can change those negative thoughts into positive ones and appear relaxed and confident. By working on using the body language of confidence, as described later in this chapter, you will gain confidence, as you will detect that your audience finds you credible.

Use positive self-talk, such as 'I have prepared my talk well. I have practised out loud and timed it, and I have put into effect all the skills discussed in this chapter. I may not be the world's best speaker at my first presentation, but my talk will be more than adequate.' With this realistic self-affirmation, you will increase your confidence and you will be able to talk about your subject convincingly. You will receive feedback, such as nods and smiles from the members of the audience, and you can then respond to that feedback. If you do not look at anyone, the only feedback will be from your inner dialogue, which will probably be negative and result in withdrawn behaviour.

Table 9.3 lists some common anxieties and the behaviour you need to adopt to overcome nervous tension and lack of confidence.

Table 9.3 Essential skills to develop self-confidence in presenting

Symptom of anxiety	Skills that you can use to deal with anxiety
A feeling of overall anxiety and a general lack of confidence; fear of appearing foolish; mentally undermining yourself	• Develop a positive attitude about the presentation. Our attitudes dictate our behaviour. We can change negative perceptions or thoughts into positive ones, and consequently our behaviour will appear confident.

→

Symptom of anxiety	Skills that you can use to deal with anxiety
Physical manifestations of nervousness, such as fidgeting, shaking knees, dry mouth, a hollow feeling in the stomach and not being able to make eye contact	• Relax areas of tension and breathe deeply. • Use the correct body language and non-verbal cues, such as direct eye contact, a composed stance and steady gestures. • Practise using your visual aids and handling equipment such as the clicker.
Fear of forgetting the content	• Use note cards with key phrases on them or informative visual aids to jog your memory. Do not write out full sentences and then read or try to memorise them. • Practise your speech several times before the presentation.
Fear of being ineffective or alienating the audience; fear that the audience might be bored or not understand what you are saying	• Analyse your audience and their needs carefully in order to plan and select your information to meet those needs. • Establish a rapport with your audience (as described in the next section).

Establish a rapport with the audience

There are several ways to establish a rapport with your audience. The most important approach is by doing a careful analysis of your audience. Carl Rogers, a noted psychologist, said that one of the major attributes of an excellent communicator is empathy; that is, the ability to put yourself in the shoes of your audience (Rogers, 1951). When they are listening to you, they should feel that you have really understood their problems or their point of view. If you can achieve this, they will be thinking things such as 'Yes, what I am hearing makes sense and could certainly convince me' or 'Hm, I don't agree with what is being said, but the speaker certainly understands why we think like that.'

The language you use – for example pronouns such as 'we' and 'you' – will underline your link with your audience. Your explanation of technical terms, if your audience is non-specialist, also shows your empathy and establishes a rapport, as does the amount of information you give them.

Another method of indicating your rapport with your audience is through the non-verbal cues you use. Non-verbal cues convey your feelings and emotions, so it is easy for your audience to pick up whether you are interested in them or not.

Is it important to get rid of your nervousness altogether? No. Remaining slightly nervous throughout your talk can be helpful, as adrenalin will contribute to your being lively and dynamic. An audience would far rather be addressed by an energised, albeit rather nervous, speaker than by a bored or tired one. (Remember: the members of the audience are all on your side; they are there to hear what you have to say.) If you can **channel your nervous energy positively**, it will enable you to:

- **concentrate** – think clearly and quickly about what you are saying and easily handle any mishaps that might occur. Remember that your audience does not mind if you make errors (because they are on your side), as long as you recover and carry on
- **engage** with your audience
- inject **vitality** and a sense of enjoyment and spontaneity into your presentation
- achieve **credibility** – the ability to make people believe in you and the role you are in and to make them trust you when you speak to them.

The Greek teacher of rhetoric, Aristotle, and modern teachers of communication such as Berlo and Hovland, have analysed the characteristics and dimensions of credibility. They have all agreed on three main attributes which you must possess if you wish to be a credible, trustworthy speaker:

1. Your **expertise, authority** or **knowledge** of your subject
2. Your **character** as per Aristotle or **trustworthiness** (Hovland, 1957) from the audience's point of view:
   a. How safe does the audience feel with you? (Berlo, 1960).
   b. Do you have any hidden agendas?
   c. Have you really thought about your audience and feel empathy for them?
3. Your **goodwill**, towards your audience, according to Aristotle, your **dynamism** (Berlo, 1960) or, as Carl Rogers put it, your **genuineness** as a communicator: are you a spontaneous and authentic communicator? (Rogers, 1951).

Table 9.4 shows how you can demonstrate your expertise, trustworthiness and dynamism in the content and delivery of your talk. In doing so, you will become a credible speaker.

Table 9.4 Demonstrating your credibility as a speaker

Credibility cue	Evidence in the content	Evidence in the delivery
Expertise	• A clear introduction, body and conclusion • Logical and coherent content, with good transitions • Concise content • Accurate, well-supported facts • Quoting evidence of own expertise and sources of others' expertise	• Appropriate dress • Correct timing • Belief in self • Confidence, self-assuredness • A relaxed posture • Variety in the use of gestures and voice

→

Credibility cue	Evidence in the content	Evidence in the delivery
Trustworthiness	• Identifying with the audience • Delivering what is promised – meeting objectives • Showing common sense • Labelling assumptions • Showing evidence of shared values • Presenting a unified message	• Eye contact • Calm, open gestures • An attitude of involvement conveyed to the audience • Authoritative non-verbal cues
Dynamism	• Active, vigorous language • Examples applicable to audience • A variety of approaches (visual or verbal) presented with the correct emphasis	• An interactive facial expression and gestures • A rapport with the audience • A variety in tone of voice; pauses • Vitality and enthusiasm

Speak with expression and projection

Many people tense their upper bodies – from the chest to the jaw – when they feel nervous. A tense chest means shallow breathing and poor volume, and a tense jaw makes the voice sound strained. It makes it difficult to make fully rounded sounds; in fact, the words will sound thin.

The moments before you start your talk

Do the following to make sure you are as relaxed as possible when you start speaking:

- While you are walking to the front of the room to give your talk, consciously relax the tense areas of your body, such as your shoulders, neck and jaw (and hands).
- Once at the front of the room, ensure you stand fully facing the audience, with your body weight on both feet. This assertive stance will make you appear confident, even if you do not feel so.
- Smile at your audience – it will relax both you and them. The non-verbal signals of confidence will be picked up by your audience, who will find you credible. They will communicate this trust to you through their eye contact and interest.
- Before you start your talk, breathe deeply two or three times, drawing breath down to your diaphragm. This deep, quiet breathing helps to relax the body and allows you to start your talk in a natural yet alert manner. Furthermore, filling your lungs to capacity enables you to project your voice strongly.

During your talk

The six most important aspects of the voice, discussed in detail in Table 9.5, to keep in mind during your presentation are:

1. clarity
2. fluency
3. careful use of pauses
4. correct pronunciation
5. variety in pitch, pace and tone
6. volume.

Table 9.5 The six aspects of the voice for a successful delivery

Aspect of the voice	Importance or value	Tips for development
Clarity: Enunciating words correctly; this is done by opening the mouth enough so that the speech muscles can move into the correct positions	Clarity prevents mumbling and indistinct speech, thereby helping the speaker to appear confident and assertive.	If you know your articulation is not sharp, you can do exercises for the tongue and lips (for example repeating 'red lorry, yellow lorry' numerous times). These help you become a clearer speaker. There are many websites with such exercises.
Fluency: Being able to express yourself smoothly, easily and articulately	The non-verbal message that a fluent speaker conveys to the audience is confidence.	Fluency comes with practising a talk out loud so that the vocabulary you wish to use is near the surface of your mind. Do not speak fast. Fluency does not mean making continuous sound – do not fill breaks between sections of the content with 'um' or 'er' when a pause is what is required.
Pauses: Short interruptions or silences in between sentences or sections	Pausing for a thoughtful silence is a powerful way to attract the listeners' attention. It also gives the speaker and the audience time to think about what has just been said. It is a useful technique to ensure that information is given at the correct pace and it makes the talk more accessible.	If you are a fast speaker, the chances are that you will deliver your speech too fast, particularly if you are nervous. You cannot change habits learnt over a lifetime, but by being aware of them, you can counteract them. You may make conscious efforts to pause after delivering a block of information or showing a slide. You may note places where you change your position. These moments of silence give the audience a moment to digest what you delivered rapidly.

Aspect of the voice	Importance or value	Tips for development
Pronunciation: English words are often not pronounced as they are spelt (for example 'wait' and 'weight'). This makes it difficult to pronounce unfamiliar words or technical terms which you have only read and not heard.	It is important for your credibility that you pronounce and accent words correctly, both general words and technical terminology.	If your talk includes technical terms which are difficult to pronounce, ensure these words appear on visual aids, such as slides. There are websites on which you may listen to soundbites of words. During your preparation, listen to the correct pronunciation of all difficult or technical words. Ensure you know which syllable of words to accent (for example 'determine' is pronounced de**ter**mine — the accented syllable is in bold). The accenting of a word may also change according to the part of speech it is functioning as (for example **de**crease = a noun, whereas de**crease** = a verb).
Variety: This is shown by the way words are stressed and how pauses are used.	Variety creates interest in your delivery and shows the audience that you have an enthusiasm for and interest in the topic.	Complete sentences have their own stress pattern, or melody. You want your talk to sound natural, not as if you are a machine reading. The variety in your speech should be an outcome of the enthusiasm you have for your subject and the audience, and it starts with your positive inner dialogue. This is an unconscious skill. Do not deliberately decide to stress a particular word in a particular way. Rather speak naturally.
Volume: The quality or power of the sound of your voice. To project your voice fully, deep breathing from the diaphragm is essential.	Volume is critical. If the audience cannot hear you, your speech is lost.	There are numerous projection exercises on the Internet. For example, hum until your lips tingle and then intone long vowel sounds: *Mmmm moo, mmmm mah, mmmm may, mmmm mee, mmmm moh.* If you have a very light voice, consider using a microphone. You will need to practise microphone etiquette. At international conferences, microphones are standard, as simultaneous interpretation is provided. In this case, never tap the mike to see if it is working, as it is unpleasantly loud for those wearing headphones.

Appropriate non-verbal cues: posture and gestures

Research has shown that non-verbal cues represent about 80% of the message that listeners receive. 'It's not what you say, but how you say it' is very true, because we convey our feelings and emotions through our non-verbal behaviour.

Our non-verbal cues are grounded in our roots; they are a grammar we learn from our parents and other significant people in our lives as we grow up. Some of us use non-verbal cues poorly, since the examples we have followed have been poor. However, because non-verbal communication is a language we learn, we can improve that language, if we choose to.

The major non-verbal cues of which you must be aware when talking to an audience are eye contact, facial expression, gestures and posture.

Eye contact and facial expression

Looking directly at the faces of your audience will portray you as a confident speaker. Members of an audience respond to the speaker as individuals, not as a group, and you can make them feel as if you are addressing them individually. If your audience is a large one, momentarily rest your gaze on a particular face – this will make the people around that person feel that you are speaking to each of them. Also **alter the focus** of your eye contact to avoid staring continuously at one member of the audience. Try to vary your head and eye movements so that they appear to be natural and spontaneous.

Coupled with direct eye contact, you need to keep your face **animated**. An audience can become alienated when listening to a speaker with a deadpan face. Your facial expression shows your feelings about your subject and the audience. If you show your enthusiasm non-verbally, your audience can relate to you more easily. Enthusiasm is contagious. A speaker who is involved with and passionate about their material will easily communicate this to the audience.

Gestures and posture

At the start of your talk, concentrate on your introduction and look at your audience – never the slides. Ensure that your opening lines are easy to remember. Even if you are nervous, you can remember the subject of your talk, its purpose and your own name.

Stand in an **alert yet relaxed** position. Keep your weight balanced on both feet and do not fidget or pace. The correct type of body language will send a message of confidence, competence and credibility, even if you do not feel it!

When you are talking, make good use of space by using **natural, spontaneous gestures**. Allow your gestures to develop spontaneously so that they emphasise what you are saying: use your hands naturally. If you are holding note cards, try to look down as infrequently as possible so that you maintain eye contact and keep the rapport with your audience. As you move through your talk and interact with visual aids and your audience, you will forget about your hands and start gesturing naturally and spontaneously to reinforce what you are saying.

Any gesture that becomes repetitive, such as fiddling with a pointer or pen or pacing up and down, becomes a barrier to presenting your ideas effectively. Your audience's focus shifts from what you are saying to what you are doing. Nervousness may cause you to gesture meaninglessly; for example waving your hands about or fiddling with a pen, your watch, etc. In this case, it is better to keep your arms loosely at your sides or even to hold your hands behind your back at the start. (If you know that fiddling with items is a problem for you, do not wear items such as a watch or necklace that day and do not carry a pen or other item in your pocket.) However, you want to avoid being completely static, with your hands in your pockets or locked behind your back all the time, as this also presents a barrier.

If you use visual aids to illustrate your major points, you will be able to **remain alert and upright** because you can glance at your aid while facing the audience. You may have a remote pointer to move through your slides, which will occupy one hand. If you are using a clicker to work slides, only use the red pointer if your hand is steady.

The closer you stand to your audience the warmer and more authoritative you will appear (do not stand too close, though). Confident, assertive people **use space well.** Do not pace up and down while you talk. Stand still and face the audience squarely until it is appropriate for you to move deliberately to the screen or towards the audience.

If possible, during a presentation, **avoid standing behind** a laptop, an overhead projector or a desk or podium, as this has the effect of separating you and your audience. However, sometimes a venue is set up in such a way that this may be unavoidable; for example, where a microphone is fixed to a lectern. Preferably have a remote microphone attached to your garment and have a remote pointer so that you are not constrained by having to be near the computer.

Visual aids and presentation software and hardware

Handling visual aids with poise and control is part of your non-verbal technique – your gestures. Move with deliberate, relaxed movements, to ensure that you are always in control and that the visual aids do not overwhelm you. (For a detailed analysis of the effective use of Microsoft® PowerPoint™, as well as details on how to create visuals, see Chapter 11.)

The visual presentation of data

Visual aids themselves provide a powerful non-verbal message about you as a presenter. If the images on your screen are overcomplicated and difficult to decipher, or if there is inadequate labelling or incorrect spelling, the audience will assume that you have rushed your preparation and that you are indifferent to both them and the subject.

If, on the other hand, your visual aids are pertinent, neat, legible and **immediately convey a message**, your audience will assume that you have taken great care to make your presentation a professional one. Some visual aids are not very suitable to a presentation. A table or detailed line graph, for example, has to be studied, read and re-read carefully. This cannot be done in a presentation. Extract only the pertinent points you wish to mention from your table or graph and put them across visually in a different way, such as a pie chart, a bar graph or a simple line graph. Figures 9.2 to 9.4 show various examples of the visual presentation of data.

R	%	dep.	int
300	1.35	6031	300
7,500	3.75	14.000	800
8,300	7.28	16.000	900
9,550	8.35	21.000	1000
12,000	9.45	26.000	1260
15,300	12.25	32.000	1890
17,250	15.12	43.000	2200

Figure 9.2 Data that is too dense

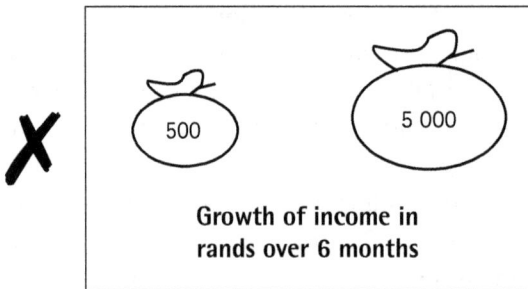

Growth of income in rands over 6 months

Figure 9.3 Data that is too simple

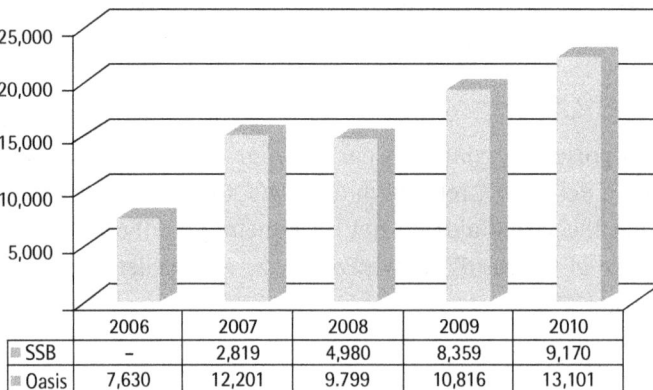

	2006	2007	2008	2009	2010
SSB	–	2,819	4,980	8,359	9,170
Oasis	7,630	12,201	9.799	10,816	13,101

Figure 9.4 Appropriate display of data

Do not use your visuals as a written summary or cue card for every point. Visual aids are used to emphasise and reinforce only those major points you wish your audience to remember.

Integrate your visuals into your presentation by the effective use of transitions. For example: 'This bar chart shows the average winter rainfall of the Western Cape compared with that of the Eastern Cape.' Introduce each visual before you discuss it in detail. For example: 'Next, I will show you an animation of the spider robot.' Do not assume your audience will decipher the visual while you go on talking. Whatever you have on your visual aid should convey the message almost immediately or else you must explain it. For example: 'The gearing of the back legs enables the robot ...'

The positioning of your laptop

If you are using Microsoft® PowerPoint™ as a visual aid, make sure that you face the audience and not the screen. Position the laptop in front of you so that you do not need to turn back to see the screen, thereby losing essential eye contact with the audience. Maintain eye contact with your audience even though their attention might be mainly on the screen. A remote mouse allows you to move, change position and look at the audience while working with slides.

Hold the remote mouse or laser pointer in the hand that is closest to the screen so that you avoid pointing across your body or turning your back on the audience when indicating detail on the screen. You will need to stand on the side of the screen that allows you to place the remote mouse or laser pointer in your dominant hand.

Projecting images onto a screen

Do not read off the projector for the entire presentation, or expect the audience to read text off the screen while you are verbalising different words. First, most audiences prefer to look at and listen to the speaker and, secondly, it is difficult to concentrate on both listening and reading. Indeed, dissonance in comprehension will occur, as an aural message and a passage of text require sequential decoding.

Screen only those points you are talking about. If other points are shown that you are not dealing with, the principle of unity is disturbed, because you appear to have irrelevant information on the screen. The principle of coherence will also be violated because what appears on the screen and what you are saying do not coincide.

If you are using Microsoft® PowerPoint™, limit your use of complicated techniques. Your audience might end up waiting to see what technique you are going to use to illustrate the next point, rather than showing an interest in the point itself. If your slides have a uniform theme throughout – created by a template bearing the same background, font, etc – it will appear as if only the text or picture on each slide is changing, and your audience will not be distracted by too many special effects.

When you do not need information on the screen, show a blank slide (that is, the template background with no text or graphics). Alternatively, you can create a slide and fill it with black to give the impression that the screen has been turned off. The same blank look can be created by pressing the 'B' button on the keyboard for a black screen, the 'W' button for a white screen (which is best depends on the presentation environment) or the 'blank screen' button on the remote presentation mouse. A blank screen rests the audience's eyes and draws their attention back towards you as the speaker, especially if you step forward and into the centre of the screen space. These techniques allow you to be in control of your audience's attention all the time.

Whiteboards, smartboards or flipcharts

The immediacy of text and drawings being created in front of the audience will always have appeal. Manual disclosure is useful if you want the audience to travel with you through an explanation, for example of a calculation algorithm. The time it takes you to write gives the audience time to process.

Write firmly and clearly: preferably in print and not cursive. Use the minimum number of words, so that the message can be immediately understood. Write phrases and not full sentences. There should be no full stops and little punctuation on visuals. For drawings and text, use space generously and use different colours for emphasis.

For a large venue, write on a smartboard or use a stylus on a tablet and then project this. Some projectors can project from paper and so allow the presenter to draw and write during a presentation or show a physical item such as map. For a small venue, a flipchart is appropriate. Flipcharts allow for some preparation as you can write key numbers or brief facts in light pencil on the flipchart paper; your audience will not be able to see these notes, but you will when you need to write over them in bold.

Physical models, maps, charts and handouts

Physical items take the pressure off the speaker and add interest. However, if you are not projecting them as described above, ensure they are large enough to be seen. Consider passing a model around, but be aware that this comes with a trade-off in the form of reduced concentration from your audience.

Maps and charts tend to be detailed, so explain them fully and give the audience time to absorb what you are showing them. Intricate parts that cannot be viewed easily and are essential to know about can be enlarged on a slide. Use the 'W' button on the computer to create a spotlight if it increases the visibility of a chart on the wall.

Be wary of distributing a handout during your talk. The audience's attention is likely to be distracted from what you are saying as they follow the progress of the handout around the room. If possible, distribute handouts at the end of the presentation.

Dress appropriately

Dress to suit the audience's expectations and the situation. Appropriate dress shows that you have analysed your audience carefully. It acknowledges that you have considered the circumstances seriously and conveys a feeling of respect for your listeners. It will also increase your self-confidence. Err on the side of being too smart rather than too informally dressed.

9.3   At the end of the presentation

Question-and-answer (Q&A) session

You need to prepare for questions at the end of your presentation, as it is often the most integral and influential part of the presentation. Maintain your professional image and remain in control right to the end.

Planning for the Q&A session

Anticipate the questions you might be asked and have some extra visuals handy that you did not use in your presentation. That always creates an extremely professional image and shows that you have both thought about and prepared your subject in depth.

Starting the Q&A session

If you are expecting questions and none are forthcoming at first, try offering an open-ended comment, such as 'What do you think about ...?'

Running the Q&A session

- If you can, acknowledge the question asked. Say something like, 'I am glad you raised that point. [*Mention your partner's name if they are to answer it*] will answer your question, as they did the most work on that aspect.'
- Repeat the question if you think that not everyone heard it. Paraphrase it to clarify the meaning for yourselves and others. This also helps you to gather your thoughts as you think of a reply.
- Allow whoever worked on that particular aspect to answer the question.
- Do not speak to the questioner exclusively. Use eye contact to include everyone.

Ways of answering questions

- If you are asked two or three questions in one, separate them and answer each in turn. Write them down if necessary, so you do not forget them.
- Do not rush your answers. A thoughtful silence while you gather your thoughts creates a professional image.

- If you do not know the answer, say so. If it is appropriate and you are to meet the audience again, say you will find out the answer. Otherwise, ask if anyone in the audience would like to make a comment.
- Maintain your sense of humour, as some questions may be deliberately disconcerting.
- Answer inappropriate questions later, privately. Or, if time is limited, suggest a more detailed discussion after the presentation.

Closing the Q&A session
- Be sensitive to your audience's non-verbal behaviour in order to judge when to end the Q&A session.
- If the Q&A session runs for an extended period, pause it and invite those who wish to leave to do so. Then no one need feel rude at disrupting a seated row to leave.
- Thank your audience and, if pertinent, give a few words of summary.
- Remain in control until the end.

Close the presentation within the time allocated

Timing is an important, often neglected, non-verbal message. Taking care to present your talk in the allotted time shows respect for the audience and an intelligent approach to selecting the correct information on your subject. Conferences monitor allotted time strictly. If your talk is too long, you will be cut off and may not be able to give the most important information or make a final, persuasive point.

Even if there is no timekeeper, members of an audience have a sense of how long they should be listening. They will cease to listen and possibly attend to other demands and distractions (such as text messages on mobile phones) if a speaker runs over the allotted time.

9.4   Overcome barriers to effective presentations

When we listen to presentations, we can often identify in the speaker certain 'faults' that prevent us from clearly understanding the message. However, it is not always easy to know how to rectify those barriers to good communication. It follows, therefore, that by identifying a problem and learning a skill to overcome it, we can make our own presentations more effective.

Table 9.6 Troubleshooting to overcome barriers to giving effective presentations

Problem/barrier	Solution	Skill
Lack of audibility, due to: • ambient sound • the speaker's voice being too soft.	Project the voice further.	Breathe deeply, lower the head slightly to avoid straining or shouting and aim for a 'vocal goal' (make eye contact with a focal point and imagine reaching that point with your voice).
The audience cannot see the speaker, because: • the lights have been dimmed • the podium is too high.	• Use a spotlight or reading light on the speaker. • Move away from the lectern or podium.	Although slides appear sharper in a darkened room, it is essential that the speaker be seen. A disembodied voice induces a lack of concentration and sleepiness.
Pronunciation problems, due to: • differing regional accents • the speaker and/or audience having English as a second language.	• Speak slowly. • Make use of visuals. • Enunciate carefully and give the audience time to adjust to your accent.	Write out difficult and crucial words, such as titles, to read off notes rather than read off the screen.
The use of jargon, for example using technical terms when speaking to a general audience	• Explain technical words. • Use different vocabulary. • Have the words written on the slide.	Use metaphors and make comparisons with everyday objects, processes and mechanisms.
A patronising attitude, communicated by cues such as a lack of eye contact, and little engagement with the audience, by a speaker who feels superior or who is shy	• Always speak to an audience with respect and avoid sounding arrogant. • Force yourself to make eye contact and try to engage.	• Ensure you have a thorough knowledge of your audience. • Anticipate as far as possible how they will respond to you and try to make them feel comfortable.
A speaker **blocking the screen** by: • obstructing the visual • standing in the projector's light • using the laser pointer.	• Place the overhead projector or laptop to the side of the screen. • Check that you are not obstructing the screen before you begin your presentation.	It is easier to stand on the left side of the screen (if you are right-handed) and use your open arm to point rather than standing to the right of the screen, using your right arm across your body to point to the screen.

✓

Checklist for well-organised and persuasive presentations

As a speaker, you can convey poise, vitality, enthusiasm and confidence through an alert yet relaxed posture, spontaneous gestures, direct eye contact, an animated facial expression, vocal expression and the way you handle your visual aids (which must be relevant and appropriate).

All these behavioural, non-verbal signals are directly linked to and based on your positive inner dialogue. This inner dialogue is the cornerstone of all effective communication.

Use the checklists below to confirm you have considered all the factors that make up an effective presentation.

Evaluate the **structure of the presentation** according to the following criteria:
- The introduction should contain:
  ▶ the objectives of your presentation
  ▶ the reason for speaking to your audience
  ▶ any relevant background information, if necessary
  ▶ an overview of your full talk.
- Clearly link the main points in the body of the talk to your objectives.
- Give factual information to support your main points.
- Use clear transitions between the main points and within each point to ensure the logical, coherent development of your ideas.
- Integrate your visual aids by using clear explanations and good transitions.
- Construct your visual aids in a clear, simple way, taking into account size and colour use.
- Make sure your visual aids emphasise only the key points.
- Ensure you are able to handle the visual aids with ease.
- Establish a rapport with your audience by:
  ▶ explaining technical terms
  ▶ using personal pronouns such as 'you', 'us' and 'we'
  ▶ unloading information and ideas at the right pace.
- Link your conclusions to your objectives – the audience should know why they have listened to you and what to do with your information.
- In your closing, reinforce the major points concisely and add a note of finality.
- Consider the Q&A session.
- If you are doing a presentation as part of a pair or team, create balance, cohesion and links between the speakers and their content.

When you prepare your **delivery**, practise it using the following criteria:
- direct eye contact, to show your poise and confidence
- good use of space, such as moving around if you are not standing at a lectern
- an alert, relaxed posture, facing the audience and showing confidence
- natural, spontaneous gestures
- animated facial expressions, showing your enthusiasm
- vocal clarity, fluency, variety and pauses
- appropriate dress for the occasion
- correct timing.

Graphics, visual aids and posters   10

We live in a visual age; our readers and listeners spend increasing amounts of time viewing information presented visually on a screen. As a result, we have become more adept at retaining data learned in this manner than data obtained through reading.

Apart from formal presentations, such as pitching a proposal or presenting a paper at a conference, there are many informal presentations you will have to take part in, such as webinars, Skype meetings and presentations.

Presenters who want an audience to remember their presentations need to use visual aids. Well-researched, well-prepared and competently managed slides – or alternative visuals, such as spontaneously created flipcharts – that support the verbal delivery are the mark of a professional presenter.

This chapter covers the use of visuals in two contexts: in written text and on posters, which may stand alone (such as at a trade fair) or be accompanied by the company representative or academic author. This chapter covers:
- the reasons for using illustrations in written documents
- conventions for using illustrations
- integrating illustrations and text
- generating illustrations
- types of tables and figures: design considerations
- guidelines for text sizes in visuals and posters
- posters as graphic representations.

After studying this chapter you will understand:
- the different types of graphics and their functions
- which type to select to display different information and for different readers.

10.1 Advantages of using illustrations

Some people understand words more easily and other people prefer illustrations. As you plan your message, ask yourself the following:
- Will this information be easier to understand if it is presented pictorially or graphically as opposed to in words?

- Will this illustration clarify and/or enhance the point I am making?
- Is it appropriate to describe the information in both text and graphics to cater for all readers' preferences?

Good illustrations can take the place of many pages of text. They can convey important information visually and they make it easy to concentrate on the key issues. They can be used to show trends and relationships quickly, accurately and clearly. Also, busy readers may read your summary and only page through the main report. Visuals can catch the eye of busy readers and make them attend to a graphically conveyed finding.

10.2 Conventions for using illustrations

The general term 'graphic' is used to refer to both figures and tables. Different types of tables and figures (as explained in detail later in this chapter) are suitable for different purposes:

- The term **'table'** refers to tables only. Tables are used when you need to show an exact set of data or results for your research. A detailed table can be used as a basis for a number of figures. Ensure you show an appropriate number of significant figures, eg '76% of people agree that ...' instead of 76.235891% of people ... '
- The term **'figure'** is used to refer to any of the full range of illustrations: line graphs, bar graphs, pie charts, annotated pictures, line drawings and photographs and so on. Graphs are effective for showing trends, relationships and approximations that would not be obvious in a table.

Graphics must conform to conventions that govern their readability and layout if all readers are to understand them. There are certain conventions to be taken into account when using illustrations in business or academic writing.

Captions and titles

Every figure and table should have a title and/or caption, which must be numbered for reference. Numbering can be done in different ways, for example:

- from the beginning of the report or thesis consecutively all the way through (Figure 1, Figure 2, etc)
- chapter by chapter, for example Figure 1.1 etc in Chapter 1 and then Figure 2.1 etc in Chapter 2.

As different spreadsheet programs (eg Microsoft® Excel™) automatically place the captions for tables and figures, ensure that they are placed where your institution requires. If a traditional layout is followed, you will need table titles to appear above the table and figure titles to appear below the figure.

In some academic fields, the title also serves as a caption and thus gives the full descriptor for the illustration. It must be complete, so that the reader does not have to search through the main text to understand the illustration. It usually runs over one line, which may in turn make the list of illustrations (or tables or figures) cumbersome if the full descriptor is carried through. In the case of long descriptors, only the first, main phrase must be inserted by using styles (see Chapter 2) for inclusion in an automated list of illustrations (or graphs or figures).

Captions for equations are generally shown next to the equation, with the equation being left-aligned, and the caption or equation number being right-aligned.

If you use the *Insert Caption* feature on the *References* tab, Microsoft® Word™ uses a built-in style called 'Caption' to enable it to automatically pull through information into the list of figures or tables. If you have a long descriptor as part of the caption, leave the main phrase in the 'Caption' style, and then start a new paragraph in a different style for the remainder. If this is the case with the majority of your graphics, then consider setting up a specific style for the caption text that you do not want to appear in the list of figures or tables. For example, you could call it 'Caption descriptor' and set it up with formatting that matches the main caption.

Placement of graphics

Treat your graphics as part of your message. Place them in the relevant part of your text. It is too distracting to have to turn pages to look for tables or figures in other places. If you cannot find space on a particular page, you can place the graphic on the opposite page or try to shift the text to make space for it.

As described in Chapter 8, you have to integrate your graphics within your text. You can do this by:

- having a descriptive title for your illustration and a caption if more information is required
- introducing the table or figure briefly in the text just preceding the graphic, eg 'Table 1 below illustrates ...'
- ensuring the x- and y-axes are clearly labelled, with the label on the y-axis written vertically, and units shown on the axes if applicable
- using shading, arrows and bold type to show key information
- analysing the information directly below the table or figure
- citing your source if the table or figure is not yours originally, or if you have adapted the graphic from a source
- pointing out key information and the interpretation of the table or figure in the accompanying text (unless the subject requires a full descriptor in the title).

If your document contains very detailed or technical illustrations, consider placing them in the appendices. You can then have a summary illustration in your text.

10.3 How to generate illustrations

Today's spreadsheet software allows you great flexibility to generate and edit professionally formatted graphics. Charts created in Microsoft® Excel™ or other spreadsheet or database programs, photographic images or other illustrations can all be copied and pasted into Microsoft® Word™ or a presentation package, for example Microsoft® PowerPoint™.

For information on how to create graphics and other types of illustrations, consult the Internet, where numerous tutorials can be found to assist you, whether for Microsoft® Excel™, PowerPoint™ or another graphics program.

If you are working in Microsoft® Word™ or PowerPoint™, you can use the options under *SmartArt*. However, it is usually preferable to create your own graphics – or at least modify the colours. The *SmartArt* options have often been used in other contexts and will not make your graphics stand out, especially if the default colours are used. Furthermore, it can be frustrating and time-consuming to try to adapt one of the pre-set options to your requirements, as their adaptability is limited.

While it is possible to insert shapes and create diagrams in Microsoft® Word™, essentially it is a text program, and so the drawing facility is not as easy to use as in Microsoft® PowerPoint™ or other graphic and mind-mapping software. It is usually more efficient to create the graphic in a visual program and copy it as a picture into Microsoft® Word™ (see the discussion of the *Paste Special* options on page 44–45 in Chapter 2).

Microsoft® Office™ provides a number of standard templates for figures and tables. These designs (particularly the basic and less extravagant ones) are useful for quickly making your tables and figures attractive. They are especially useful in large documents where it is important to use a uniform design for tables and figures. Once you have chosen a template, each design can be changed further to suit your needs. The formatting of the design is done on the table or figure. It is easiest to change the number of decimal points displayed in a figure by changing the source data in Microsoft® Excel™.

When choosing or constructing graphics in a program, consider the design options available. This is particularly relevant for bar graphs and pie charts that will be printed in black and white. For example, two or more grey bars or slices of pie next to each other can lack differentiation, and can be clarified by the use of **outlining, contrast between light and dark, cross-hatching** and **labels**. The examples shown in Figure 10.1 are all bar graphs, but many of these principles apply to other types of graphics as well. (Later in this chapter, the characteristics of different types of tables and figures will be discussed in detail.)

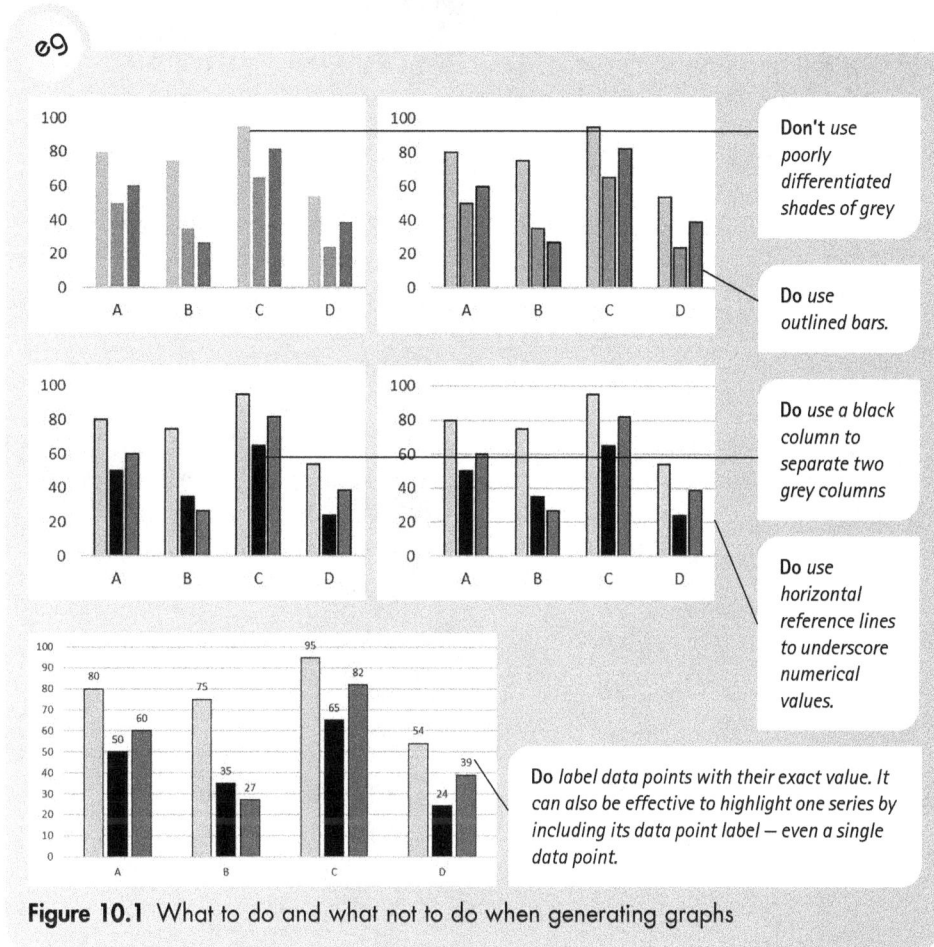

Figure 10.1 What to do and what not to do when generating graphs

10.4 Tables

A table is made up of rows and columns of cells that you can fill with text and graphics. Tables are often used to organise and present information, but they have other uses as well. The major function of tables is to impart specific information to the reader. You can use tables to align numbers in columns and then sort and perform calculations on them. You can also use tables in Microsoft® Word™ to arrange text and graphics in such a way that the information is conveyed more effectively than in a paragraph. This aids the readability of the message. For example, consider the information given in the paragraph below:

e9

In 2018, Floral Kingdom showed an increase in sales of flower seedlings. For clivias in three colours – red, yellow and orange – 15 435, 17 896 and 16 493 trays were sold respectively, while sales in 2017 were 14 327, 15 677 and 12 393 trays respectively for the three colours. In 2018, 4 692, 3 987 and 2 165 trays of hibiscus in the same three colours were sold, while 2 178, 1 982 and 2 075 trays were sold in 2017, respectively.

Now try to find out how many trays containing yellow clivias were sold in 2017. It is rather confusing. However, if we put this information into a table, it becomes far clearer.

e9

Table 1: *Sales of seedlings in 2017 and 2018*

	Clivia	Hibiscus
	2017	2017
Red	14 327	2 178
Yellow	15 677	1 982
Orange	12 393	2 075
	2018	2018
Red	15 435	4 692
Yellow	17 896	3 987
Orange	16 493	2 165

This information can also be ordered as shown in the following example.

e9

Table 2: *Sales of seedlings in 2017 and 2018*

	Clivia		Hibiscus	
	2017	2018	2017	2018
Red	14 327	15 435	2 178	4 692
Yellow	15 677	17 896	1 982	3 987
Orange	12 393	16 493	2 075	2 165

The spaces between the two seedlings columns and between the two years ensure easy visual discrimination. Clear row and column headings tell your reader exactly what specific data is there.

Note that a sans serif font is used in tables even if a serif font is used for the main text. A little formatting or shading can sometimes make a table easier to read. Compare Table 1 with Table 3 in the following example. You will note that the shading gives added emphasis to certain data and makes the table easier to read.

Table 3: *Sales of flower seedlings in 2017 and 2018, emphasising sales of red and orange seedlings*

	Clivia seedlings	Hibiscus seedlings
	2017	**2017**
Red	14 327	2 178
Yellow	15 677	1 982
Orange	12 393	2 075
	2018	**2018**
Red	15 435	4 692
Yellow	17 896	3 987
Orange	16 493	2 165

It is important to note the integral function of tables. All illustrations and text are closely related, but while some illustrations are additional to the text (eg a photograph), tables supplement and support written content without replacing it. A written explanation of the material in the table is required to ensure that it is understood. Without this accompanying explanation, readers may skim over a table in their reading of the paper and so miss important information.

Readers are not expected to absorb the information within a table as if they were simply continuing to read the text. Instead, tables such as the example below require that readers stop and reflect on the arrangement of facts.

e9

Table 4 *Results of an English language competency test given to students in three types of tertiary institutions*

	Total score								
	Types of institution								
Classes of students	Type 1 Professional			Type 2 Arts			Type 3 Teacher training college		
	No	Mean	Std deviation	No	Mean	Std deviation	No	Mean	Std deviation
Entering students	1 800	60.3	9.2	9 000	55.6	9.3	2 200	58.1	9.4
1st-years	1 400	62.4	9.2	7 500	57.4	9.3	2 000	51.3	9.4
2nd-years	5 500	64.0	9.3	27 000	59.3	9.4	8 000	54.2	9.5
3rd-years	700	65.2	9.4	4 000	60.5	9.5	1 200	65.3	9.5
4th-years	600	66.2	9.4	2 500	61.6	9.5	600	59.5	9.6
Totals	10 000			50 000			14 000		

Tables may be placed at the end of a document, but it is preferable to place them within the text. In this case the table must be clearly distinguished from the text by, for example, an outline. There are various table layouts, which can all be accessed via the ribbon in Microsoft® Excel™ and Word™. (See Chapter 2 for more on creating and working with tables in Microsoft® Word™.)

Parts of a table

Every table has five essential parts, as shown in Figure 10.2, namely:
1. the table number
2. the title of the table, above the table
3. row headings
4. column headings
5. the body of the table, containing the data.

Note the referencing.

Table 14: Mesh statistics and simulation solution times for the three CFD models
Source: Williamson, M.E. and Wilson, D.I. (2009) "Development of an improved heating system for industrial tunnel baking systems
(91) 64-71

CFD Model	Nodes	Elements	Iterations	Solution time (min)
First	45 825	145 101	200	35
Second	59 770	206 759	106	54
Third	388 495	147 072	171	37

Note the use of an attractive
given table design.

Figure 10.2 Parts of a table

Unlabelled tables in text

Information may be tabulated and placed in the text as an integral part of a written statement. In this case it needs no number, title or caption, because it is a continuous part of the text and not an illustration.

The example below includes portions of the surrounding text to show how the sense of the table ties in with that of the preceding and following text.

e9

The relative effectiveness of these four nematocides (a type of chemical pesticide) can be seen in a study done at Gardens University where the nematode population was studied in treated Oregon pine seedling beds.

The percentage reduction in the nematode population reduced in each case was as follows:

Methyl Bromide	= 99.2%
D-D	= 85%
Mylone	= 68%
Vapam	= 64%

Methyl Bromide was thus the most effective material for controlling plant parasitic nematodes in the Oregon pine seedbeds.

Using unlabelled tabulated information has many advantages over standard text:
- The information uses a minimum number of words and therefore saves space.
- It assists readability by breaking up pages of solid text.
- It signals that something different or special is being said.

However, this type of tabulated information should be restricted to small amounts of relatively straightforward data.

10.5   Figures

All types of graphs and charts are referred to as figures. Line and scatter graphs convey accurate information and are effective in a written document. However, in a presentation they should only be used to show a trend, as they are too detailed to be read on a screen during a presentation.

The terms 'graph' or 'chart' are used when numeric data is presented in graphic form. The ability to generate graphs and charts is always included in spreadsheet programs and presentation programs. Graphs and charts are used as a means of providing a spatial, pictorial perspective on numerical data in order to:
- explain, summarise and simplify
- synthesise or deduce relationships
- add interest by introducing an extra perspective.

The type of figure you choose depends on:
- **the target audience**: non-specialist, mixed or technical, taking into account their particular background and needs
- **contact**: whether the message will be written or spoken and how much spoken time or written space will be available
- **the nature of the raw data**: the amount and complexity of the data.

This section covers, in particular, those figures used to communicate business or technical information for non-technical or mixed audiences.

Parts of a chart

Figure 10.3 illustrates the various parts of a chart. The type of chart illustrated is a bar graph, but many of these features are common to other types of figures as well.

Chart title

Smart phone ownership by age group in different continents

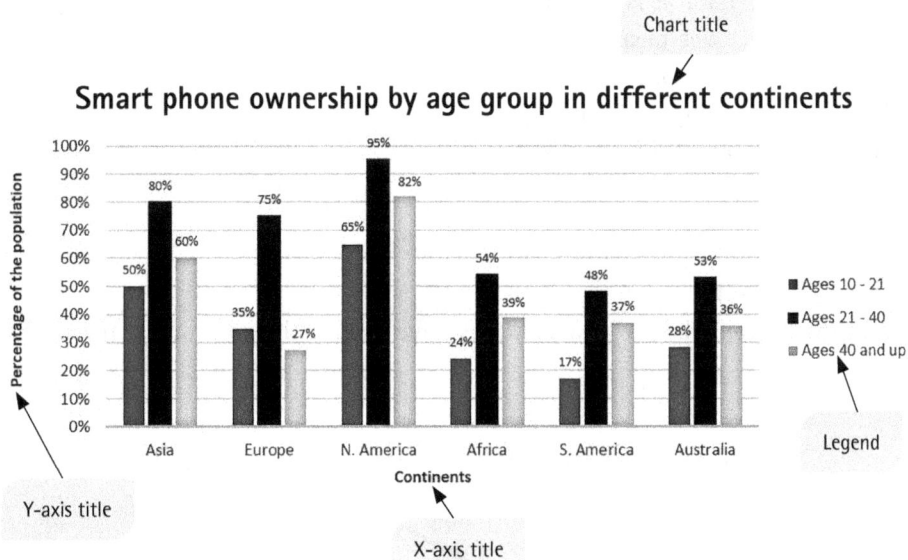

Y-axis title

X-axis title

Legend

Figure 10.3 Parts of a bar graph

Line graphs

Line graphs are specific and factual. They are therefore suitable for representing continuous information and for showing technical and specific data to knowledgeable, professional audiences. The term 'curves' applies to line graphs even if the lines are broken. You can use a line graph to show the behaviour of two variables, namely:

1. the independent variable on the horizontal axis
2. the dependent variable on the vertical axis.

As shown in the examples in this section, a complete graph will include axis titles and, if necessary, a legend for explaining what each of the data series represents. Make sure the measures on the y-axis (the vertical axis) are major values, such as R0, R10m, R20m, R30m, etc for a graph that shows data from R0 to R50m. Do not clutter the axis with unnecessary detail; for example, for a graph that shows data up to R50m, do not use values such as, R0m, R2m, R4m, R6m, etc. For accuracy, you can include the gridlines; or, to show trends, you can leave them out (especially in a screened presentation).

Different types of line graphs are used for different purposes:

*   **Simple line graphs** show trends. They can include gridlines or not.
*   **Multiple line graphs** show comparative trends. These need a well-planned key to distinguish each line.
*   **Cumulative line graphs** are not good for accurate detailed information.

For data that is appropriate as a line graph, plot a scatter graph and then fit a trend line to the data. It is also important to indicate errors associated with each data point, if this was measured or is a factor. Note that for some information, a line graph is not appropriate. In these cases, avoid plotting line graphs, as it can be misleading. For example, if you want to show values between 0 and 100% along the x-axis, but you only measured 1%, 2%, 5%, 10%, 25%, 50%, 75% and 100%, plotting a line graph implies that you made measurements at each percentage point.

Simple line graphs

Note in the example below how gridlines have been included to assist the reader.

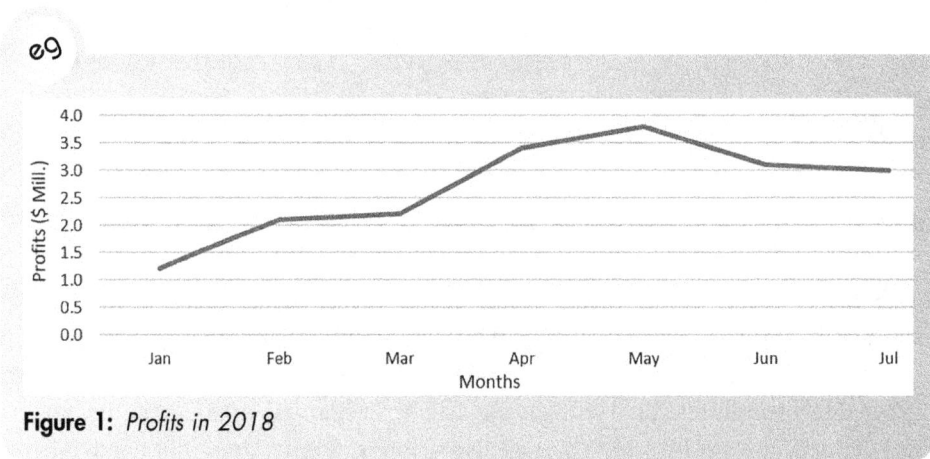

Figure 1: *Profits in 2018*

In the next example, the gridlines have not been included, which makes readability more difficult. In a screen presentation, however, this graph could show a trend well without making the graph look too cluttered, especially if the trend is more relevant than the absolute figures.

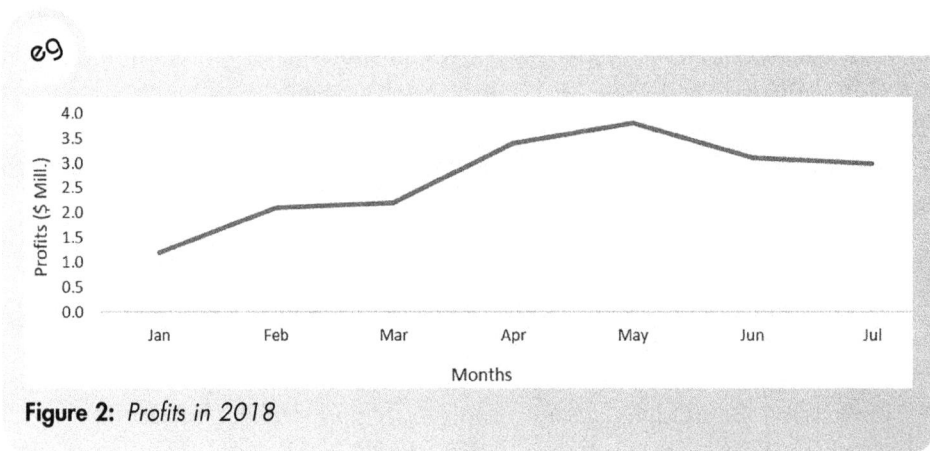

Figure 2: *Profits in 2018*

Multiple line graphs

These graphs can be used to present complex trends. The following is an example of a multiple line graph. Care has been taken to distinguish the lines from one another.

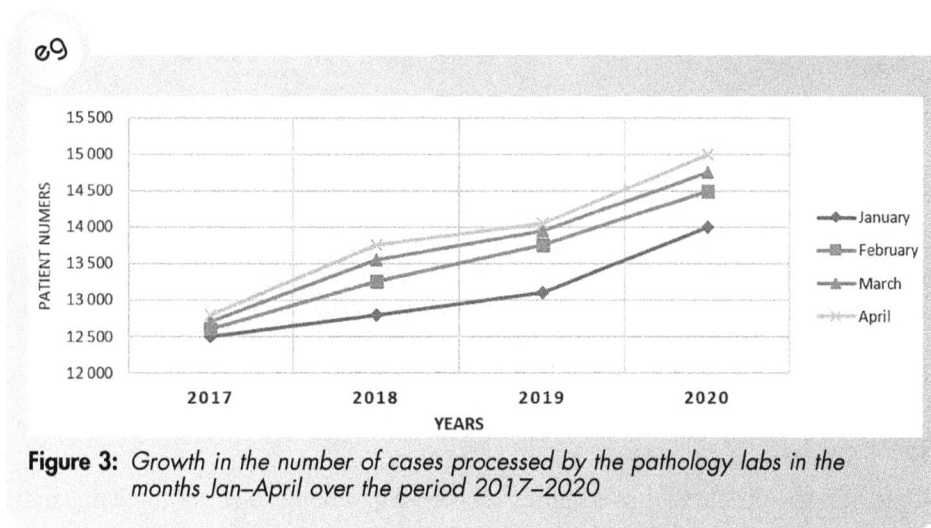

Figure 3: *Growth in the number of cases processed by the pathology labs in the months Jan–April over the period 2017–2020*

Make sure that the lines are sufficiently different from one another. The lines shown in the example above are easily distinguishable. The graph would be more difficult to read if the lines crossed one another, as is shown in the next example (a cumulative line graph, Figure 4). Use colour, dashed lines and different shapes for data points to differentiate between the lines, but beware of relying only on colour – the differentiation will be lost if the graph is printed in black and white.

Cumulative line graphs

These graphs are a cross between a line and a cumulative bar graph. They are very useful for showing trends at a quick glance. They are not good for showing accurate information. Yearly totals would have to be worked out separately.

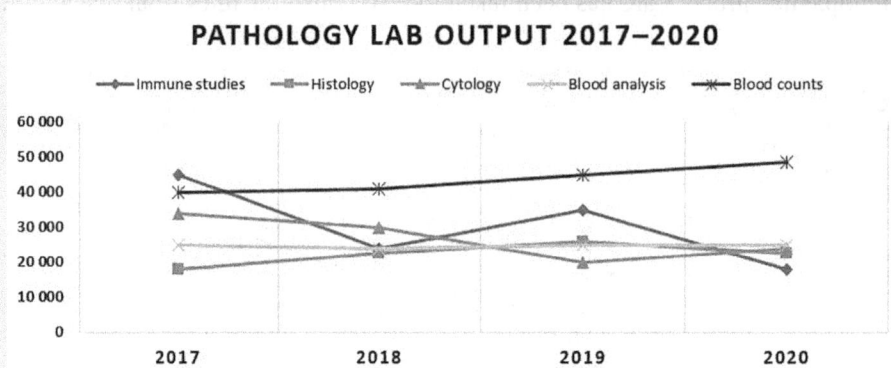

Figure 4: *Pathology lab output for the period 2017–2020*

Bar graphs

While line graphs show a continuous relationship among data points, bar graphs are useful for showing discrete and comparative information. The bars may run vertically or horizontally (and are named either bar or column graphs in processing tools, depending on the orientation). However, bear in mind that people expect certain comparisons, such as altitude, to be read vertically, whereas distance would be more easily read horizontally.

In order to increase visual impact and accuracy, it is useful to use reference lines. You can also place exact numbers at the top of each bar or, if you are using cumulative bar graphs, within each bar.

Several options for bar graphs exist. Your choice will depend on the focus of your message:

- **Simple bar graphs** compare a series of values for one item.
- **Grouped bar graphs** compare two or more items.
- **Cumulative bar graphs** compare the component parts of several totals as numbers or as percentages of the whole.
- **Two-scale bar graphs** are useful for showing complex information, both discrete values and comparative relationships.
- **Bilateral bar graphs** are used to show negative amounts.

Simple bar graphs

These graphs are good for comparing the values of one item over time.

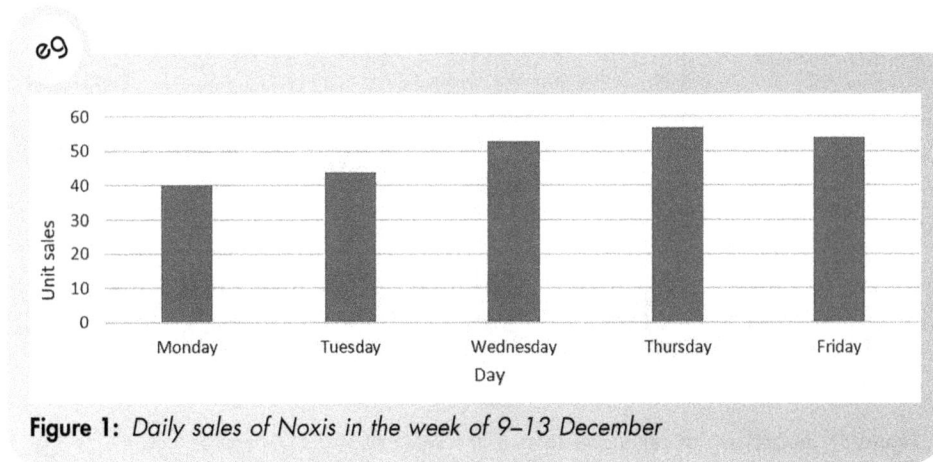

Figure 1: *Daily sales of Noxis in the week of 9–13 December*

Grouped bar graphs

Grouped bar graphs can be used effectively to compare more than one item, as shown in the following example.

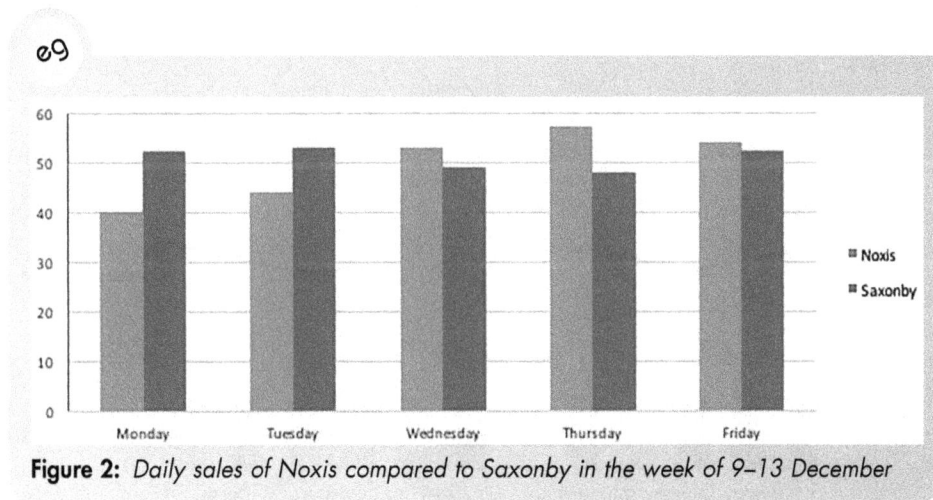

Figure 2: *Daily sales of Noxis compared to Saxonby in the week of 9–13 December*

Cumulative bar graphs

Cumulative bar graphs compare the component parts of several totals as numbers or as percentages of the whole. They are good for giving a quick visual impression of the data, but not for an accurate representation. In order to rectify this, you could:

- add numbers inside the bars to make them read more accurately (as in the example that follows)

- use a legend or key to explain each component of the graph
- use a key or legend to explain the colours or shading.

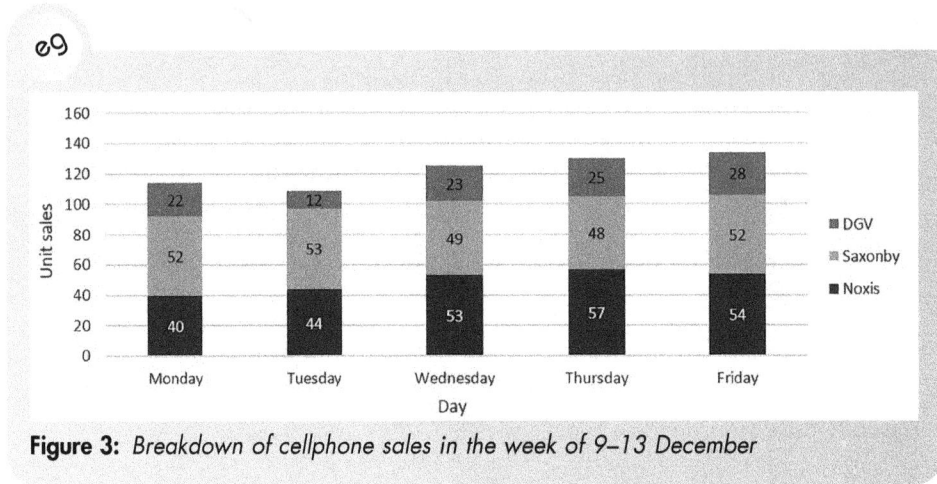

Figure 3: *Breakdown of cellphone sales in the week of 9–13 December*

Two-scale bar graphs

Two-scale bar graphs (see the example that follows) are useful for showing relationships that are difficult to show in any other way. The line graph shows the relation of Noxis pre-ordered sales to the other types of sales shown in the bars. The bars and key describe different information on the bars.

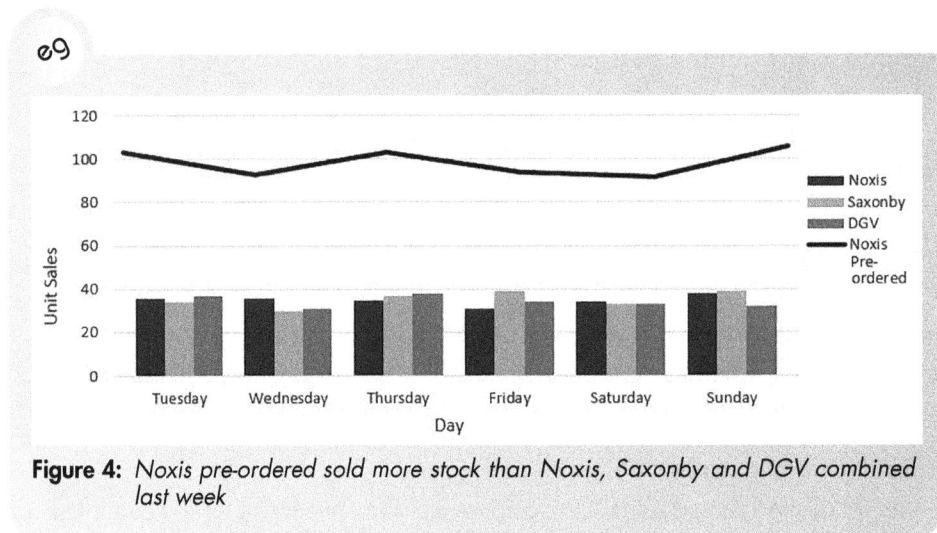

Figure 4: *Noxis pre-ordered sold more stock than Noxis, Saxonby and DGV combined last week*

Bilateral bar graphs

Bilateral bar graphs need to show negative amounts very clearly. Note how the zero line in the following example distinguishes positive numbers from negative numbers.

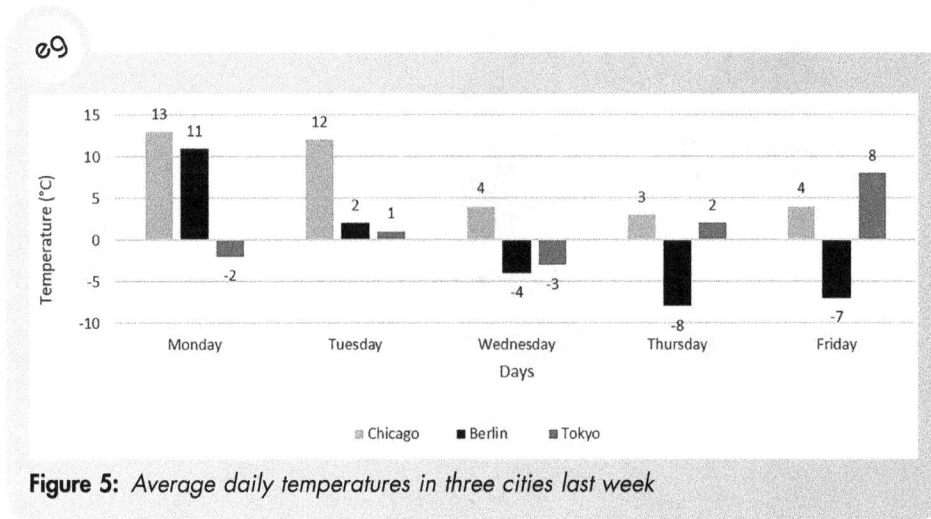

Figure 5: *Average daily temperatures in three cities last week*

Pie charts

Pie charts are useful for showing parts as a percentage of a whole, but they do not indicate relationships and trends. As pie charts are not visually precise – particularly three-dimensional (3D) pie charts – they are not favoured by the scientific community. However, they are effective in conveying a general impression and are easily understood by non-specialist audiences.

It is sometimes difficult to distinguish between slices in a pie chart when it is printed in a single colour, even if there is a legend accompanying the pie. To offset this, write the values or labels within the pie segments. Consider the use of shading or other fill effects to enhance your graphic if you are not able to reproduce colour. However, patterns and shading within slices of a pie chart should be used with care, as they can make the graphic overwhelmingly busy and the text difficult to read. You may also consider giving emphasis to a critical segment through a pop-out.

When creating a pie chart, start at 12 o'clock with the largest slice and work around in a clockwise direction, from largest to smallest. The example that follows is a simple flat pie chart showing population figures.

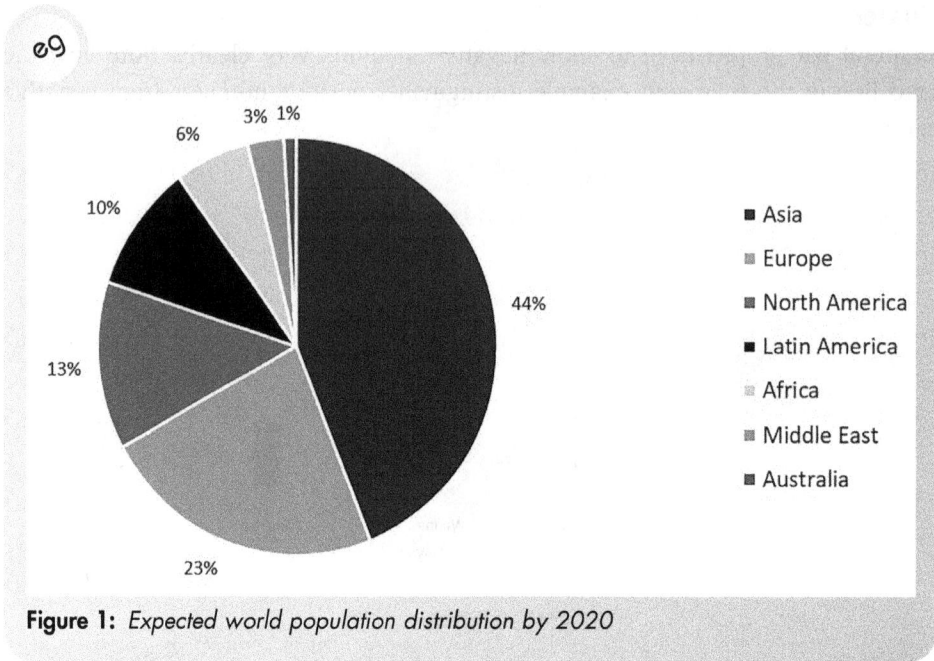

Figure 1: *Expected world population distribution by 2020*

Avoid the temptation of using three-dimensional pie charts, particularly in screen presentations, as the visual impact of the facing segment is sometimes enhanced, thus distorting the message. See the examples that follow.

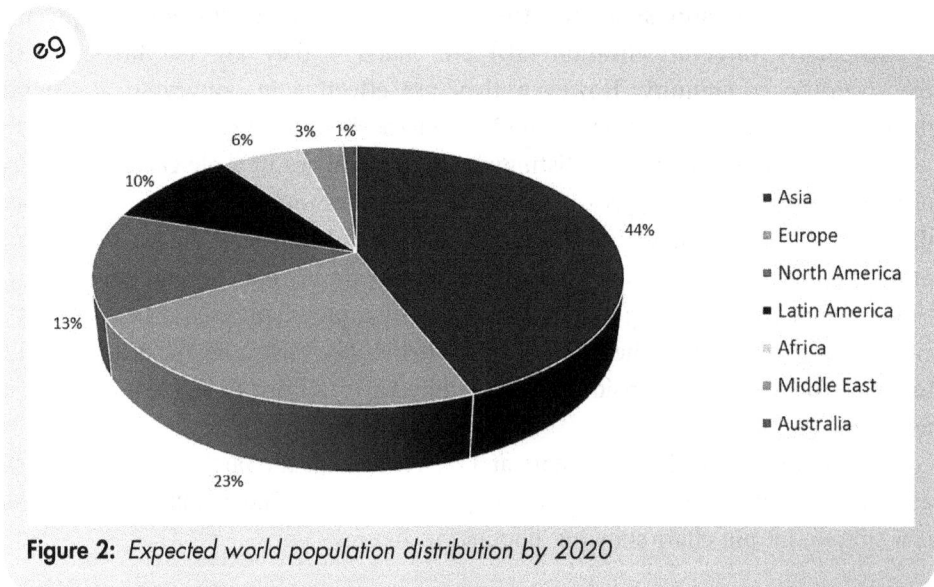

Figure 2: *Expected world population distribution by 2020*

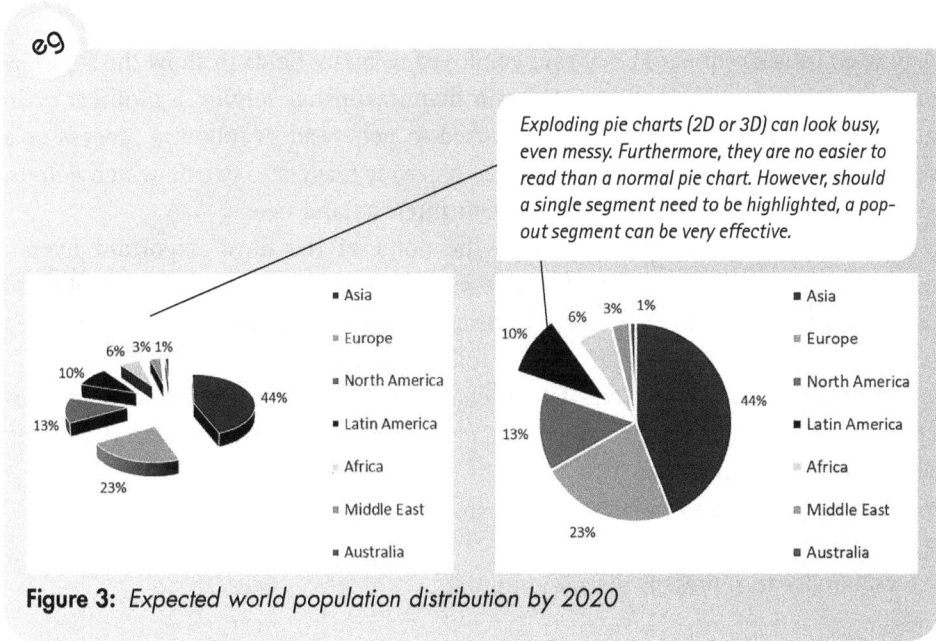

e9

Exploding pie charts (2D or 3D) can look busy, even messy. Furthermore, they are no easier to read than a normal pie chart. However, should a single segment need to be highlighted, a pop-out segment can be very effective.

Figure 3: *Expected world population distribution by 2020*

Pictograms

In pictograms, representational forms are used to show statistical information. These graphs are not accurate. They are most useful for conveying broad information to a wide audience who are not used to seeing graphics and can relate to the pictorial element as shown in the example that follows. Pictograms are often used to liven up a presentation but should be used with caution in an academic presentation.

e9

Projected Saudi Arabian oil production

2017   2018   2019   2020   2021

Figure 1: *Projected Saudi Arabian oil production for five years: 2017–2021*

Flow charts

A flow chart is a sequential diagram employed in many fields to show the stepwise procedures used to perform a task, as in manufacturing, solving a problem or in an algorithm. In flow charts, lines are used to help readers follow a process or a set of possibilities. A flow chart makes it easier for readers to decide which details, circumstances or conditions relate to their interests and needs.

The information is arranged from the point of the most important overall question, and then follows a decision-making sequence through a number of points or questions and comments. Information which can be ignored is indicated (see the word 'NO' in the example that follows).

Conventions in the design of flow charts are that the main body of the flow chart should run down the centre of the page from top to bottom and left to right. The symbols used include:

- rounded squares to indicate the starting or finishing point
- diamonds to indicate questions
- rectangles to represent discussion points.

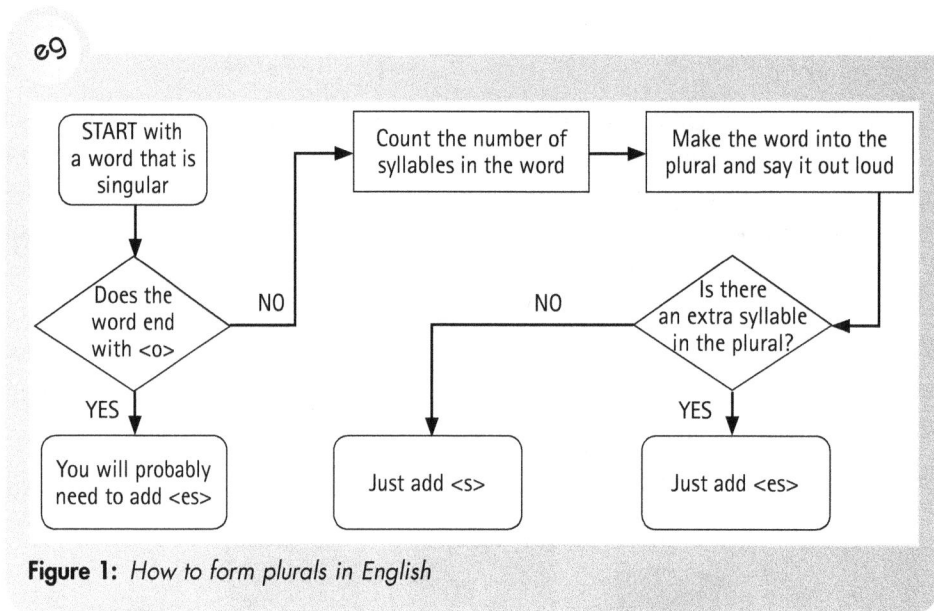

Figure 1: *How to form plurals in English*

The Shapes option on the *Insert* tab in Microsoft® Word™, PowerPoint™ and Excel™ contains a section of flow chart shapes.

Flowchart

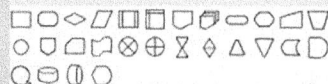

Gantt charts

A Gantt chart is a horizontal bar chart developed as a production control tool in 1917 by Henry L Gantt, an American engineer and social scientist. Henry Gantt and Frederick Taylor are generally credited with being the 'fathers' of scientific management or project management as we know it today. Henry Gantt's charts are built on the principles of scientific management to depict complex time-work schedules visually.

Gantt charts are therefore visual representations of intended tasks, their sequence and the proposed allocation of time for each task over a specific period. They are frequently used in project management to provide a graphical illustration of a schedule that helps people to plan, co-ordinate and track specific tasks in a project. Gantt charts are an integral part of technical or academic proposals.

A Gantt chart must include a statement of events or undertakings in the left column. The number of days, weeks or months that each task will take are represented graphically by means of horizontal bars, as shown in the example on page 290.

It is usual to state the names of specific individuals or their designations unless the chart reflects the work of a single person. Notice the key supplied in the example above to explain the bars.

Gantt charts may be simple versions created on a wall chart, for example, showing the use of rooms or various resources over time. More complex versions can be created using Microsoft® Excel™, and automated Gantt charts can be created using project management applications such as Microsoft® Project, Microsoft® Smartsheet™ or GanttProject (a free downloadable project scheduling and management tool available at ttps://www.ganttproject.biz).

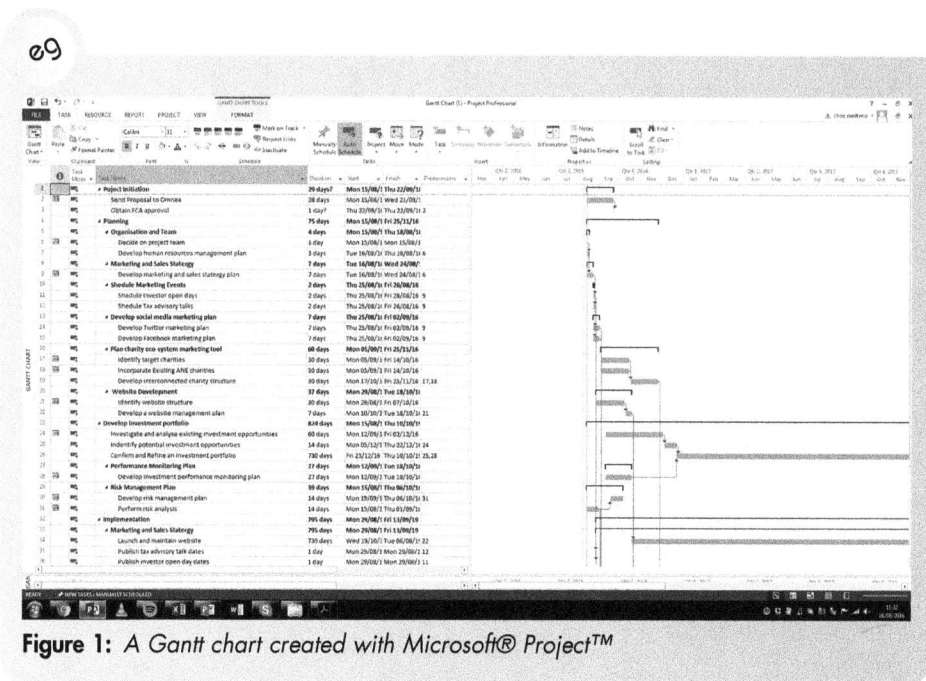

Figure 1: *A Gantt chart created with Microsoft® Project™*

Figure 2: *A simple Gantt chart*

ID	Task name
1	Inventory and research
2	Inventory artifacts
3	Arrange loans – other museums
4	Pick up donations
5	Design and development
6	Create exhibit space
7	Photograph artifacts
8	Design artwork and graphics
9	Prepare audiovisual segments
10	Create titles and labels
11	Construction
12	Install new lighting system
13	Install clocks
14	Installation complete

Task resources: Researcher; Chief archivist; Donations curator; Chief archivist, researcher; Chief archivist; Photographer; Graphic artist; Audiovisual technician; Graphic artist; Chief archivist, researcher, don; Audiovisual technician

Project: Project 2
Date: Friday 02/09/--

Task
Progress
Milestone

Summary
Rolled Up Task
Rolled Up Milestone

Rolled Up Progress
Split

Project Summary
External Tasks

Scientific models

Research in science, medicine and engineering includes the extensive use of technical diagrams and models. The example that follows shows a design created for a specific project.

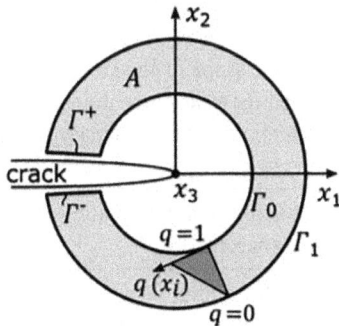

Figure 2: J area integral, contour path (Γ_0, Γ_1, Γ^+ and Γ^-), crack tip local coordinates and q function schematic

Figure 1: *A diagram drawn in Microsoft® Project™ for a specific project (Molteno, MR & Becker, TH. 2015. 'Mode I–III Decomposition of the J-integral from DIC Displacement Data'. Strain 51(6): 492–503)*

See pages 25–26 in Chapter 1 for detail on typefaces and their various qualities, such as the comparative font sizes of different typefaces. The visual impact made by a font with a large body and short ascenders and descenders contrasts with one in the same point size but with a small body and long ascenders and descenders.

10.6 Posters

Posters are a key component of communicating your research or business proposals, and an important element in a successful business or academic career. (See Chapter 13). Posters, although different to oral presentations or published papers, still delivers high-quality content. Posters are intended to engage colleagues or investors in a dialogue about the content. It can be accompanied by a representative or it can stand alone at events such as conferences or trade fairs. A poster requires careful planning so that it can be tailored to a particular audience and purpose.

You will need to decide what you want the passing reader to do – engage in a dialogue, collaborate or be sufficiently interested to seek further information. You will have to design your poster accordingly.

Rules for research and business posters

Rule	Reason and method
Decide on content to fit the audience and purpose.	By identifying the audience and the purpose, you will be able to select the relevant material and the extent of the detail.
Attract attention.	Make the first impression striking, as you will probably have to compete with other posters in the room. Be sure to state the topic and purpose boldly and clearly. The banner title describes the topic and holds the material below it together. It could pose a decisive question, define the scope of the study, hint at a new finding or establish the need for a new invention. Above all, the title should be short and comprehensible and easy to read from far away.
Distil the information.	Use only key points. Avoid details and information overload. The content should be self-explanatory.
In an academic poster, include the necessary information.	The poster must contain a title, author names and affiliations, the supervisor's name, an introduction, methodology, results, conclusions and future work, references and acknowledgements.
Use as much illustrative material as possible.	Use illustrations to replace text. Use photographs, charts, tables and diagrams to simplify complex material. Create clear, concise captions, headings and labels. In academic posters, you need to give literature citations, but keep them to a minimum.
Ensure the images are large enough.	This ensures that they do not pixelate when they are enlarged on a slide or projected.
Keep the design simple.	Consider the layout carefully so that the eye can move in a logical manner. Typically, use three to five columns and arrange the material vertically from top left to bottom right. This is the easiest for the reader. However, other designs can be appropriate, for example a horizontal or circular sequence. Use arrows or numbering if necessary to guide the reader through the data in the correct sequence. Keep some open space so the information does not appear crowded.
Ensure the text is readable.	Follow the guidelines given in Section 10.7 of this chapter to make sure your text is clear and legible.
Use colour for effect.	Aim for a striking impression with your use of colour. A suitably transparent watermark can be effective as a background. Use contrasting colours to help isolate text for easy readability. Use space to avoid the poster appearing cluttered, but avoid large, bland areas of colour. Avoid combinations of complimentary colours, such as green and red.
Include professional product photographs wherever possible.	An enlarged product photograph can help emphasise and reinforce the impact long after the exhibition is over.

Guidelines for text sizes in posters

If you use text in a poster, keep in mind that you need to be able to read the text on your computer screen for your poster to be read from approximately two metres away. This will give you an idea of how the audience will experience reading from your poster. Follow these guidelines to make sure your text is readable:

- Use text blocks with clear titles and headings.
- Keep the text to a minimum, as clarity and precision of expression is important.
- Avoid full sentences.
- Avoid upper case.
- Keep the font size legible (not less than 24 points). Use the following font sizes for these features:
  ◗ Title: 72 pt
  ◗ Subtitle or authors' names: 48 pt
  ◗ Affiliations: 36 pt
  ◗ Section headings: 36 pt
  ◗ Text: 28–32 pt
  ◗ References and acknowledgements: 24 pt
- Use a sans serif font, such as Ariel, Calibri, Tahoma or Verdana.

Finally, it is important to laminate your poster with either a glossy or matt finish. This is a practical and professional way to display the poster easily. A large sheet of paper has a tendency to tear or look worn. See an example of a well-designed poster in Figure 10.4.

eg

An electro-mechanical walking-assist device for drop-foot

*Have you ever wondered how Luke Skywalker could control his robotic hand? It's all possible with **Electromyography**.*

Clear heading

1. What is drop-foot?

Drop-foot is a medical condition
- the inability to raise the foot at the ankle
- patients drag their foot along when walking.
- commonly caused by stroke and nerve damage.

Effective use of watermark

2. Rehabilitation

Usually drop-foot patients use a plastic brace which holds the foot in the 'lifted' position. This helps with walking.

Active movement of the foot has been shown to improve muscle control. But
- this takes months of professional help
- the patient is unable to walk effectively.

Electromyography (EMG) is a technique for detecting and amplifying the electrical signals produced by muscles when they contract.

Numbering; clear directional logic (can be with graphic connectors)

Devices (see below) currently exist that use EMG to help patients to rehabilitate and have been shown to accelerate rehabilitation. Unfortunately, these are bulky and expensive.

Same typeface with suitably varied size

Legible graphics

3. How this device works

The device is designed to fit inside the shoe and trouser leg and functions as follows (see fig below):

Good illustrative material

- the muscle signal which controls the device is obtained through electrodes and screened wires (1)
- muscle signals are exceedingly weak (80mV 30mV) These are susceptible to noise and must be amplified to be of any use. For this, a high gain differential amplifier and band pass filter is used (2, 3)
- a microproc   *Key points only*   ) and uses position input   introl power to the foot (6) which is done using an h-bridge (4).
- the actuator, which is a brushed DC motor, an epicyclic gearbox and slip clutch, then moves the foot.

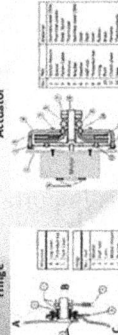

Hinge   Actuator

4. How to use it

With rehabilitation, patie
degrees of muscle contro
device is designed with th
patient to adjust performance and sensitivity of
the device (see below)

Catchy subheading

The geometry of the device is also easily changed. The
drive system may be installed and adjusted to cater for
the specific needs of each patient (see 1,2 below)

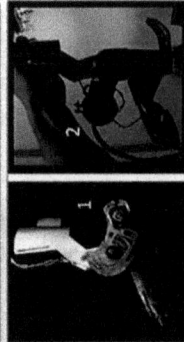

5. The future

This project
future de
mechanis

The devic
of acceler
affordable repair.

Focused conclusion and 'future'

solutions for
nge-actuator

ther evidence
ow for

Figure 10.4 Elements of a well-designed poster (final-year thesis poster by Matthew Molteno on the design of an electro-mechanical walking-assist device for drop-foot for BSc [Eng], UCT, 2011)

✓

Checklist for creating graphics

Poor graphics and visual aids will not only detract from any message you intend to convey, but may even distort it. It is essential to use clearly laid out and appropriate graphics and tables to create maximum impact, whether in written text or on a poster. This is particularly important as some readers may engage with a poster or written message when you are not there to explain what it means. Use the following checklist to ensure your graphics are effective:

- Be clear about what the graphic is intended to convey.
- If you are using generic graphics, adapt them to your context. Alternatively, create your own.
- Source photographs of good quality.
- Choose the correct style or format, especially for charts and graphs, to display the information clearly and accurately.
- Keep explanatory text to a minimum and rather use arrows or other highlighting techniques to focus the audience's attention.
- Use animation sparingly but with a view to assisting the audience to focus more easily on important elements.
- Use notes pages or handouts to provide detailed data to accompany graphics. (This will allow the graphic to promote understanding rather than just impart information.)
- Check whether there are any issues of copyright infringement that you need to pay attention to.

11 Visuals to support oral messages

In the modern, digital environment, we rely as much on visuals to understand a message as on the spoken or written word. This means that oral presentations will be enhanced by the use of well-designed presentation visuals. They can help a speaker communicate more effectively, hold the attention of an audience and imprint powerful memories related to key points or messages. Unfortunately, the overuse of text on slides or poorly designed visuals can detract from the speaker's message and even have a negative impact on the company's or individual's professional reputation. This chapter covers information on:

- using visuals in oral messages
- generating and working with visuals to accompany presentations in Microsoft® PowerPoint™, including the use of animation
- creating dynamic and interactive presentations
- creating non-linear presentations.

By working through this chapter, you will learn that visuals as part of your oral delivery are useful to:

- clarify processes or explain procedure
- simplify complexity
- denote order and show connectivity and relationships
- demonstrate moving parts
- show spatial locations.

11.1 Importance of using visuals in oral messages

When you need to do a presentation, you may be tempted to simply transfer tables and graphs from written text to a Microsoft® PowerPoint™ slide. Although it might seem convenient to use material that has already been formulated and used in a text, invariably the size and amount of detail is unsuitable for a visual presentation. Text-heavy slides will not just bore an audience, but will also create the impression that little thought has been given to the presentation and the main points to be made.

Dangers of bullet points

Microsoft® PowerPoint™ has become ubiquitous in the world of business presentations, and this has not always been to the benefit of the presentations themselves. It is a versatile and easy-to-use program that has enormous capacity. However, it has also acquired a poor reputation because of some presenters tending to overuse bullet points in an attempt to avoid writing down all their content on a slide. While it may appear advantageous to have short phrases neatly captured on a slide to help your audience follow a presentation, lists of bullet points more often than not indicate a lack of thought about how best to present information. They may even prove counterproductive, as audience members' attention easily drifts away when they are confronted by the monotony of bulleted slide after bulleted slide. Neither is a long list of bullets mitigated by the speaker making the bullet points appear one by one either on a control transition or the click of a mouse. Furthermore, such a presentation almost always requires the presenter to face the screen more than the audience and, often, to read from the screen bullet point by bullet point.

Research from the 1980s onwards has consistently shown significantly improved retention of information from slides containing visuals. Message retention after three days has been shown to be up to 50% to 65% for slides containing visuals versus 10% to 25% for slides with text and bullets only, with a corresponding increase in the chance of achieving presenter objectives (Gutierrez, 2014). Figure 11.1 is an example of a visual representation of these figures – significantly more memorable than the same information provided in this paragraph.

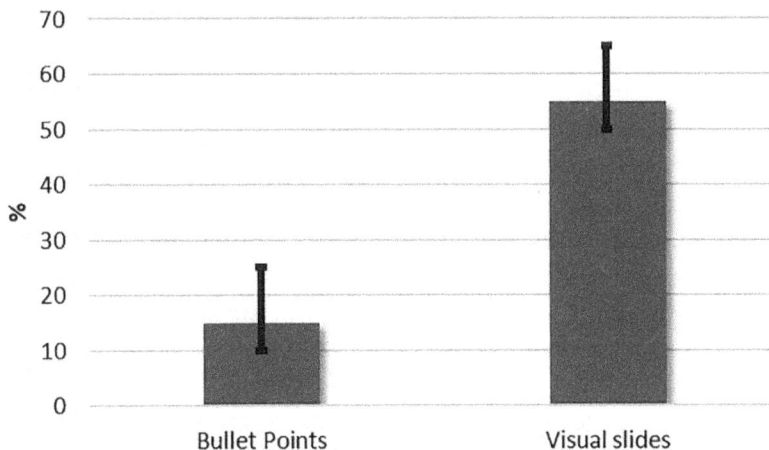

Figure 11.1 Message retention after three days when using bullet points vs visuals

Presenters often excuse the use of text in oral presentations by suggesting that the presentation will serve as a record which, when viewed again later by a member of the audience, will act as a reminder of the information provided. This approach is commonly used with lecture presentations. Slides are not, however, an easy reading medium and in reality people rarely read back over the slides of presentations or lectures for recall. Audience members rather rely on the notes they took at the time (perhaps on a handout with reduced copies of slides). They may also rely on a fact sheet that adds detail to a memorable message provided by a visual, but in this case it will be the visual that draws the audience back to the fact sheet or notes, and not vice-versa.

Effective visuals in presentations

The aim in a presentation is therefore to include well-considered, targeted visuals that enhance understanding or emphasise key points. (The effective design of visuals will be discussed in the next section of this chapter.) Many programs are available for preparing slide presentations, including Microsoft® PowerPoint™, Prezi and Keynote, or a combination of them.

Inserting multimedia, such as short movie clips and moving data from the Internet, is becoming more common in oral presentations. You can use Google Images, Instagram and other sites to source images – some sites are free and some may charge, but you should be clear that you have permission to use any externally sourced images or clips. Furthermore, as quality images are important, it is usually well worth sourcing a good image even if it requires a small fee, particularly if the presentation or poster is likely to be used multiple times.

Infographics are great examples of how text and research can be visually combined. Before designing a presentation, a quick Internet search of infographics around your subject may give ideas for visuals if you are uncomfortable with generating ideas for graphics. But do make your own graphics after you have found some ideas, not just because of copyright issues but also because a graphic from one context is rarely completely suitable in another.

Some go so far as to believe that a presentation should contain the minimum amount of text (no more than six words per slide – usually in the heading to make a point) or even no text at all. In such a case, detailed facts and information would be provided in an accompanying handout or fact sheet (should that be required). This is particularly viable since programs such as Microsoft® PowerPoint™ and Keynote allow you to prepare presentations that include slides, audience handouts and speaker's notes.

As Microsoft® PowerPoint™, Prezi or other presentation media are designed to be visual, that is what should be on the slides. If detailed figures or information is required in the presentation, consider accompanying the presentation with a handout of relevant facts and figures rather than cramming them all onto the slides. Afterwards, the information provided will be enhanced for the audience members by their memory of the accompanying visual on the slide. Information can easily be set up to accompany a presentation in Microsoft® PowerPoint™, for example by formatting the layout of the *Notes Page* view to match the presentation or company style and then adding the relevant facts, figures, quotes and other evidence for reference (rather than relying on handouts containing just the slides). These pages can then be printed out to accompany either specific slides or the presentation as a whole. These accompanying notes can also be set up as a guide or manual in a training presentation, or just as a useful reminder of the presentation content for the presenter at a later date.

11.2 Guidelines for the design of effective visuals

It is not enough to merely create and use visuals, as poorly designed visuals can ruin your presentation. Elaborate, complex or cluttered visuals will not necessarily be perceived as excellent. In addition, including more visuals rarely compensates for a lack of quality visuals – too many visuals can be just as counterproductive as too much text. Table 11.1 highlights good and poor practice in the creation and use of visual aids.

Table 11.1 Designing successful visual aids

Poor visual aids	Good visual aids	Example of a good visual aid
Too many unnecessary slides	Slides that are fully integrated into the speech with relevant information on the slides	Using 10 slides for a 10-minute presentation
Wrong choice of graphic (eg a complex table instead of a simple chart)	Data that is presented in proportionally sized shapes, eg pie charts and bar graphs; animations used to highlight important factors	A solid bar graph with an animated graph line coming in to show the trend only
Use of clip art or poor quality images	Photographs or high-quality images that show up sharply and cleanly when projected as well as on screen	A relevant photograph with a simple caption and minimum text, or a clear diagram with easily read labels

→

Poor visual aids	Good visual aids	Example of a good visual aid
Poor choice of colour (eg tones which have little differentiation or that clash)	Slides that have a background and contrasting text to suit the venue — depending on whether the venue is light or dark.	Not orange and brown but white and blue and other strong contrasts in colour and tone
Data in tiny, illegible letters or minute colour blocks	Data within the visual, and sufficiently large to be legible	Data shown in proportional sizes of pie chart or bar graph, and with descriptor added
Unnecessary decoration, too many special effects or a completely white background	Using an appropriate template in keeping with professional image; sans serif text; an off-white background; animations only to disclose material and even then sparingly	A discreet banner giving own or company name or logo above or below main body of slide
Too much text on a slide and overusing bullet points	Text of approximately 40 pt for headings and 24–32 pt for text, for readability and to limit the amount of text on any one slide; limited use of bullets	Slides with images that replace or support text

In particular, you need to pay attention to the use of text and colour in slides.

Use of text on slides

The typeface you choose, and the size of the typeface, can affect the legibility of text on slides. Follow these guidelines for readability:

- Use a **sans serif font** (eg Arial, Calibri, Tahoma or Verdana); it is easier to read from afar.
- For **content text,** the font size should be at least 22 to 28 pt. However, also bear in mind that some fonts have a large body and short ascenders and descenders, and others have a small body and long ascenders and descenders. This will create the impression of a difference in size even if the fonts are in the same point size.
- The size of text and numbers on **graphs** should be between 22 and 28 pt, to ensure that they are legible when projected.
- For **title text,** the size needs to be about 40 to 44 pt.
- Stick to **one font** throughout the body text. A second font may be used for headings.
- **Avoid special effects** such as text shadows in your slide, as this can reduce the legibility of the writing.
- Keep text to a **minimum** — full sentences are not usually required.

Use the slide title to make a statement or assertion highlighting the key point of your slide and use the rest of the slide to provide evidence for your point, preferably in visual form with minimal text. If you do this, make sure the title is left aligned to make it easy to read across. This technique helps you remember the key point you need to make on that slide, allowing you to focus more on the audience.

Do not read out the slide title. The audience can read it faster than you can say it, and it is therefore irritating when a presenter reads out slide titles of any kind, or the table of contents slide, should you have one.

Use of colour on slides

The visibility of your text is affected by your choice of colours:

- **Light backgrounds** are beneficial if the environment is likely to be darkened, as they tend to give a clean, uncluttered look. Light backgrounds often benefit from gradient shading to soften them.
- **Darker backgrounds** can project better and be easier to view than light backgrounds in certain environments, especially very light ones.
- **Do not make backgrounds too dark.** Blue or grey is better than black, which can appear quite intimidating. Red as a background colour is hard on the eyes.
- **Use contrast** between the colours that you choose, for example dark on light or vice versa.
- **Do not use multiple colours.** Use a maximum of two colours. Rather use bold for emphasis than a colour change. Red text especially can be hard to see.

Data projectors in lecture halls, board rooms or conference venues may distort colours. What seems bright and legible on your computer screen may not always be so on the larger screen in the room. Check in advance, where possible, and adjust your colours accordingly.

11.3   Slides in Microsoft® PowerPoint™

Create templates

When you open Microsoft® PowerPoint™, you have two options. You can either use one of the variety of installed design templates, with pre-set colours, graphics, fonts, and so forth, or you can use a blank presentation, which allows you to choose and change all the design elements.

Just as in Microsoft® Word™, PowerPoint™ allows you to set up templates that can be used over and over. As with documents, finding an old presentation and using the *Save As* command before replacing unwanted material means you run the risk of the slide design becoming degraded over time, with fonts and so on becoming inconsistent. A Microsoft® PowerPoint™ template has a different file extension to a regular presentation (.potx rather than .pptx). This allows it to launch a presentation identical to the template, but leaving the template untouched for the next time it is needed and thereby preserving the design.

Using a pre-set Microsoft® PowerPoint™ template may initially appear to be a timesaver, but it can also prove restricting where the design does not fit all the elements of your presentation. Adapting the template can take as long as, if not longer than, setting up your own design template. Furthermore, there is always the risk that an installed design template could have inappropriate or distracting associations should an audience member have seen that design in a different context. It is therefore preferable to create your own slide design so that you are able to manipulate various elements to suit your needs.

If you work for a company or organisation, it is important to maintain the company's brand at all times. Even if the company does not have a required template to use for presentations, it is a good idea to ensure that your slide design follows the company's style sheet, particularly regarding the colour palette and the use of the corporate logo. If no style sheet is available, then the organisation's website is a good guide to the look and feel that should be embodied in your slide design.

If your presentations are for your own purposes, having your own design template is still advisable, as it contributes to your personal or professional brand.

Slide Master

The Slide Master function, accessed via the *View* tab on the ribbon, acts as a convenient one-stop shop for setting up a presentation in Microsoft® PowerPoint™, whether to use once or to save as a template. Making the effort to get the master slide right saves hours of extra work formatting every separate slide.

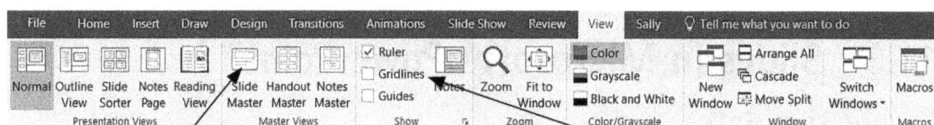

Clicking this button on the *View* tab opens the *Slide Master* view and a contextual tab on the ribbon called *Slide Master*.

This tab also allows you to see the ruler around the slide in *Print Layout* view and the gridlines, to help with lining up objects on the slide.

Figure 11.2 Useful viewing options accessible from the *View* tab

The Slide Master function allows you to set the fonts, colours and layout you would like to appear on each slide, which could include the company logo, for example. Once the master slide is set up, you can then adapt the specialised slide layouts available in Microsoft® PowerPoint™. This is shown in Figure 11.3.

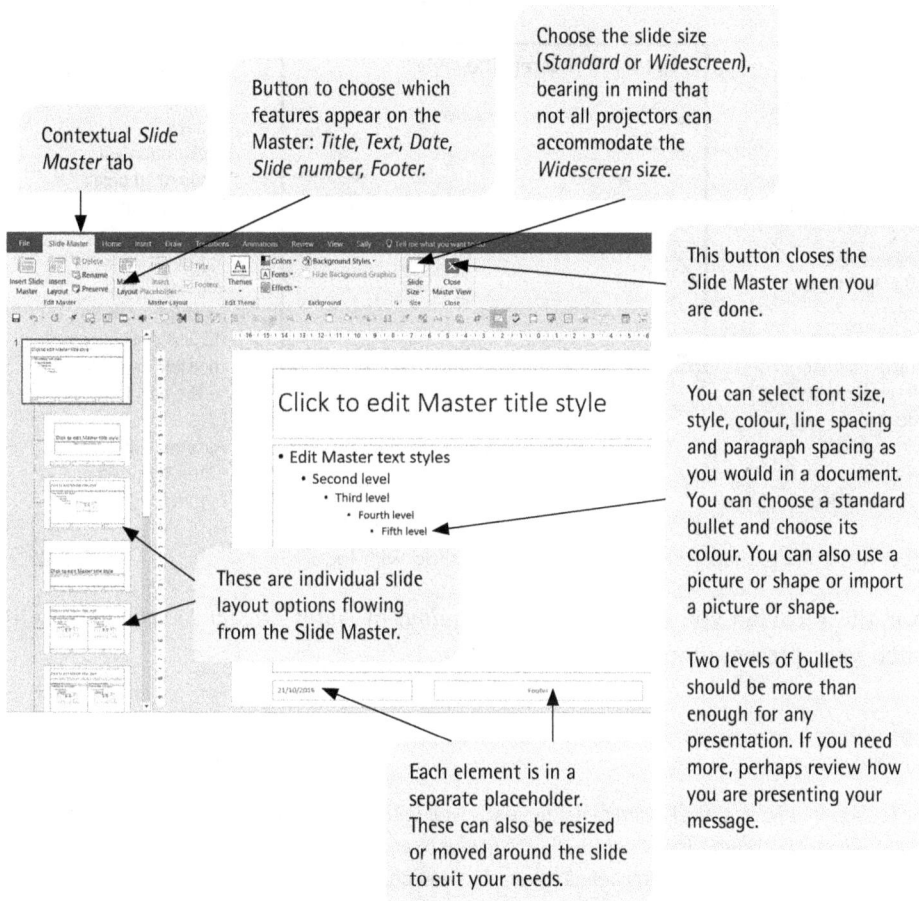

Figure 11.3 Editing with Slide Master

When you open the Slide Master, by default it shows the title page slide layout option. In the panel to the left, scroll up and click on the very first slide to ensure that you are working on the actual master slide. The dotted lines in that panel show how all the other slides take their cue from this one. A single presentation can, however, contain more than one master slide, especially if slides have been copied from other presentations with a different look. Always check you are working on the correct master slide.

Figure 11.4 is an example of a formatted master slide, showing a logo. Once you have formatted your master slide, each new blank slide will share the same look, albeit with different layouts depending on the option you select for each slide. For example, the logo could be in the same place, for continuity of the theme. Your text formatting will be maintained throughout.

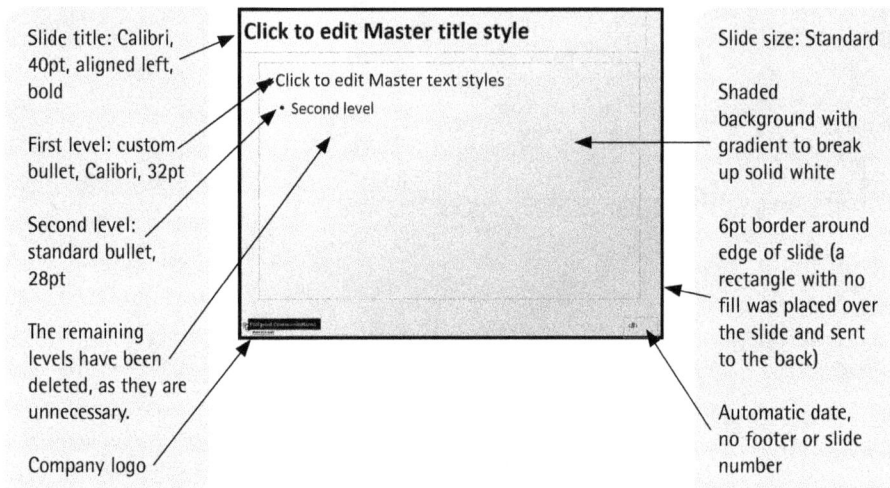

Slide title: Calibri, 40pt, aligned left, bold

First level: custom bullet, Calibri, 32pt

Second level: standard bullet, 28pt

The remaining levels have been deleted, as they are unnecessary.

Company logo

Click to edit Master title style

Click to edit Master text styles
• Second level

Slide size: Standard

Shaded background with gradient to break up solid white

6pt border around edge of slide (a rectangle with no fill was placed over the slide and sent to the back)

Automatic date, no footer or slide number

Figure 11.4 An example of a formatted master slide with logo

From the *View* tab you can also access *Handout* or *Notes Master* to set them up to match your presentation design.

If you work in Microsoft® PowerPoint™ regularly, you will use certain commands often. Just as in Microsoft® Word™ (see Chapter 2), it is useful to customise the Quick Access Toolbar to contain all your regularly used commands so that you do not have to keep moving between different tabs on the ribbon for the required actions. You can do this in one of two ways:

1.   Right-click on the ribbon and select *Show Quick Access Toolbar Below the Ribbon.* Now right-click on any command you use frequently and choose *Add to Quick Access Toolbar.*
     OR

2.   Go to the *File* tab and click on *Options* to bring up the *PowerPoint Options* dialog box. Choose Quick Access Toolbar and add the commands that you want.

Alternatively, you can customise the ribbon itself by adding a new personalised tab to include all your required commands. Using the *Options* button on the *File* tab to bring up the *PowerPoint Options* dialog box, select *Customise Ribbon* and click on the *New Tab* button below the pane on the right-hand side. You can then add one or more groups to the tab and select commands from the left-hand pane to add, as with the Quick Access Toolbar (see Figure 11.5). Both the tab and the custom groups can be renamed to identify them.

→

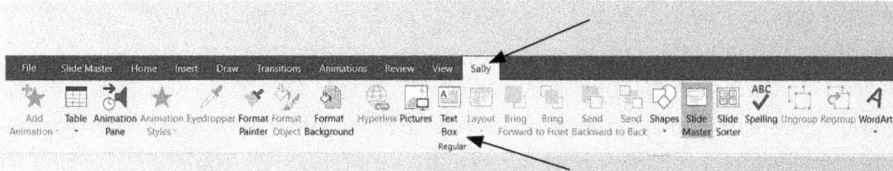

Figure 11.5 Customising the Quick Access Toolbar and ribbon

Save your master slide as a template

To save your design as a Microsoft® PowerPoint™ template, click on the *Close Master View* button on the *Slide Master* tab and then save your slide as a template by using the *Save As* command. Select 'PowerPoint Template' from the dropdown options in the *Save as type* box at the bottom of the *Save As* dialog box.

If you save your presentation as a Microsoft® PowerPoint™ show (.ppsx), your presentation will open directly in slideshow mode — effectively as a 'read only' presentation.

If you need to edit a show, select the file or show you want to edit, click *Open* and carry on editing as normal. When you save it, the file will still be a show.

If you do not want your show to be edited, or you need send out notes, handout pages or selected slides, consider saving the presentation as a PDF to protect it. After selecting .pdf from the *Save as type* dropdown box, click on the *Options* button to open the *Options* dialog box and then select which slides you want to save as a PDF.

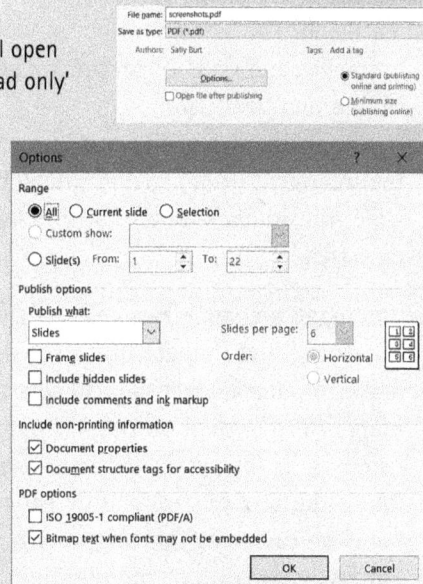

Figure 11.6 Opening the *Options* dialog box when saving as a PDF

How to insert a graphic or chart

To insert a chart, you can either create one via the *Chart* option on the *Insert* tab or you can import one you have already created in Microsoft® Excel™. Creating a simple chart directly in Microsoft® PowerPoint™ is straightforward, although you will still be prompted to add data in Microsoft® Excel™ via a pop-up window once the chart type has been selected. However, as most people present work already done elsewhere, it usually ends up being easier to copy and paste from Microsoft® Excel™. You can do an ordinary copy and paste, which still allows you to edit the chart by double-clicking on it to access the Microsoft® Excel™ base data. You can also paste the chart as a picture (in which case it will be unchangeable) or as a link (see pages 45–46 in Chapter 2 for information on how to use the *Paste Special* options).

Get the formatting and look of the chart correct in the original program before you paste it into your presentation.

Animations

Animation is a useful tool in presentations, as there is inherent meaning in the movement of images or text apart from and in addition to the visual impact of the content itself. The animation options in Microsoft® PowerPoint™ include:
- entrances and exits of text or images
- timing and triggers
- motion pathways of moving images around the screen
- the treatment of clips from films or YouTube
- slide transitions – note that these can make the presentation appear fussy if overused.

The following are some examples of the effect of animation:
- **Revealing text** (bullet points) to coincide with the moment the speaker makes a point allows the listeners to focus on one point at a time. This is more effective than putting up the whole list and revealing too much to the listeners, as this would mean they are ahead of the speaker.
- **Revealing sections on a flow chart incrementally** allows the audience to focus on each stage of the process.
- The **use of arrows** or highlighting tools that point out significant elements on the slide as they occur in the presentation helps focus the audience.
- **Animating parts** of machinery or specific elements within a diagram can help clarify complex movements.
- The appearance of **correctional material superimposed** on existing faulty or incomplete sections is more effective than two static slides showing 'before' and 'after'. Also note, however, that two consecutive slides can achieve the same effect as an animated addition onto a slide.
- A **moving diagrammatic version** can be clearer than a photograph that lacks clarity.

It is important, however, not to get carried away with animations, as you then run the risk of their dominating the content and distracting from the real purpose of the slide.

Figure 11.7 is a screenshot of the *Animations* tab and the listed animations on the *Animation* pane.

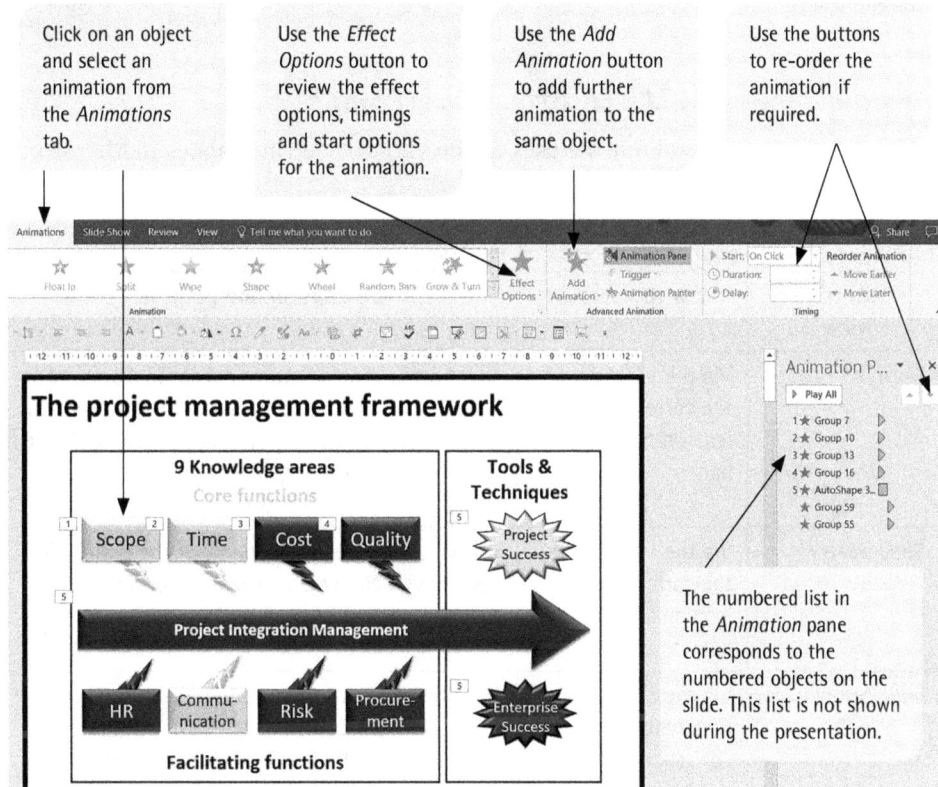

Figure 11.7 The *Animations* tab and the *Animation* pane in Microsoft® PowerPoint™

Keep the number of animations per slide to the minimum, as the animations can actually hold you up while you are presenting — you can adapt what you want to say to fit an audience and the flow of the presentation, but it is not possible to cancel the animations mid-presentation. This is especially problematic if you do not have a presenter mouse, as you can end up trapped by constantly needing to trigger the animations at the laptop or keyboard. Less can be more.

Animation should be used only to the extent that it enhances understanding and facilitates retention.

Animation should not be overused, as it can distract from the points being made in the presentation.

Viewing modes in Microsoft® PowerPoint™

Table 11.2 gives details about the uses of the various viewing modes in Microsoft® PowerPoint™.

Table 11.2 Viewing your slides in working modes

Presentation view	How to access it	Description and purpose
Normal	Via the *View* tab or the corresponding icon on the status bar	Numbered slide miniatures appear in a pane to the left of the main slide, giving you an overview and allowing you to easily move around or delete slides. This is the standard view for working on slides.
Slide Sorter	Via the *View* tab or the corresponding icon on the status bar	This view provides an overview of the entire slide deck so you can delete or rearrange slides by cutting and pasting or dragging selected slides.
Slide Show	Via the *Slide Show* tab, the corresponding icon on the status bar or F5/Function F5	This allows you to show your presentation. The *Slide Show* tab contains various options for ways to present the show as well as to rehearse the timings and record narration.
Presenter View	Via the *Slide Show* tab (see figures 11.8 and 11.9)	This option is only available for selection when the computer is attached to another monitor or screen for presenting. It shows the current slide, the notes page, the next slide, your timing and various show options, including a laser pointer and drawing tool. These allow you to be interactive with the slide during the presentation.

Holding the Shift button down and clicking on the first and last slide in a sequence selects all of them. Holding the Control button down allows you to select discrete slides that are not next to each other.

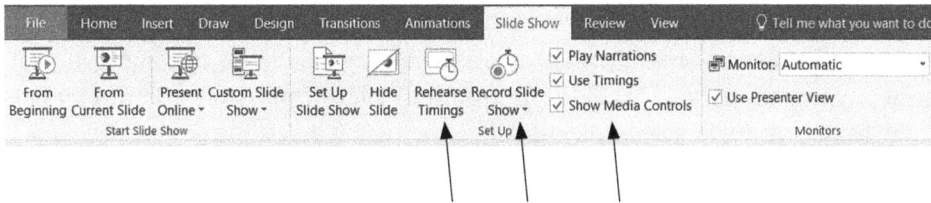

Figure 11.8 The *Slide Show* tab with options for viewing the completed presentation and rehearsing timing

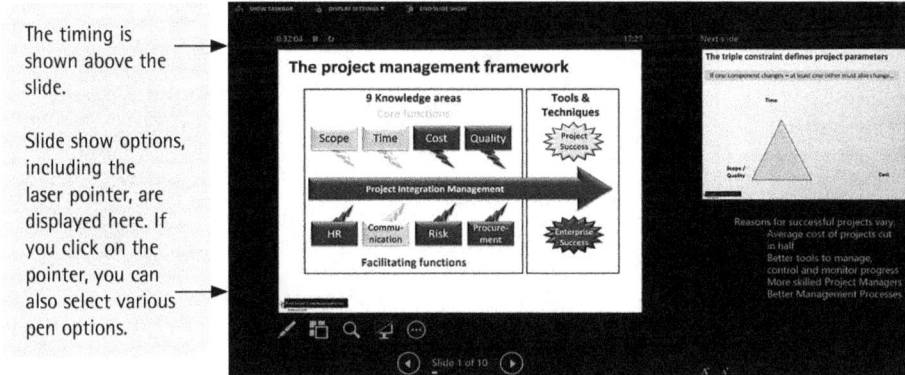

The timing is shown above the slide.

Slide show options, including the laser pointer, are displayed here. If you click on the pointer, you can also select various pen options.

Figure 11.9 *Presenter View*

11.4   Non-linear presentations

Non-linear presentations in Microsoft® PowerPoint™

One of the drawbacks often cited about Microsoft® PowerPoint™ presentations is that they have little flexibility. Once you have begun on a sequence of slides, the order is fixed even if the presentation itself takes a different turn. In addition, fixed-order, linear presentations preclude spontaneous changes to presentations where the agenda is set by the audience as much as the speaker. This is particularly relevant for small-group presentations aimed at promoting discussion. This drawback can be effectively countered by developing a deck of slides with optional routes through individual slides or short sequences of slides.

Rather than having a range of presentations for similar (or even widely different) audiences or topics, you can rather build up or create a comprehensive deck of slides compiled from all your presentations. If they are not all designed using the same template, then the first requirement is to make sure that they are. One of the most common presentation errors (and timewasters) is to take slides from different presentations and create a new presentation, the problem being that it takes time to format the slides to look the same. The chances are that differences and inconsistencies will creep in, which in turn make their way into the next presentation and the next as slides are re-used and adapted.

Hyperlinks in Microsoft® PowerPoint™

Once you have created a master deck of slides all in the same template, you can create hyperlinks to specific slides or groups of slides from your title or contents slide, as shown in Figure 11.10. Should a particular question or the need for a specific explanation arise, this organisation allows the presenter to go straight to a relevant group of slides in response to the enquiry or topic that has arisen.

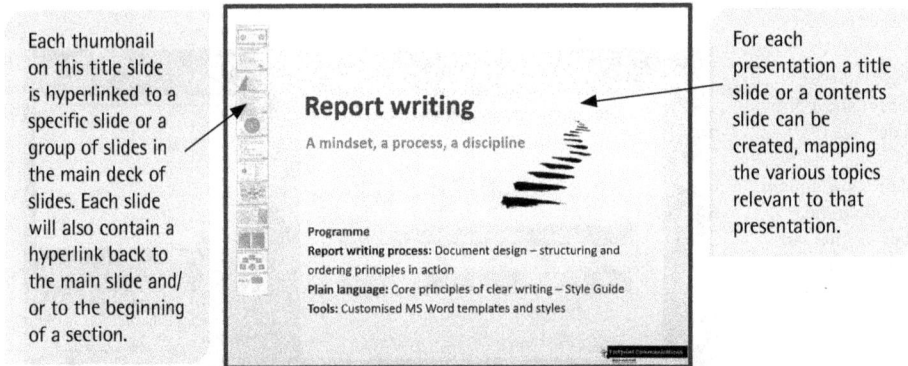

Figure 11.10 An example of a title slide showing the hyperlink dashboard

It is not necessary for the hyperlink triggers to be slide thumbnails, but it is convenient to do this as a reminder of the slide content. Do the following to create slide thumbnails with hyperlinks:

1. Either take a screenshot of the relevant slide you want the hyperlink to lead to, or copy the slide in *Slide Sorter* view. Then use *Paste Special* to paste it onto the title slide as a picture, and then resize and position it in a convenient place.
2. If the thumbnails look too prominent, apply a faint colour format to the image to make it appear semi-transparent. Do the same for all other target slides.
3. Click on one of the slide miniatures and do the following to insert a hyperlink to the relevant place in the presentation:
   a. Select the *Hyperlink* option from the *Links* section on the *Insert* tab (or press Ctrl+K). This will make the *Insert Hyperlink* dialog box appear.
   b. Select *Place in This Document* and scroll through the slides to select the slide that you want the hyperlink to lead to, as shown in Figure 11.11.
   c. Click *OK*.

Select *Place in This Document* to get a list of slides in the presentation. The list also contains generic options, such as 'First Slide'.

The *Slide preview* box indicates the content of the selected slide.

If a link is no longer valid or has changed, use the *Remove Link* option.

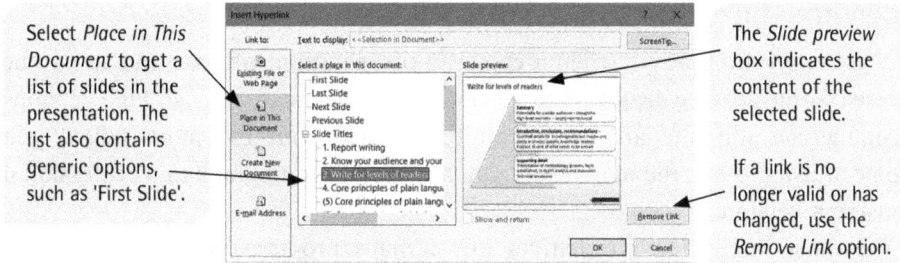

Figure 11.11 The *Insert Hyperlink* dialog box

Once all the hyperlinks have been set up to the required slides or groups of slides, you need to add a hyperlink to each individual slide to enable the presenter to link back to the title or contents slide. You can add a hyperlink to any shape or item, but a sensible option is to add an invisible rectangle in the same place on each slide (for example, the bottom right-hand corner) as a hyperlink. The invisible hyperlink can be on top of a logo and will not interfere with any text or graphics on the slide). The hyperlink is therefore not obvious to the audience, but is there for you to use. Follow these steps:

1. Draw a shape using the *Shapes* dropdown menu on the *Insert* tab.
2. Size the shape appropriately and position it, for example, in the bottom right-hand corner of one of the presentation's content slides.
3. Select the pasted shape and format it to have no colour and no outline.
4. Select *Hyperlink* from the *Insert* tab.
5. In the *Insert Hyperlink* dialog box, select *Place in This Document*.
6. Choose a specific slide (eg the contents slide) or one of the generic options, for example 'First Slide'.
7. Click *OK* to finalise the hyperlink.

Having set up one of these invisible hyperlinks, copy the hyperlink object and paste it onto each slide. This means each slide is now hyperlinked to the primary slide which contains a dashboard of links to all the other slides or groups of slides.

Working in this way means that at a moment's notice you can access almost any slide you have ever created. Alternatively, you can set up more than one deck of slides and set up a hyperlink to your other decks as well as to slides in the deck you are currently in. It takes a short time to open the new presentation via the link and you do not have to exit your presentation to find the one you now want. This method relies on the decks remaining stored in the same location, but it can be very useful for locating a particular set of slides very quickly.

Other non-linear presentation software

There are many alternatives when it comes to presentation software and, as can be expected, some are free or have free versions and others carry a cost. Free versions of commercial software are usually quite adequate, but the more skilled you become at using them, the more likely you are to want to upgrade to a professional or business version.

The most interesting alternatives are perhaps programs such as Prezi (see https://prezi.com/) or Focusky (see https://focusky.com), both of which have free versions. Essentially, they are like an open, blank canvas on which you can create a concept map or poster style presentation. Having created all the presentation elements, you can map a pathway through the different areas, zooming in and out to go into greater detail. Emphasis and hierarchy are created through size of text or images and placement of material. You can also include material to enable you to respond to questions in an ad hoc manner without being forced to include the material in the initial pathway. They also allow you to have an overview of the entire presentation – rather like the *Slide Sorter* view in Microsoft® PowerPoint™ but more interactively, showing links and relative importance.

These programs, with capacity for embedded video, audio and imagery like traditional programs, are designed to be more visual and interactive than traditional presentation platforms. The presentations can be shared easily online, although the offline editing functions in the free versions can be limited. It may take a while to become proficient at these programs, but they are definitely worth exploring.

Microsoft has added Zoom for PowerPoint™ (only available through Office 365 subscriptions at the time of publication of this book) and Microsoft® Sway™ to its suite of standard programs. Creating a Zoom allows you to jump to and from selected slides, sections, or portions of the presentation as you present, so it effectively allows you to choose the order, similar to the dashboard slide mentioned above, rather than following a linear route through the presentation. Microsoft® Sway™ is an online, digital storytelling app, which can be used to create presentations as well as interactive reports, newsletters, personal stories – all of which can be shared online by sending a link.

✓

Checklist for presenting with visual aids

Presenting is a multifaceted activity. While some presentations may be successful without any form of visual support, appropriate and well-planned visuals not only enhance the presentation itself but also facilitate both understanding and retention. The visuals, however, should be just that: visuals. Too much text on a slide may even be counterproductive. Use the following checklist when you prepare visuals for a presentation:

- Choose an appropriate title for the presentation.
- Try to minimise the amount of text on your slides. Summarise your points with phrases rather than whole sentences. Your oral presentation will include the more detailed explanations, so there should be no need to put much text on the slides.
- Keep charts and graphs simple, without too many elements such as lines, colours and textures.
- In an audio-visual presentation, show trends rather than detailed data.
- Use bright and contrasting colours to help your audience read the text easily. Do not use too many colours throughout your presentation; choose two main colours and be consistent (you can use shades of those colours if you need more).
- Make sure your lines are thick enough for easy visibility.
- Make sure your labels and numbers are legible.
- Consider whether there is appropriate lighting and equipment in the venue. For example, you do not want too much light on the screen or a poor quality data projector that will not be able to reproduce colour definition.

12   Foundations: approaching the research journey

Taking on a research task, be it for an academic assignment, a marketing report or a business proposal, can be a daunting prospect. Yet, we engage in research on a daily basis. Before buying a product, we weigh up the pros and cons of different options. When going on a holiday, we prepare by reading up about the climate, culture and food we can look forward to. We may even search for information online about our new employer before we meet him or her in person!

It is therefore clear that going in search of the information we need is, in many cases, second nature to us. Ready access to the Internet means that most people are able to locate exactly what they need to know more quickly and efficiently than has ever been possible. Yet, too often, this haste can lead to research that is sloppy, superficial and inadequate.

The aim of this chapter is to introduce the main elements you will need to master to become a confident, competent researcher. To do this, you will consider:
* the appropriate paradigm and approach for your research
* locating your research question
* strategies to promote ethical research
* referencing and citation.

After studying this chapter, you will be:
* informed of the theory supporting approaches to research
* apprised of options for managing your data
* able to select appropriate and ethical approaches to accessing and recording information
* equipped to integrate literature into your text and be able to cite and reference these readings according to your discipline.

12.1   Research paradigms and approaches

Once you know the research task you need to complete, it can be tempting to dive right in. Yet, you would do well to set time aside before you begin to consider the approach that you plan to adopt for the task.

Research paradigms

First, you need to decide which **research paradigm** is appropriate to your work. A paradigm is the particular worldview you bring to a task. In research, this involves careful consideration of two factors: **ontology** and **epistemology**. Ontology refers to your understanding of reality and epistemology refers to how we, as humans, can know this reality. These two factors will affect all elements of your research, from formulating your research question to the research methods you adopt and your research design.

For example, if a researcher believes that reality is stable and unchanging, he or she will believe that it is possible to objectively know this reality. This is known as a **positivist** paradigm, and researchers working in this paradigm adopt methods that quantify and measure this reality, such as surveys and questionnaires. On the other hand, if a researcher believes that there is no single, stable reality and that people only 'perceive' the world as working in a particular way, knowledge becomes far more subjective. This **interpretive** paradigm calls on research methods such as interviews and focus groups that delve into people's experiences. Table 12.1 presents an overview of two of these paradigms.

Table 12.1 Positivist and interpretive paradigms (adapted from Terre Blanche & Durrheim, 2006: 6–7)

Paradigm	Ontology	Epistemology	Examples of methods
Positivist	There is a stable, fixed reality.	It is possible to know this reality.	• Surveys • Questionnaires
Interpretive	Reality is subjective.	It is possible to know people's interpretations of this reality.	• Interviews • Ethnographic observation

The research paradigm you adopt will depend on the nature of your task. Research in the sciences and the built environment field most often requires a positivist paradigm, while humanities fields such as sociology or education often sway towards the interpretive. Sometimes you will be guided by your methodologies or the nature of the research topic. For example, if you are required to survey customers' product preferences for a report, you are researching for a single correct answer, which means your paradigm is positivist. As an advanced student, for example at PhD level, you will need to locate the paradigm that makes the most sense for your piece of work. This forethought lays the groundwork for a well-designed, coherent piece of research. Terre Blanche and Durrheim (2006: 6–7) provide a more thorough analysis of the various research paradigms.

Research approaches

Another element to consider before beginning your research task is whether the research approach you adopt will be **quantitative, qualitative** or a **mixed approach.**

Quantitative research is characterised by three main qualities (Maree & Pietersen, 2007: 145):

1. It is **objective** because it is trying to portray the truth about a situation. For example, quantitative research could be used to find out how many students at a university use WhatsApp for group projects.
2. It draws on **numerical data** because its findings are quantifiable. In the previous example, a survey could be administered across campus to determine the percentages of students who do and do not use WhatsApp for group projects.
3. It is **generalisable** because the findings can be applied to other contexts. For example, if 73% of students at a certain university use WhatsApp for group projects, this can give us a sense of WhatsApp usage at other similar universities too.

Qualitative research, in contrast, focuses on exploring the 'why' **questions** of research (Nieuwenhuis, 2007: 51). Instead of seeking out a single 'truth', it looks to find ways of explaining the way the world works, or what Nieuwenhuis calls 'the processes and the social and cultural contexts which underlie various behavioural patterns' (2007: 51). This often means learning about how individuals and groups perceive the world and make meaning for themselves. To use our previous example, a qualitative study on the use of WhatsApp for group projects could therefore involve trying to understand the reasons why students do or do not use WhatsApp in their projects. Students could be interviewed, with these interviews being analysed for deeper meaning.

Qualitative research differs from quantitative research in that the findings are not normally generalisable. Thus, a qualitative study would incorporate information about the specific context of the university where the research was carried out, meaning that the findings would not necessarily be relevant to other universities.

Figure 12.1 summarises the main qualities of quantitative and qualitative research.

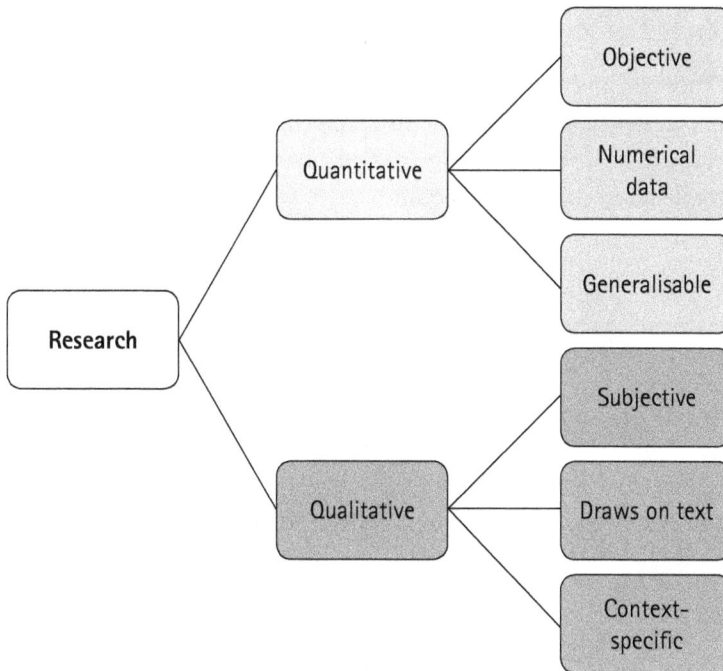

Figure 12.1 Qualitative and quantitative research

When determining your own research approach, remember that it can be helpful to think of quantitative and qualitative research as two poles on a continuum. This means that it is possible to tackle a research task that has both qualitative and quantitative elements, although it may lean more towards one approach. For example, look at the following research topic:

e9

Graduates today are required to enter the workplace with strong communication skills. How confident are the students in your class about their communication skills? Explain and discuss.

For this particular topic, you may decide to develop a questionnaire which you administer to all the students in your class, asking them to rank their confidence levels from 'poor' to 'very strong'. You may also decide to interview five students to obtain a clearer picture of their perspectives. In this scenario, you are drawing on both quantitative and qualitative techniques to inform your study. This is known as a **mixed approach** and it can yield rich results for a researcher.

12.2 How to locate your research question

Part of producing a focused piece of research is having a strong awareness of the research question that underpins your work. All research is guided by a question that involves something that you are trying to find out. Sometimes this will be quite overt. For example, a research topic could be:

> ℮9
>
> What are the factors that lead to attrition in the engineering industry in South Africa?

Here, the research question is clearly stated in the topic, giving the researcher a strong sense of what must be investigated.

Other times, the research question may be implied. For example:

> ℮9
>
> Discuss the relationship between matric results and the orientation to learning adopted by first-year accounting students.

While this is phrased as a statement (and not a question), the topic is clearly asking the researcher to explore a question (Ratele, 2006: 540).

At more advanced levels of research, such as postgraduate studies, you may be required to formulate your own research question. This can be challenging, given the almost endless possibilities available. Immersing yourself in the current literature around your field will be helpful, as this will give you a sense of what research already exists and what still needs to be explored further.

A strong research question is important for several reasons:
- It can help define the boundaries of your study, giving you a sense of what you need to include and what you can leave out.
- It can help you decide what research methodologies to adopt, as these will be guided by what it is you are trying to find out.
- Certain research projects can take years to complete, during which time you may stray off task. A strong research question can be a directive that pulls you back to the initial objectives.
- Developing a strong research question at the start of the study can save you time (and other resources) later on, as this will keep your study on track.

The following questions will be helpful as you develop your research question:

- **Is my question answerable?** For example, a question such as 'How do all South African doctors feel about vaccinations?' will be impossible to answer, as the scope is far too wide.
- **What questions have been asked previously?** Valuable research, particularly at PhD level, should develop new knowledge. As such, your question should not simply replicate those that have come before.
- **How is my research question phrased?** A question such as 'Does religion influence career choice?' requires a yes/no answer. A question such as 'In what way can religion influence career choice?' is open-ended and leaves scope for more in-depth responses. The former is better suited to a quantitative approach, while the latter is better suited to a qualitative approach.
- **Is my research question theoretically rich?** Jansen (2007: 4) compares a good research question to an onion. Just as a peeled onion reveals more layers as you go deeper, so too a good research question should create space for the emergence of other interesting research questions.
- **Is my question easy to understand?** While your research study may deal with complex concepts and ideas, your research question should be clear and concise. This is especially important, as it will guide your study throughout the research process. A complex research question could obfuscate your process.

Once you have developed your research question, consider sharing it with respected peers, colleagues or, if you are undertaking postgraduate studies, your supervisors. Their feedback can help you assess whether your question adequately encompasses the full scope of the issue and whether your findings will be a valuable addition to the body of knowledge in your field. Remember, your research question might change over the course of your studies as your understanding of an issue evolves. This is perfectly acceptable since research, by its nature, is dynamic. Nevertheless, taking time at the start of your study to articulate a strong research question is one of the most valuable tasks you can undertake as you begin your research journey. See pages 374–376 in Chapter 14 for detailed information on writing research questions and hypotheses.

12.3 Research ethics

Another issue you will need to consider before starting your research is whether the task that you are undertaking is based on ethically sound principles. This is most obvious when research involves human participants, particularly those who are vulnerable to exploitation, such as children. However, it is also a consideration in other fields such as medicine, science and engineering.

Research ethics often yield issues that are not clear-cut. One example of this is animal testing. Another is research involving the study of people without their knowledge. The researcher often has to weigh up issues of transparency and integrity versus the greater good that the research findings could lead to.

For this reason, many institutions such as universities have strong procedures in place to manage the research that is undertaken. This entails getting **ethical clearance** from university and/or faculty ethics committees before starting your research project. To do so, you will need to indicate that you have taken ethical issues into consideration and developed appropriate strategies to deal with these.

Wassenaar (2006: 67–68) highlights four widely accepted philosophical principles that you will need to consider to determine whether your research is ethical:

- **Autonomy and respect for the dignity of persons:** This relates to your study participants, for example interviewees. It could also relate to people with whom you are working on joint projects, for example in a laboratory setting.
- **Non-maleficence:** This refers to inflicting the least harm possible in order to fulfil the aims of your research.
- **Beneficence:** This refers to action done for the benefit of others. What is the potential benefit of your research and how does this weigh up against the potential risks thereof?
- **Justice:** You should treat research participants with fairness and equity throughout the research process.

Once you have built these principles into your research, you will also need to consider whether your research findings are **valid**. Threats to validity, according to Maxwell (2013: 123), are answers to the question 'How might I be wrong?' These relate to ethics because they have to do with how your identity as a researcher could impact your research findings. The following are some potential threats to your research validity:

- **Insider research** relates to how you are located in relation to your research. Some people believe that if your research setting is an area you are very familiar with, you are unable to study it in an objective way. For example, if you are a nursing student researching how patients respond during the admission process, you may take certain things for granted and let your own anecdotal experience from working with patients overtake your research findings.
- **Reactivity** refers to how you, as researcher, could influence the setting or individuals studied (Maxwell, 2013: 124). Particularly in the social sciences, it relates to whether you can be sure that your interviewees will answer your questions openly and honestly. If you are observing a staff meeting in order to research effective corporate practices, can you be sure that the staff members are behaving as they usually do?

- **Researcher bias** entails any prior beliefs, values and perspectives that you bring to the research that you are undertaking. It can be challenging to shed your personal frames of reference, but as a researcher you will constantly be enacting bias, from the topic that you choose to focus on to the sources that you choose to include or leave out.
- **Lack of response variability** can be an issue in spaces where you are conducting research with groups, such as focus group interviews. Some participants may be reluctant to share personal experiences or ideologies, while others may overpower the group. How will you ensure that you obtain a variety of inputs from different participants, which will lead to rich research?

While these validity threats may be challenging, there are strategies that can be implemented to support the four principles of ethical research mentioned above. These include:

- **Triangulation:** Use two (or more) sources to ensure that your findings are consistent. For example, check that your observations of how students behave in academic libraries match up to how they describe their own behaviour in interviews and how the literature says they behave.
- **Informed consent:** Ensure that you have participants' consent to be involved in your research. Be sure to draw up a consent form that outlines the background to your study, the goals thereof and the extent of the participants' involvement. Always keep this for your records. Participation in your study should always be voluntary.
- **Confidentiality:** Always take active measures to protect the confidentiality of your participants. Where appropriate, use pseudonyms when writing up your results and, if necessary, also change the name of study locations and institutions. Video or audio recordings should be destroyed once the research is complete.
- **Member-checking:** You can test emerging theories and results with your study participants to ensure that you are adequately representing their contributions. This can be done during the research process to ensure the integrity of your work.
- **Researcher reflexivity:** This entails a thorough exploration of your own researcher identity. What prior beliefs are you bringing to the study? How might your ideology, status and/or experiences affect the way you interpret your data? For example, how might a psychology student's research on family structure be affected if that student is an only child, is strongly anti-monogamy or has religious beliefs that prohibit divorce? Researchers need to acknowledge their own identity in order to understand how this could impact their research and how to build ways to deal with this into their research design.

12.4 Referencing and citation

Acknowledging the work of those who have come before you is a cornerstone of research, whether you are writing in the academic or professional sphere. The concept of 'standing on the shoulders of giants' is relevant here, as it refers to the idea of building new knowledge on the foundations of what has come before.

Plagiarism is often cited as the main reason why it is necessary to reference the work you cite in your research. Plagiarism is when you pass off the work of others as your own. This can range from submitting essays downloaded from the Internet as your own to using an idea that you read about in a book without acknowledging it. There are severe consequences for plagiarism, including loss of reputation and, in some cases, expulsion from university or loss of employment.

However, while the consequences of plagiarism serve as a warning, it is also possible to view referencing from a more positive perspective. Referencing the ideas of another author connects you to a global, dynamic body of knowledge that is constantly evolving. When researchers use other researchers' ideas in their work, they are building on what has gone before to create something new. At the same time, those researchers are laying the platform for others to do the same with their work, and so on.

There are a number of reasons why someone may neglect to reference, beyond deliberately stealing another person's ideas. Referencing is seen as time-consuming and tedious, taking precious research time away from the actual task at hand. Also, referencing can seem overwhelming and difficult, and researchers may refrain from doing it because they do not know how to. However, once the principle of referencing is understood, it is straightforward.

Basics of referencing

No matter which referencing system you are using, referencing consists of two main aspects: in-text citation and a reference list, as shown in Figure 12.2.

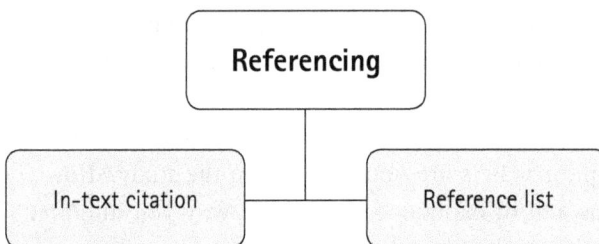

Figure 12.2 The two aspects of referencing

In-text citations are the references to where you located an idea, concept or quote that you are using within the text itself. For example, you could find the following paragraph within an essay on team dynamics:

> *℮୨*
>
> However, team dynamics can also be understood as heavily influenced by the effects of context (Chansa, 2016). This includes geographic context, meeting site, demographics of the company and material resources at the disposal of the group leader …

Here, you know that the researcher has used Chansa's idea, written in 2016, about team dynamics.

A **reference list** appears at the end of the study and includes full details about all of the sources that you have referenced within your essay. Thus, in the example above, the reference list would provide more details about the publication in which Chansa's idea was found. Below is the reference list entry for the book by Chansa:

> *℮୨*
>
> Chansa, Z. 2016. *Team dynamics in practice.* Cape Town: Corporation Press.

The purpose of a reference list is that another reader should be able to easily locate all the sources that you have used.

A **bibliography** is not usually essential for research reports. It is similar to a reference list in that it provides the details of sources, but it differs in that it can include any sources you used in your research, not only those that you cite directly in your study. It can thus be useful if you want to show the full scope of your research or provide a supplementary reading list.

In-text citations and a reference list are standard when referencing. However, there are a number of different referencing systems that exist. While each system may differ in format, the principles of referencing remain the same. Referencing systems are categorised into two main sets: **author–date methods** and **number methods**.

Author–date methods

Author-date methods of referencing include the Harvard system, the Modern Language Association (MLA) and the American Psychological Association (APA) system. They are so named because when you reference a source within the text, you include the name of the author and the date in which the source was published. When you have used a direct quote or an idea from a specific page, you also include a page reference. This method is used in this book.

The following examples provide a guide of how to apply the Harvard system of referencing. Remember, each system has developed correct ways of referencing all kinds of sources, including telephone conversations, YouTube videos and blogs. The following examples are not exhaustive, but should serve as a guide.

In-text citations

When the author's name forms part of the sentence, only include the year and page number (if relevant) in brackets in the text.

> ℮9
>
> Nene (2013: 12) is a strong proponent of the concept of discourse as language-in-use.

When the author's name is not part of the sentence, it should appear within the brackets.

> ℮9
>
> One way to understand discourse is as language-in-use (Nene, 2013: 12).

When there is more than one author, the first time you cite the reference you should refer to all the authors. Thereafter, you can use 'et al' after the first author's name.

> ℮9
>
> It is therefore evident that matric scores for South African students are directly linked to early childhood development initiatives (Pieterse, Lameez & Newton, 2011). This can be understood as a 'step forward for educational planning' (Pieterse et al, 2011: 44).

The reference list

In the Harvard system, the reference list is arranged alphabetically. The following section provides some common methods for referencing different kinds of sources in your reference list (and in-text citations). Note aspects such as the use of italics and punctuation. These vary according to the different systems you may be required to use. See Chapter 8 for the inclusion of a reference list in a report.

A guide to referencing different types of sources

Referencing books

When referencing a book, you need to include the author's initials and surname, the year of publication, the title of the book, the name of the publisher and the place where the book was published.

A book with a single author:

Smith, A. 2016. *Engineering tomorrow: An industry in transition.* Cape Town: Capitol Publishing.

A book with more than one author:

Dinler, H, Behr, L & Dlamini, K. 2015. *Watershed moments.* Pretoria: Harfeld Press.

A later edition of a book:

Mboweni, Z. 2009. *Healing hands: Tertiary health education.* 3rd ed. London: Exactfile.

Referencing a chapter or section in a book

Note the inclusion of the page numbers of the chapter or section:

Terre Blanche, M, Durrheim, K & Kelly, K. 'First steps in qualitative data analysis', in *Research in practice: Applied methods for the social sciences,* edited by M Terre Blanche, K Durrheim & D Painter. Cape Town: University of Cape Town Press: 320–344.

Referencing a journal article

When referencing a journal article, you need to include the title of the journal article, the name of the journal in which it appears, the year of publication, the authors' names and the page numbers. Where relevant, you must also include the volume and issue of the journal.

> e9
>
> Ni, X, Wong, ZJ, Mrejen, M, Wang, Y & Zhang, X. 2015. 'An ultrathin invisibility cloak for visible light'. *Science* 349(4): 1310–1314.

Referencing a website

When referencing an online source, include the author (if known), the date on which the document was created, the title, the URL and the date on which you accessed the page.

> e9
>
> Botes, P. 2016. Shooting the struggle. *Mail & Guardian*. Available: http://mg.co.za/article/2016-07-04-shooting-the-struggle. (Accessed 9 July 2016).

Referencing personal communication

Personal communication includes private emails, letters, interviews and telephone conversations. When referencing these, only use in-text citation. Do not include any entry on the reference list. The in-text entry should include the author, year, format, day and month of the communication.

> e9
>
> Strong oral communication skills emerged as the most important focus for employers when choosing a candidate (P Naidoo 2016, personal communication, 23 August).
> OR
> In an interview conducted on 23 August 2016, Paul Naidoo explained that strong oral communication skills were the most important focus for employers when choosing a candidate.

Referencing a secondary source

Sometimes authors refer to another author's work in their writing. Ideally, you should track down this original source if you wish to use it in your research, but if you are unable to do so, only include the source you did read in your reference list. In-text, the words 'cited in' indicate that you are referring to a secondary source.

> e9
>
> Of the students at Klipford College, 86% use their cellphones for research purposes (Sithole, cited in Mahlangu, 2015).

In the reference list, include the full reference for both the authors citing Mahlangu's publication and then write 'cited in' Sithole – and give the full details for this work.

Number methods

Number methods of referencing include the Vancouver system, the American Institute of Physics (AIP) system and the Institute of Electrical and Electronics Engineers (IEEE) system. According to these systems, in-text citations are signalled by a number (either in brackets or superscripted). These either refer to a numbered note at the bottom of the page or a numbered reference list at the end of the text. The following examples are of the IEEE system. Again, remember that the precise formatting will change depending on which system you are utilising.

In-text citations

When you refer to a source in-text, the number signalling the citation may either be located within the sentence or at the end of the sentence.

Perhaps this is a result of another benefit of insider research: that of increased credibility and rapport with research participants [1]. Furthermore, logistically, insider research is often more practical [2] in that it is cheaper and easier.

The reference list

According to the IEEE system (and other number methods of referencing), the reference list is organised according to the chronological appearance of sources within your work. Thus, the reference list for the above example would look like this:

[1] J Mercer. 'The challenges of insider research in educational institutions: wielding a double-edged sword and resolving delicate dilemmas'. *Oxford Review of Education*, vol 33, no 1, p 7, 2007.

[2] P Trowler. 'Researching your own institution: higher education'. *British Educational Research Association online resource.* Available: http://bera.dialsolutions.net/system/files/Researching%20your%20own%20institution%20Higher%20Education_0.pdf 2011. (Accessed 28 May 2014).

Some footnote systems will require you to have a bibliography at the end of your text that lists all the sources that you have used. These should be organised into categories of different kinds of materials, for example books, articles, cases (for legal writing), Internet sources and newspaper articles. Within these categories, sources should be listed alphabetically.

A guide to referencing different types of sources

Referencing books

A book with a single author:

[1] R Soulsby, *Dynamics of marine sands: a manual for practical applications.* London: Thomas Telford, 1997.

A book with more than one editor:

[2] WF Chen & L Duan, eds. *Bridge Engineering Handbook: Construction and Maintenance.* Boca Raton: CRC Press, 2014.

A later edition of a book:

[3] JP Gee. *Social linguistics and literacies: Ideology in discourses.* 3rd ed. London: Routledge, 2008.

Referencing a chapter or section in a book

[4] J Garraway, 'Higher education and the world of work' in *Higher education in South Africa: A scholarly look behind the scenes,* E Bitzer, ed. Stellenbosch: SUN Media, pp. 229–254, 2009.

Referencing a journal article

Note the abbreviated journal title:

℮9

[5] M Kipping and I Kirkpartrick, 'Alternative pathways of change in professional services firms: The case for management consulting, *JMS*, vol 50, no 5, pp 777–807, 2013.

Referencing a website

℮9

[6] K Kruger. *'South Africa leads the way in mobile health services which will change healthcare.'* Available: http://www.engineeringnews.co.za/article/south-africa-leads-the-way-in-mobile-health-services-which-will-change-healthcare-2012-03-14-1, 2012. (Accessed 11 July 2016).

Footnote styles

If you are using a system that uses footnotes, for example the South African Law Journal house style or the Chicago citation style, the footnote number should always be inserted **after** the punctuation in the text.

℮9

Current discourses on graduates' employability focus on how higher education prepares them for the labour market.[1]

This number will relate to the details of the source from which you have drawn your information, which can be found at the bottom of the page. The first time you cite a source, include a full citation.

℮9

1. Michael Tomlinson 'Graduate employability: a review of conceptual and empirical themes' (2012) 25 *Higher Education Policy* 408.

If you refer to the same source again, you need to use Latin abbreviations to refer to previous references. Explanations and examples of three of these can be found in Table 12.2.

Table 12.2 Latin abbreviations in footnote referencing

Abbreviation	Use	Example
ibid (in the same place)	This indicates the same source as the footnote immediately above. Include page numbers if these are different.	1. Benjamin Sulcas *Discourse in practice in higher education* (2006) 115. 2. Ibid. 3. Ibid at 120.
loc cit (in the place cited)	This indicates a source and page number already used, but not immediately above.	1. Gloria Dall'Alba 'Learning professional ways of being: ambiguities of becoming' (2009) 41 *Educational Philosophy and Theory* 36. 2. Roy Bhaskar *A realist theory of science* (1975) 146. 3. Dall'Alba, loc cit.
op cit (in the work cited)	This indicates a different page number of a source already used, but not immediately above.	1. Gloria Dall'Alba 'Learning professional ways of being: ambiguities of becoming' (2009) 41 *Educational Philosophy and Theory* 36. 2. Roy Bhaskar *A realist theory of science* (1975) 146. 3. Dall'Alba, op cit, 45.

Online referencing tools

Many resources online can help you master referencing, including extensive style guides that will provide you with the correct formatting for referencing even the most obscure types of sources. In addition, Google Scholar (see www.scholar. google.com) has a 'cite' function that shows you how to reference each source in its database according to a variety of different systems, including MLA, APA and Harvard.

However, as a savvy researcher, you would do well to acquaint yourself with one of the numerous online referencing tools that currently exist, including Zotero (see Figure 12.3), Mendeley, Refworks and EndNote. These programs provide innovative ways to manage your references. While they differ in specifics, each offers most (if not all) of the following functions:

- collecting sources directly from your web browser with a single click
- gathering your sources in a single, searchable interface
- organising your sources into collections and sub-collections
- tagging your sources for easy searches
- creating citations simply in Microsoft® Word™ via a plugin (See Figure 12.3)
- formatting according to any referencing style
- creating reference lists instantly
- synching across various devices.

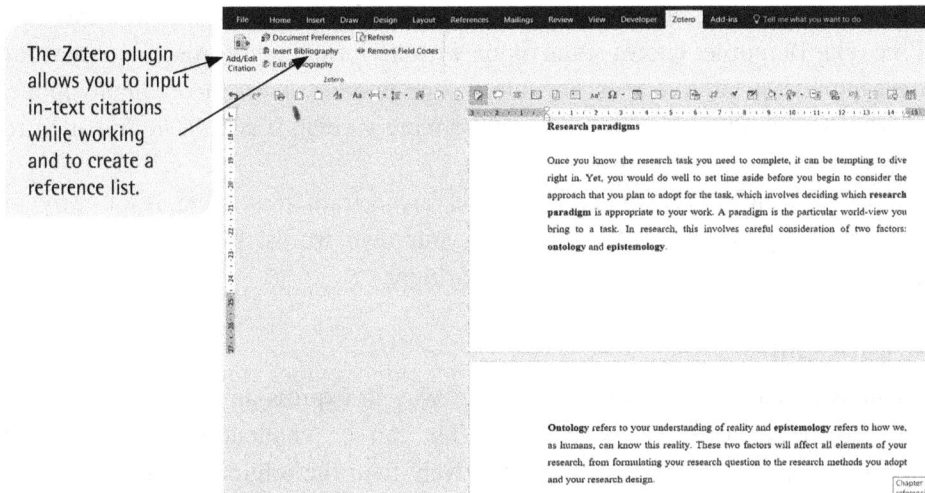

The Zotero plugin allows you to input in-text citations while working and to create a reference list.

Figure 12.3 The Zotero plugin for Microsoft® Word™

These online referencing tools are free and fairly intuitive to use. Each site provides comprehensive support in the form of guides, tutorial videos and discussion forums where you can post specific queries. Visit the following sites to learn more about these tools:

- **Zotero:** http://www.zotero.org
- **Mendeley:** http://www.mendeley.com
- **Refworks:** http://www.refworks.com
- **EndNote:** http://www.endnote.com

In addition to these online tools, Microsoft® Word™ has an in-built referencing function. See Chapter 2 for more information on this.

12.5 Integrating sources into your work

Once you have located an idea, quote or concept in a source that you wish to use in your research, you have two options. You can either **quote** or **paraphrase** the author.

Quotes

Consider the following extract:

Case's definition of a profession as 'a distinct body of individuals who take charge of a particular domain of knowledge for the purposes of practice in society' (2013: 75) locates the emergence of engineering as a profession around the time of the industrial revolution.

In the example above, notice how the quotation has been integrated into the flow of the text. Do not let quotes stand alone with no introduction. Also, note that for direct quotes the citation must include a page number, as in the example above. If it is a longer quotation (normally 40 or more words), it should be indented to stand out clearly from the rest of the text.

Only use direct quotations when you are certain that there is no way to adequately express the author's idea in your own words. If you do use direct quotations in your writing, do so very sparingly.

Paraphrasing

Paraphrasing consists of finding your own way to express an idea from a source that you are using in your research. This can be challenging when it feels impossible to state something more effectively than the original author.

When paraphrasing, it is not sufficient to simply change a few words of the original. Rather, find a way to encompass the whole idea the author has presented. The best way to do this is by breaking away from the original source. Once you have read the source and located an idea you wish to use in your work, close the book or put away the journal article and write down how you understand the idea. Check to see whether this corresponds to the original idea. You may need to refine this to ensure clear expression.

Look at the following extract from a journal article. Note that this extract is from page 551 of an article written in 2013 by an author called L Holmes:

> By opening up, rather than closing down, the analysis, we can see that the employability-as-possession approach to graduate employability has major flaws. One alternative, that is based on notions of social positioning, provides little clear and positive guidance on how we might intervene at the level of the curriculum. The third, the processual approach, particularly in terms of identity project, it has been argued, avoids the problems with the other two approaches.

The following is an illegitimate paraphrase of the source content given above:

> By broadening the analysis, we can see that the employability-as-possession approach to graduate employability has many issues. One alternative, based on ideas of social positioning, does not provide clear and positive guidance of how to intervene in the curriculum. The third, the processual approach, particularly in terms of identity project, avoids the problems with the other two approaches.

In this example, the author has simply substituted certain words from the original. Also, the author has not provided any in-text referencing.

The following is an example of a legitimate paraphrase:

e9

Of the three approaches to graduate employability, the processual approach, which relates to identity development, is the most effective. Both graduate employability as possession and as positioning are problematic (Holmes, 2013: 551).

Here, the author has reworked the concept from the original example into his or her own words. The author has also included an in-text citation. Note the page number which is included, as it is a reference to a particular idea.

See Chapter 1 for more information on good discourse and writing style.

✓

Checklist for the savvy researcher

The research journey begins long before the researcher enters the field and begins to collect data. Strategies need to be developed and plans put in place in order to ensure that the research will be of high quality. This involves careful decisions around paradigm, approach, research question and ethics and validity. In addition, you will save time by referencing from the very start of the project. Use the following checklist to guide you as you undertake your research task:

- Select an appropriate research paradigm and approach.
- Formulate a well-articulated research question.
- Consider the ethical implications of the study and develop a strategy to address these.
- Implement a referencing system which includes, where appropriate, using an online referencing tool.

13 Working with data and research methodologies

Whether you are working on a feasibility study, newspaper article or academic thesis, your research project will require you to use external sources as part of your information gathering. The data that you use will come from two kinds of sources:

1. **Primary sources** provide direct, first-hand evidence about your object of study. They are original documents and objects. These would include interviews, experimental results, speeches, historical and legal documents, statistical data, emails, fieldwork and surveys.

2. **Secondary sources** discuss data that was originally presented elsewhere. This always involves some level of interpretation of the data. Some examples of secondary sources are newspaper and magazine articles, scholarly journal articles and textbooks.

Books can be considered primary or secondary sources, depending on their content. An autobiography is a primary source, as it presents a first-hand account. A history book dealing with a particular subject, however, is a secondary source, as it synthesises different data sources and incorporates the author's interpretation.

This chapter provides an overview of how to use sources to strengthen your research. It does so by describing:

- strategies to locate data sources
- quantitative and qualitative research methodologies
- techniques for data analysis
- research presentation.

Once you have read this chapter, you will be able to:

- find appropriate sources of data that you can use in your literature review
- design your qualitative and/or quantitative research strategy
- analyse any data you generate
- deliver your research in a document or presentation.

13.1 How to locate sources

If your research project requires you to complete a literature review, your initial groundwork will consist of locating appropriate sources. With the Internet enabling unfettered access to a mass of information at any time, it becomes more and more important to base your research on sources that are credible. This entails knowing **where** to search and **how** to search. Both aspects are covered in this section.

Libraries

While much research, both academic and professional, is moving into a virtual space, it is still a good idea to begin your research journey at a library. Many libraries have access to the most recent books and journals, as well as up-to-date technology that can aid your literature search. In addition, reference librarians are specially trained to help you locate relevant sources that will help your research. Some libraries even have specialist librarians for different areas of study.

Most academic libraries will have access to services such as online library catalogues and electronic journal databases (described in the following sections) that you can draw on when locating sources.

Online library catalogues

The online library catalogue can be used to browse through all the material (including books, DVDs, theses and journals) the library has available or to look for a specific source.

When doing a **general search** to locate sources on a topic, you can do a keyword search of the whole catalogue. This will return a list of sources that contain your keyword(s). Use the Boolean operators (AND, OR and NOT) to aid your online search, as illustrated in Table 13.1.

Table 13.1 The Boolean operators

Operator	Function	Example
AND	Narrows the search	A search for 'dogs AND cats' will return any sources with the word 'dogs' and the word 'cats' as keywords.
OR	Widens the search	A search for 'dogs OR cats' will return any sources with either 'dogs' or 'cats' as keywords.
NOT	Excludes terms from the search	A search for 'dogs NOT collies' will return sources with the keyword 'dogs', but not those that have 'collies' as a keyword.

You can combine the Boolean operators in various ways as needed. For example, the search '(Dogs AND Cats) NOT (Collies or Siamese)' can deliver a more targeted search.

If, after using keywords and the Boolean operators, your search still produces an overwhelming number of results, consider using the 'advanced search' function to limit the results to the most recent publications only or to those that relate to a particular field, such as the humanities or the built environment.

Alternatively, you can use a source's title and/or author to locate the **specific source** on an alphabetically organised list of all available sources. Here, you would search using the title and/or author. This method will be ideal if you already know the sources you need to locate from a reading list or a bibliography. If the source is already out on loan, many libraries offer a service whereby you can use the online catalogue to request that it be returned promptly.

Electronic journal databases

The benefit of using journal articles in your research is that you know that the research will be up to date. Also, because journals are reviewed by academic experts before being published, you can be sure that the source will be valid. If you know that you need to access journal articles for your research, use electronic journal databases to locate general sources or to search for a specific source. There are various online databases that cater for different research areas, for example:

- **Engineering Village:** engineering
- **LexisNexis:** law
- **PubMed:** biomedical
- **JSTOR:** multidisciplinary
- **EBSCOhost:** multidisciplinary

A number of these databases are subscription-based. This means that you must access them via an institution, such as a university, that has a subscription agreement with the database. In this case, you would need to either use a computer in the library, or access the database after logging on to the library's website.

Databases may differ in the level of results that they yield. Some provide the citations of relevant journal articles, which you can then use to search your own library. Others provide abstracts or summaries of the articles, which can provide you with more information about the article before you decide whether you want to search for the full version. Finally, there are some databases that provide the full text versions of articles. You are then able to print or download the articles as you need them.

The Internet

Inevitably, you will use the Internet in the course of your research project. Consisting of billions of pages, the Internet is an incredible source of data. This does, however, mean that during your search you will encounter a lot of content that is irrelevant, invalid or of questionable integrity. Targeted, purposeful use of the Internet will ensure that you are able to find credible sources that aid your research. There are various ways of searching the Internet. Some are discussed in the following sections.

Search engines

Most people access the Internet via search engines such as Google, Yahoo, Bing, AOL or ask.com. A search engine is a software system that allows you to search the World Wide Web (WWW) using keywords that you generate. The search engine works in three basic stages:

1. **Web crawling:** Sites on the Internet are visited by an automated spider or robot.
2. **Indexing:** The content is analysed and placed in a huge database.
3. **Retrieval:** The search engine returns a list of sites related to your search.

There are a number of strategies that you can implement in order to increase the relevancy of the sites that the search engines yield:

- **Choose keywords carefully.** Remember, the search engine will yield sites that contain the words you search for. Therefore, use keywords that would appear on the pages you want. Also, be specific. A search such as 'jobs South Africa' will yield far more irrelevant results than 'marketing jobs Cape Town'.
- **Use Boolean operators.** Boolean operators (see Table 13.1 on page 335) can also aid your web search by specifying the bounds of your search.
- **Use double quotation marks when searching for an exact phrase.** For example, the search "a rolling stone gathers no moss" will return pages with these exact words in this order.
- **Limit the date.** Many search engines will allow you to limit your search according to when the website was created.
- **Use the 'advanced search' feature.** Most search engines offer an advanced search feature that allows you to specify factors such as country of origin, date of publication and the type of document you are searching for.
- **Get to know your search engine well.** Search engines differ in terms of their specific tools. It is therefore worthwhile to get to know the one you use regularly, including shortcuts, so that you can maximise your searches.
- **Use a different search engine.** Search engines employ different algorithms. As such, the same search may yield different sites on different search engines. If you are struggling to locate the sites you need, consider using an alternative search engine.

Google Scholar (see Figure 13.1) is a particularly useful search engine for academic research, as it indexes the full text or abstracts/summaries of scholarly literature such as journal articles, books, theses and conference presentations. You can browse articles according to key words (using the strategies explained earlier to focus your search) and arrange the results according to year or relevance. Google Scholar also allows you to create a library as you work, where you can save search results to read or cite later. You can access Google Scholar at www.scholar.google.com.

Stand on the shoulders of giants

Figure 13.1 The Google Scholar home page

Directories

Web directories differ from search engines because they are compiled by human beings, not robots. This means that while a search on a directory will yield fewer sites, these will be more relevant. On a directory, sites are organised hierarchically by categories and subcategories and the user navigates through these in order to locate the topic area. Most directories are general in scope, but some are more specific. Some examples of comprehensive directories are the Open Directory Project (www.dmoz.org), the WWW Virtual Library (www.vlib.org) and the Best of the Web Directory (www.botw.org).

Other ways to search the Internet

The following are some additional tools you can use for Internet searches:

- Gateways and subject databases: These consist of collections of sites and databases, arranged by subject, which are organised, maintained and evaluated by specialists. Some examples are Chemdex (www.chemdex.org), which focuses on chemistry; Zunia (www.zunia.org), which focuses on social development; and TechXtra (www.techxtra.tradepub.com), which focuses on engineering, computing and mathematics.

- **'Invisible web' searches:** Standard search engines and directories are only able to search the limited amount of the content on the Internet that has been catalogued. The rest of the content is known as the 'invisible web' and is by far the largest component of the Internet. The content on these sites may contain information that is valuable for your study. Several tools have been developed to help you access the invisible web. These include Find Articles (www.findarticles.com), the Directory of Open Access Journals (www.doaj.org) and the OAIster Database (www.oclc.org/oaister.en.html).

- **Real-time searches:** This is the concept of searching for and finding information online as soon as it is produced. This allows you to stay abreast of the most current information available. One way of doing a real-time search is by using the search function on social media sites such as Twitter or Instagram. Another way is to use a social media search engine such as Social Searcher (www.social-searcher.com) or Social Mention (www.socialmention.com). These allow you to search across various social media sites.

13.2 Research methodologies

When your research project requires you to generate your own data, you will need to employ quantitative, qualitative or mixed methodologies in order to do so. (See Chapter 12 for more about these approaches to research.)

Sampling

Whichever approach you choose for your research, you will need to determine the size and composition of your **sample**. This refers to the portion of a population that you choose to use in order to generate your data. There are various techniques one can use for sampling.

Probability sampling

These techniques rely on random selection, meaning that different subsets of the population have an equal chance of being selected for the study. This means that the sample is more representative and the findings are generalisable over a wide group. Some methods of probability sampling are shown in Figure 13.2.

Simple random sampling:
The sample is selected from the whole population completely at random, often electronically.

Cluster sampling:
The population is divided into clusters, often based on geography. A sample of these clusters is then randomly selected and used for the study.

Stratified random sampling:
The population is divided into subgroups (for example, by age or race) and then a sample is randomly selected from each group.

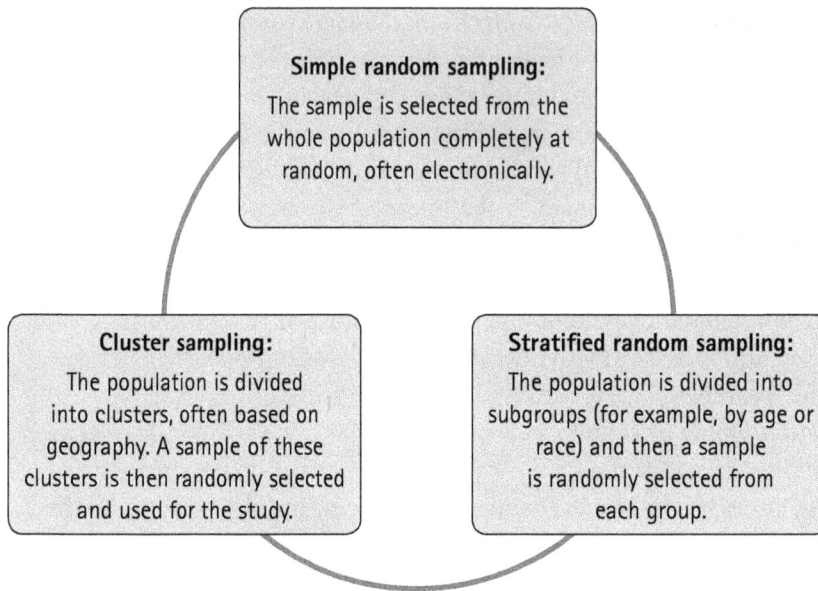

Figure 13.2 Methods of probability sampling

Non-probability sampling

This refers to the purposeful, non-random choosing of particular subjects for the study. There are various methods of non-probability sampling, as shown in Figure 13.3.

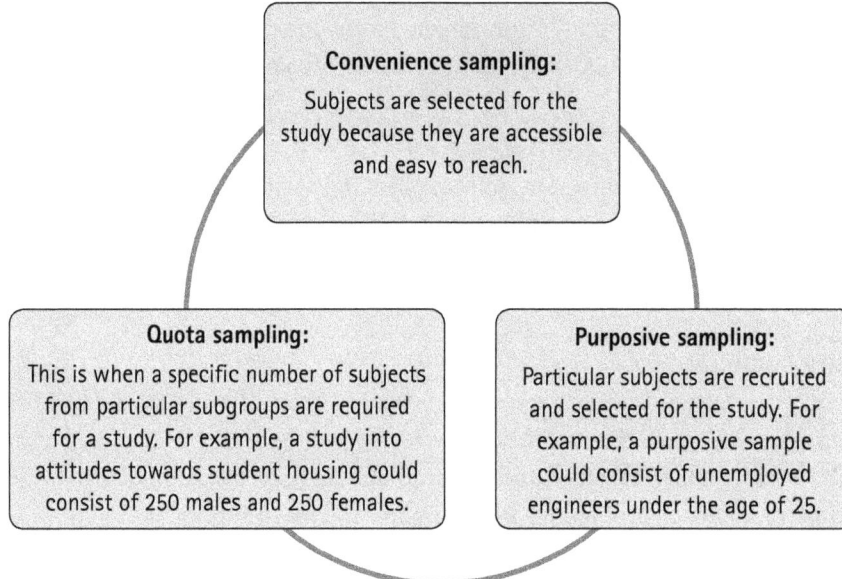

Convenience sampling:
Subjects are selected for the study because they are accessible and easy to reach.

Quota sampling:
This is when a specific number of subjects from particular subgroups are required for a study. For example, a study into attitudes towards student housing could consist of 250 males and 250 females.

Purposive sampling:
Particular subjects are recruited and selected for the study. For example, a purposive sample could consist of unemployed engineers under the age of 25.

Figure 13.3 Methods of non-probability sampling

The size of the sample that you use in your research will differ depending on the nature of the task. For example, quantitative research often relies on large samples because of the requirement that the findings be generalisable across other contexts. Contrastingly, in qualitative research, with its focus on understanding in context, there is often a stronger emphasis on a well-selected sample than on attaining a large sample size. In fact, some qualitative research only focuses on one subject, for example an in-depth, ethnographic study of a particular school.

Quantitative methodologies

Once you have decided on your approach to the research, your next decision will be what methodologies to implement in order to gather your data. In the natural sciences, quantitative research methodologies involve empirical investigation or the observing and recording of natural phenomena. In the social sciences, on the other hand, this usually involves surveying a target population for factual information, experiences, opinions or behaviour, depending on the purpose of the research.

There are different ways of going about carrying out a survey. Two of these are **questionnaires** and **interviews**. Your decision about which data gathering tool to use will be based on a number of factors:

- What **financial resources** do you have to carry out the study? Questionnaires are cheaper to administer than face-to-face interviews.
- How big is your required **sample size**? It may not be feasible to interview hundreds of subjects.
- Is your sample **literate**? This will affect whether you can use a written survey.
- Can you guarantee that your sample will read, complete and return a written survey? '**Survey fatigue**' means that people often ignore requests to complete yet another form.
- Is the sample **geographically dispersed**? If so, it could be difficult to carry out face-to-face interviews.

Constructing your survey

Once you have decided whether you wish to use a questionnaire or an interview to gather your quantitative data, it is necessary to design your survey carefully. You may choose to use **closed questions** or **open questions** in your survey.

Closed questions prescribe the range of possible responses. Below are some examples of closed questions:

- **Dichotomous question:** This is a question that has only two possible responses. These may be Yes/No, Agree/Disagree or True/False. For example:

> ✐
>
> It is a woman's responsibility to arrange childcare. Agree/Disagree?

- **Multiple-choice question:** The respondent is asked to choose a response from a number of possible options.

> ✐
>
> What is your role within the factory?
> A.   Worker
> B.   Shop steward
> C.   Manager
> D.   None of the above

- **Likert scale:** The respondent must choose a response out of possible responses spanning a five-point scale.

> ✐
>
> The course has shifted your perception of what it means to be a professional.
>
> ─○──────○──────○──────○──────○─
> Strongly   Disagree   Neutral   Agree   Strongly
> disagree   agree

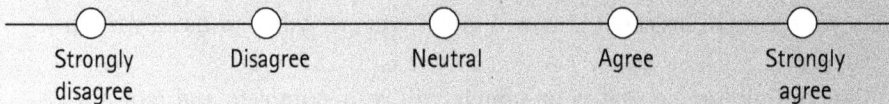

- **Filter questions:** These can filter out some of your respondents so as to direct them to a particular subsequent question.

> ✐
>
> Do you have a master's degree? Yes/No
> If yes, please indicate the faculty in which this was achieved.
> A.   Humanities
> B.   Law
> C.   Engineering
> D.   Business

Open questions leave space for a variety of answers from respondents.

> *e9*
>
> Describe one skill you have learnt as part of the soft skills workshops.
>
> Please complete the following sentence in your own words: An effective engineer.....

Open questions afford a level of personal engagement and depth of response that is not possible with closed questions. However, bear in mind that these may lead to difficulties at the data analysis stage, as they require complex coding.

Questionnaires

If you choose to administer your survey via a questionnaire, there are a number of guidelines to adhere to with regard to its design:

- Pay attention to the **appearance** of the questionnaire. A messy, hard-to-read and poorly laid-out questionnaire will lower the response rate. Ensure that there is plenty of space for questions and answers and that the font is large enough to read easily.
- Instructions should be **simple and clear** to avoid ambiguity.
- Begin the questionnaire with an explanation of the **purpose** of the research. Where appropriate, also include assurances of confidentiality and anonymity.
- Use **headings and subheadings** to guide the respondent through the various sections of the questionnaire.
- Adhere to the rules for **Plain English**, given in Chapter 1. Avoid jargon where possible.
- End the questionnaire by **thanking** the respondent and include your contact details for any further correspondence.

Interviews in quantitative research

In a quantitative research approach, interviews tend to be highly structured. This means that the interviewers will ask the questions exactly as they have been formatted by the survey designer and will record the responses. This structure is important in order to ensure that the research remains objective, the study can be replicated and the answers can be collated across multiple interviews. Once an interview becomes less structured, the approach shifts towards the qualitative. This type of interviewing will be discussed later in this chapter.

Quantitative interviews can be carried out face to face or telephonically. Interviewers should be well trained so as not to influence the answers that are given.

New technologies for quantitative research

In **mobile surveys**, material is collected via smartphones or tablets. This can result in wide dissemination and rapid response time. In addition, online software also exists to administer surveys via text message, which would work well in contexts where respondents have access to more basic technology.

Online surveys have become common in the field of marketing, but can also be useful for academic research. They are fast, simple and easy to disseminate. However, they have been associated with lower response rates than traditional paper surveys. Another advantage of online surveys is that they offer powerful tools for response collation and analysis, thus saving the researcher work at a later stage.

Computer-Assisted Telephone Interviewing (CATI) sees computer software being used to facilitate the interviewing process. The computer dials a telephone number, and the interviewer then follows the computer prompts, reads the questions to the interviewee and notes the answers. The computer contributes to data accuracy and analysis at later stages. **Automated Computer Telephone Interviewing (ACTI)** sees the entire interview being carried out by a computer with voice recognition capabilities.

Qualitative methodologies

As discussed in Chapter 12, qualitative research differs from quantitative research in that the findings are not generalisable or directly comparable between various contexts. Rather, the research aims to describe and interpret the research material in an in-depth manner, in contrast to the quantification- and measurement-based explanations common in quantitative research. Whereas quantitative research is strongly structured, qualitative research is often more open-ended and inductive, with a level of flexibility that allows for dynamism in the research process.

There are a number of qualitative methodologies and approaches that one can use. The sections that follow discuss some examples of these.

Case studies

Case study research refers to an in-depth research focus on a particular person, organisation, event or situation. Once the case has been selected, multiple research methods (both qualitative and quantitative) may be used to develop a rich understanding of the subject within a real-life context over a sustained period of time.

For example, adopting a case study approach to a research project about mathematics education may see the researcher picking one particular high school maths class to focus on as a case study for a full term. The researcher might decide to observe the classes, interview the teacher and administer surveys to the learners at the beginning and end of the term. The researcher would then use these methods to develop a full description and explanation of the maths class. While the findings in this case study would not be generalisable to every other maths class in the country, they could help us better understand how learning takes place within a maths class. As such, the value of case study research lies in the in-context descriptions and explanations that it can develop, strengthening previous research and opening up areas for future research.

Different kinds of case studies that you may choose to use for your research are discussed in Table 13.2.

Table 13.2 Types of case studies

Type of case study	Description
Illustrative case study	This is a case study that illustrates a particular instance or situation. For example, a particular brand of canned drink could be used as a case study to illustrate how beverages move to market.
Exploratory case study	This is a small-scale case study carried out as a pilot. The purpose is to determine the advantages and pitfalls of the methodologies that are implemented in preparation for the full study.
Critical instance case study	This is a case study that highlights a unique research situation. For example, if a school abolished homework altogether, this could form the location for a critical instance case study for new approaches towards primary education.

Individual qualitative interviews

Individual interviews provide an important data gathering tool for qualitative research projects, as they are a way to glean a large amount of in-depth, rich information from research subjects. Qualitative interviews differ in their levels of structure, as described in Table 13.3.

Table 13.3 Types of qualitative interviews

Type of interview	Process or structure
Structured interview	The interviewer has a set script of questions from which he or she does not deviate.
Semi-structured interview	The interviewer has an interview schedule with some questions, but the conversation may shift from this.
Unstructured interview	The interviewer may use a prompt to begin the conversation, but thereafter there is significant flexibility and the interviewer follows the interviewee's lead in determining the interview focus.

Before embarking on individual interviews, consider logistics such as the time available and financial resources. Interviews can be time-consuming to organise and carry out, and transcription is very labour-intensive. If your project needs to take place in a short timeframe, this may not be a feasible method. Also, finances may be necessary to pay interviewers, to organise a space to carry out your interview, for equipment such as a recording device, and to pay for transcription.

Qualitative interviewing requires a high level of focus from the interviewer, who should be able to use questions effectively to maintain a focus on the aims of the research, while still remaining flexible enough to follow potential valuable threads that may arise. Critical listening and responding are thus important skills for an interviewer.

When carrying out interviews, it is important to be well prepared. Consider how you will record the interview. For example, will you use a digital voice recorder, a video camera, or simply paper and pen? Whatever you choose, ensure that all equipment is in working order prior to the start of the interview.

If you decide to carry out individual interviews, the following are some ethical issues that you should keep in mind:

- Avoid **leading questions** that can influence the data you gather. For example, the question 'How many times have you felt unsupported by your employer?' carries the implicit assumption that the interviewee has felt unsupported by his or her employer. However, this may not actually be the case. A better phrasing could be: 'Describe the levels of support provided by your employer.'
- Be aware that even in formulating your interview schedule you will inevitably be influencing the research by **choosing to focus on some areas** over others. Ensure that you are aware of the influence this could have on the data that is collected.
- Consider the influence that you could have **as an interviewer**. For example, if you are a manager at a company interviewing employees, they may be unwilling to share information about bullying in the workplace for fear of repercussions, given your higher status within the company.
- Some interviewees may be uncomfortable with the idea of having their words recorded and saved on a digital voice recorder or video camera because of issues around **confidentiality**. It is standard practice to delete any recordings once the study is complete.

Focus group interviews

Focus group interviews involve carrying out an interview with a group (usually between six and ten participants) as opposed to an individual. The advantage of this research methodology lies in the interaction between the group members. Rich data can emerge from their conversations with one another and through their agreements, disagreements and discussions. This is the kind of data that may not come to the fore in an individual interview.

In a focus group interview, the interviewer should take the role of a facilitator, creating a safe, enabling space where the views of the participants can predominate. There are various ways of encouraging conversation. These include the use of stimulus material such as newspaper articles, images or objects; role-play scenarios; and/or creative activities such as drawing or free writing.

Again, consider the ethical implications of choosing to gather your data via a focus group interview:

- Consider the impact of **group dynamics**. For example, a polite, friendly group may be unwilling to disagree about issues, resulting in a lack of response variability. Also, particular group members could be overpowering during the discussion, which would have an impact on the opportunity for disparate perspectives to emerge.
- Consider **your role as an interviewer**. Again, how the participants perceive you could impact on what they are willing to share with you.
- While you can ensure that you respect the **privacy** of your participants and keep the contents of the interviews confidential, you cannot guarantee that all the participants will do the same.

Observation

Observation as a data gathering tool involves in-depth immersion in a real-life context. It can vary from straightforward observation to participant observation, where the researcher becomes a member of the group he or she is observing. For example, straightforward observation could involve sitting in a restaurant, observing how customers interact with waiters. In participant observation, on the other hand, the researcher could actually become a waiter and spend some shifts serving customers in a restaurant and noting what emerges from this.

When using observation as a method for qualitative research, there is much reliance on the notes developed by the researcher, which need to adequately capture the sights, sounds, atmosphere and details of the situation. Consider how best to record your experiences. For example, will you take notes or use a video camera? Note that these may be obtrusive and interrupt the natural flow of events, thus threatening the validity of the data you gather.

One of the ethical issues around observation involves the impact that the researcher may have on the research setting. It is unethical to carry out covert research without the participants' permission; however, if participants are aware that an 'outsider' is present, they may alter their behaviour, thus affecting the data that is gathered. In addition, observations always occur through the perceptions of the researcher and as such will always be affected by some level of bias. It is important for researchers to be aware of their impact on the research. A research journal in which the researcher tracks his or her evolving perceptions can be an important way of making these explicit.

13.3 Data analysis

Quantitative data analysis

Once you have implemented your quantitative research methodologies, you will have generated raw data, such as completed questionnaires or transcripts of interview surveys. These will provide you with lists of numbers that represent the responses to your questions. Next, you will need to turn your attention to the analysis of this data so that you can draw valid conclusions to answer your research question.

There have been entire textbooks and courses dedicated to the statistical methods behind quantitative data analysis. This in-depth approach is beyond the scope of this chapter. Our discussion here will, however, set you on the path to working with your quantitative data and point you in the direction of tools that can support your work in this field.

Durrheim (2006: 188–193) highlights three steps that are necessary in order to prepare your data for analysis. They are coding, entering and cleaning, as shown in Figure 13.4.

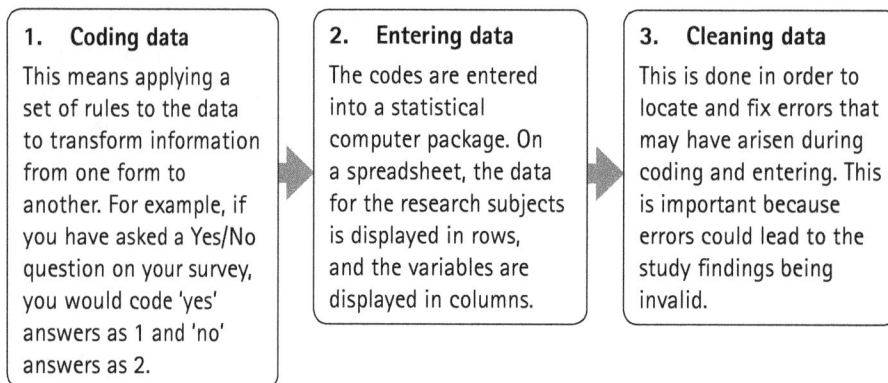

1. Coding data	2. Entering data	3. Cleaning data
This means applying a set of rules to the data to transform information from one form to another. For example, if you have asked a Yes/No question on your survey, you would code 'yes' answers as 1 and 'no' answers as 2.	The codes are entered into a statistical computer package. On a spreadsheet, the data for the research subjects is displayed in rows, and the variables are displayed in columns.	This is done in order to locate and fix errors that may have arisen during coding and entering. This is important because errors could lead to the study findings being invalid.

Figure 13.4 Steps in preparing data for analysis

Once the data has been coded, entered and cleaned, it is ready to be statistically analysed. There are two methodologies for quantitative data analysis (Durrheim, 2006: 196):

1. **Descriptive data analysis** techniques describe the data by investigating the different scores for each variable and determining whether these are related.
2. **Inferential data analysis** techniques see the researcher draw conclusions about wider populations based on the sample data from the study.

A number of computer software applications have been released in recent years that can aid the quantitative data analysis process. These have the benefits of reducing calculation errors and supporting data management processes. However, users should remember that while applications can support analysis, the researcher still needs to manage the process. Some of the most popular applications are the following:

- **SPSS (Statistical Package for the Social Sciences):** This package supports the entire quantitative data analysis process, from planning and data collection to analysis, reporting and deployment. An intuitive interface allows for high levels of functionality for both beginners and more advanced users.
- **STATISTICA:** This advanced data analysis package offers a comprehensive variety of statistical techniques and covers thousands of functions, algorithms, tests and methods. In addition, it has strong data visualisation capabilities, allowing the creation of unique 2D and 3D graphs.
- **Stata:** This is an interactive data analysis program that has capabilities including data management, statistical analysis, graphics and custom programming. It can import data in a variety of formats (including from other statistical packages, spreadsheets and data sets) and can be used across Microsoft, Mac and Linux/Unix computers. In addition, there is a version called Small Stata which is designed specifically for students.

Qualitative data analysis

Once you have completed your qualitative data gathering, you will have collected a large number of texts, be they interview transcripts, field notes, memos or relevant documents. Remember that analysis should begin while you are still collecting the data, as this is when it is most fresh in your mind. You can start thinking about ways to link the different data you come across, noting similarities, differences and ideas that arise from them. Be sure to write these burgeoning ideas in your research journal.

Terre Blanche, Durrheim and Kelly (2006: 322–326) break the qualitative data analysis process into five steps. These are shown in Figure 13.5.

1. Familiarisation and immersion

This initial stage is an opportunity for you to get to know your data very well. This means reading the texts, making notes and brainstorming so that it becomes very familiar.

2. Inducing themes

This means inferring themes from the data itself as opposed to applying predetermined conceptions. It could be said that this stage requires you to 'listen to the data' to see what ideas emerge.

3. Coding

Maxwell (2013: 107) defines coding as the act of fracturing the data and rearranging it into categories that allow for the comparison of elements and the development of theory. Here, you run through the data, marking different sections (including words, phrases, sentences and paragraphs) as being instances of the themes you have developed.

4. Elaboration

This relates to the careful examination of the data categorised under each code in order to capture the nuances that lie in the selections that you've made.

5. Interpretation and checking

At this stage, you develop your interpretation of the data. Having done so, it is important to check your interpretation critically in order to ensure that it is valid, reliable and ethical.

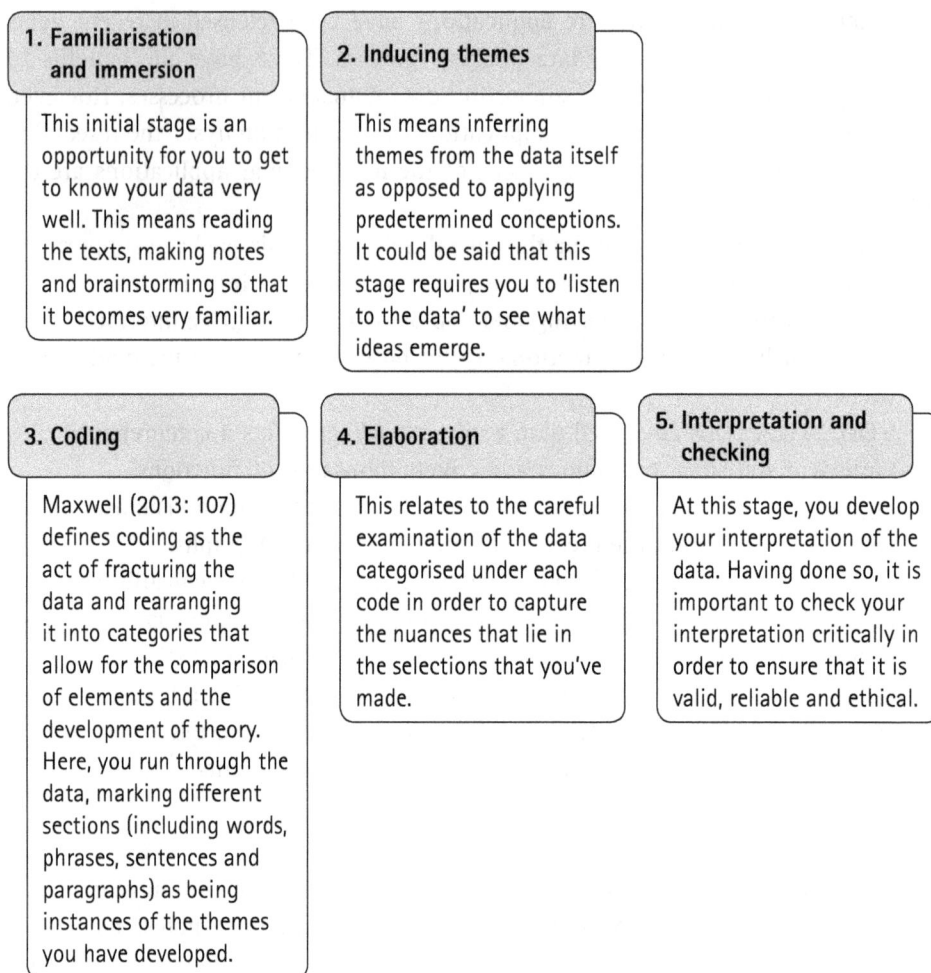

Figure 13.5 Steps in analysing qualitative data

Again, whole books have been devoted to the topic of qualitative data analysis, and the brief explanation in this chapter simply presents an overview of the process. The novice researcher may find it useful to become familiar with one of the many software packages designed specifically for qualitative data analysis. This software is called Computer-Assisted Qualitative Data Analysis Software (CAQDAS).

CAQDAS facilitates the organisation, management and analysis of qualitative data, providing ways of storing and retrieving data and coding and sorting this. Some can support the development of theory by allowing you to attach memos to particular codes and to create concept maps. The following are some examples of CAQDAS:

- NVivo allows the researcher to import and analyse text or multimedia files and to code these using coding stripes. The researcher can then work within these codes, add memos and notations, and create word clouds, mind maps, diagrams and other visualisations.

- ATLAS.ti aims to help researchers uncover complex phenomena hidden in qualitative data by allowing for the coding and annotation of primary data material and the provision of a number of powerful tools to facilitate visualisation of the relationship between elements. A useful feature is PDF support, which allows you to work seamlessly with PDF files.
- **CAT (Coding Analysis Toolkit)** is a free, open source, web-based service that provides a way to code raw text data. It offers tools to work with multiple collaborators and is a reliable and safe program to use if working on a team project.

13.4 How to present your research

Academic writing

Assignments that are written in an academic context, such as a college or a university, require that you adhere to a particular genre of writing. This involves adhering to particular conventions regarding structure, style and tone. The following sections discuss approaches to academic writing.

A proper approach to the assignment

Before you begin writing your assignment, ensure that you have taken time to properly analyse the topic. This will ensure that the response that you develop matches the requirements of the topic.

One way to analyse the topic is to look for two types of words: **process words** and **content words**. The process words will give you a clear sense of what you need to do in the assignment, and the content words will tell you what you need to research. For example, look at the following assignment topic:

> List the traits required for becoming a successful entrepreneur. Discuss the various financial incentives offered by government to promote entrepreneurs. (1 000 words)

In this topic, the process words are 'list' and 'discuss', because these tell you what the topic is asking you to do. Note how these are requiring you to do two different things. The word 'list' requires you to mention a number of different elements, while 'discuss' requires you to go further than this by weighing the elements up and adding your own input.

Many different process words may appear in your assignment topic. Here are some examples, along with the action they require you to take:

℮9

- **Assess:** Weigh up to what extent something is true, taking into consideration evidence. Conclude strongly.
- **Contrast:** Look at two or more different elements and point out how these are dissimilar.
- **Define:** Offer a precise meaning.
- **Explore:** Consider something from a variety of different viewpoints.
- **Justify:** Make a case for an argument, providing different lines of evidence.
- **Summarise:** Give a condensed version of something.

The content words in a topic provide focus for your research. Returning to the example used earlier, the content words are 'entrepreneur(s)', 'financial incentives' and 'government'.

Plan your assignment structure

Once you have a clear sense of the topic requirements, the next step is to develop a rough structure of the assignment, which will form an outline for your writing. Start by determining how long the assignment is. Next, look at previous samples of your work and example essays to determine the average length of your paragraphs. This will give you a sense of how many paragraphs you will need to write.

For example, in the essay topic above, based on an average of 120 words per paragraph, you will know that you need to write approximately seven paragraphs. With the first and last paragraphs containing the introduction and conclusion, this leaves five body paragraphs for content.

Next, you may find it helpful to use your process words to begin to develop a rough outline. For example, you may decide that of the five body paragraphs, the first will be used to 'list the traits required for becoming a successful entrepreneur' and the remaining four will be used to 'discuss the financial incentives offered by government'.

Do bear in mind that this structure is very flexible and may change during the course of your research and writing. However, having a sense of the essay structure early on and using this to develop your outline will help you remain focused during the process.

Introductions and conclusions

The **introduction** of your assignment is the first time your reader will engage with your writing, so it is important that you create a positive impression. You also want to hook your reader to compel him or her to read on. Here are some strategies to use in your introduction:

- **Define key terms.** If the topic contains any terminology that may be unfamiliar to the reader, you may define it in the introduction. Do, however, avoid the clichéd sentence: 'The Oxford English Dictionary defines X as ...' Rather, work the definition into the flow of your text.
- **Catch the reader's attention.** There are various ways to do this. You may include an interesting statistic, a relevant quote or an alternative perspective on the topic.
- **Provide an overview of the assignment.** This will prepare the reader for what to expect in the body of the writing.
- **Be succinct, brief and crisp in style.**

The **conclusion** is the section that will most likely stay with the reader once he or she has finished reading your assignment. This is your opportunity to leave a lasting impression. The following are some strategies to do this effectively:

- **Reiterate your argument.** This is important, as it will tie together the argumentative thread running through the paper.
- **Summarise the main points.** Do this in order to remind the reader of the gist of your writing.
- **Leave food for thought.** One way to do this is to include a reference about your topic's implications for the future. For instance, using the example topic used earlier, you could leave the reader thinking about how government may incentivise entrepreneurship in the future.
- **Suggest areas for future research.** This shows that you are aware of the longevity of the subject area.

Academic style

See Chapter 1 for guidelines on writing effectively. These principles, with a particular focus on the writing style for Plain English, will stand you in good stead with your academic writing. The following are some additional stylistic elements that are unique to academic writing:

- Unless explicitly stipulated (for example, in a reflective assignment), **use the third person** for academic writing. Avoid the personal pronoun 'I'.
- Use the present tense when incorporating the work of other authors.

e9

Van Niekerk (2015) explains that ... Mbongeni (2013) describes the context ...

- Avoid unnecessary words.

> *e9*
>
> Instead of writing:
> In his book Anatomy of Freedom (2016), Bertrand Make effectively discusses the various approaches towards conceptualising models of social freedom.
>
> Rather write:
> Make (2016) discusses approaches to social freedom.

- Be specific when mentioning people and dates.

> *e9*
>
> Instead of writing:
> Many people believe communication skills are important for engineering students.
>
> Rather write:
> Communication skills are important for engineering students (Johnson, 2012; Govender, 2016; Ndlovu, 2010).
>
> Instead of writing:
> Greenside University recently opened a new Science Centre.
>
> Rather write:
> Greenside University opened a new Science Centre in December, 2015.

- Avoid asserting your personal opinions too strongly.

> *e9*
>
> Instead of writing:
> Nkosi (2011) has an excellent approach to the topic ... .
>
> Rather write:
> Nkosi's (2011) approach is significant because ... .

Formatting and proofreading

Adhere to the guidelines for readability given in Chapter 1, including typefaces, headings and subheadings, and columns. These will contribute to the overall quality of your document.

Also, proofread your document carefully before submitting it to ensure that you eliminate any errors. After working on an assignment for a significant period of time, it can be hard to pick up mistakes. In this case, follow these tips for proofreading:

- Read the document sentence by sentence in reverse order, from the end to the beginning. By breaking up the logic of the piece, you should be able to spot small technical errors.
- If you have been working off a computer screen, consider printing the document out and proofreading a hard copy.
- Read the paper aloud.
- Recruit a friend to proofread your work. A fresh pair of eyes may pick up errors that you miss.
- As you work through various assignments, develop a list of your common errors. Pin this up in your work area and refer to it as you write.

Collaborative writing

In some situations, you may be required to complete a group academic writing assignment. It can be challenging to distil different people's styles and content into a cohesive piece of writing, so it is worth deciding on a strategy with your group before commencing the work.

On the one hand, you may decide that all members of the group will work on all sections of the assignment together, from conceptualisation to the finished product. The positive aspect of this approach is that the assignment will truly be a group effort. The negative aspect is that the process will most likely be unwieldy, with many conflicting contributions and much debate.

On the other hand, one person may take on the role of primary writer, with some feedback from the other group members. This process will likely be more efficient, but the assignment may lack the richness of diverse contributions.

Ideally, formulate a strategy that falls between these two options. This could see the group planning the assignment together face to face, working on different sections separately, and then coming back together to assemble the final version. Alternatively, some group members may focus on the research part of the process, while others write up the work.

Whatever strategy you develop for your group writing, there are some principles you can implement in order to achieve consistency in the group assignment:

- Develop a **style guide** with your group. This can include aspects such as the template, length of paragraphs and vocabulary. This style guide can be dynamic and will change over time.
- **Brainstorm** the topic together and use the guidelines above to agree on the assignment's outline. This will ensure that all group members are working towards the same vision.

- **Plan your time carefully.** Schedule meeting times with your group and agree on benchmarks for progress. Allow plenty of time for revision.
- Work **review mechanisms** into your assignment scheduling. This means that at various points in the process, different group members will have an opportunity to review and report back on the process of the assignment.

Writing collaboratively over a distance

With distance learning and part-time study becoming viable options for students internationally, you may find yourself needing to complete a written assignment with group members who are geographically dispersed. In this scenario, there is a wide variety of technological support available in order to ease the process:

- **Doodle** (www.doodle.com) is a scheduling tool that allows you to set up convenient meeting times with your group members.
- **Skype** (www.skype.com) can be used to video-call with up to 25 group members. This provides an opportunity for face-to-face communication.
- **Google Docs** (www.docs.google.com) allows you to share files between group members. These are instantaneously updated as they are worked on, with the changes appearing automatically in the document seen by all members.
- **Dropbox** (www.dropbox.com) provides a way to share up to 2GB of files with different users. These can be accessed via any computer through the Dropbox website.
- **Wiggio** (www.wiggio.com) is an online group collaboration tool which brings together a number of the functions in the applications named above, including scheduling meetings, sending messages, hosting conference calls, sharing files and polling group members.

These are just some of the online tools available, and the options are expanding rapidly. Most of these applications are highly intuitive, but online help is available through the sites or on YouTube (www.youtube.com). See Chapter 2 for more about online collaboration tools.

New media for your research

While academic essays and journal articles remain the most ubiquitous formats for the dissemination of research, researchers are constantly developing new and innovative ways of sharing their work. The benefit of this is that your research can reach unfamiliar and diverse audiences who may not have access to the more formal academic channels. Utilising new media can also challenge you to find ways to make your work accessible to non-experts and can help you see your research in fresh ways. The following sections discuss three alternative ways to share your research.

Blogs

A blog (short for weblog) is a personal online site created and maintained by individuals or small groups. There are millions of blogs online dealing with all manner of subjects, from sports to the arts, from history to science. The differentiating factor for blogs, as opposed to static websites, is that they are highly interactive, inviting visitors to comment and authors to respond, thereby stimulating networking.

Researchers create blogs for different reasons. For example, a researcher working on an in-depth project may share his or her experience, from fieldwork to data analysis and write-up of the findings. Another person may chart his or her development as a researcher over time from a personal perspective. Another could use a blog to make his or her work accessible to a wider audience than would be possible through formal academic publishing. Figure 13.6 shows an example of a blog that deals with a specific field.

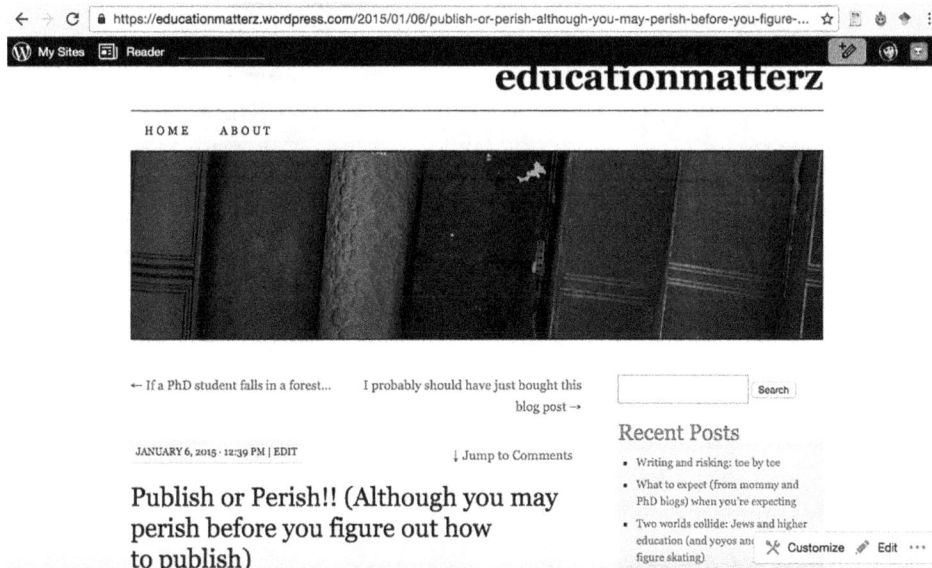

Figure 13.6 A WordPress blog on higher education (personal blog by Gabrielle Nudelman)

There are a number of free online platforms one can use to create a blog. These include WordPress, Blogger and Tumblr. Online tutorials are available via the platforms themselves and YouTube, and these can guide you through the process.

E-portfolios

Like a traditional portfolio, an e-portfolio is a space for you to store samples of your work. However, an e-portfolio is unique in that it is an online space and, as such, you can store a variety of different media types, such as videos, audio clips, images and documents. Using free, easy-to-access software such as Wix.com,

WordPress or Pathbrite, it is simple to create a customised website to showcase your work. This becomes your e-portfolio. See Figure 13.7 for an example of an e-portfolio.

Figure 13.7 An e-portfolio home page (by Puleng Lelala for BSc [Geomatics], UCT)

You may choose to use your website to focus on one research project, such as your thesis or an investigation you have carried out at work. In this case, you could incorporate a variety of different media. For example, you may include a video of the experiment you carried out, an audio recording of an interview with your supervisor and a PDF document of the completed full paper.

Alternatively, you could use your e-portfolio to showcase the full spectrum of your research over time. You could upload all your articles or essays to date, organised according to logical categories, as well your CV in order to show your credentials.

A major positive aspect of e-portfolios is that you can include links to external sites, such as YouTube videos, organisations' home pages, the work of researchers in related fields, and social media pages. This is useful for creating networks between your work and the field in which it is situated, thus showing its relevancy within a wider context.

Posters

If you plan on showcasing your research at a conference, trade fair or expo, you may be required to create a poster. In this context, your poster needs to be able to stand alone, as you will not always be around to explain the content. As such it needs to be comprehensive enough to present the gist of your research to the audience. This means that you need to refer to your research problem, findings, conclusions and recommendations on the poster.

However, remember that your poster is primarily a visual medium. As such, it should not be too word-heavy. Also, bear your audience in mind. If the audience may include non-experts in your field, steer away from the use of jargon as far as possible. Explain all technical terms as appropriate.

Figure 13.8 is an example of a research poster that will accompany a presentation by a speaker.

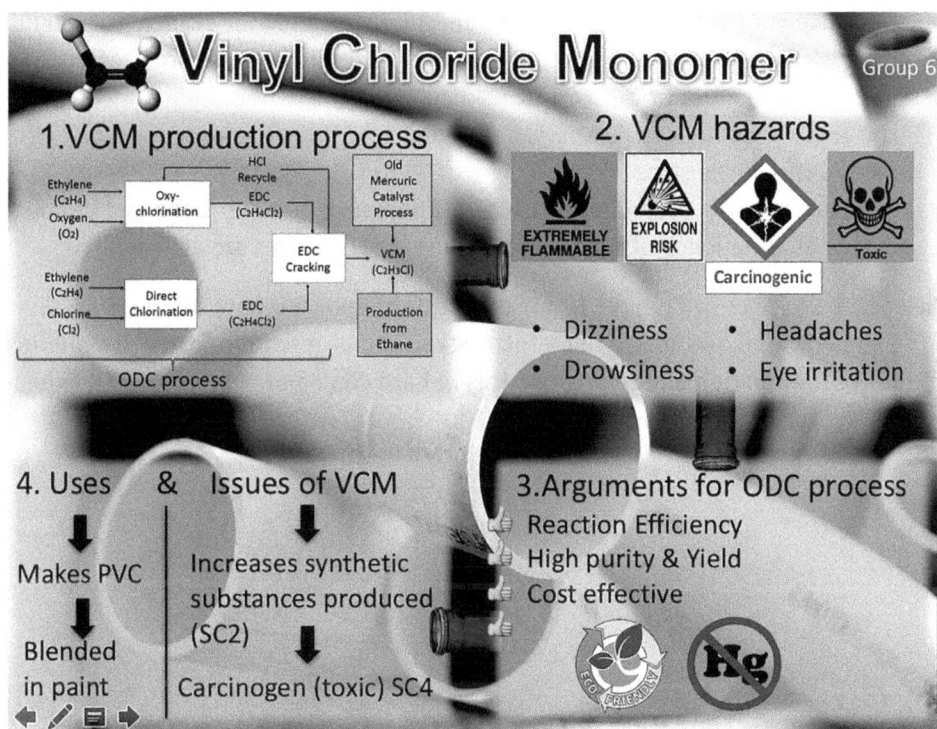

Figure 13.8 A research poster for a chemical process, created to complement a delivery by a speaker (poster by Mark Hambrock for a BSc Chemical Engineering project)

Here are some tips to consider as you develop your posters:

- Ensure that the font you use is **readable** from a distance.
- Use **graphics** where possible instead of text. Consider the inclusion of tables, graphs, diagrams and images where appropriate. All graphics should be labelled and clearly integrated.
- **Design** your poster taking into consideration the theme of the research. This means choosing fonts, colours and graphics that are appropriate to the topic. For example, a poster dealing with environmental issues may incorporate earthy colours (for example green and brown).
- **Organise** your information logically and intuitively for the reader. This could mean using a clockwise layout, or moving from the top left corner of the poster to the bottom right corner.
- Use **text connectors** such as arrows to guide the reader from section to section of your poster.
- Remember to include **important information** such as your name and contact details and the logos of any organisations to which you are affiliated.

See pages 291–293 in Chapter 10 for more information on how to create posters.

Figure 13.9 shows an example of a stand-alone research poster. It contains extensive information and references. It is in hard copy and very large (AO), which means the type can be read with ease.

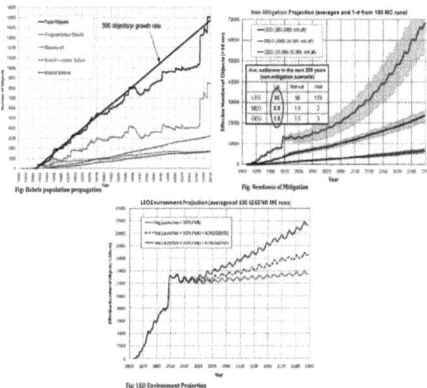
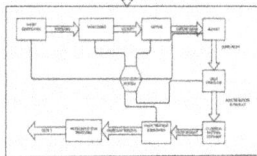
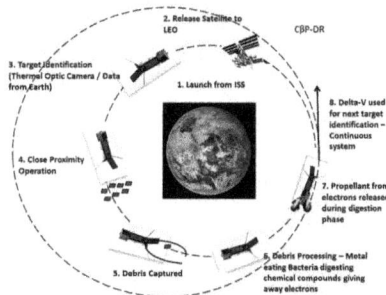
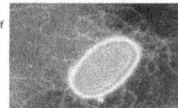
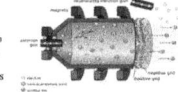
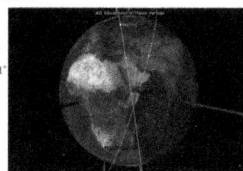

Figure 13.9 A stand-alone research poster for a process for clearing space debris (poster by Louis Feng and Abhijit Nath for an MSc in Space Studies)

✓

Checklist for working with data

Working with data can be challenging, stimulating and frustrating. Particularly when your research deals with human subjects, the process can be unpredictable, requiring you to be flexible and dynamic in your approach. However, research can also be extremely rewarding, particularly when understood as the creation of new knowledge. As you collect, analyse and present your data, use the following checklist:

- Use the library's resources to search for relevant sources, including the catalogue, electronic journal databases and librarians.
- Search the Internet purposefully, utilising search engines, directories, gateways, the 'invisible web' and real-time searches as and when appropriate.
- Determine whether you will use quantitative or qualitative methodologies to generate your data, or whether you will use a combination of these.
- Formulate a plan for data analysis, supported by software packages.
- Implement the principles for good academic writing, including effective structure, introductions and conclusions, academic style, and formatting and proofreading.
- Consider the use of new media to showcase your research, including blogs, e-portfolios and posters.

Academic proposals, dissertations, theses and papers

14

A thesis for a postgraduate degree is a scholarly work that presents an integrated, well-supported argument. Requirements for the degree depend on the level of the degree: honours, minor or full master's and doctorates all have different requirements. At master's level, the thesis must show that the candidate has learnt the various crafts needed to conduct research, but the thesis does not necessarily have to introduce new knowledge. A PhD thesis must display novel ideas and concepts, complexity and originality in thought, critical thinking and publishable outcomes. It must make a contribution to the knowledge in the field explored.

All academic writing has a cyclical nature. While this chapter describes the process chronologically, many of the stages, such as reading literature, writing up the literature review and handling the empirical work, happen simultaneously or are revisited.

This chapter will introduce you to the requirements of an academic submission such as a proposal, a thesis or a journal paper. From this you will learn about the:
- process of writing up research
- writing of academic proposals to take a master's or doctoral degree
- main elements of a proposal
- writing academic theses
- sections of a thesis
- timetable for writing a thesis
- style for a proposal and thesis
- presentation of a thesis
- writing journal papers and articles.

After studying this chapter, you will be able to:
- plan and manage your research so that you write it up timeously and in stages
- write persuasively about research when submitting a proposal
- select appropriate data for each section of the proposal
- know the requirements of a postgraduate thesis and its sections
- manage your time to write each section to the appropriate length
- use appropriate style and tone, while applying prescribed formats, when writing your proposal, thesis or paper.

14.1 How to manage the process of writing up research

Write from the start of your degree programme. Do not wait until you have completed all the research – both deskwork and fieldwork – in order to write. Some theses do not reach fruition because the researcher becomes absorbed in the reading and practical work and leaves writing up until the end, in the belief it is a quick and easy task. Although writing is taxing, it is an exercise that, like all exercise, becomes easier as you become fitter at doing it. A trend for PhD theses is to write up sections as academic papers as you complete them. Thus, by the time the final writing-up stage is reached, you may have written and even published a few papers which are the foundation of chapters, for example on the literature, on the methodology or on some of the results.

It is particularly important to write about the literature you are reading as you read it, to avoid losing the links to the paper when you eventually do get to writing and referencing. Likewise, it is advisable to write the methodology section as you experience it – or else you run the risk of forgetting what you did or why you made certain decisions along the way.

Take care of yourself during this period of research, as writing can be a lonely task. Join writing groups with other postgraduates so you can review each other's work and provide support and encouragement. One way to try to insure yourself against potential problems is to have a clear Memorandum of Understanding (MoU) drawn up between your supervisor (the representative of the university) and yourself regarding meetings, preparation for meetings, feedback and extent of support. A good MoU will outline your role and that of your supervisor and include important details, such as the number of meetings, the work required for the meetings, whose names will be given as authors on publications arising out of the thesis and in what order these names will be given.

A university, with the author, owns copyright on all theses. It remains the right of the author to cede copyright of his or her thesis to another party; however, the university will always hold the thesis and protect the knowledge.

14.2 Academic proposals

Many of you will have to write academic proposals as part of your degree studies. These proposals set out your plans to undertake academic research. They are similar to business and industrial proposals, but have additional sections relating to the theoretical basis of your research. They stress your theoretical approach and record the academic reading you have done. They include a possible chapter outline of your proposed thesis. Most proposals also require a timeline or Gantt chart (see Chapter 10) and an outline of predicted expenses.

In your proposal, you tell your department, potential supervisors and possible funders exactly what research you plan to undertake. A well-researched proposal is the essential basis for a successful research programme. It helps your department to decide whether your project is worth accepting and supporting. It helps your supervisor to understand your focus and your proposed methods. The department will need to choose an external examiner. If your work is interdisciplinary, it must be housed in a core discipline in which the main supervisor and external examiner will be based.

In terms of writing academic proposals, the following sections of this chapter discuss:
- how to identify the problem and research methodology
- the main elements of a proposal
- a suggested layout for your proposal.

Once your proposal has been approved and the necessary systems put in place (for example funding) you can continue with the research. The proposal forms the basis for the introduction chapter in the thesis.

Identify the problem and research methodology

In your proposal you identify a particular problem or topic before you investigate it. You will need to review current literature on the subject and on your chosen methodology. Your problem statement may come out of a gap in the literature (accepted body of knowledge) or be part of a continuum of current research. You identify your proposed research methodology so that others can judge whether or not your project is worth supporting. You will need to review current literature on the subject and on your chosen methodology.

Before you embark on new research, the following are possible questions to ask yourself:
- What is the problem I have to investigate?
- What is the significance and originality of the proposed study in its field?
- Is the research likely to produce new data or will it confirm existing hypotheses?
- Will the hypothesis/es be valid? And how will the hypothesis/es be tested?
- What procedures – such as Finite Experimental Methods (FEM) – will I use to investigate the problem?
- Will there be a representative sample if a field study is required?
- Are the facilities, equipment, funding and other resources adequate for the proposed work?
- What are the ethical considerations?
- Is there an appropriate supervisor in the system I am studying who can guide the work?

Main elements of a proposal

A proposal may be as few as 3 pages or be up to 10 or, even, 30 pages. It may include some, or all, of the following elements (which are all discussed in the sections that follow):

- A **title page** with a provisional title for your research project
- A **glossary**: A definition of the technical terms and concepts that you will be using. This section is very important if you are using unusual terms or newly coined terms.
- The **introduction**, including details about:
  - ▶ the background to your thesis topic and reasons why you think the study is worth undertaking
  - ▶ a statement of the main problem to be investigated, or the main topic to be covered
  - ▶ the overall aim of the study
  - ▶ some of the possible sub-problems to be investigated
  - ▶ the scope or limits of your study. You could, for example, state the boundaries within which the investigation will be confined, for example time, geographical area, cultural groups, statistical sampling and age groups
- The **motivation**: The significance of the specified problem in relation to business or industry or your academic discipline
- A **preliminary literature review**, which will identify gaps in the literature
- **Hypothesis/es and key questions** that will be used as a way to unpack or investigate the elements of each hypothesis
- The **proposed methodology**, detailing your methods of empirical data gathering, such as field research, opinion surveys, focus groups, tests, rating scales, interviews, questionnaires. For example, you may include sample questionnaires that you wish to use, or a preliminary list of the names of those whom you wish to interview and their companies.
- The **expected outcomes**: A sample layout or chapter headings of your proposed thesis will give an indication of the expected outcomes.
- **Possible conclusions and recommendations**, including:
  - ▶ some tentative conclusions, particularly implications for further study or for applications
  - ▶ some tentative recommendations that focus particularly on action to be taken
- A **proposed budget**
- A **timeline**
- A **reference list** (see Chapter 12 for details on citation and referencing) that will include:
  - ▶ the references used in the proposal
  - ▶ other reading of appropriate literature undertaken.

Suggested layout for your proposal

The following sections are suggested for your research proposal. Do not, however, feel constrained by this layout. Your research proposal will differ in format according to the purpose and the type of research you propose to undertake.

Title page

The title page should contain the following:
- Title of the proposed research (provisional, as the research may change)
- Proposal for honours, master's or doctoral thesis
- Prepared for: Supervisor's name and institution
- Thesis in partial fulfilment of the requirements for the degree of ... (special field)
- Prepared by: Author
- Date of proposal.

Summary or abstract

As most proposals are only a few pages, a summary is usually not included. However, if the proposal is lengthy, a short, half-page summary should be included.

Your summary should contain information about:
- the topic
- the essential background, description and motivation (introduction)
- essential literature that may form the departure point of the proposed study (if applicable)
- the hypothesis/es developed
- the main purpose of the study
- a brief outline of the procedure
- the expected conclusions and recommendations.

Some universities refer to this section as an abstract. An abstract is a short summary sent to a journal or conference for consideration for publication. Depending on the requirements of the publishing body, your abstract may be as many as 300 words or as few as 150 words. Some abstracts are now presented graphically, as illustrated in Figure 14.1.

Figure 1. Overview of work packages

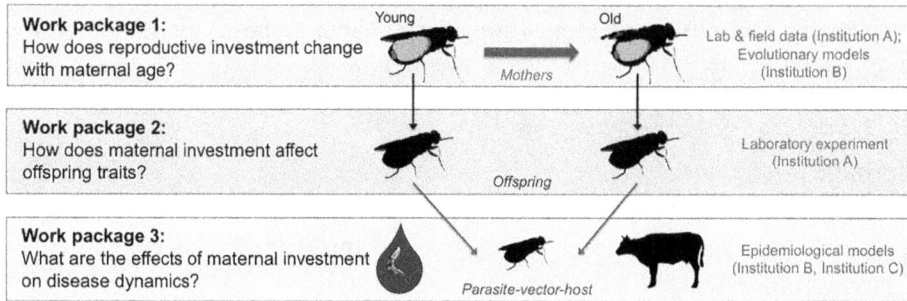

Work package 1:
How does reproductive investment change with maternal age?

Young   Old

Mothers

Lab & field data (Institution A);
Evolutionary models
(Institution B)

Work package 2:
How does maternal investment affect offspring traits?

Offspring

Laboratory experiment
(Institution A)

Work package 3:
What are the effects of maternal investment on disease dynamics?

Parasite-vector-host

Epidemiological models
(Institution B, Institution C)

Figure 14.1 Abstract for funding submission for a research grant by Dr Sinead English, University of Cambridge

Introduction

This section may or may not carry subheadings. Ensure that it includes:

- a description of the **topic**
- the **background** to the study
- details about the **core problem** to be solved, or the hypothesis to be proved
- a **motivation** for the topic through its importance, for example, to research, society, industry or commerce
- an **outline** and **justification** of the major limitations that might be placed on the research, for example time constraints and access to data. It is essential that known or predicted limitations and/or assumptions that are being made be considered at the outset of the study.

Description of proposed research

Describe exactly what you propose to do. Make it clear to what extent you see the project being manageable and where you predict there may be challenges. It is sensible to be realistic from the outset. For example, if your empirical work needs to take place in another location, logistical matters need to be in place, such as funding.

Justification for research

This section describes the significance of the research in relation to your academic discipline. Research is not finite, but a continuum. Your research will contribute to this continuum within its given field, be it business, the social sciences, medicine or industry. Describe the position of the research in relation to historical and current knowledge and, if pertinent, discuss the impact it may have on current or future work in the given field. Your research may be justified according to several aspects:

- Describe the specific **outcomes** of the research and their importance; for example discuss a model that might be developed or a checklist that might be compiled where none exists at present.
- Indicate **gaps in the literature**, if there are any.

- Discuss the possible **contribution** your research will make to the existing body of knowledge, for example by:
  - ▶ filling gaps in the literature
  - ▶ providing unusual or new methodology
  - ▶ benefiting the outcomes of future research, future policy and practice
  - ▶ benefiting industry or business (the size of the industry or enterprise involved may be relevant here).
- Mention the **role** of your work in the continuum of research, such as:
  - ▶ a conference at which a paper about the research could be presented
  - ▶ a journal in which your paper may be published as an article.

Preliminary literature review

In this section, give a brief review of your reading to date:
- Show how this reading gives a good theoretical base to your proposed research.
- Start from the most general perspective and then narrow your review to specific theory.
- Expand on the major issues in the literature that led to your research proposal and/or hypothesis.
- Describe where your research will fill gaps in the literature.
- Discuss some likely research questions or hypotheses you might use that arise from these gaps. They could become the focus of your data collection and data analysis.

See Chapter 13 for more information on how to find appropriate sources.

Proposed methodology or procedure

Use some or all of the following subsections and give literature references to support this (for example field research, opinion surveys, your methodology and analysis):
- methods of selecting the sample or sources of data (qualitative research)
- methods of undertaking experiments (quantitative research)
- description of instruments to collect data, for example field research, proposed interviews or focus groups
- planned administration of instruments and procedures for analysis, for example SPSS, NVivo (see Chapter 13) and rating scales to be used (describe your proposed rating scales if these are relevant)
- limits of the methodology (for example time, geographical area, selected cultural groups, types of statistical sampling, selected age groups).

You may use a graphic to show your intention for methodology developing in relationship with the analysis of the literature, as illustrated in Figure 14.2.

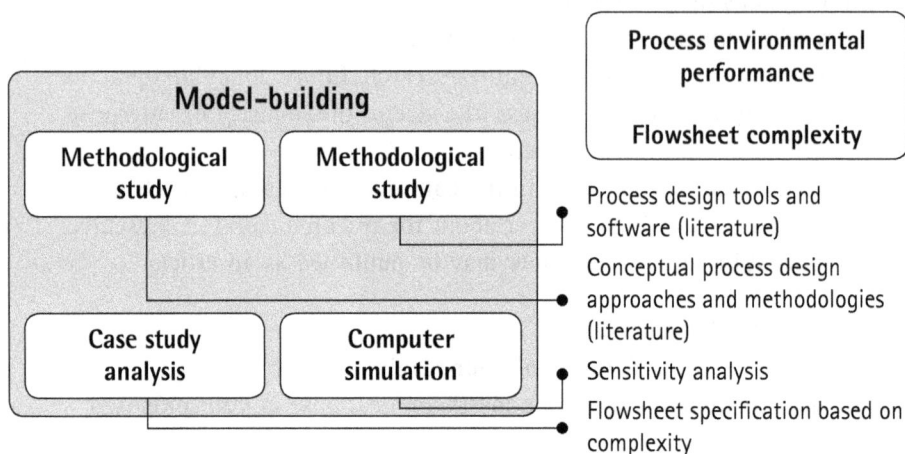

Figure 14.2 Research design for methodology

Background of researcher

If appropriate, describe any pilot studies that you have done, your research qualifications and work experience and/or word lengths of dissertations. Such background should be described so as to give the context of the proposed work in relation to your previous work. Also, particularly in qualitative research, your identity as a researcher can impact your findings. This section shows that you have taken this into consideration.

Tentative outline of your proposed thesis

The following outline is suggested. If possible, give specific headings relevant to your proposed thesis that may become the chapter headings. These are the headings and subheadings that inform your reader about your expected outcomes. The following example is based on a thesis that contained 11 chapters:

e9

Chapter 1: Introduction

Chapter 2: Literature review

Chapter 3: Methodology

Chapter 4, 5, 6 and so on: The findings or facts

Chapter 7: Discussion of results

Chapter 8: Conclusions

Chapter 9: Recommendations
            (and implications for future research)

Chapter 10: References

Chapter 11: Bibliography

Appendices

This section can be divided into a number of chapters. Use specific headings relevant to your thesis.

Optional: the discussion may also fall into the chapter in which the findings are given.

Tentative at this stage

Now often absorbed into the list of references

Given letters A, B, C, etc and titles

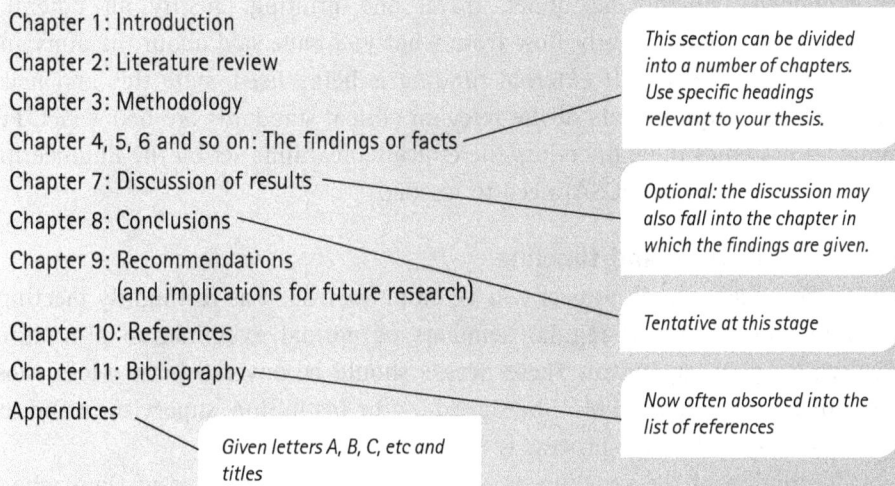

At this point, a mind map, such as the one in Figure 14.3, is often made. It may be used in giving a presentation on the proposal.

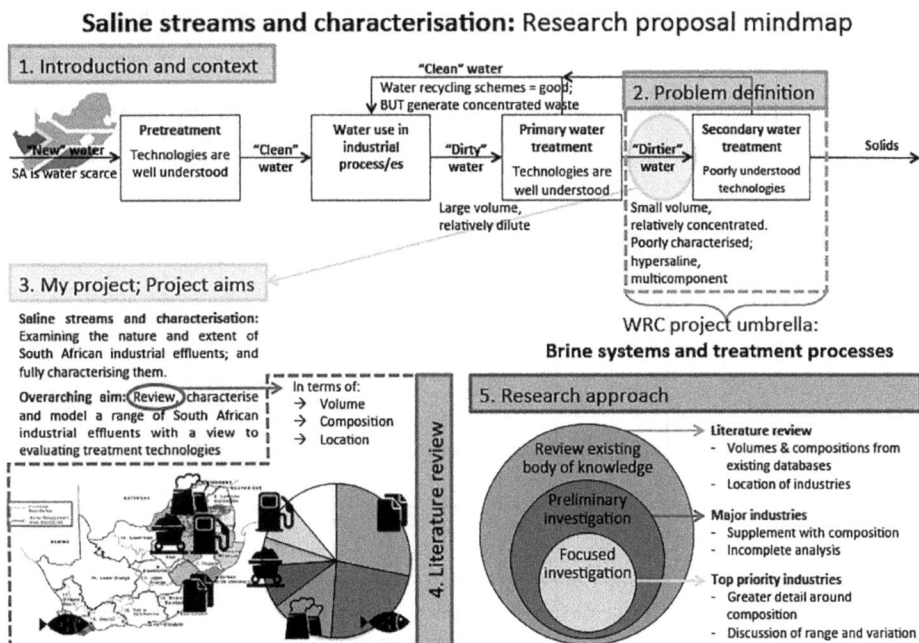

Saline streams and characterisation: Research proposal mindmap

Figure 14.3 Mind map of an MSc thesis plan by Genevieve Harding, University of Cape Town, 2016

Resources requirements

Give a tentative estimate of all refunding needed, for example IT needs, laboratory and equipment, support personnel, travel and printing. Justify all potential expenses. These should clearly flow from what you have said about the aims and designs of your research. If external funding is being used, state this and make it clear that the requirements of the relevant ethical standards are being met. For example, for studies in engineering, the ethical constraints set by the Engineering Council of South Africa (ECSA) need to be met.

Proposed evaluation and timeline

Mention how the research project will be monitored, such as fortnightly meetings with your supervisor and regular seminars or normal examination procedures organised by your supervisor. These details should be covered in an MoU. Most institutions require that the MoU be signed by the institution, supervisor/s and the student, to ensure that due process is followed.

A description of the timeline or work plan (and accompanying Gantt chart) shows that you have planned your research and the key experimental work that is needed. If possible, speak to your supervisor about whether your timeline plan is realistic. See Figure 14.4.

Date	6–12 Sept	13–19 Sept	20–26 Sept	27–3 Oct	4–10 Oct	11–17 Oct	18–24 Oct	25–31 Oct	1–7 Nov	8–14 Nov	15–21 Nov	22–28 Nov	29–5 Dec	6–10 Dec
Week	1	2	3	4	5	6	7	8	9	10	11	12	13	14
Submit research proposal	✓													
Request access to company	✓	✓												
Develop in-depth interview questions		✓	✓											
Conduct interviews			✓	✓	✓	✓								
Transcription of interviews			✓	✓	✓	✓								
Interpret data			✓	✓	✓	✓								
Data findings							✓	✓						
Submit 1st draft to supervisor									✓					
Revise draft									✓	✓	✓			
Submit 2nd draft to supervisor												✓		
Revise draft and prepare for final submission												✓	✓	
Print & bind													✓	
Submit final														✓

Figure 14.4 A proposed timeline for an honours thesis

Preliminary bibliography

List the material that you have read and propose to read. In addition, summarise exploratory work. For example, describe the initial laboratory work or list the interviews that you have already conducted and propose to conduct. If these references cover various forms, it is expedient to list your material under the following subheadings:

- Books
- Journals
- Web/Internet
- Unpublished sources (eg theses, company reports).

14.3   Academic theses

A dissertation or thesis conveys the research context, the theoretical approach to and the results of an investigation into a specific area. Every thesis or dissertation should present an argument. It can also develop a purely theoretical approach to a topic. The most important task of the writer is to communicate these findings or theoretical approaches clearly and effectively. This section covers the sections of a thesis and an approach to writing them.

Sections of a thesis

Most institutions give the limit on length for a thesis. For example, a master's thesis may be between 40 and 80 pages of text and a doctoral thesis between 90 and 110 pages of text. This would not include the appendices. The thesis may include some or all of the following elements (which are discussed in the sections that follow):

- **Title page**
- **Preliminary pages**, eg table of contents, list of illustrations, glossary, nomenclature
- **Acknowledgements**
- **Summary or abstract** with key words
- **Introduction:** This includes the research design, problem statements and/or hypotheses.
- **Literature review:** Content headings apply, as the literature may encompass a number of chapters, each of which must include an introduction and summary section.
- **Methodology:** This includes a justification for the choice of methods and details of ethical considerations.
- **Analysis of data:** Content headings apply, as this section may encompass a number of chapters.
- **Conclusions:** Each hypothesis requires a conclusion, and the overall research question needs to be concluded.
- **Further research:** Suggest a next step or steps in this study.
- **Reference list**
- **Appendices**

As the thesis evolves from the proposal for work and research design, have an overall **mind map** of your thesis which you develop. It is effective to continue to develop the mind maps done for the proposal. Figure 14.5 illustrates the inter-relationship between all the sections of a thesis.

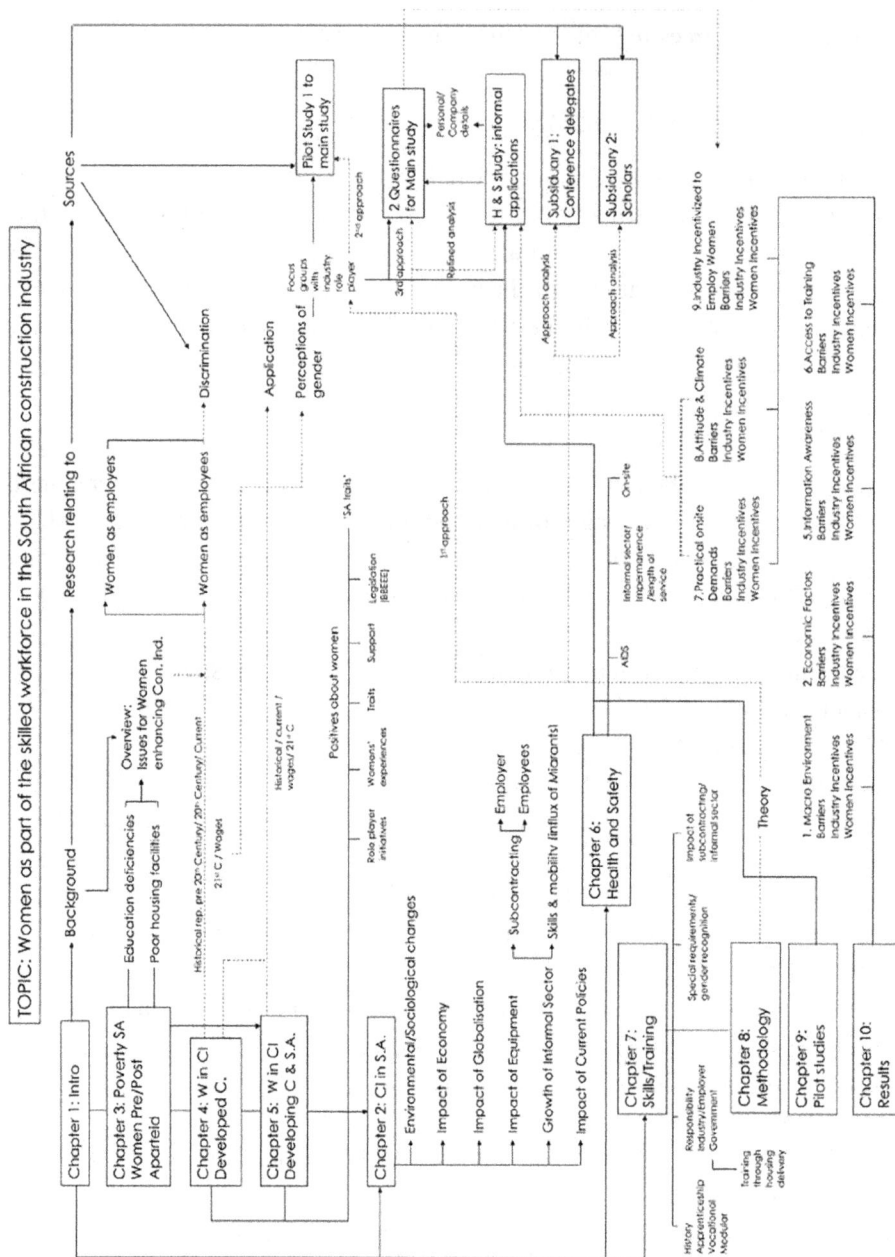

Figure 14.5 Schematic for a PhD thesis showing the inter-relationship between all sections (English, J. 2007. The development of women in the South African construction workforce in terms of employment, training and skills acquisition. Unpublished thesis. Scotland, Glasgow Caledonian University: 30)

Write up each section of work as you complete it. This writing will be easier if you do it while you are working in the area and while your focus is there, rather than leaving it for months or even a year later. By that time, you will have covered other empirical work and written up other sections, and lost touch with this work. At the end of writing up, when you are tired, you will be grateful to have clear and informative introductions and conclusions from each chapter which can be pulled together as a basis for the summary or synopsis.

Preliminary pages

The template of your institution will give you the requirements for the title page, summary, table of contents and lists of tables and figures. (See Chapter 8 for a full description of these standard sections.) In a thesis, you may also need a glossary, nomenclature and acknowledgements.

Glossary or definitions of technical terms, acronyms or symbols/ nomenclature

A glossary lists definitions of the technical terms and concepts that you will be using. This section is very important if you are using unusual terms or newly coined terms. To help you compile the glossary, it is useful to have a non-expert (eg a family member or friend) read the text and make a list of the words they do not understand.

The nomenclature section lists symbols used. This is particularly important if your work includes many equations with various Greek (or other) symbols.

Acknowledgements

This section is not a requirement, but often writers want to thank professional or personal connections who have offered help and support through this long process. Keep a list of those who assist you from the time you start so as not to forget anyone. You are not under any obligation to include those who were paid to do work.

When you submit your thesis, make contact with the people on your acknowledgements list. Communicate to them that you have submitted and thank them for their assistance. Attach a soft copy of the thesis, if appropriate.

Introduction

This section sets out your intention for the thesis. Some of this content would have been researched for your proposal, with the addition of the detailed problem analysis or presentation of hypotheses. The following example shows the possible subheadings for an introduction:

℮9

1.1 Topic of and background to study

1.2 Problem statement ———————————————

Describe the main and sub-questions or -problems to be investigated, and state why these problems are worth investigating.

1.3 Significance of the specified questions or problems

1.4 Brief reference to literature out of which the hypothesis is presented

1.5 Major and minor hypotheses

1.6 Scope and limitations of the study

State the significance of your specified problems in relation to your academic discipline, business or industry. A full motivation may be given in a separate section if warranted.

Present problems and purposes as hypotheses to be proved or disproved by the study.

Researchers in the humanities and the social sciences tend to explore questions, while researchers in science and engineering tend to solve problems and state hypotheses.

If you are working on a design for your research, you should go through the following stages:

1. **State the research question or problem and the aims you have to answer or solve it.** What exactly is the question or problem that you have been set? Can you describe it precisely so that you can attempt to answer or solve it? Have you isolated the fundamental question or problem? Have you narrowed down its scope?

2. **State your hypothesis.** Alternatively, you may work with hypotheses which may be expressed positively or negatively or as a null hypothesis. Hypotheses are tentative answers to questions. They are educated guesses to be verified or disproved by gathering data and by the logical analysis of relationships between data. Formulate your hypotheses after conducting an initial literature review.

Hypotheses: Major and minor, and research objectives

A hypothesis should be justified by the reasons it will be proven.

The following are two examples of a **positive hypothesis** in the area of communication studies:

℮9

A communication-needs analysis of students and employees in organisations will result in an improved communicative syllabus. This is because ...

Or:

The academic achievements of accountants who do aerobics are significantly higher than the achievements of those who do not do aerobics. This is because ...

An example of a **negative** hypothesis would be:

> The evaluation of driving competence in the driver's test is inadequate to assess the ability of drivers when confronted by extreme weather conditions.

Two examples of a **null** hypothesis would be:

> There is no significant difference in driving competence between drivers who pass the test and those who do not.
>
> Or:
>
> There is no significant difference between the academic achievements of accountants who do aerobics and those who do not.

To solve a problem, for example the need to increase the number of women in the construction industry, you would have the following **aim**:

> The thesis aims to establish the barriers that must be overcome for women and to define the skills and employment uptake that needs to be provided for their employment in construction.

Emerging from this aim you could have a major hypothesis which is supported by a number of **minor hypotheses**. These, in turn, are unpacked through objectives.

An example of a main positive hypothesis could be:

> In order to achieve this aim, the following hypothesis is tested: Women can be employed as artisans on construction sites in South African industry.

A minor positive hypothesis which arises from the main hypothesis could be the following:

e9

A sub-hypothesis arising from this is that:

A process and methods can be developed for the improvement of skills in the construction industry through the employment of women, and that this development will contribute to:
- an environment for economic growth, particularly for entrepreneurship and the development of SMMEs as a route to growth
- improved infrastructure and services
- increased human resources, particularly skills, labour training systems and employment creation.

In order to test the hypotheses, the thesis has detailed **research objectives** which set out what you wish to achieve by your research. Key questions may also provide a way to unpack the hypothesis and answer it in parts.

e9

The research objectives of this study are to:
- ascertain the image of construction and the level of self-awareness of employability in construction held by women
- analyse the barriers that need to be dismantled in order to enable more women to enter the construction industry, either as employees or as entrepreneurs
- assess the attitudes to and the priorities of the industry in relation to the inclusion of women in the construction workforce
- establish a database of levels of education, work histories, patterns of skill acquisition and job status which are available to women working in construction in the spectrum of the skilled workforce
- define the initiatives needed to facilitate the entry of women into the construction industry workforce.

Literature review

A literature review is a chapter in a thesis that debates relevant research read and studied by the writer and which has led to the writer's approach to the work. The literature review brings together readings describing different approaches in the subject. You use these approaches, formulated by experts, to support your theoretical approach. Thus the literature review of prior theory is part of the development of the methodology.

Your use of prior knowledge is extremely important, because it gives you credibility and places your study in context. It shows how your research project relates to the broad environment of similar research done by others. The fundamental view of researchers is that the more you know about other people's work in your field, the better you can approach your own research.

There are three main purposes in undertaking a literature review, namely to:

1. gain help in approaching your research problems by finding investigations similar to your own and learning how others tackled problems similar to your own
2. gain theoretical knowledge that enables you to keep your research central
3. evaluate your own research by comparing it with that of others.

First, your literature review shows that you have read widely in your chosen topic, your field and/or a field close to it. Secondly, a good literature review synthesises all the theoretical viewpoints into a whole. It sets these viewpoints under headings in a systematic order, for example from general to specific. Thirdly, your literature review should not only report on previous work in the field, but should also interrogate, compare and critique previous work. You aim to synthesise different pieces of work to draw greater conclusions or highlight areas of confusion, uncertainty or disagreement. This analysis is very important, because it shows your readers that, besides understanding the theory, you are also able to make the connections between different theories in a systematic way.

Make a conscientious and thorough review of the literature. For your supervisor to see you have gained this knowledge, you need to discuss and paraphrase material you have read. Synthesise and paraphrase the work in your own words to indicate your understanding of it. If you repeatedly quote directly from the text, you are not indicating your understanding of the text: you are reproducing, not reviewing.

The following is an approach to **managing the reading of sources**:

1. On accessing a document such as a journal article for the first time, read for the overarching message. Therefore, read closely the introduction and conclusions only and scan the bulk of the article. In this initial reading, you will avoid becoming absorbed in the detail – for example, being slowed down by needing to understand complex equations – and you will focus on the main message.
2. If the content you read is pertinent to your study, re-read and absorb the whole article.

The following are approaches to **managing the writing of the review**:

- Constantly group other people's studies and relate them to one another, as well as to your own study.
- Compile a hierarchy of information.
- Connect your special area of interest to the broad historical horizon from which you can gain perspective for your work.

- Emphasise relationships and state exactly what these are.
- Write a cohesive account of previous research, not simply a chain of pointless isolated summaries. Do not, for example, say: 'X says ...; Y says ...; Z says ...'. In other words, review the literature, do not simply reproduce it.
- Do not quote long passages from the literature. Use short, direct quotations.
- File the work you are reading in a logical, easy-to-search way. This may mean including key words or summaries for each piece of literature. Use a referencing tool.

For details on how to avoid plagiarism and on citing and referencing, see Chapter 12. For sourcing and locating data, see Chapter 13.

Methodology or research design

You will have selected appropriate research methods before writing your proposal. Methodology is selected according to your discipline and intended outcomes. Your supervisor will assist you.

Pay attention also to the methodologies undertaken in literature that is relevant to your study; these may suggest approaches useful for you. For detail on working with data and different methodologies, see Chapter 13.

Results

You have to lead your reader through each stage in your argument and negotiate your findings with your reader. The results will fall across a number of chapters. Each chapter must have a topical, content-based heading. The results must discuss, in the text, the graphical material included; that is, tables and figures which are required for understanding the thesis.

The results are interpreted by the author for the reader within the context of the literature and the theory, and within the context of the problem or hypotheses. You should therefore argue as logically as you can and be aware of the bases for argumentation discussed in Table 14.1.

Table 14.1 Bases for argumentation

Aspect	Checklist of questions to ask yourself
Facts and opinions	• Have I differentiated between fact and opinion? • Have I judged the reliability and qualifications of my sources?
Inferences	• What are the bases for my inferences? • How reliable are they? • How important are they to my conclusions?
Assumptions	• Can I justify my assumptions? • How reliable are they? • How important are they to my conclusions?

$\rightarrow$

Aspect	Checklist of questions to ask yourself
Analogies	Are there enough similarities between the objects or ideas compared to justify an analogy?
Logic	• Have I pretended to use logic when in reality my argument is illogical? • Have I used effective discourse words to reflect my logic? (See Chapter 1.)
Primary and secondary information	Have I used both primary and secondary information? (Primary information is information that you have generated, whereas secondary information is information that you have gained from other people's work. Always ensure that you acknowledge other people's work in your text through an appropriate citation method. See Chapter 12.)

Conclusions

When you draw a conclusion based on research evidence, make sure that you and your reader are aware of the general principles upon which your argument rests. These general principles establish a logical connection between your findings and your conclusions. They explain why your findings are relevant to your conclusions.

If your thesis presented hypotheses, each of these requires a conclusion. Always check your underlying principles or assumptions to make sure that they link to your findings and your conclusions reliably. The conclusions to your study should reflect all or some of the following:

• A systematic progression from the known to the unknown
• Verifiable and accurate results
• Research conducted objectively
• Conclusions clearly drawn from facts by logical reasoning.

Future work or recommendations

Based on the conclusions, you may suggest future work arising out of your study and conclusions. This future work may be further research to be conducted by a researcher, or it may mean actions to be adopted or changes to be made in systems described. It is desirable to include this section, as all research is part of a continuum and you need to show that your work is not isolated.

References

The list of references (which may be called a reference appendix) comes at the end of the main thesis chapters but before the appendices. Before you seek articles and other reference material, set up a system for automated citation and referencing, such as RefWorks or Zotero. Programs such as these enable you to store and access your readings. See Chapter 12 for more on these programs.

Appendices

Any data which should be absorbed by the reader as part of the understanding of the document must be presented in the main document; that is, in the appropriate chapter in the results. However, a study of the breadth and depth of a postgraduate thesis may contain information that is too detailed, complex or simply not sufficiently relevant to the main argument to be contained in the document. Such information can be contained in an appendix and must be referred to in the text of the thesis. Increasingly, the appendices are placed on a CD, even where the thesis is printed in hard copy.

Examples of data appropriate for the appendices are:
- computer printouts
- codes for mathematical modelling
- detailed mathematical calculations
- examples of questionnaires
- transcriptions of recorded dialogue
- illustrations such as sets of photographs and plans
- supporting correspondence.

Appendices are not part of the document, so are not given a chapter number or title. They are listed by letters of the alphabet and with the title of each appendix given.

e9

Appendix A: Acts and Promulgations
Appendix B: Acts and Regulatory Bodies

Appropriate style for a thesis

You should take great care over your style:
- For some disciplines (eg engineering) you are required to write in a **formal, impersonal style** which, in keeping with the scientific approach, emphasises your research work rather than you as the experimenter. For others (eg the social sciences), a **personal voice** is required, as it demonstrates the writer taking ownership of the opinions expressed.
- Check your argument for **clarity and conciseness**: sentences in a paragraph must have a logical narrative flow.
- Write in the **active voice** rather than the passive voice.
- The **past tense** is commonly used, as work is completed when written up. The introduction may be written in the present tense, as it describes the thesis, which is current. Avoid mixing tenses in one section.

- Choose your **vocabulary** well and use a low average number of words per sentence. Use effectively chosen discourse words (conjunctions, conjunctive adverbs, pronouns) to ensure your argument flows well.

Finally, start the process early to give yourself time to review the document and for others to read it and give you feedback. Do not leave the writing until a few days before the deadline; a carefully crafted paper takes time to create but will have more chance of acceptance or publication.

For more details on effective writing style, see Chapter 1. Also see Chapter 13 for a discussion on academic writing style. These principles also apply to writing an academic proposal.

Presentation of a thesis

A written message is both a verbal and a non-verbal message. The appearance of the text and in particular the elements mentioned in the list below affect the readability of that text. Always make sure that your thesis is as appealing to the eye as possible and that the text is easy to follow. In this way you will avoid two of the major barriers to clear communication: a badly set out text and a dense style that is hard to follow.

A thesis is a structured document with major and minor numbered headings to guide the reader through the essential components of the text at a glance. Some institutions provide templates pre-set with the desired formatting. For journal articles, numbering is not required. All journals provide strict guidelines or a template.

If you are not given one, create a template. A well-constructed template will ensure that your document looks professional and is easy to edit, particularly if it includes built-in functions such as cross-referencing to make editing and formatting easier over time. See Chapter 2 for more on templates and using Microsoft® Word™ effectively.

Most institutions and all journals specify a template. However, if you need to create or choose one, there are various important elements to consider, namely the:
- cover
- layout of the title page
- typeface chosen
- use of white space throughout the text
- numbering system
- effective use of type styles to indicate the hierarchy of material and text emphasis
- built-in, automated functions for all captions, illustration titles, equations, cross-references and citations
- colour to direct the eye to key points in diagrams or other graphics.
  However, keep in mind that if the thesis is to be printed, the graphics need to be readable in greyscale.

Timetable and tasks for writing a thesis

Allow two months at the beginning for settling in and at the end to put the finishing touches to the whole thesis. If there is a lead-in or follow-up study to the main methodology, allow a few more months. A timetable such as the one in Table 14.2 could be shown in detail for each chapter. The word counts and timelines given in Table 14.2 are a guideline – these details will depend on your institution and on whether you are submitting a thesis at honours, master's or PhD level.

Table 14.2 Guidelines for writing a PhD thesis

Chapter	Section*	%	Words	Months**
1	Introduction	5	3 500	3
2	Literature review	30	21 000	6
3	Methodology	20	14 000	4
4	Data analysis	25	17 500	5
5	Conclusions and implications	20	14 000	6
		100	70 000	24

* Some sections may be written in a different order or concurrently.

** Suggestions for minimum time are given.

Table 14.3 summarises all the tasks that need to be completed and ways to approach them.

Table 14.3 Summary of your thesis-writing tasks

	Thesis task	Description of task	How to do the task
1.	Prepare your thesis proposal.	Think about what research you wish to do. Think about your problem statement and the exact purpose of your research. Read widely around the research topic.	Follow the guidelines in this chapter and prepare a detailed research proposal that communicates to your supervisor.
2.	Once your proposal has been accepted, work on your terms of reference (your MoU) with your supervisor.	The terms of reference is a statement of your supervisor's instructions to you. These instructions will show the purposes and scope of your research. You and your supervisor must agree on these terms of reference.	• Seek written approval of your proposal and terms of reference. • Apply for ethics clearance if pertinent. • Confirm your MoU.

→

	Thesis task	Description of task	How to do the task
3.	On the basis of your reading and research, create a topic outline of your thesis.	This is a detailed numbered topic or heading outline in the correct order.	• Generate a master document in Microsoft® Word™. • Use *Outline* view in Microsoft® Word™ to draw up a detailed outline to guide your writing. (See Chapter 2.)
4.	Read about the theories on which you will base your research. Work out your own theoretical base. This is your literature review.	The literature review brings together all the theories that give you a basis for your research. It also positions your research in the context of work that has already been done. Where novelty is required (eg for a PhD) it highlights where the gap/s in the literature is/are.	• Use your library to find relevant books, journal articles, theses and other sources. • Use the Internet to find information. However, you need to check your sources very carefully. Include a disclaimer in your literature review, especially if you are not using refereed sources. • Make sure that you synthesise theories. Do not simply say 'X says ...' or 'Y says ...'.
5.	Prepare a list of the research procedures that you have followed. These procedures are also called your methodology.	This is a detailed description of the exact research procedures that you have followed. Describe all experimental apparatus and your techniques for gathering information. This will include technical descriptions. Include a range of illustrations here, especially diagrams.	• Describe exactly what you did, in such detail that your reader is able to repeat your procedure. • Use the past tense to describe what you did. • Write in an impersonal, active style.
6.	Present your findings or results.	This is a detailed statement of what you found out as a result of your research. It is a factual account.	• Set out your facts in a logical order. • Use a range of illustrations, including flow charts, tables, graphs, diagrams and photographs. • Integrate your illustrations into your text. Show your supervisor where to look by using arrows and shading. • Write in a factual, impersonal style.

→

	Thesis task	Description of task	How to do the task
7.	Discuss your findings or results.	Interpret the significance of your facts in terms of your theoretical approach. Use this section to prepare your reader for your conclusions. You may position your results in the context of and in comparison with the literature.	• Make sure that you show the differences between facts, your interpretation of the facts, others' opinions and speculation. • If you draw inferences, state whether they are strong or weak. • Indicate your confidence in the results, discuss errors and uncertainties, and explain how you minimised these.
8.	Draw conclusions.	Conclusions are not a summary of your findings. They are inferences drawn from your results.	• Use implication language, with the correct use of modifying and qualifying words such as 'however', 'if' and 'nevertheless'. • Do not introduce new information at this stage.
9.	Recommend action.	This is the exact action that should be taken as a result of the conclusions. This action stresses further research required, better designed experiments or better designed research. Your research may have implications for policy makers, the corporate world, industry etc. In this case, include recommendations applicable to these groups.	• Use imperatives here. • Stress the exact action to be taken. • Do not introduce new information at this stage. Your recommendations must flow from your conclusions, which should flow from your findings.
10.	Put together all your references.	The development of your reference list should be ongoing and preferably managed via referencing software. You may also have a bibliography. This includes your general reading and related work that you have read but have not referenced. See Chapter 12 for guidelines on citation and referencing.	• Use the Harvard method of referencing (unless otherwise specified — check with your supervisor). • In your reference section, record only those works that you read, used directly or quoted from. • If you have a bibliography, this should include work that you read but did not use directly.

→

	Thesis task	Description of task	How to do the task
11.	Write your summary.	This is a summary chapter. It must be so well written that it replaces your thesis for the busy reader. It is commonly one or two pages, except in some institutions which require up to 10 pages. It is placed at the beginning of your thesis and has a high impact.	• Summarise all the sections of your thesis. • You may include a good summary illustration, such as a photograph or diagram. • Write this section last.
12.	Check that your preliminary sections are correct. They are an important lead-in to your thesis.	Check that the table of contents and list of illustrations have been updated in the template. Check that the glossary and nomenclature are there and are complete.	Use your formatting styles correctly. You can then generate your table of contents and your list of illustrations automatically.
13.	Draw up an index, if your supervisor considers this necessary.	An index is an alphabetical list of all the important ideas and concepts used in your thesis. The pages on which these ideas are listed are given.	Use your word processer to put together your index. If you cannot do this, write each idea on a card, with the relevant page number. Then put your cards into alphabetical order.
14.	Edit your thesis. Confirm that the formatting is correct.	This is a final check to get rid of all errors in content (eg references) and presentation (eg layout, numbering and pagination).	• Use your software to check your spelling and grammar. (See Chapter 2.) • Have another person or several other people read your whole thesis to check for errors.
15.	Assemble the final master copy.	Online and soft copy theses are becoming more common. For hard copy, allow up to a week for copying and binding.	There is a required number to be printed: one for the university library, one for each supervisor and each examiner, and the number you want for yourself. Thus you may need a minimum of five copies.

14.4 Papers and journal articles

Many theses are comprised of a number of academic papers which were written in the course of the research and presented at conferences or published in journals. Your research is your passion, but it may not necessarily be your reader's prime interest. Even if also in your field, others will not necessarily have your background, as they may not have been drilling down into the same detail. Readers and listeners will not remain interested if your content is not well explained.

Follow these guidelines when you present your work as a paper or journal article:
- Present your work in the context of other research.
- Ensure you define all terms and concepts.
- Minimise theoretical sections in favour of experimental, new material.
- Avoid overloading the text with detail (eg pages of equations) which is only relevant to the full thesis.

A paper must tell a story about a section of the work. The first paper may be based on the literature study, a following one on methodologies, and more than one may come out of the results. The introduction to a paper needs to attract the reader: motivate, state what is particularly pertinent about this work and how it relates or not to other work. Give the structure of the paper.

Figure 14.6 shows how the layout accommodates illustrative matter.

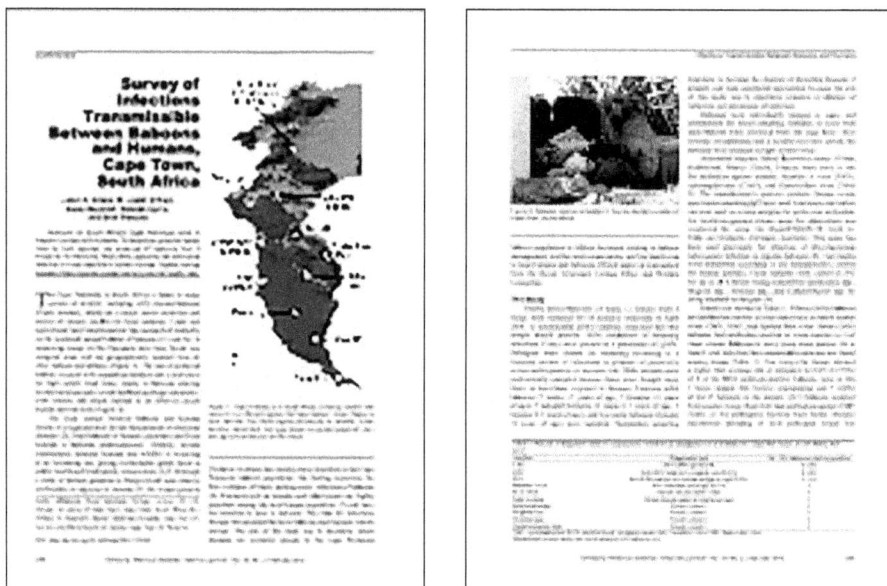

Figure 14.6 An academic journal paper in a template that accommodates two columns (Drewe, JA, O'Riain, MJ, Beamish, E, Currie H & Parsons, S. 2012. 'Survey of Infections Transmissible between Baboons and Humans, Cape Town, South Africa'. *Emerging Infectious Diseases* 18(2), February: 298–301)

✓

Checklist for a well organised and coherent proposal, thesis or article

For your research to be effective, it must be accessible to the reader. Consider the following pointers:

- Make sure the **background** to the thesis is clear. The reader should know why the study was undertaken.
- Clearly set out the **objectives** in the introduction.
- If there are **hypotheses**, set them out clearly in the introduction or in the literature review. Justify them.
- Set out the specific **problems** either in the introduction or in a separate chapter.
- Organise the chapters **logically**.
- In the final chapter, draw together all the **arguments** and **findings** in the thesis.
- Make sure the **overviews** and **summaries** for each chapter are adequate.
- Check that the thesis is an **integrated whole**, with every graphic device in the right place and properly referred to.
- Make sure the reader knows how to **interpret** complex tables and other graphics.

Go through this checklist regarding the parts of the thesis:

- The **title page** should be well set out.
- The **synopsis**, **summary** or **abstract** should reflect the entire content of the thesis.
- The **table of contents** should be informative.
- Avoid obscure one-word **headings**. These should be expanded for clarity.
- Make sure all the **illustrations** and **equations** are listed, each one with a number and a clear title.
- Check if you need to include a **glossary** or **nomenclature**.
- Make sure your **introduction** is clear.
- Include a specific chapter on **method** if required.
- Make the **chapter headings** clear and specific.
- If **conclusions** are drawn, set them out clearly in a conclusions chapter.
- If **recommendations** are made or suggestions for **future work**, set them out clearly in a separate chapter.
- Set out the **references** at the end of each chapter according to the chosen specifications.
- Organise the **appendices**. Refer to each appendix in the main body of the thesis. Make sure the reader knows how to interpret the information in the appendices.

Go through this checklist regarding the discourse structure and logic:

- Use proper links between the **chapters** so that the reader can follow your arguments.
- Use proper links between **paragraphs**.
- Use **sentence links** within paragraphs so that your reader can follow your arguments.
- Adhere to the principles of **unity, coherence** and **emphasis**.
- Avoid **leaps in logic or unsupported generalities** in the argument.
- Label your **assumptions** as such and justify or reference them.
- Label your **inferences**.
- Justify any **analogies**.

→

Go through this checklist regarding the language and readability:
- Use **referential** (factual) language.
- Base your arguments on **facts**. (For example, do not write 'obviously' when there are no facts to support this emotive statement.)
- Choose your **vocabulary** carefully to reflect on the topic.
- Pitch your writing at the correct level of **formality**.
- Check your **grammar**. For example, check that subjects and verbs agree in number.
- Set your word processor to the correct **spelling** for your area.
- Write paragraphs of **reasonable length** (100–200 words). Avoid large blocks of continuous writing.
- Write sentences that are **coherent** and of reasonable length (on average about 15–20 words per sentence).
- Avoid overly **complex** sentences with convoluted arguments. Rather simplify these.
- Create a **template** that is inviting to the eye.
- Make sure there is good **cross-referencing** between sections: body of document to appendices, chapter to chapter, section to section, text to graphics and literature references.
- Present an **integrated message**.

Bibliography and suggested reading

Barkley, EF, Cross, KP & Major, CH. 2005. *Collaborative learning techniques: A handbook for college faculty.* San Francisco: Jossey-Bass.

Berlo, DK. 1960. *Process of Communication.* New York: International Thomson Publishing.

Bolman, LG & Deal, TE. 2008. *Reframing Organizations: Artistry, Choice and Leadership.* 4th edition. San Francisco: Jossey-Bass.

Case, JM. 2013. *Researching student learning in higher education: A social realist approach.* London: Routledge.

Chetty, S. 2012. Tackling interview questions. UCT Careers Service Guide 2012. Available: http://www.careers.uct.ac.za/sites/default/files/image_tool/images/37/tackling_interview_questions.pdf. (Accessed 29 September 2016).

Cleary, S, Harran, M, Luck, J, Potgieter, S, Scheckle, E, Van der Merwe, R & Van Heerden, K. 2010. *Communication: A Hands on Approach.* Claremont: Juta.

Curry, DE. 2005. *Developing and Applying Study Skills: Writing Assignments, Dissertations and Management Reports.* London: CIPD.

De George, RT. 2015. A history of business ethics. Available: http://www.scu.edu/ethics/practicing/focusareas/business/conference/presentations/businessethics-history.html. (Accessed 2 October 2016).

Durrheim, K. 2006. 'Basic quantitative analysis', in *Research in practice: Applied methods for the social sciences.* Cape Town: UCT Press: 188–214.

Engineering Council of South Africa: Rules of Conduct for Registered Persons: Engineering Profession Act, 2000 (Act No. 46 of 2000). Available: https://www.ecsa.co.za/regulation/RegulationDocs/2014_Code_of_Conduct.pdf (Accessed 13 December 2016).

Giordano, L. 2016. The ultimate guide to job interview preparation. Available: https://www.livecareer.com/quintessential/job-interview-preparation. (Accessed 29 September 2016).

Gustavii, B. 2008. *How to Write and Illustrate a Scientific Paper.* 2nd Edition. United Kingdom: Cambridge University Press.

Gutierrez, K. 2014. Studies confirm the power of visuals in elearning. Available: http://info.shiftelearning.com/blog/bid/350326/Studies-Confirm-the-Powerof-Visuals-in-eLearning. (Accessed 23 October 2016).

Hamilton, C. 2010. *Communicating for Results: A Guide for Business and the Professions*. 9th Edition. California: Thomson/Wadsworth.

Holmes, L. 2013. 'Competing perspectives on graduate employability: Possession, position or process?' *Studies in Higher Education* 38(4): 538–554.

Hovland, CI. 1957. *The Order of Presentation in Persuasion*. New Haven: Yale University Press.

Hudson. 2016. Career advice. Available: http://au.hudson.com/job-seekers/helpfultips-career-advice. (Accessed 29 September 2016).

Jansen, JD. 2007. 'The research question'. In *First steps in research,* 2nd Edition, edited by K Maree. Hatfield, Pretoria: Van Schaik: 1–13.

Kitchin, R. & Fuller, D. 2005. *Academics' Guide to Publishing*. Thousand Oaks: Sage

MacLeod, L. & Zanders, E. 2010. *Presentation Skills for Scientists: A Practical Guide*. United Kingdom: Cambridge University Press.

Maree, K & Pietersen, J. 2007. 'The quantitative research process', in *First steps in research*, 2nd edition, edited by K Maree. Pretoria: Van Schaik: 145–153.

Maxwell, JA. 2013. *Qualitative research design: An interactive approach*. 3rd edition. Thousand Oaks: Sage.

Nieuwenhuis, J. 2007. 'Introducing qualitative research', in *First steps in research*, 2nd edition, edited by K Maree. Pretoria: Van Schaik: 47–68.

O'Hair, D, Friedrich, G and Dixon, L. 2011. *Strategic Communication in Business and the Professions*. 7th Edition. Cape Town: Allyn and Bacon.

Pease, A & Pease, B. 2011. *Body Language in the Work Place*. London: Orion.

Porter, ME. 1985. *Competitive advantage: Creating and sustaining superior performance*. New York: Free Press.

Ratele, K. 2006. 'Postcolonial African methods and interpretation', in *Research in practice: Applied methods for the social sciences*, 2nd edition, edited by M Terre Blanche, K Durrheim & D Painter. Cape Town: UCT Press: 539–556.

Rogers, CR. 1951. *Client Centred Therapy: Its Current Practice, Implications and Theory*. London: Constable and Company Limited.

Samovar, L, Porter, R & McDaniel, E. 2010. *Communication between Cultures*. 7th Edition. Wadsworth: Cengage Learning.

Sandler, C & Keefe, J. 2004. *1001 Letters for All Occasions: The Best Models for Every Business & Personal Need*. Cincinnati: Adams Media.

Seely, J. 2005. *The Oxford Guide to Effective Writing and Speaking*. Oxford: Oxford University Press.

Seglin, JL. 2002. *The AMA Handbook of Business Letters*. New York: AMACOM American Management Association.

Terre Blanche, M & Durrheim, K. 2006. 'Histories of the present: Social science research in context', in *Research in practice: Applied methods for the social sciences*, 2nd edition, edited by M Terre Blanche, K Durrheim & D Painter. Cape Town: UCT Press: 1–17.

Terre Blanche, M, Durrheim, K & Kelly, K. 2006. 'First steps in qualitative data analysis', in *Research in practice: Applied methods for the social sciences*, edited by M Terre Blanche, K Durrheim & D Painter. Cape Town: UCT Press: 321–344.

Tubbs, S. 2007. *A systems approach to small group interaction.* 9th edition. New York: McGraw-Hill.

Tubbs, S & Moss, S. 2008. *Human communication: Principles and contexts.* 11th edition. New York: McGraw-Hill.

Tufte, ER. 2001. *The Visual Display of Quantitative Information.* 2nd edition. Cheshire: Graphics Press.

Turabian, K. 2007. *A Manual for Writers of Research Papers, Theses and Dissertations.* 7th Edition. Revised by WC Booth, GG Colomb & JM Williams. Chicago: University of Chicago Press. Available: http://www.press.uchicago. edu/ucp/books/book/chicago/M/bo5059214.html (Accessed 5 August 2011).

Van Staden, E, Marx, S & Erasmus-Kritzinger, L. 2011. *Corporate Communication: Getting the Message Across.* 2nd Edition. Pretoria: Van Schaik.

Virtual Dr. 2016. [Forum discussion] Available: http://discussions.virtualdr.com/ showthread.php?212865-Silly-Analogies. (Accessed 17 October 2016).

Von Brocke, K. 2012. The Marketing Mix. [illustration]. Available: https://vonbrocke. files.wordpress.com/2012/10/the-marketing-mix-or-4ps-of-marketing.png. (Accessed 4 October 2016).

Wassenaar, DR. 2006. 'Ethical issues in social science research', in *Research in practice: Applied methods for the social sciences*, 2nd edition, edited by M Terre Blanche, K Durrheim & D Painter. Cape Town: UCT Press: 60–79.

Weil, V. 2003. Emerging technologies and ethical issues in engineering: Papers from a workshop, October 14–15, 2003. Chapter: Ethics in engineering education. Ethics across the curriculum: Preparing engineering and science faculty to introduce ethics into their teaching. Available: http://books.nap.edu/ openbook.php?record_id=11083&tpage=119. (Accessed 17 October 2016).

Williams, K, Krizan, A, Logan, J and Merrier, P. 2011. *Communicating in Business.* 8th Edition. USA: South Western Cengage Learning.

Wordhippo.com. 2016. What is the meaning of the word gobbledygook? Available: http://www.wordhippo.com/what-is/the-meaning-of-the-word/gobbledygook. html. (Accessed 17 October 2016).

Index